WORLD WAR BLUE

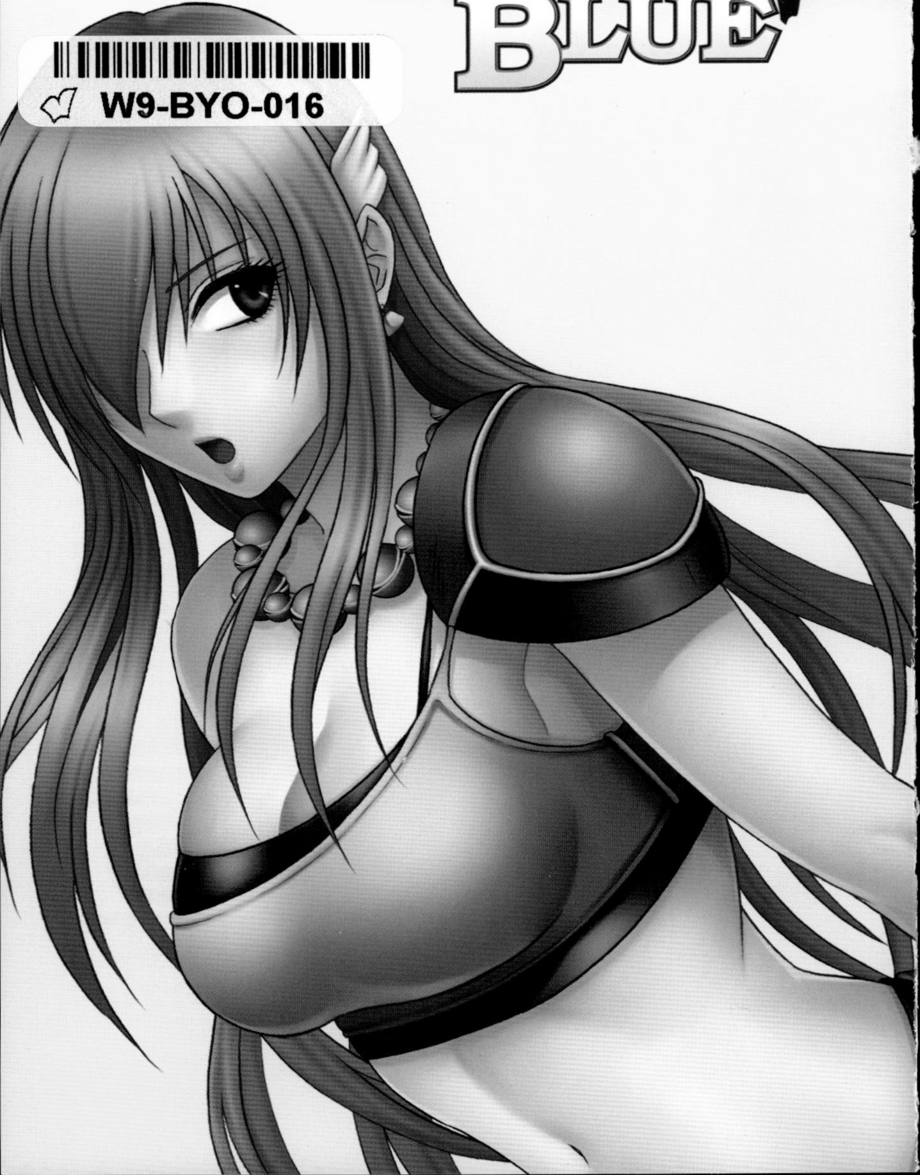

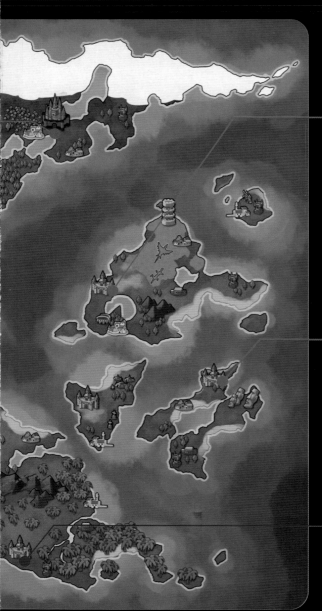

KINGDOM OF NALUA

This powerful and influential neutral nation is famous for its delicious gyoza and succulent cherries. Nalua's grand towers, stadiums, and historic geoglyphs make it a popular tourist destination.

CORTONA THEOCRACY

A neutral nation with very strict laws. Cortona's residents are huge sports fans. Its mysterious stone statues are considered to be a world treasure.

KINGDOM OF SEGUA

The Ninteldo Empire's rival for control of the continent. As a southern nation, Segua has a warm, humid climate.

CONTINENT OF CONSUME – MAP 2

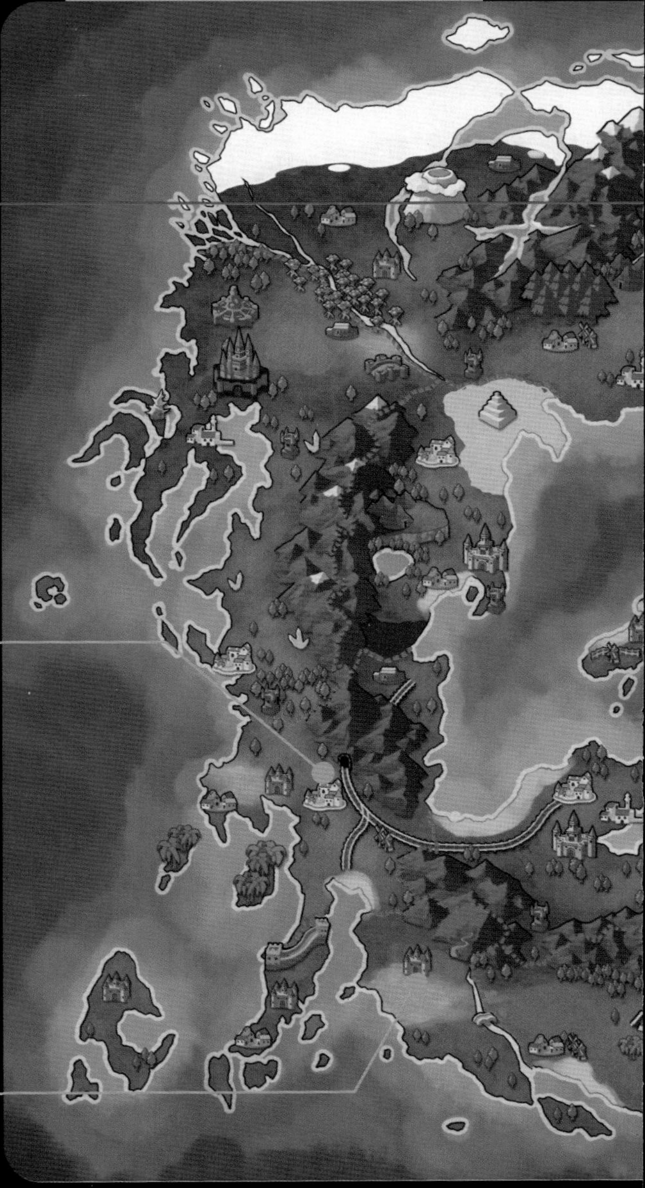

NINTELDO EMPIRE

The largest power on the continent of Consume, its northern reaches are covered in snow throughout most of the year. The Holy Mountain dominates its landscape.

REPUBLIC OF HABEED

An advanced nation in both science and business, Habeed has a thriving railroad industry. Merchant caravans from Habeed are a common sight throughout Consume.

DECORAN

Famous for its unique and unusual culture. Mushrooms are the primary ingredient in the most popular local dishes.

WORLD WAR BLUE

vol. 2

art by **Crimson**

story by **Anastasia Shestakova**

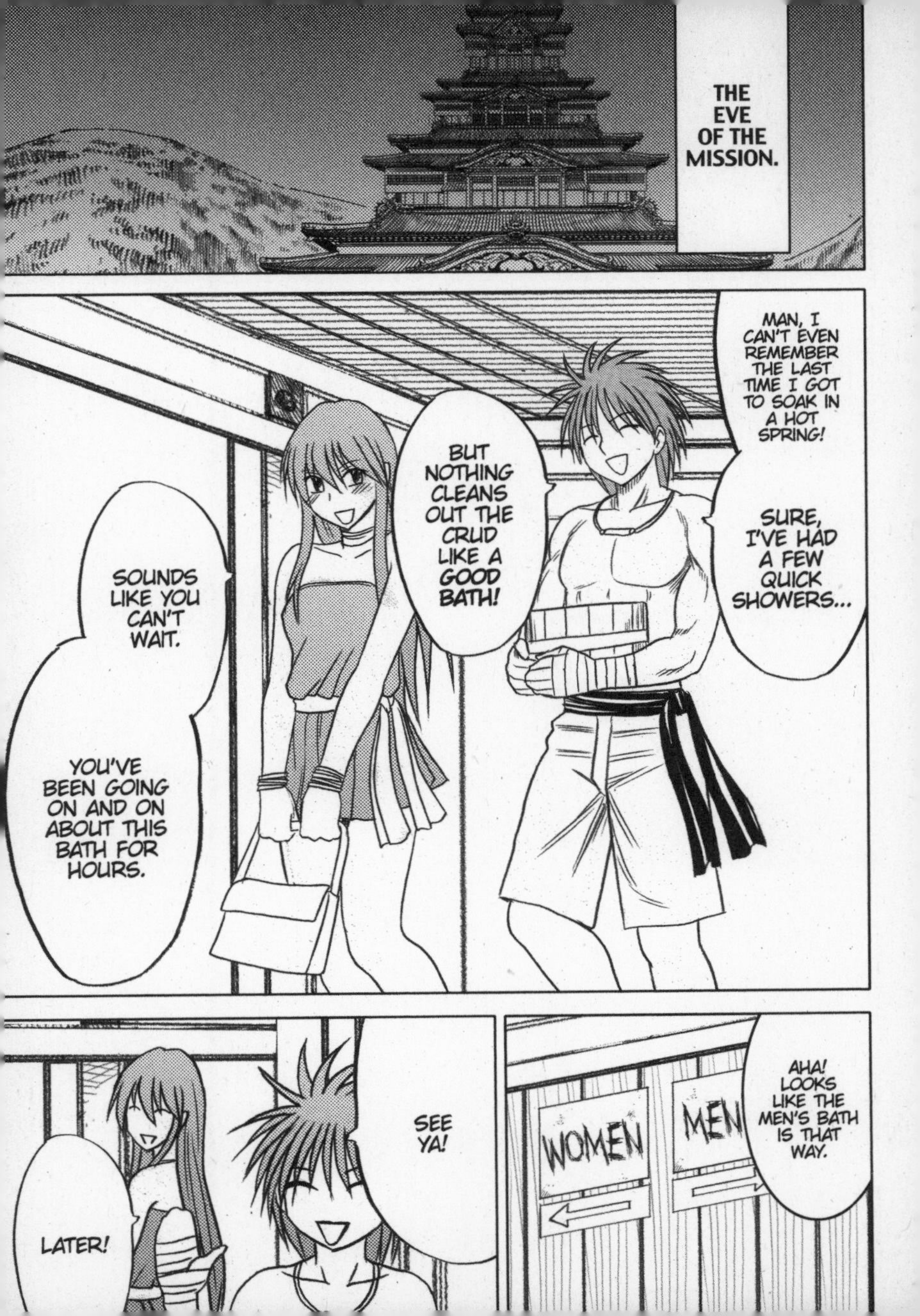
THE EVE OF THE MISSION.
MAN, I CAN'T EVEN REMEMBER THE LAST TIME I GOT TO SOAK IN A HOT SPRING!
SURE, I'VE HAD A FEW QUICK SHOWERS...
BUT NOTHING CLEANS OUT THE CRUD LIKE A GOOD BATH!
SOUNDS LIKE YOU CAN'T WAIT.
YOU'VE BEEN GOING ON AND ON ABOUT THIS BATH FOR HOURS.
AHA! LOOKS LIKE THE MEN'S BATH IS THAT WAY.
MEN
WOMEN
SEE YA!
LATER!

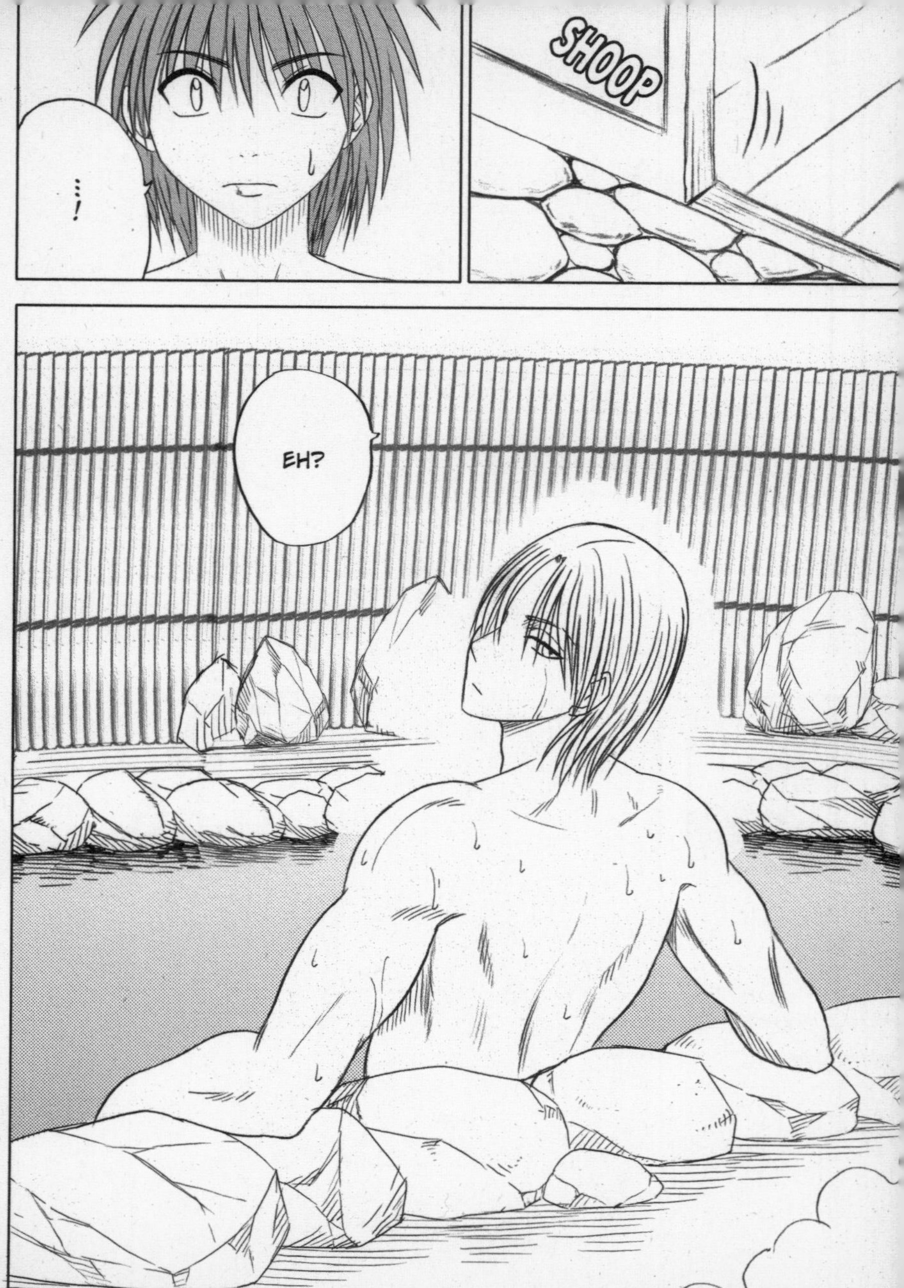
SHOOP
...!
EH?

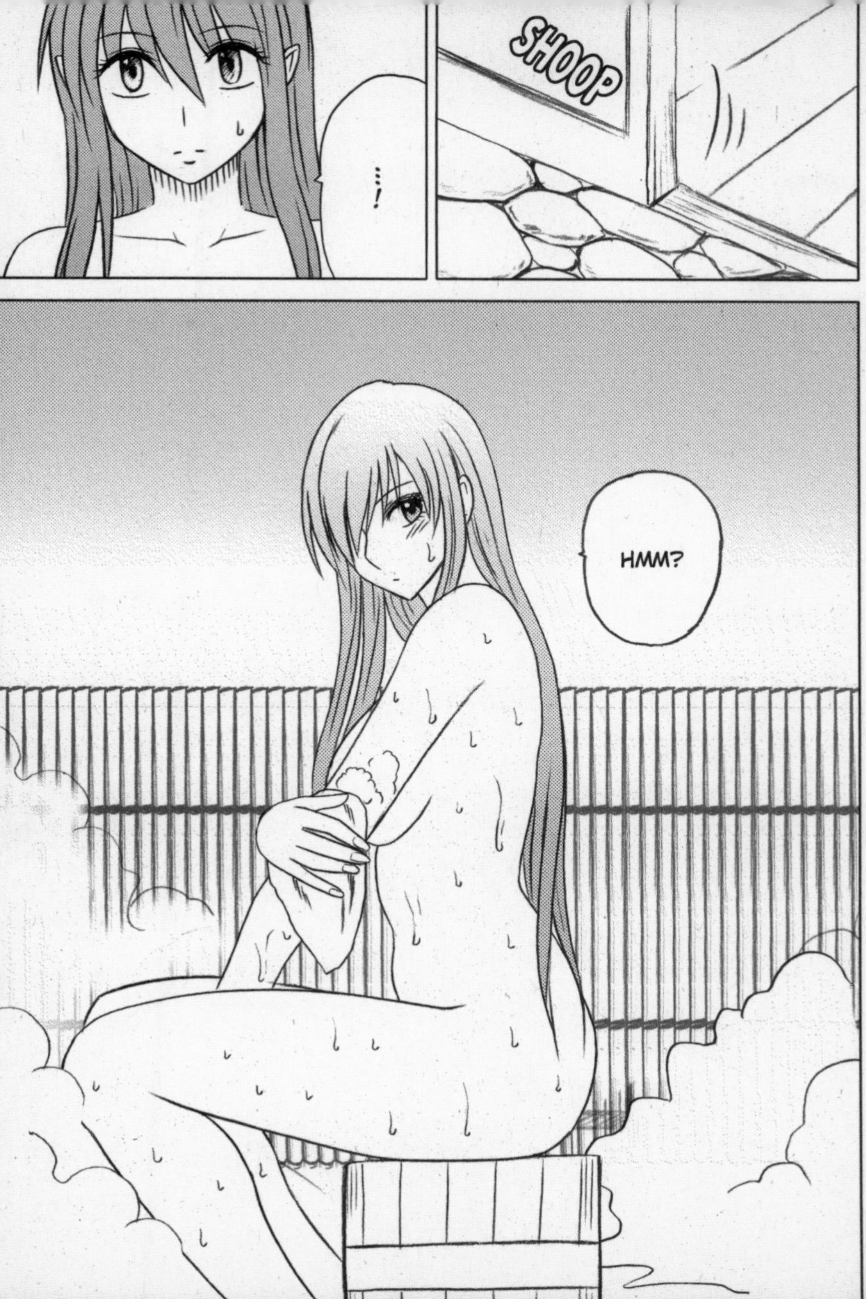
SHOOP
...!
HMM?

CHAPTER 7

Q&A TIME AT THE HOT SPRINGS

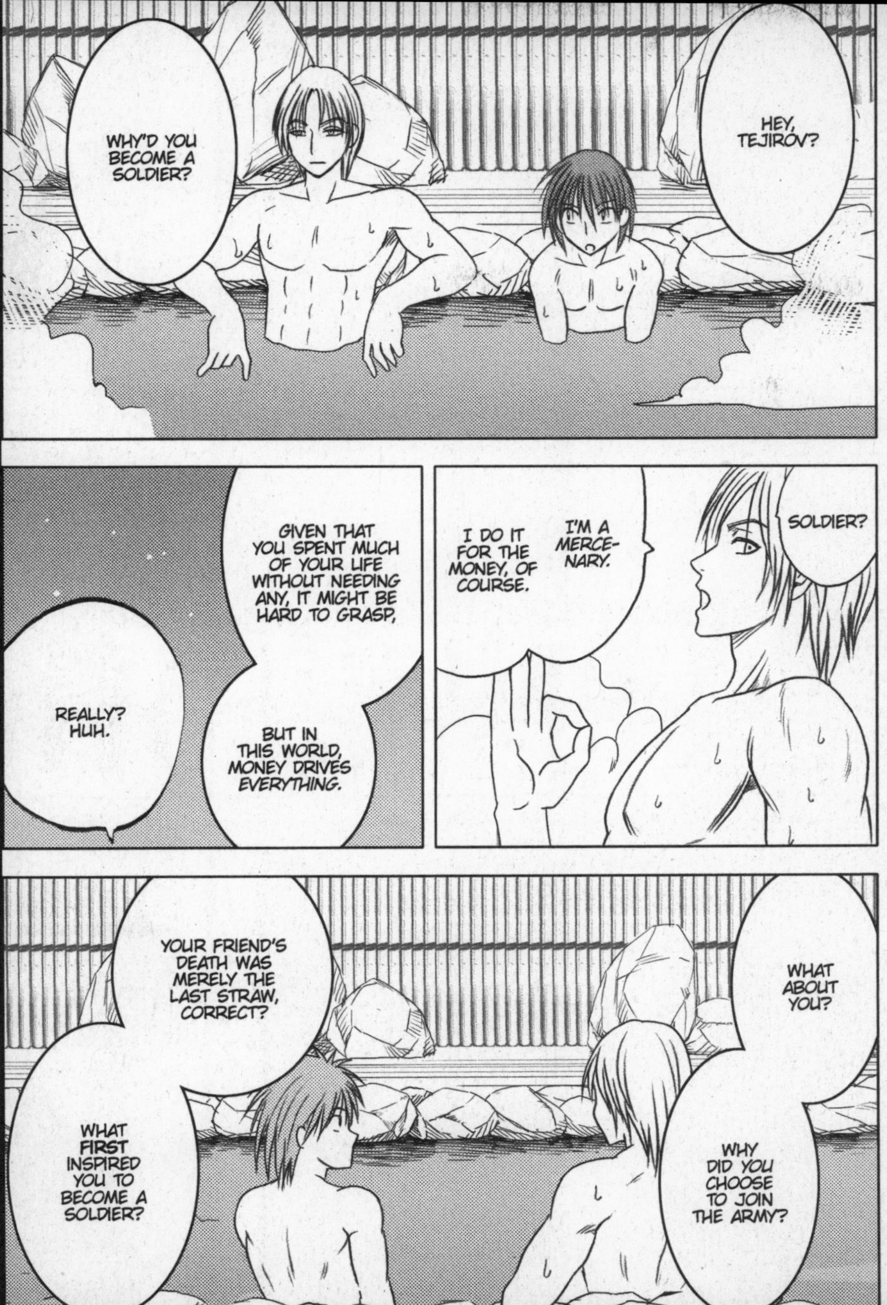
HEY, TEJIROV?
WHY'D YOU BECOME A SOLDIER?
SOLDIER?
I'M A MERCE-NARY.
I DO IT FOR THE MONEY, OF COURSE.
GIVEN THAT YOU SPENT MUCH OF YOUR LIFE WITHOUT NEEDING ANY, IT MIGHT BE HARD TO GRASP,
BUT IN THIS WORLD, MONEY DRIVES EVERYTHING.
REALLY? HUH.
WHAT ABOUT YOU?
WHY DID YOU CHOOSE TO JOIN THE ARMY?
YOUR FRIEND'S DEATH WAS MERELY THE LAST STRAW, CORRECT?
WHAT FIRST INSPIRED YOU TO BECOME A SOLDIER?

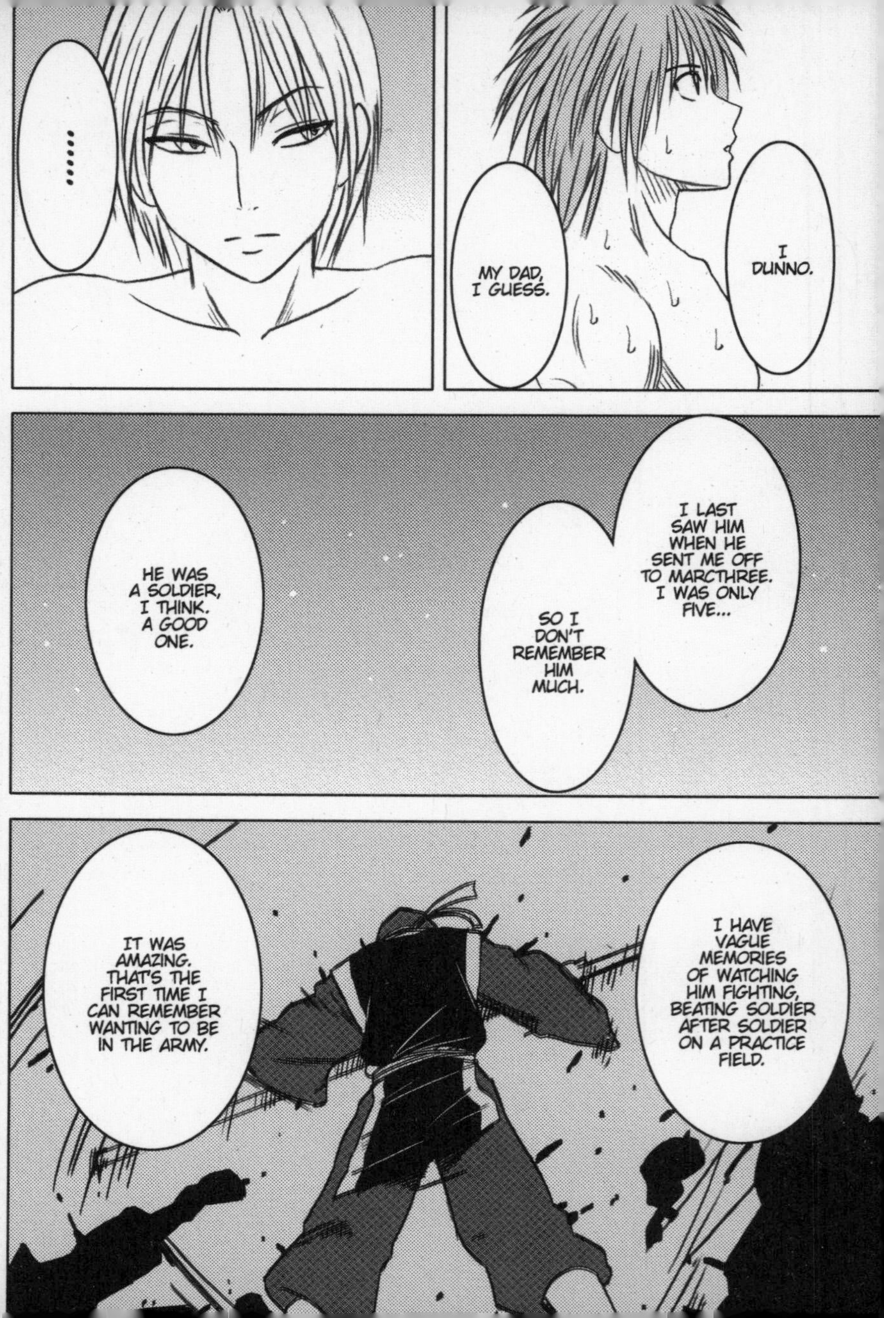
I DUNNO.
MY DAD, I GUESS.
......
I LAST SAW HIM WHEN HE SENT ME OFF TO MARCTHREE. I WAS ONLY FIVE...
SO I DON'T REMEMBER HIM MUCH.
HE WAS A SOLDIER, I THINK. A GOOD ONE.
I HAVE VAGUE MEMORIES OF WATCHING HIM FIGHTING, BEATING SOLDIER AFTER SOLDIER ON A PRACTICE FIELD.
IT WAS AMAZING. THAT'S THE FIRST TIME I CAN REMEMBER WANTING TO BE IN THE ARMY.

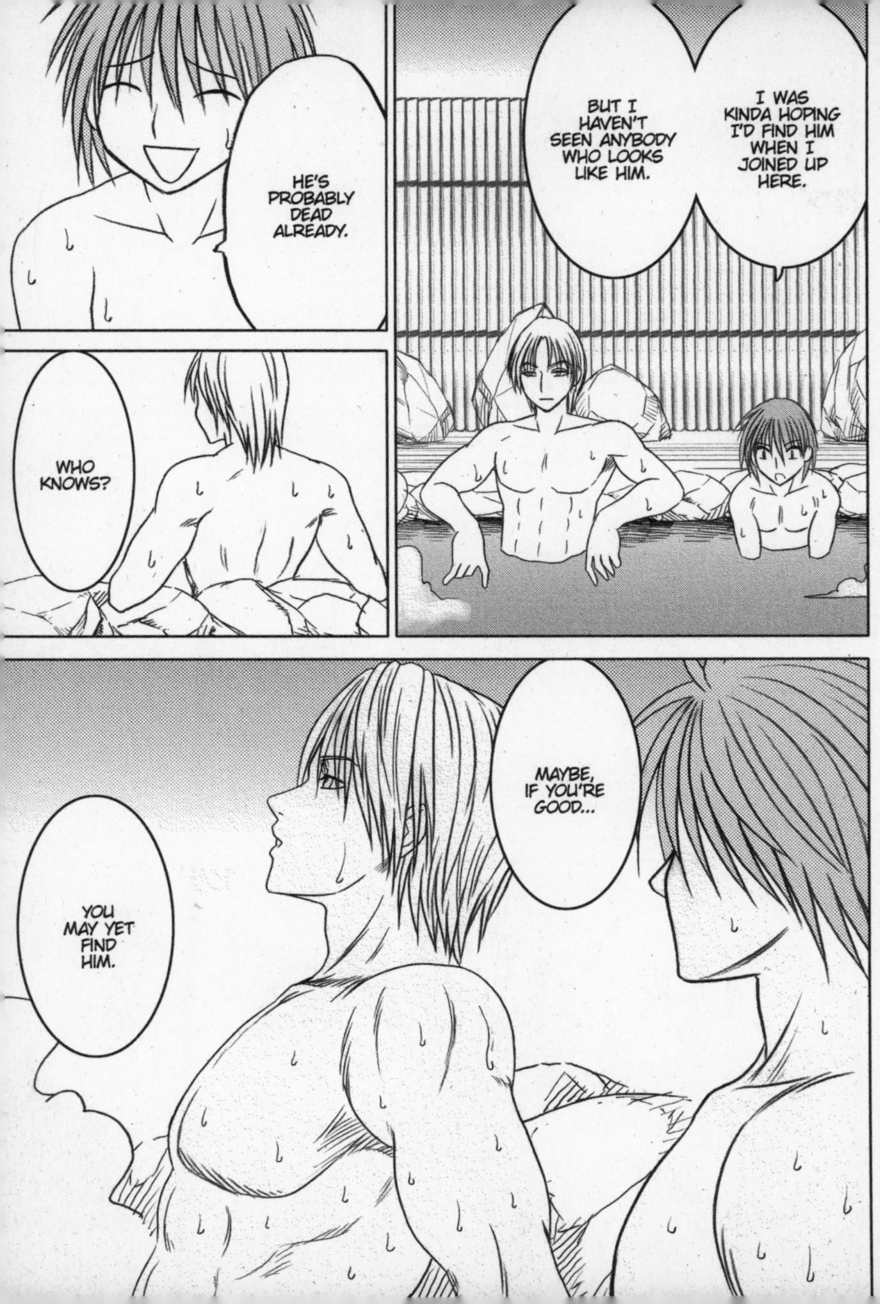
I WAS KINDA HOPING I'D FIND HIM WHEN I JOINED UP HERE.
BUT I HAVEN'T SEEN ANYBODY WHO LOOKS LIKE HIM.
HE'S PROBABLY DEAD ALREADY.
WHO KNOWS?
MAYBE, IF YOU'RE GOOD...
YOU MAY YET FIND HIM.

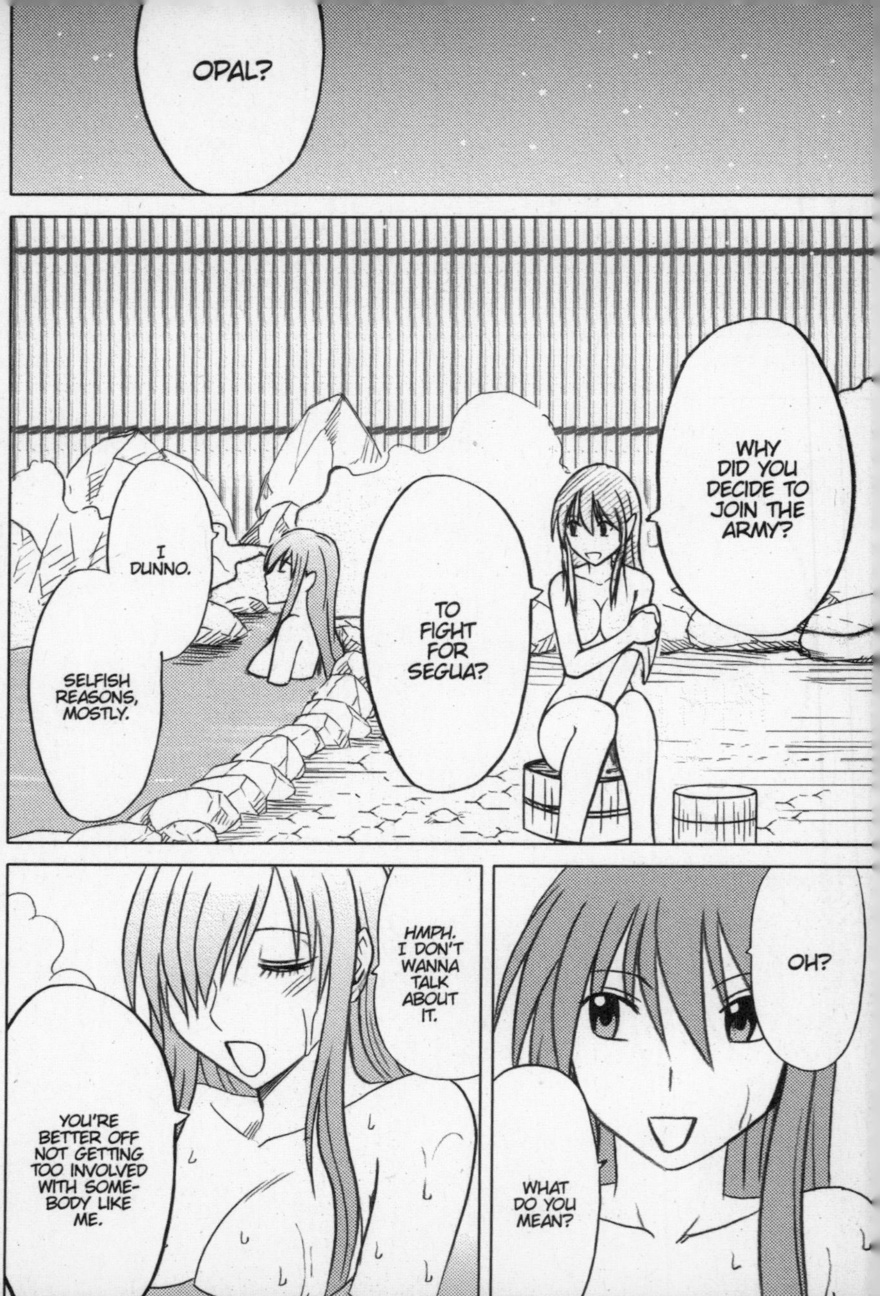
OPAL?
WHY DID YOU DECIDE TO JOIN THE ARMY?
TO FIGHT FOR SEGUA?
I DUNNO.
SELFISH REASONS, MOSTLY.
OH?
WHAT DO YOU MEAN?
HMPH. I DON'T WANNA TALK ABOUT IT.
YOU'RE BETTER OFF NOT GETTING TOO INVOLVED WITH SOME-BODY LIKE ME.

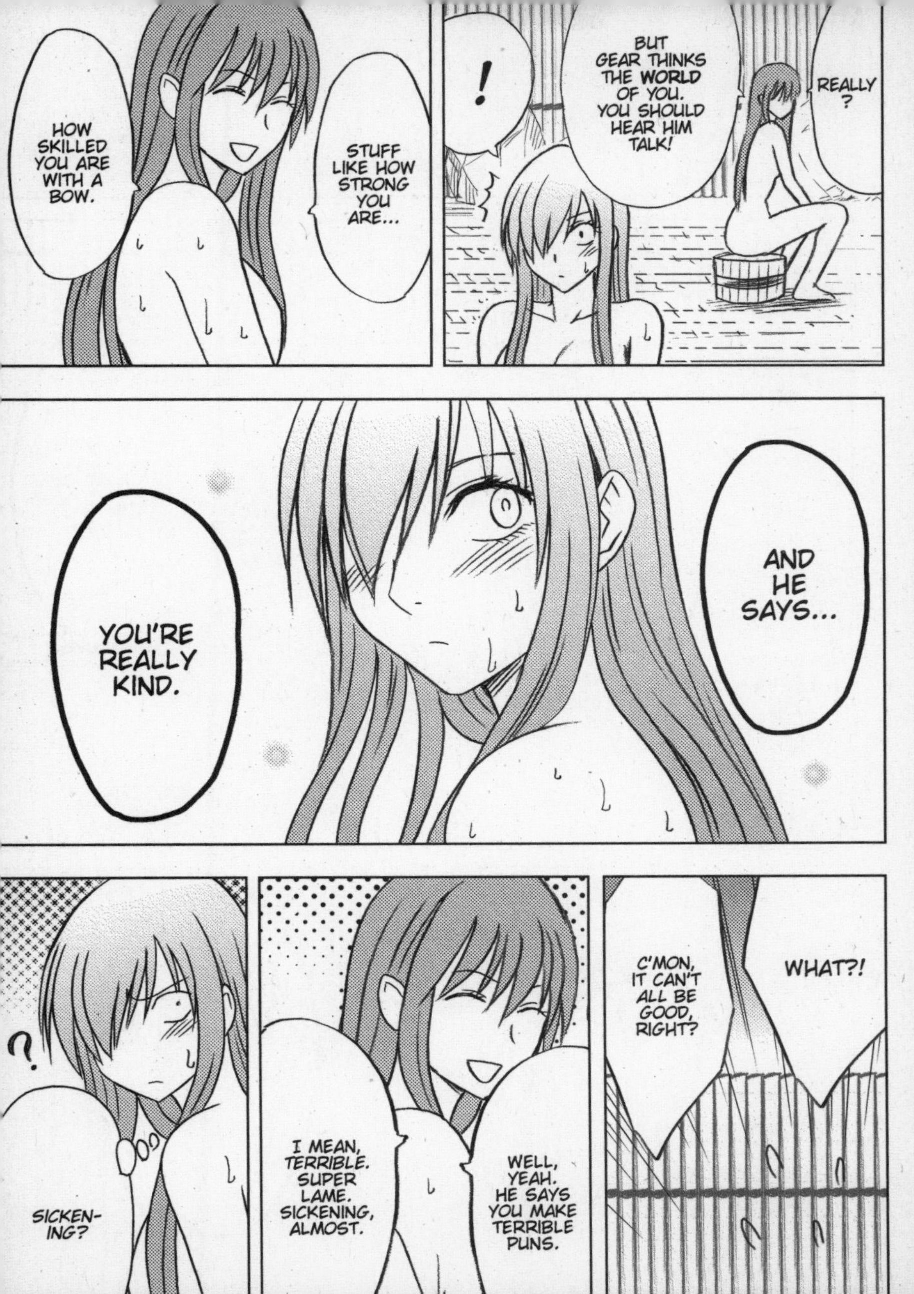
REALLY?
BUT GEAR THINKS THE WORLD OF YOU. YOU SHOULD HEAR HIM TALK!
!
STUFF LIKE HOW STRONG YOU ARE...
HOW SKILLED YOU ARE WITH A BOW.
AND HE SAYS...
YOU'RE REALLY KIND.
WHAT?!
C'MON, IT CAN'T ALL BE GOOD, RIGHT?
WELL, YEAH. HE SAYS YOU MAKE TERRIBLE PUNS.
I MEAN, TERRIBLE. SUPER LAME. SICKENING, ALMOST.
?
SICKEN-ING?

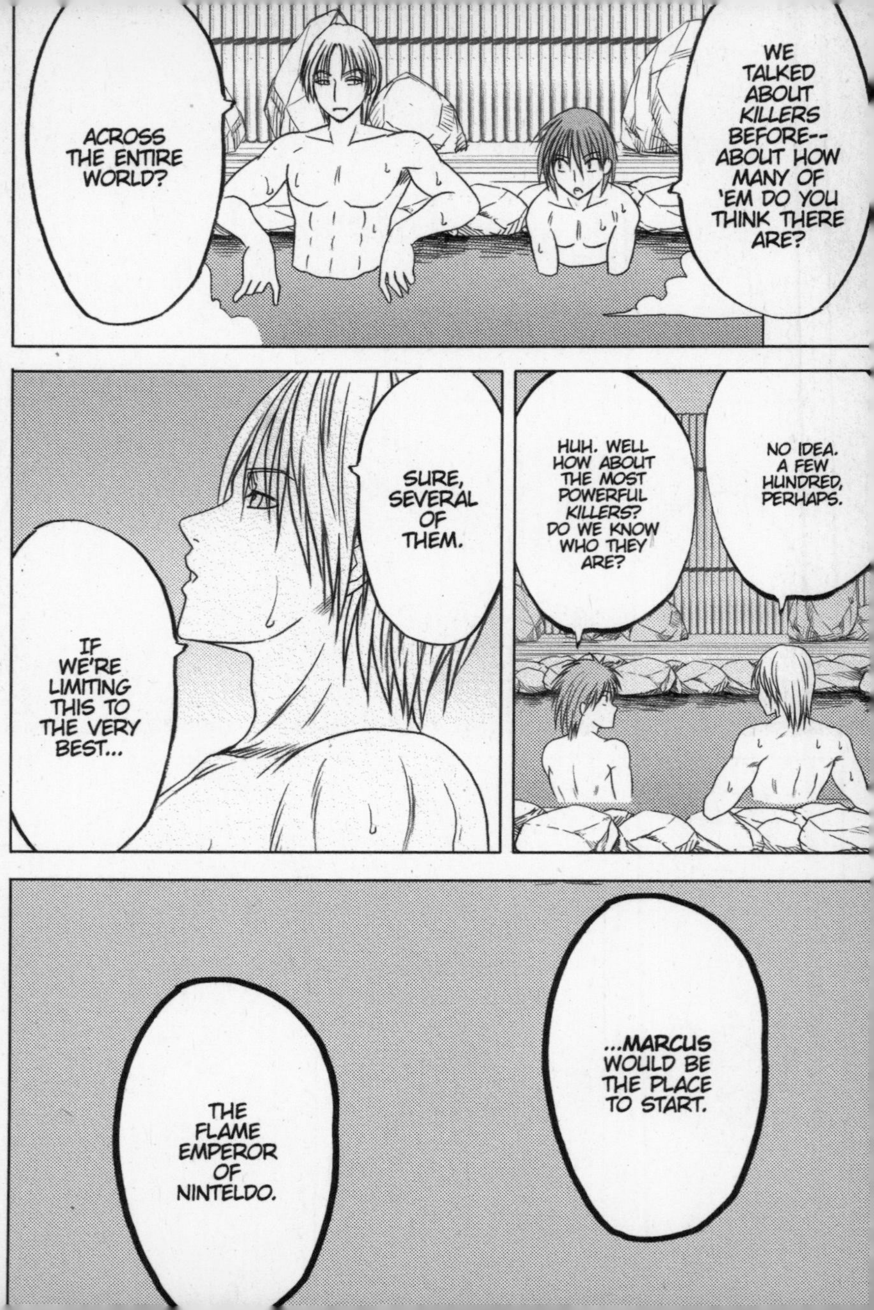
WE TALKED ABOUT KILLERS BEFORE-- ABOUT HOW MANY OF 'EM DO YOU THINK THERE ARE?
ACROSS THE ENTIRE WORLD?
NO IDEA. A FEW HUNDRED, PERHAPS.
HUH. WELL HOW ABOUT THE MOST POWERFUL KILLERS? DO WE KNOW WHO THEY ARE?
SURE, SEVERAL OF THEM.
IF WE'RE LIMITING THIS TO THE VERY BEST...
...MARCUS WOULD BE THE PLACE TO START.
THE FLAME EMPEROR OF NINTELDO.

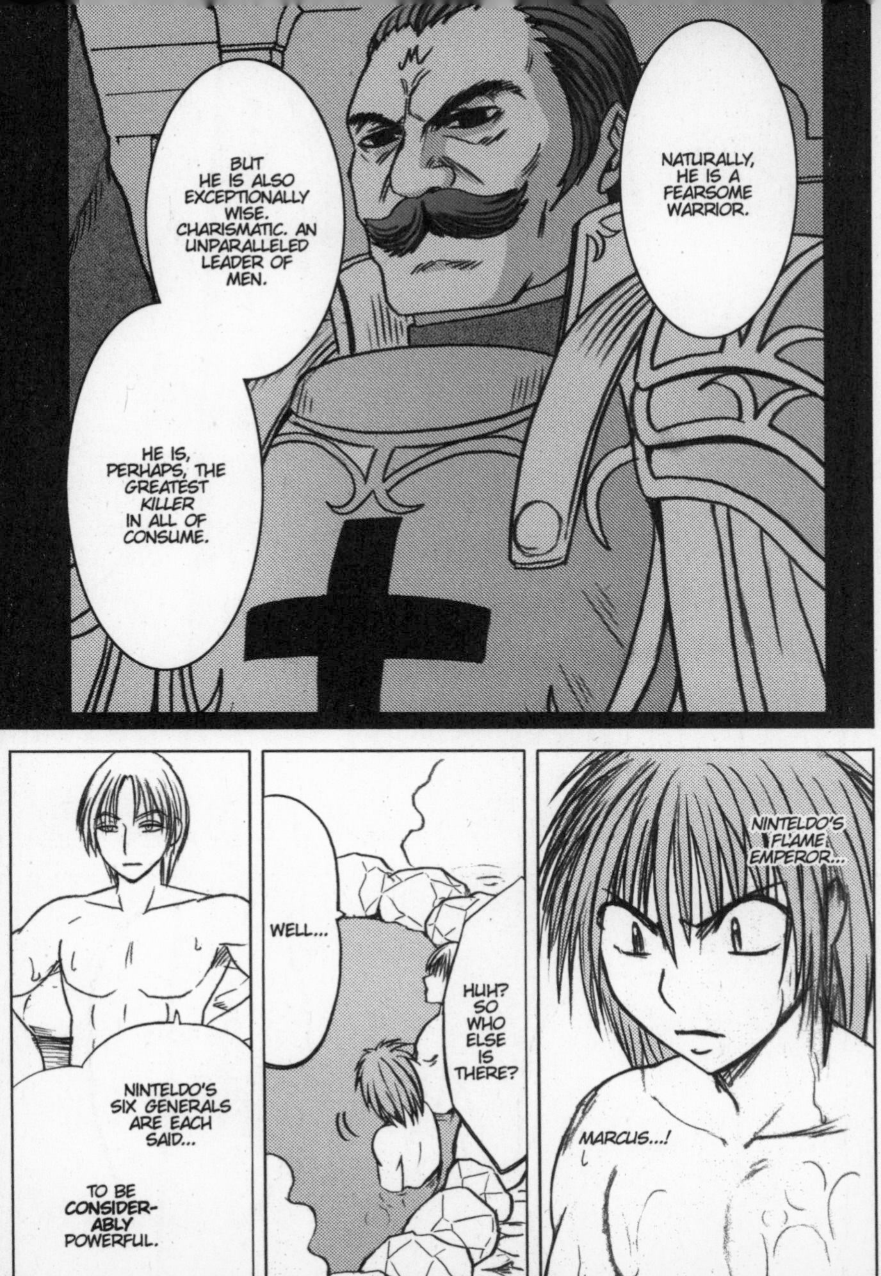
NATURALLY, HE IS A FEARSOME WARRIOR.
BUT HE IS ALSO EXCEPTIONALLY WISE. CHARISMATIC. AN UNPARALLELED LEADER OF MEN.
HE IS, PERHAPS, THE GREATEST KILLER IN ALL OF CONSUME.
NINTELDO'S FLAME EMPEROR...
MARCUS...!
HUH? SO WHO ELSE IS THERE?
WELL...
NINTELDO'S SIX GENERALS ARE EACH SAID...
TO BE CONSIDER-ABLY POWERFUL.

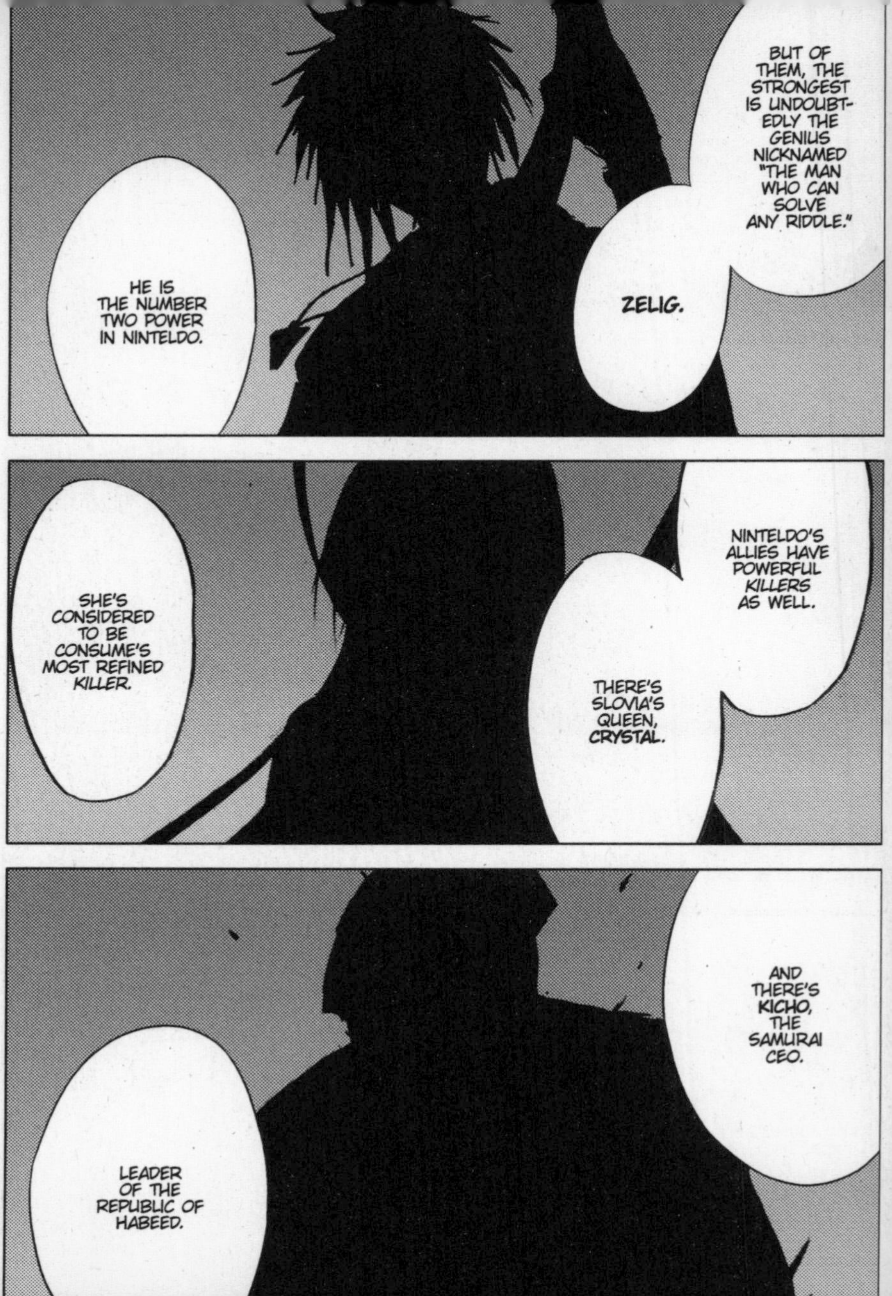
BUT OF THEM, THE STRONGEST IS UNDOUBT-EDLY THE GENIUS NICKNAMED "THE MAN WHO CAN SOLVE ANY RIDDLE."
ZELIG.
HE IS THE NUMBER TWO POWER IN NINTELDO.
NINTELDO'S ALLIES HAVE POWERFUL KILLERS AS WELL.
THERE'S SLOVIA'S QUEEN, CRYSTAL.
SHE'S CONSIDERED TO BE CONSUME'S MOST REFINED KILLER.
AND THERE'S KICHO, THE SAMURAI CEO.
LEADER OF THE REPUBLIC OF HABEED.

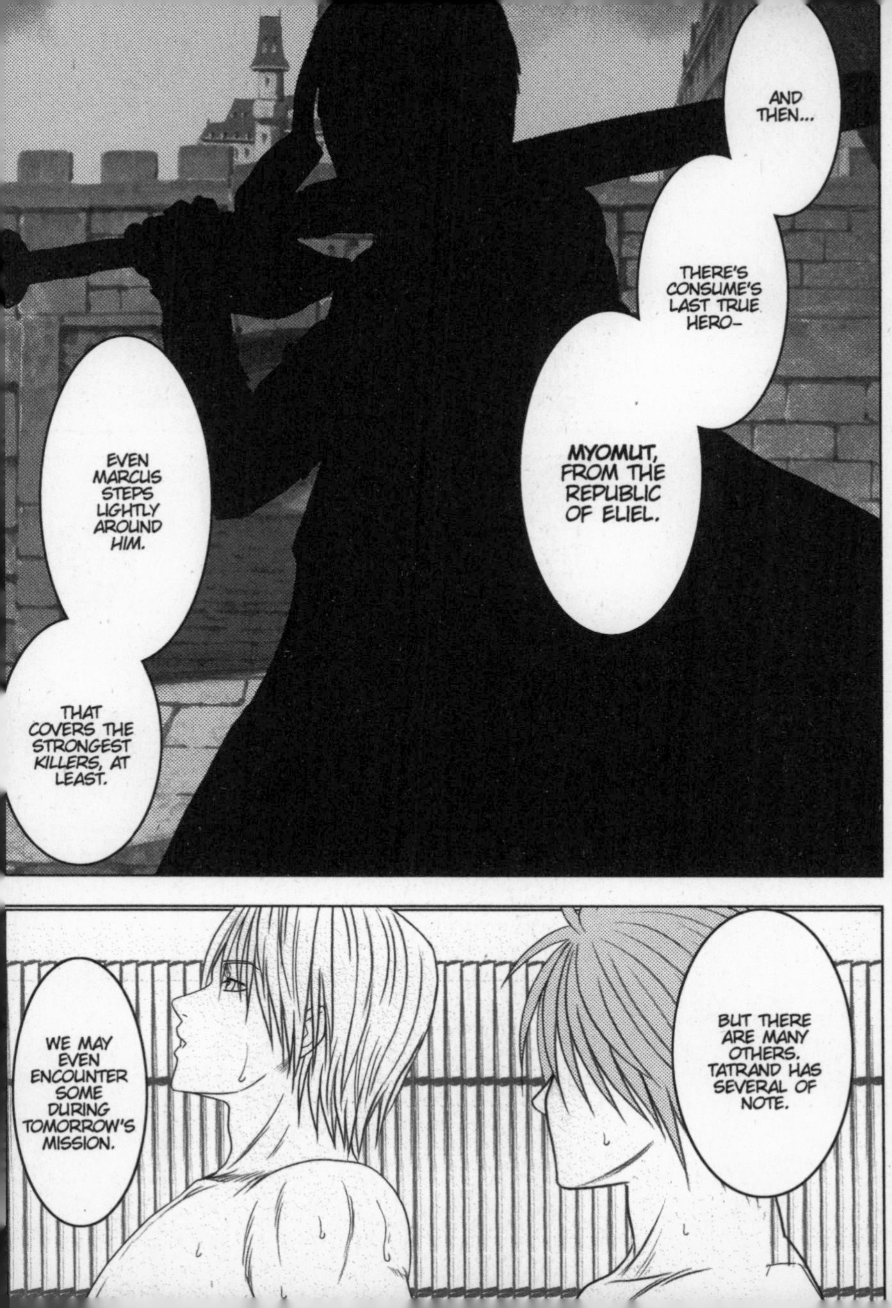
AND THEN...
THERE'S CONSUME'S LAST TRUE HERO–
MYOMUT, FROM THE REPUBLIC OF ELIEL.
EVEN MARCUS STEPS LIGHTLY AROUND HIM.
THAT COVERS THE STRONGEST KILLERS, AT LEAST.
BUT THERE ARE MANY OTHERS. TATRAND HAS SEVERAL OF NOTE.
WE MAY EVEN ENCOUNTER SOME DURING TOMORROW'S MISSION.

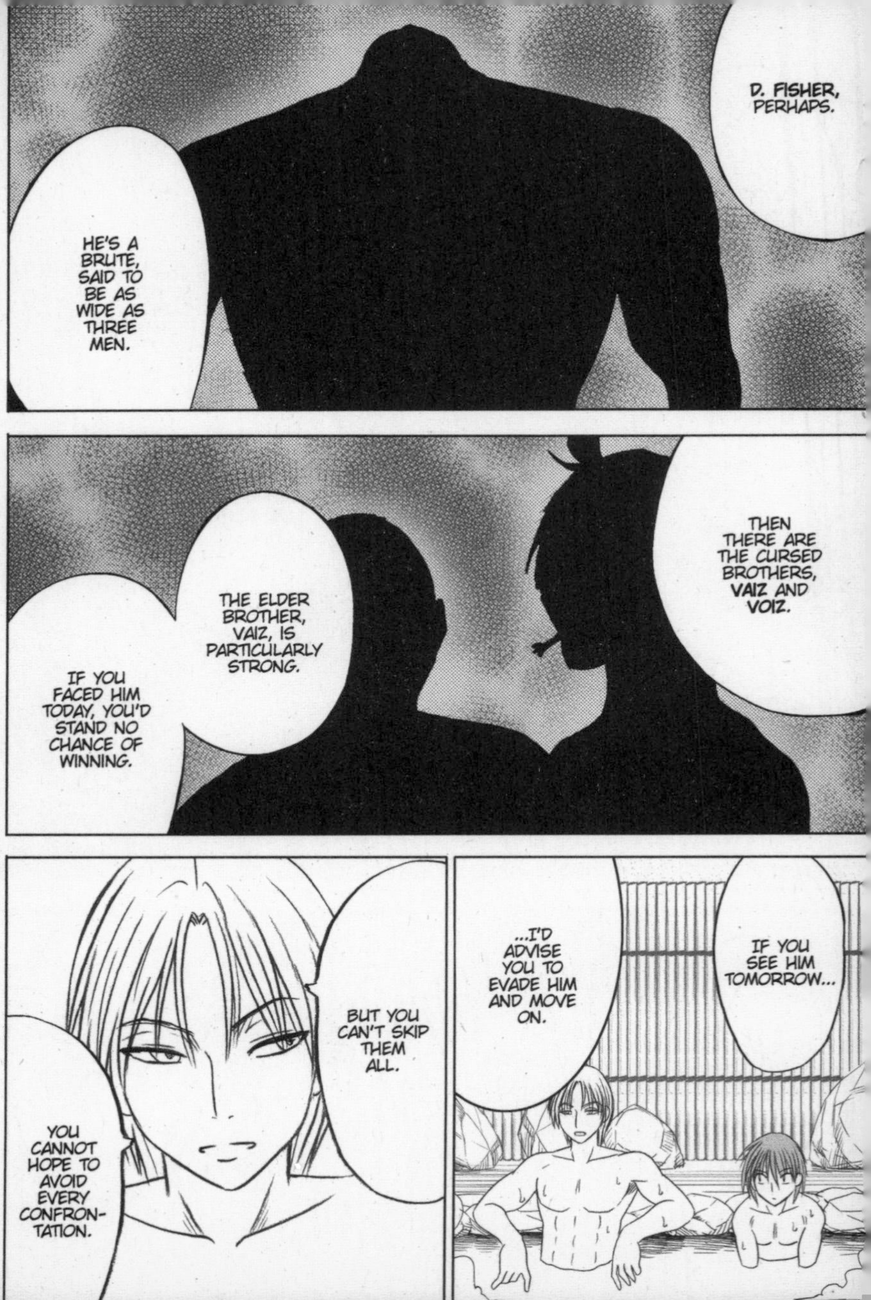
D. FISHER, PERHAPS.
HE'S A BRUTE, SAID TO BE AS WIDE AS THREE MEN.
THEN THERE ARE THE CURSED BROTHERS, VAIZ AND VOIZ.
THE ELDER BROTHER, VAIZ, IS PARTICULARLY STRONG.
IF YOU FACED HIM TODAY, YOU'D STAND NO CHANCE OF WINNING.
IF YOU SEE HIM TOMORROW...
...I'D ADVISE YOU TO EVADE HIM AND MOVE ON.
BUT YOU CAN'T SKIP THEM ALL.
YOU CANNOT HOPE TO AVOID EVERY CONFRON-TATION.

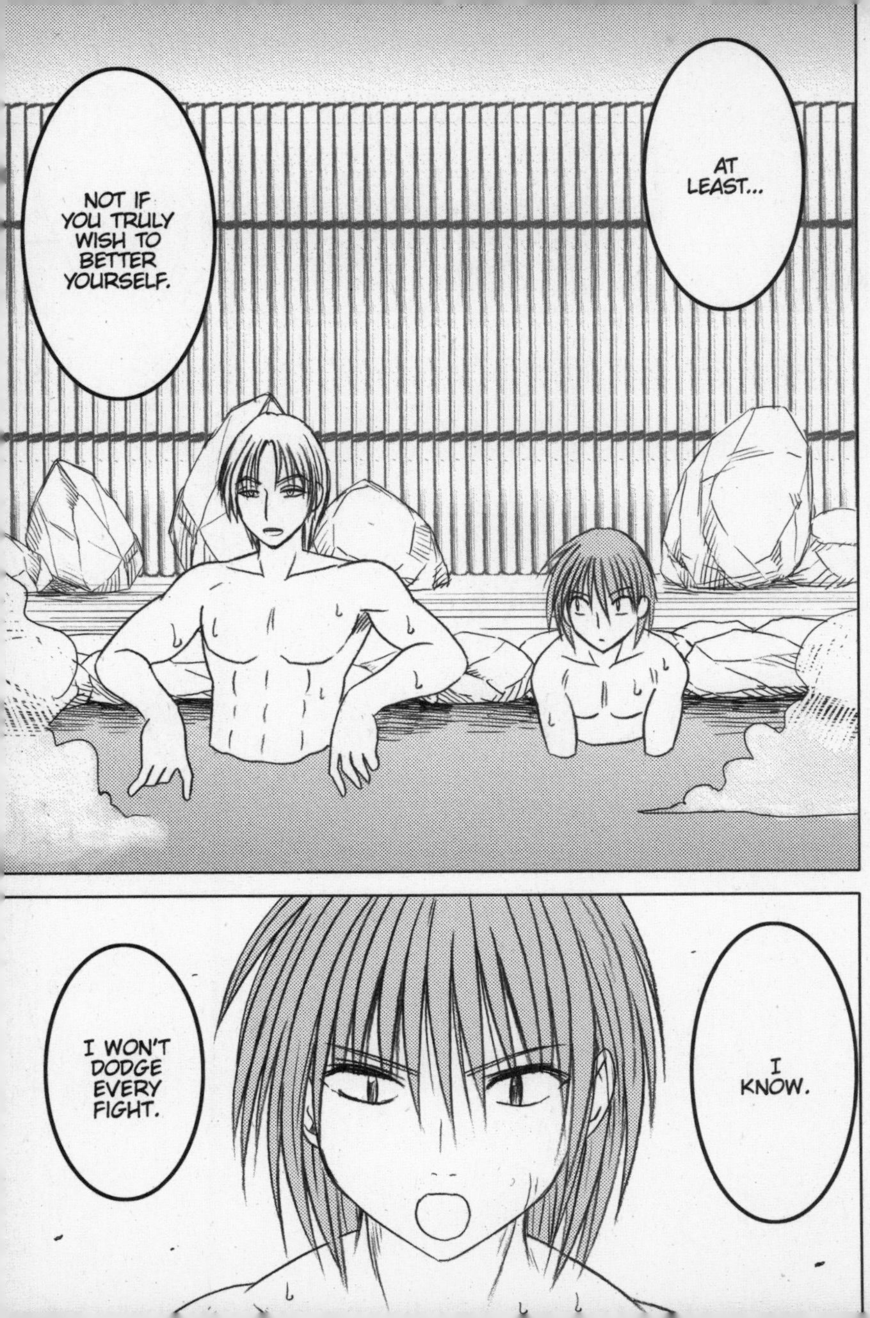
AT LEAST...
NOT IF YOU TRULY WISH TO BETTER YOURSELF.
I KNOW.
I WON'T DODGE EVERY FIGHT.

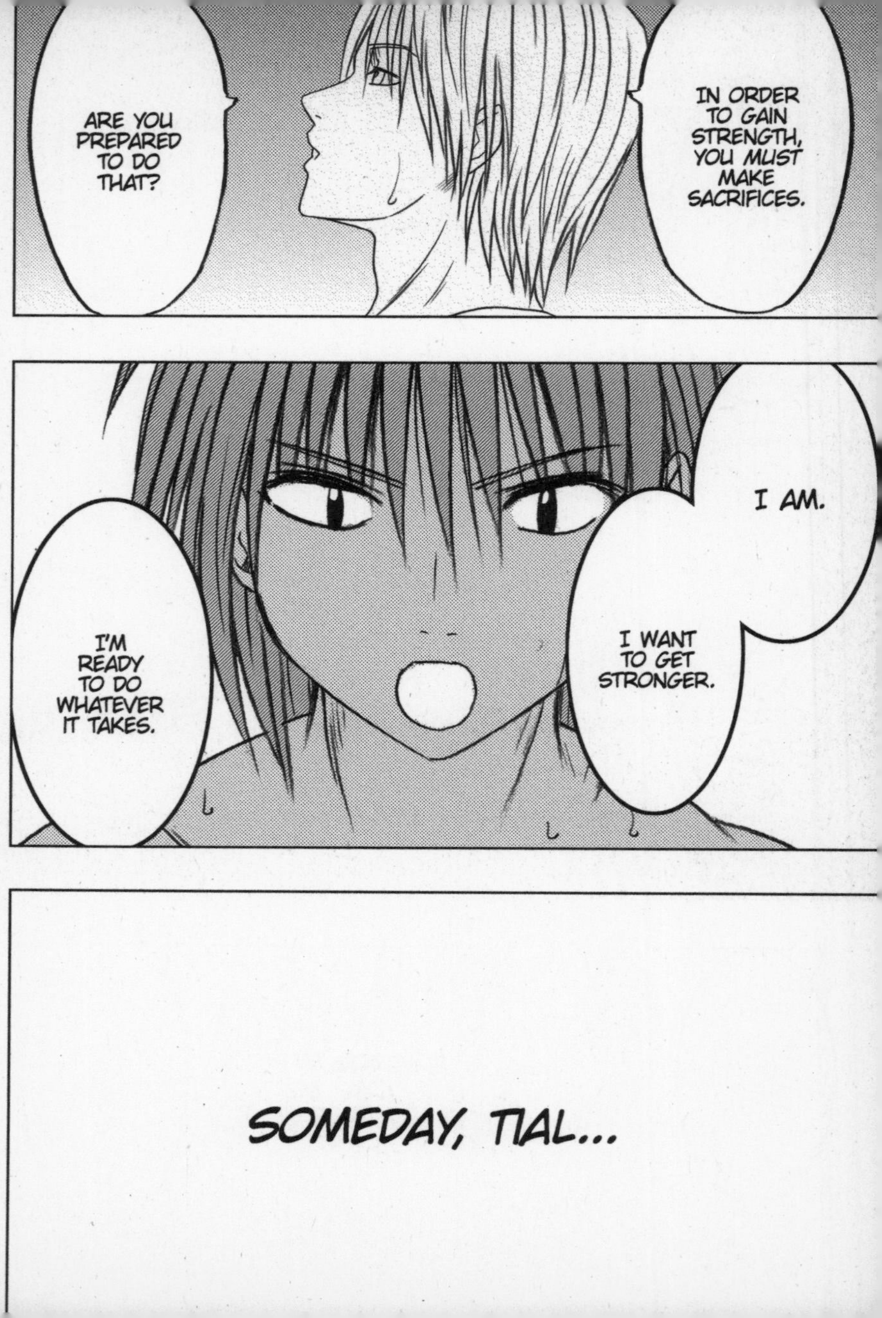
IN ORDER TO GAIN STRENGTH, YOU MUST MAKE SACRIFICES.
ARE YOU PREPARED TO DO THAT?
I AM.
I WANT TO GET STRONGER.
I'M READY TO DO WHATEVER IT TAKES.
SOMEDAY, TIAL...

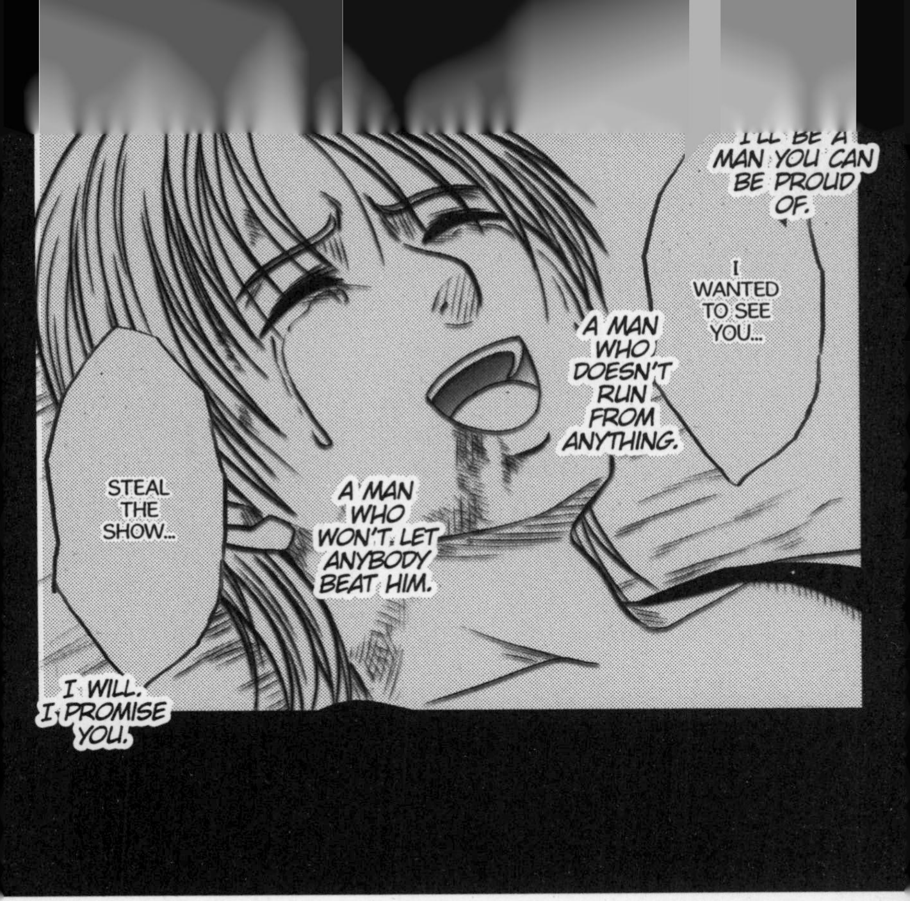
I'LL BE A MAN YOU CAN BE PROUD OF.
I WANTED TO SEE YOU...
A MAN WHO DOESN'T RUN FROM ANYTHING.
A MAN WHO WON'T LET ANYBODY BEAT HIM.
STEAL THE SHOW...
I WILL. I PROMISE YOU.

TOMORROW I'LL TAKE MY FIRST STEP IN THAT DIRECTION!

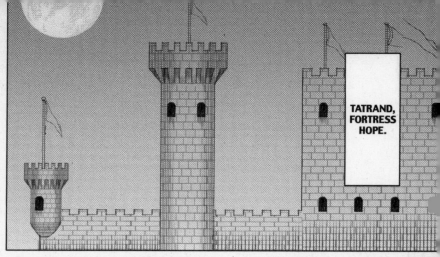

TATRAND, FORTRESS HOPE.
NOTHING BEATS SQUISHIN' FISH EGGS.
I LOVE WATCHING THEM POP.
GURK ...!
GAK ...!!
SPLAT
IT'S LIKE BUSTIN' A WATER BALLOON.

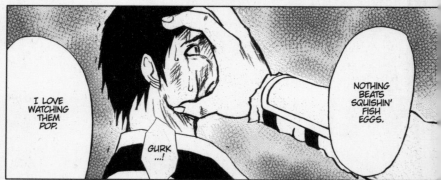

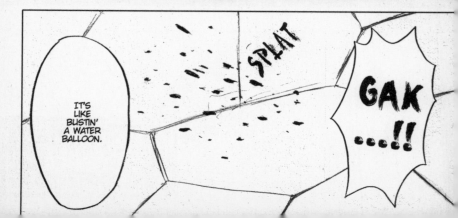

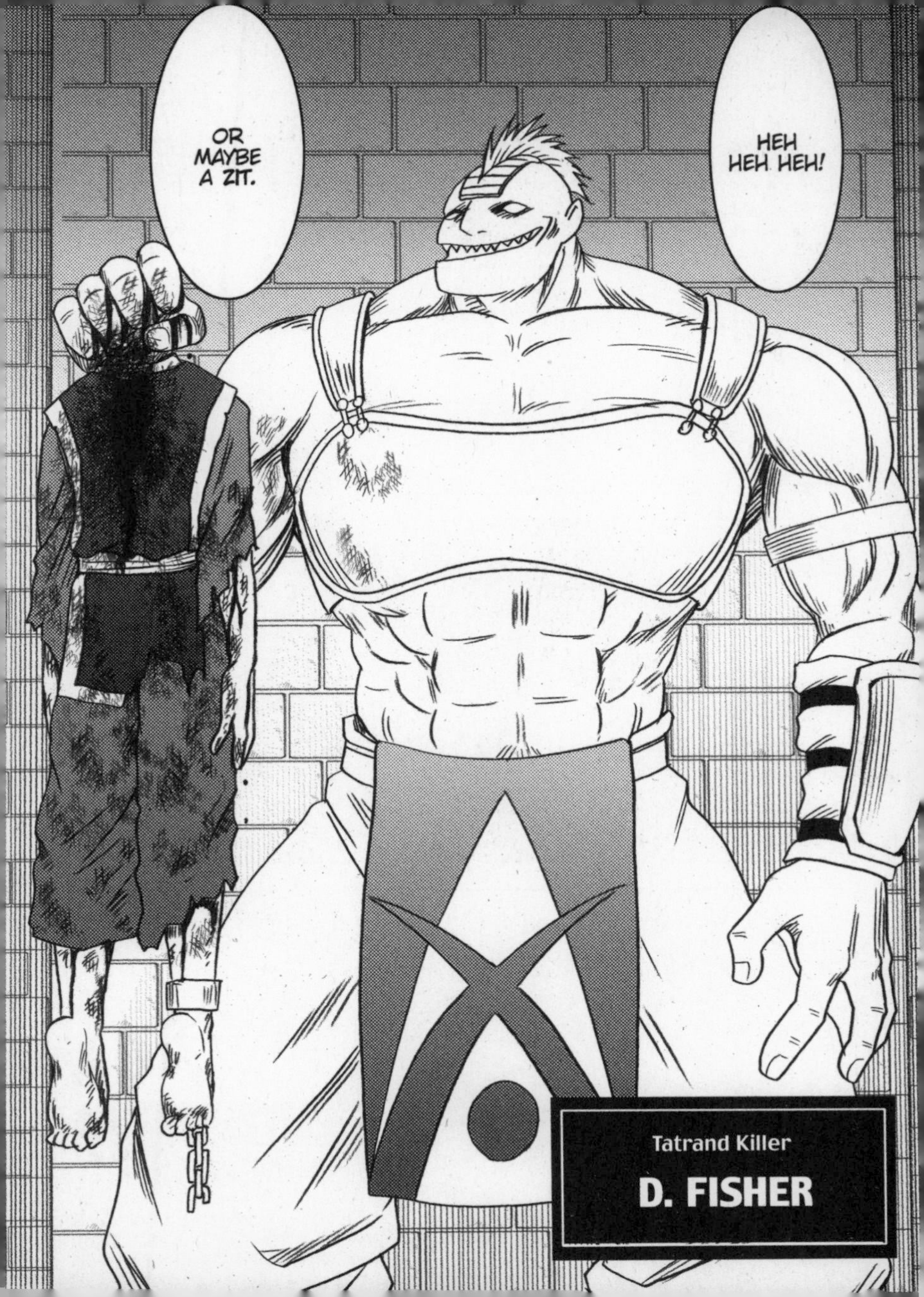
HEH HEH HEH!
OR MAYBE A ZIT.
Tatrand Killer
D. FISHER

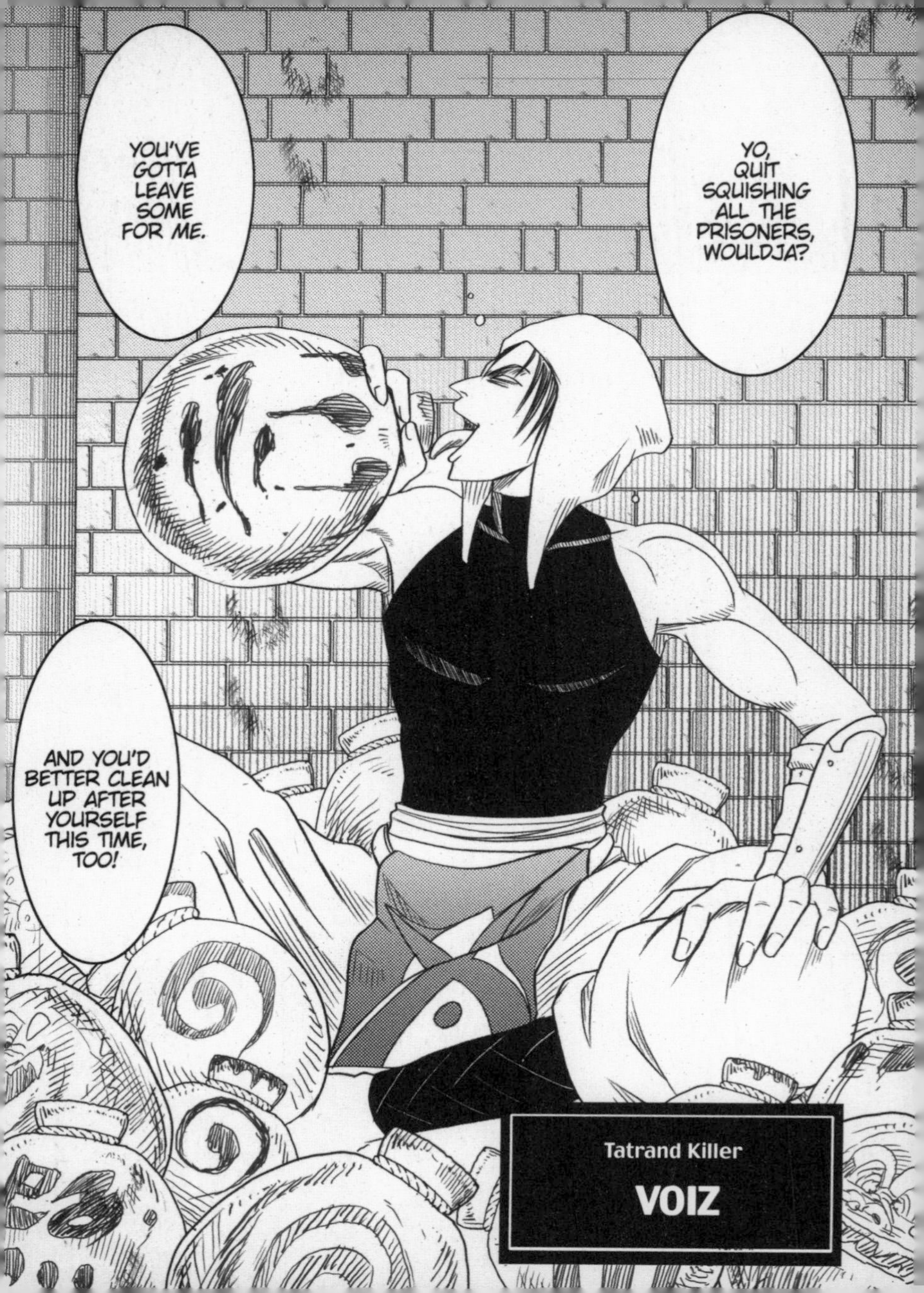
YO, QUIT SQUISHING ALL THE PRISONERS, WOULDJA?
YOU'VE GOTTA LEAVE SOME FOR ME.
AND YOU'D BETTER CLEAN UP AFTER YOURSELF THIS TIME, TOO!
Tatrand Killer
VOIZ

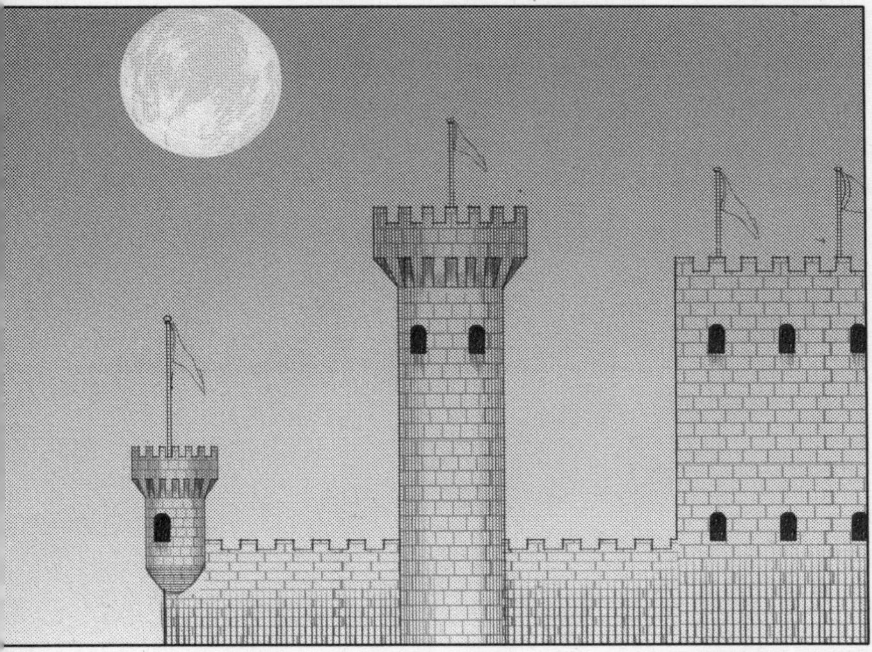

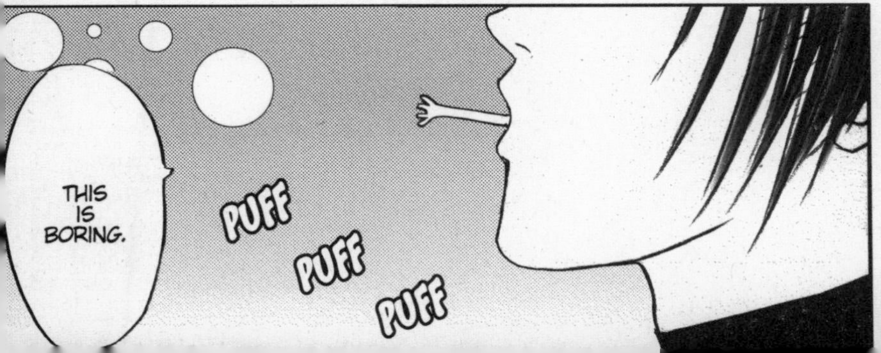
PUFF
PUFF
PUFF
THIS IS BORING.

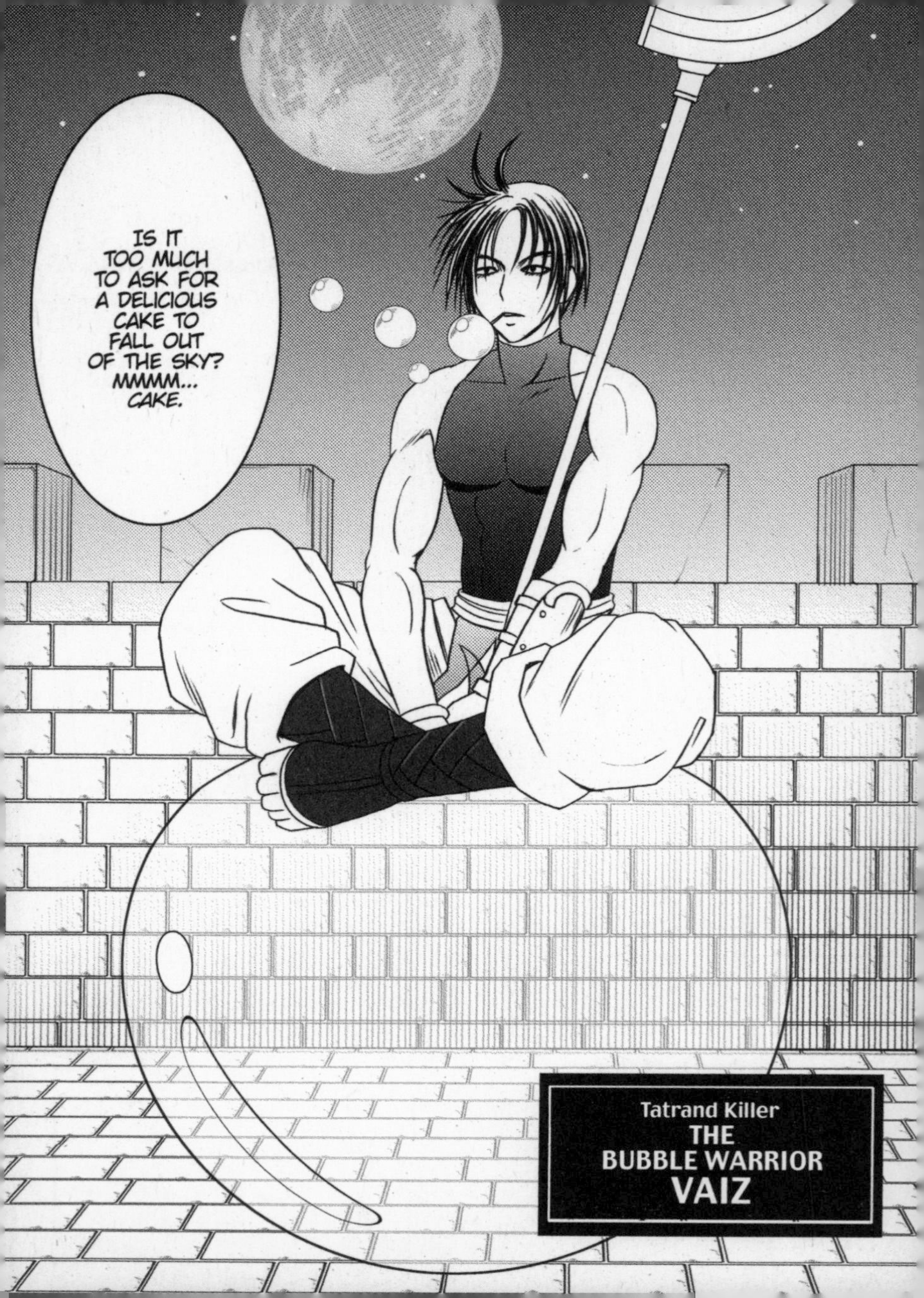
IS IT TOO MUCH TO ASK FOR A DELICIOUS CAKE TO FALL OUT OF THE SKY? MMMM... CAKE.
Tatrand Killer
THE BUBBLE WARRIOR
VAIZ

WORLD WAR BLUE
CHARACTER INTRODUCTION

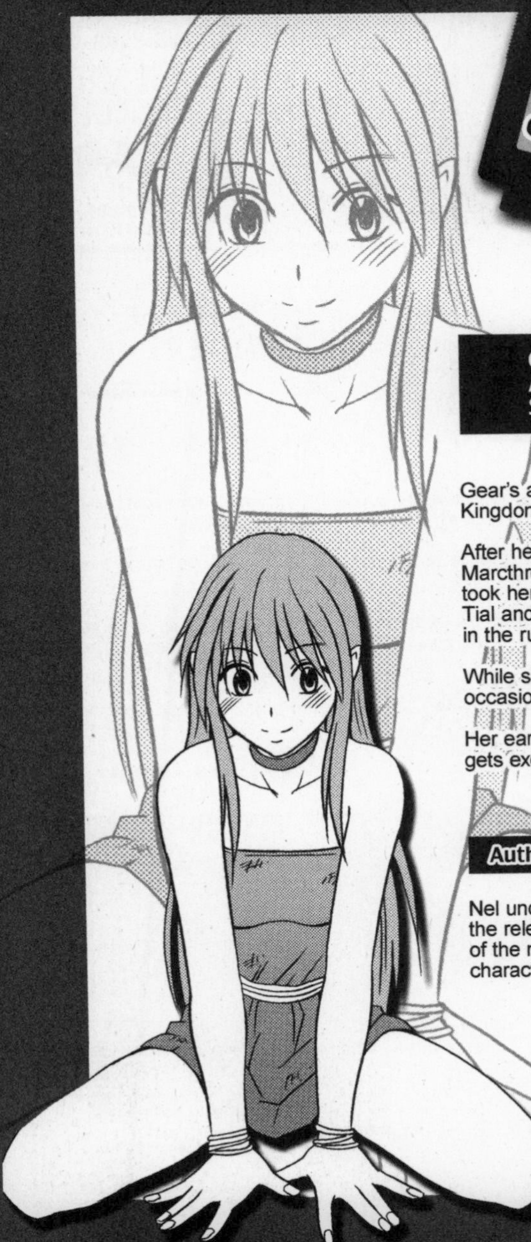

Gear's Adopted Sister: NEL

Gear's adopted sister is a native of the Kingdom of Segua.

After her mother was killed in the Marcthree massacre, Gear found her and took her in. From that point forward, Gear, Tial and Nel stayed together as a "family" in the ruins of the village.

While she is very kind, she can occasionally be sharp-tongued.

Her ears are slightly pointed. When she gets excited, they seem even more pointy.

Author Comment

Nel underwent a few changes with the release of this updated version of the manga. "Little sister" characters are hard to get right.

NEL

ON THE EDGE OF THE BLUE WORLD

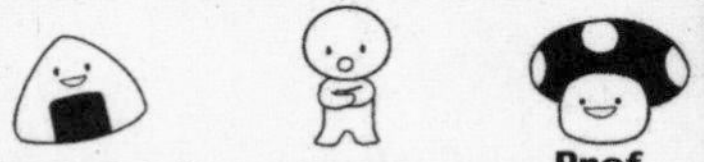

Dr. Onigiri Mr. Why Prof. Mushroom

Today's Topic

THIRD PARTY DEVELOPERS

Mr. Why: Hello, everyone! In this chat corner, the Doctor, the Professor, and I are going to talk a little about video games and their history. Just as a warning, it's not going to have much to do with what's going on in the story.

Dr. Onigiri: Hi! I'm Dr. Onigiri. Onigiri are best when they come in sets of two. Two is always better than one.

Prof. Mushroom: Yo! I'm Professor Mushroom. My special talent is walking sideways.

Mr. Why: So this time we're talking about Third Party Developers. I don't get it. Did the first two parties run out of punch and pie?

Prof. Mushroom: Exactly! The first party had a little too much dubstep, the second party served only diet colas, and the third party...wait, no.

Dr. Onigiri: <sigh> Put simply, they're outside contractors game companies hire to make games.

Prof. Mushroom: Right. Companies who make games for their own consoles are first-party developers, like Nintendo and Sega. At least, when Sega still made consoles, they were a first-party developer.

Dr. Onigiri: Well we're talking about a time when both Nintendo and Sega had consoles, so they're first-party! So there!

Prof. Mushroom: Okay, okay! Yeesh. Anyway, when companies that *aren't* Nintendo make games for Nintendo's consoles, they're called third party developers. Got it?

Dr. Onigiri: Basically, it's one company doing contract work for another.

Mr. Why: Oh, okay.

Prof. Mushroom: Now, Sega mostly released games developed in-house. But Nintendo made use of third party developers in the very early days of the NES.

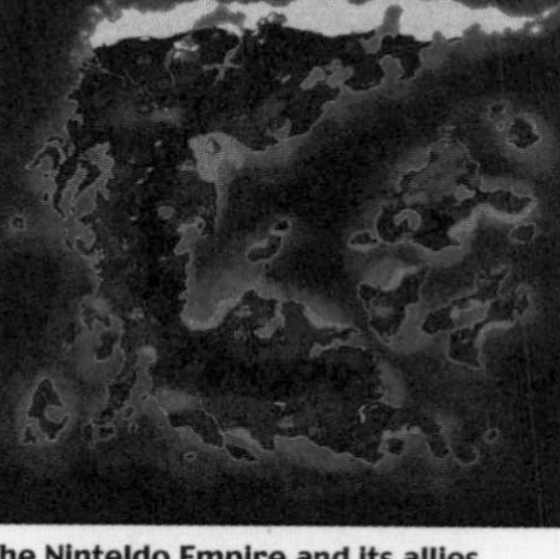

The Ninteldo Empire and its allies control 90% of the Consume continent.

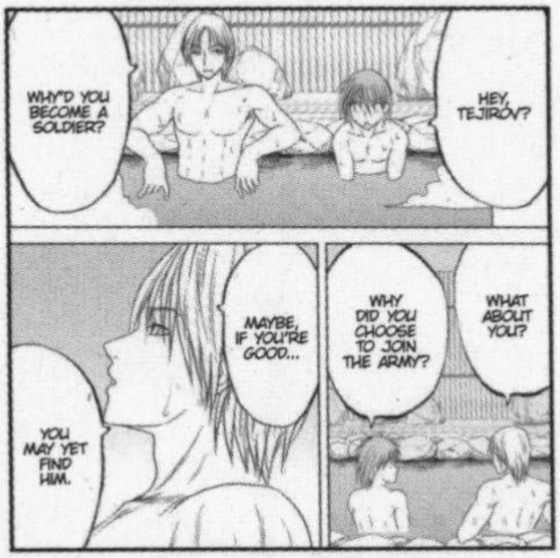
HEY, TEJIROV?
WHY'D YOU BECOME A SOLDIER?
WHAT ABOUT YOU?
WHY DID YOU CHOOSE TO JOIN THE ARMY?
MAYBE, IF YOU'RE GOOD...
YOU MAY YET FIND HIM.
The outcome of a battle is often determined by the number of Killers on either side.

Prof. Mushroom: Thus, Nintendo wound up with a super-diverse lineup of games, which made them popular with lots of different gamer demographics.

Mr. Why: Wow. So what kind of games did they have?

Prof. Mushroom: Okay, if we're gonna start with the big ones first, you've got to mention SquareSoft. Their RPG *Final Fantasy* helped define the genre. Hudson Soft was also up there, with their *Momotaro Dentetsu* series. Then there was Enix and *Dragon Quest*, which stood shoulder-to-shoulder with Mario for popularity. Oh! And you can't forget Taito and Data East and a whole host of others.

Mr. Why: Wait, I thought the same company made both *Final Fantasy* and *Dragon Quest*.

Prof. Mushroom: Well, they're the same company *now*, but back then, they were separate.

Mr. Why: Oh, okay.

Prof. Mushroom: By the way, *Dragon Quest* and *Final Fantasy* were flagship titles for their creators. People would buy the whole console just to play those games, and so they were called "killer apps." Naturally a console with more killer apps would do better.

Dr. Onigiri: Going back to the days of the Sega Mark III, *Fantasy Zone* and *Phantasy Star* were killer apps.

Prof. Mushroom: And the NES had the *Mario* and *Zelda* titles as killer apps developed in-house. But then it also had lots of other killer apps it distributed for third party developers. That's one of the big reasons why Nintendo had such great success.

To Be Continued...

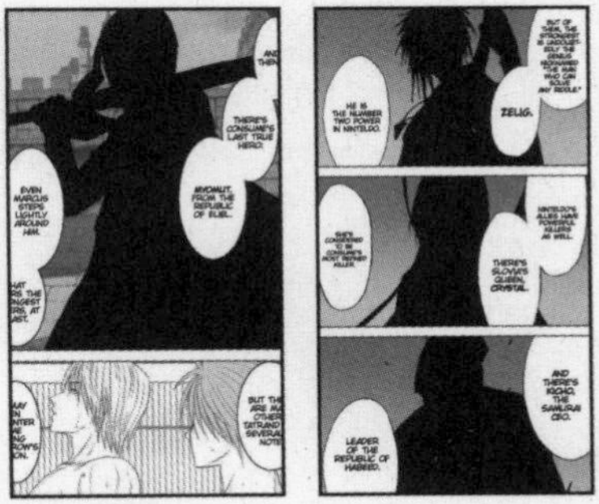
ZELIG.
HE IS THE NUMBER TWO POWER IN NINTELDO.
NINTELDO'S ALLIES HAVE POWERFUL KILLERS AS WELL.
THERE'S SLOVIA'S QUEEN, CRYSTAL.
LEADER OF THE REPUBLIC OF HABEED.
THERE'S CONSUME'S LAST TRUE HERO!
EVEN MARCUS STEPS LIGHTLY AROUND HIM.
Various Killers of Consume.

WORLD WAR BLUE

CHARACTER INTRODUCTION

MARCUS

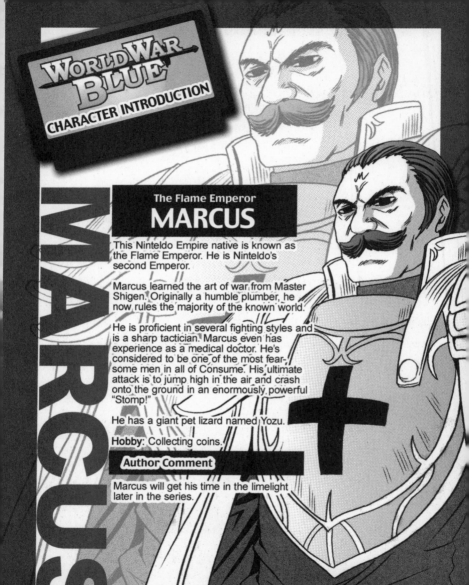

The Flame Emperor
MARCUS

This Ninteldo Empire native is known as the Flame Emperor. He is Ninteldo's second Emperor.

Marcus learned the art of war from Master Shigen. Originally a humble plumber, he now rules the majority of the known world.

He is proficient in several fighting styles and is a sharp tactician. Marcus even has experience as a medical doctor. He's considered to be one of the most fearsome men in all of Consume. His ultimate attack is to jump high in the air and crash onto the ground in an enormously powerful "Stomp!"

He has a giant pet lizard named Yozu.

Hobby: Collecting coins.

Author Comment

Marcus will get his time in the limelight later in the series.

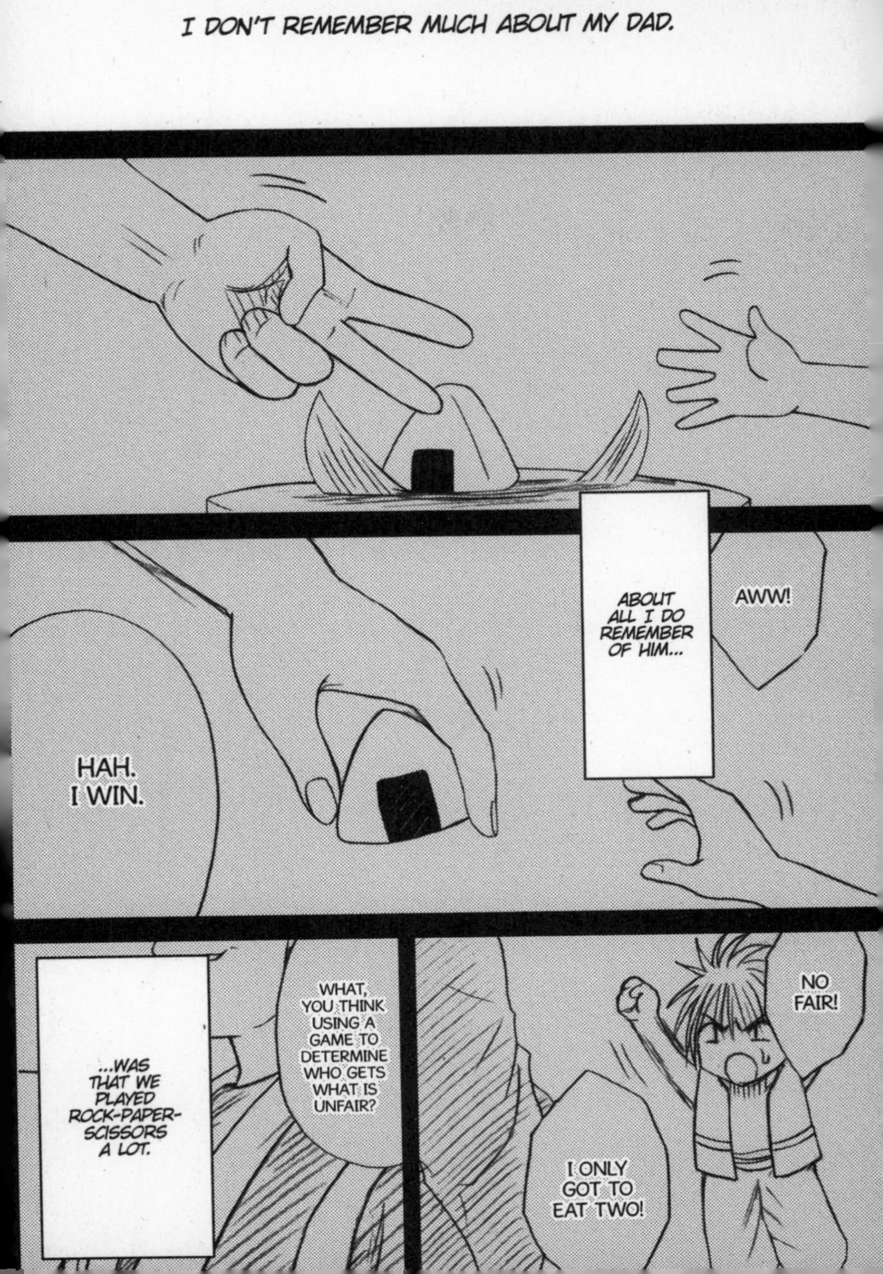
I DON'T REMEMBER MUCH ABOUT MY DAD.
AWW!
ABOUT ALL I DO REMEMBER OF HIM...
HAH. I WIN.
NO FAIR!
I ONLY GOT TO EAT TWO!
WHAT, YOU THINK USING A GAME TO DETERMINE WHO GETS WHAT IS UNFAIR?
...WAS THAT WE PLAYED ROCK-PAPER-SCISSORS A LOT.

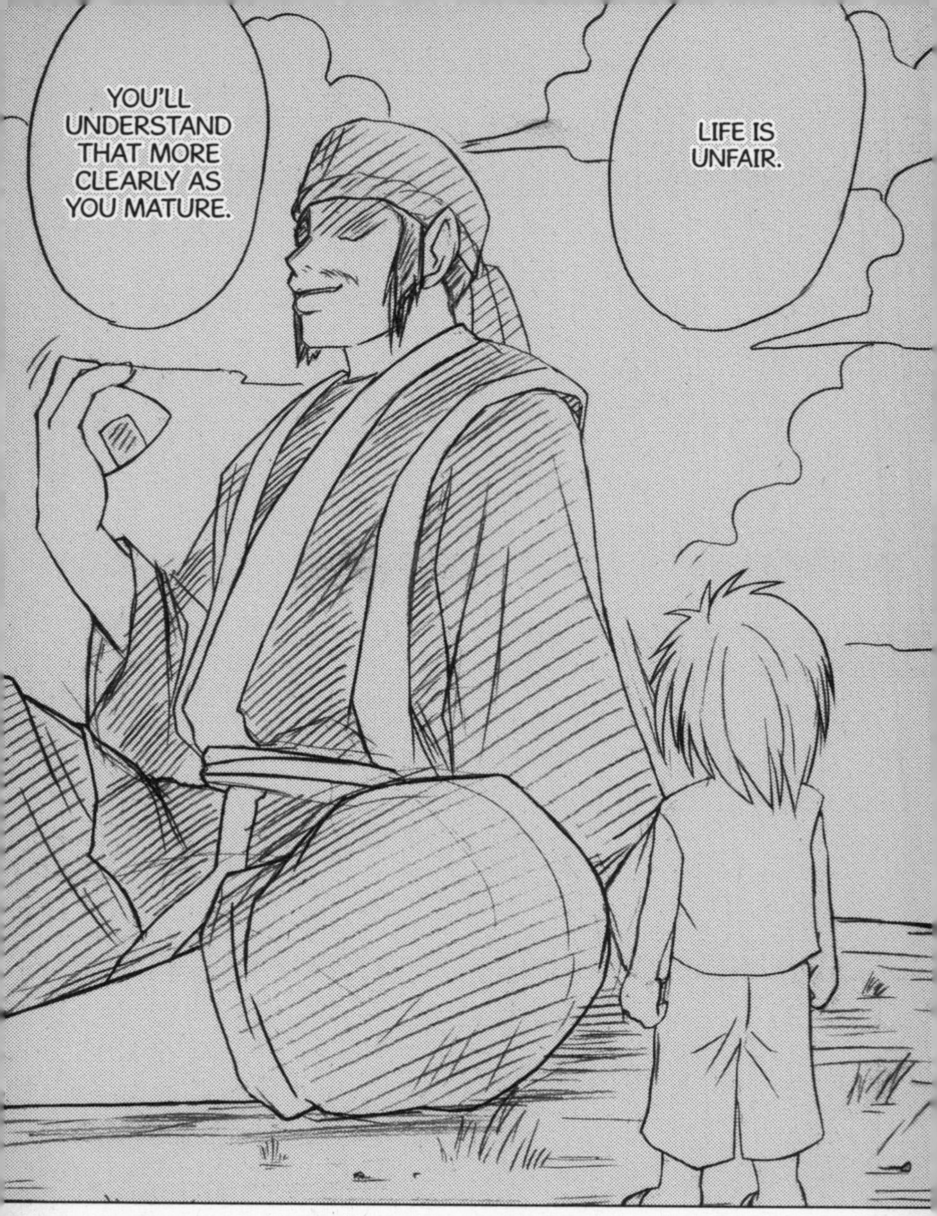
LIFE IS UNFAIR.
YOU'LL UNDERSTAND THAT MORE CLEARLY AS YOU MATURE.

I DO REMEMBER WHEN HE SAID THAT.

AT THE TIME,
I DIDN'T GET
WHAT HE MEANT.

BUT FOR SOME
REASON, THE WORDS
STUCK IN MY
HEAD.

LOOKING
BACK ON IT
NOW...

IT'S ALMOST
LIKE HE KNEW
WHAT WAS
COMING.

CHAPTER 8

OUR POWERS COMBINED

Part 1

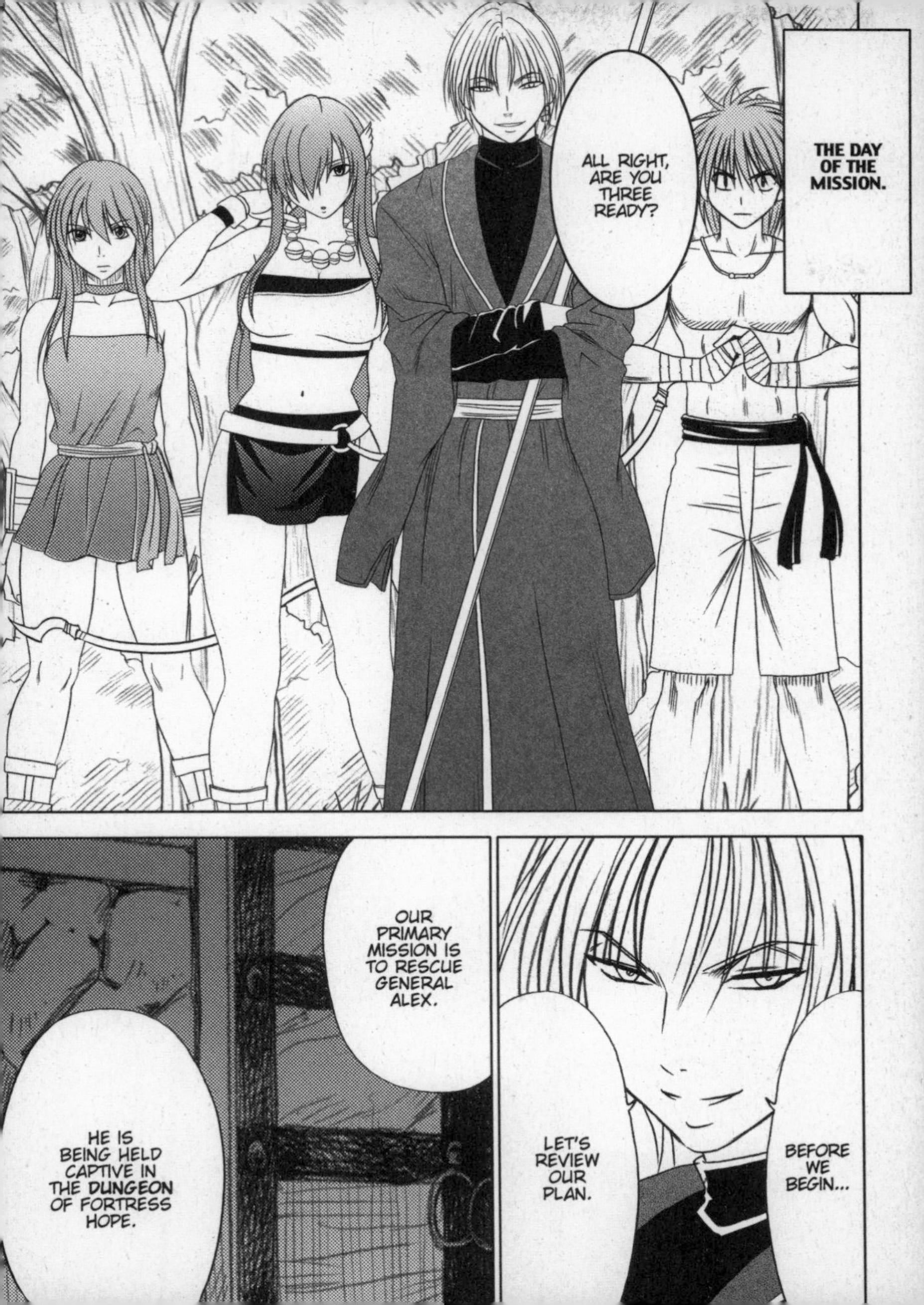
THE DAY OF THE MISSION.
ALL RIGHT, ARE YOU THREE READY?
BEFORE WE BEGIN...
LET'S REVIEW OUR PLAN.
OUR PRIMARY MISSION IS TO RESCUE GENERAL ALEX.
HE IS BEING HELD CAPTIVE IN THE DUNGEON OF FORTRESS HOPE.

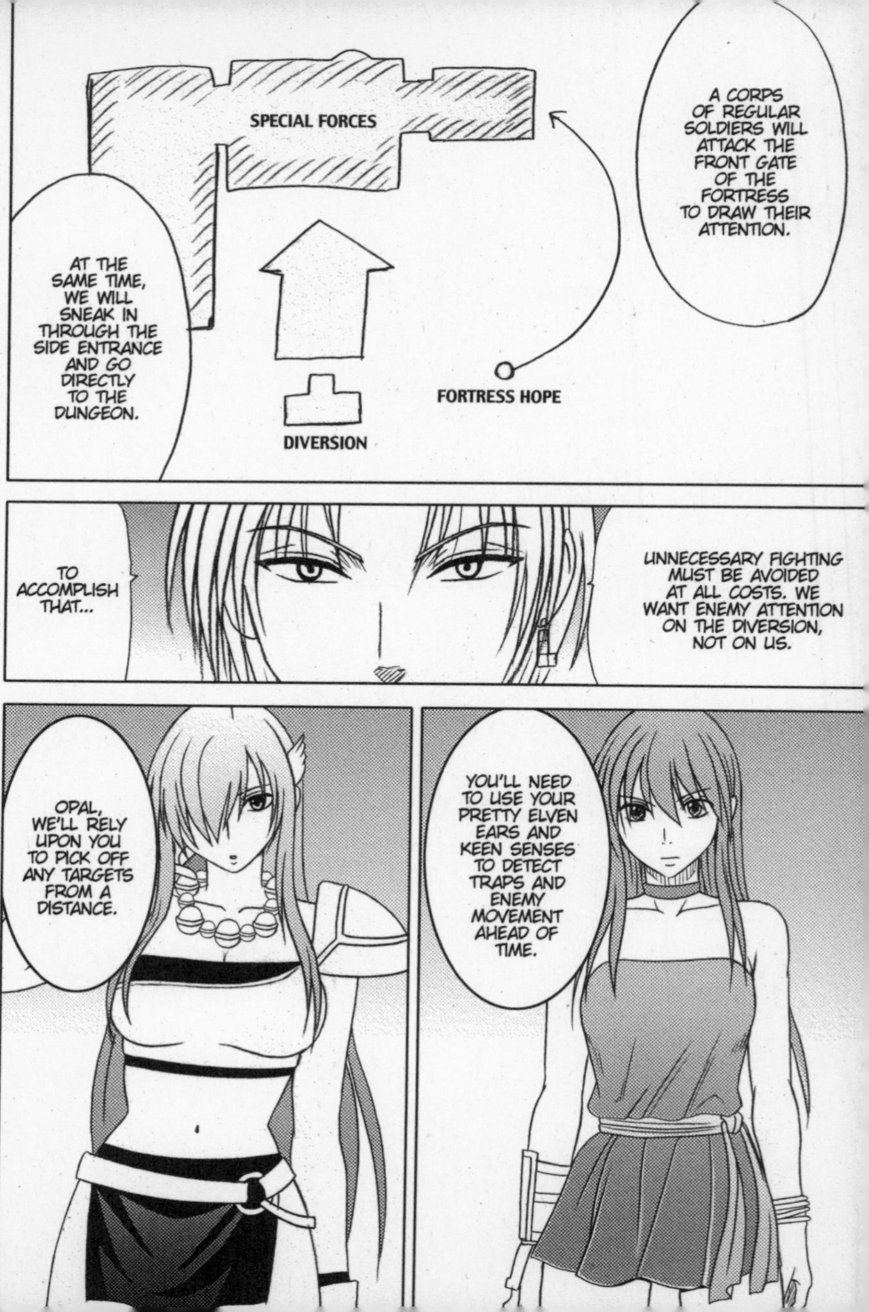
A CORPS OF REGULAR SOLDIERS WILL ATTACK THE FRONT GATE OF THE FORTRESS TO DRAW THEIR ATTENTION.
SPECIAL FORCES
AT THE SAME TIME, WE WILL SNEAK IN THROUGH THE SIDE ENTRANCE AND GO DIRECTLY TO THE DUNGEON.
FORTRESS HOPE
DIVERSION
UNNECESSARY FIGHTING MUST BE AVOIDED AT ALL COSTS. WE WANT ENEMY ATTENTION ON THE DIVERSION, NOT ON US.
TO ACCOMPLISH THAT...
YOU'LL NEED TO USE YOUR PRETTY ELVEN EARS AND KEEN SENSES TO DETECT TRAPS AND ENEMY MOVEMENT AHEAD OF TIME.
OPAL, WE'LL RELY UPON YOU TO PICK OFF ANY TARGETS FROM A DISTANCE.

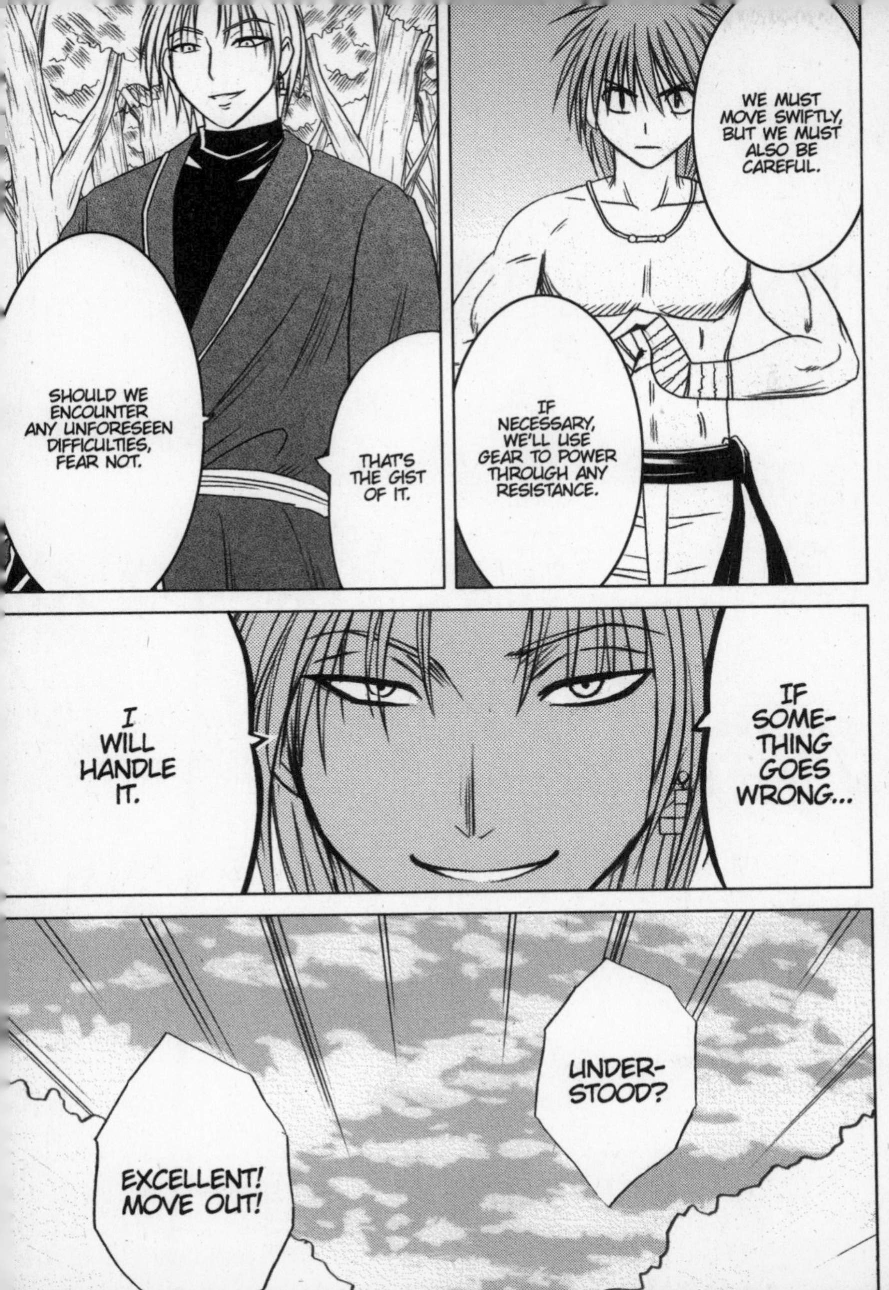
WE MUST MOVE SWIFTLY, BUT WE MUST ALSO BE CAREFUL.
IF NECESSARY, WE'LL USE GEAR TO POWER THROUGH ANY RESISTANCE.
THAT'S THE GIST OF IT.
SHOULD WE ENCOUNTER ANY UNFORESEEN DIFFICULTIES, FEAR NOT.
IF SOME-THING GOES WRONG...
I WILL HANDLE IT.
UNDER-STOOD?
EXCELLENT! MOVE OUT!

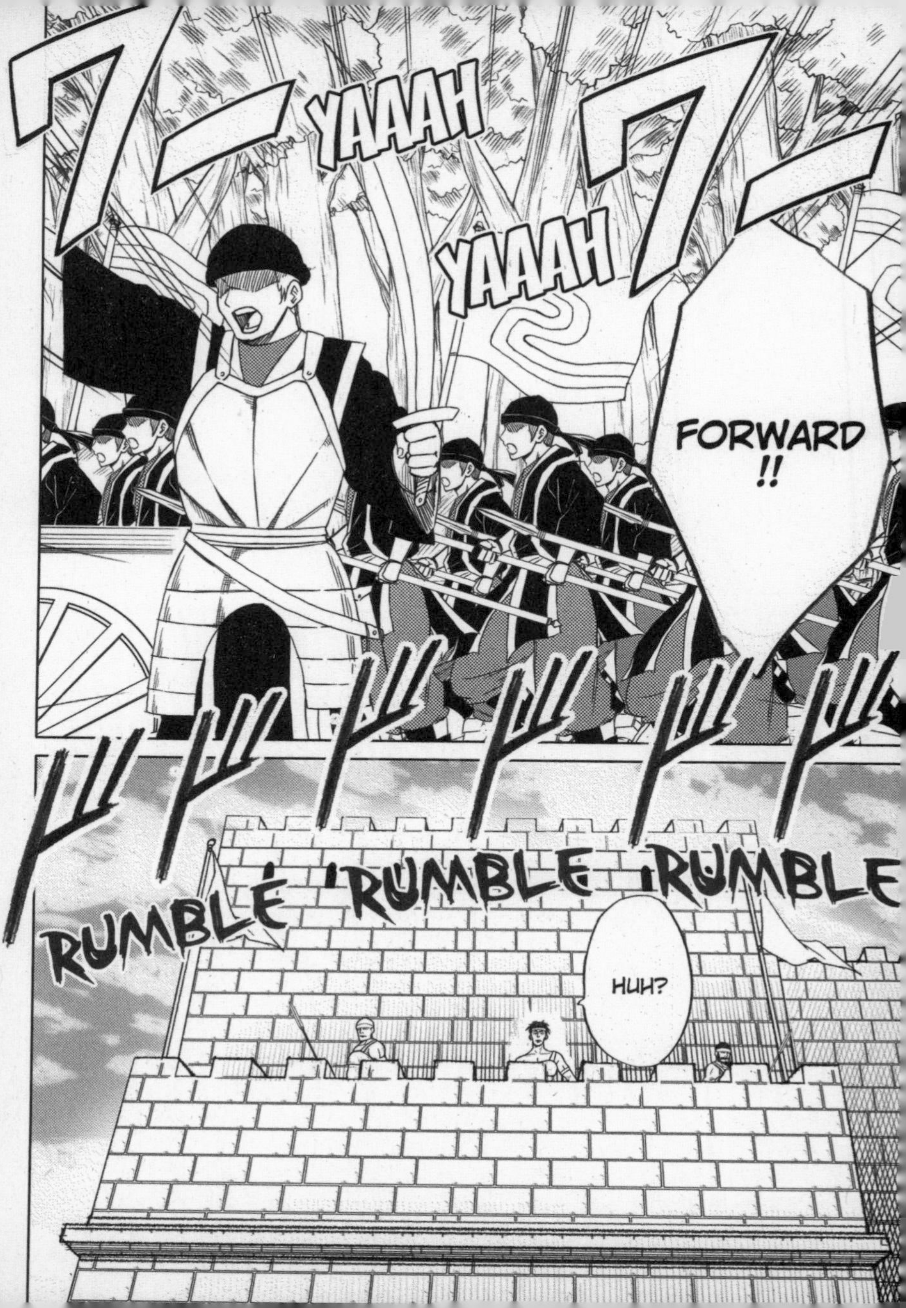
YAAAH
YAAAH
FORWARD !!
RUMBLE
RUMBLE
RUMBLE
HUH?

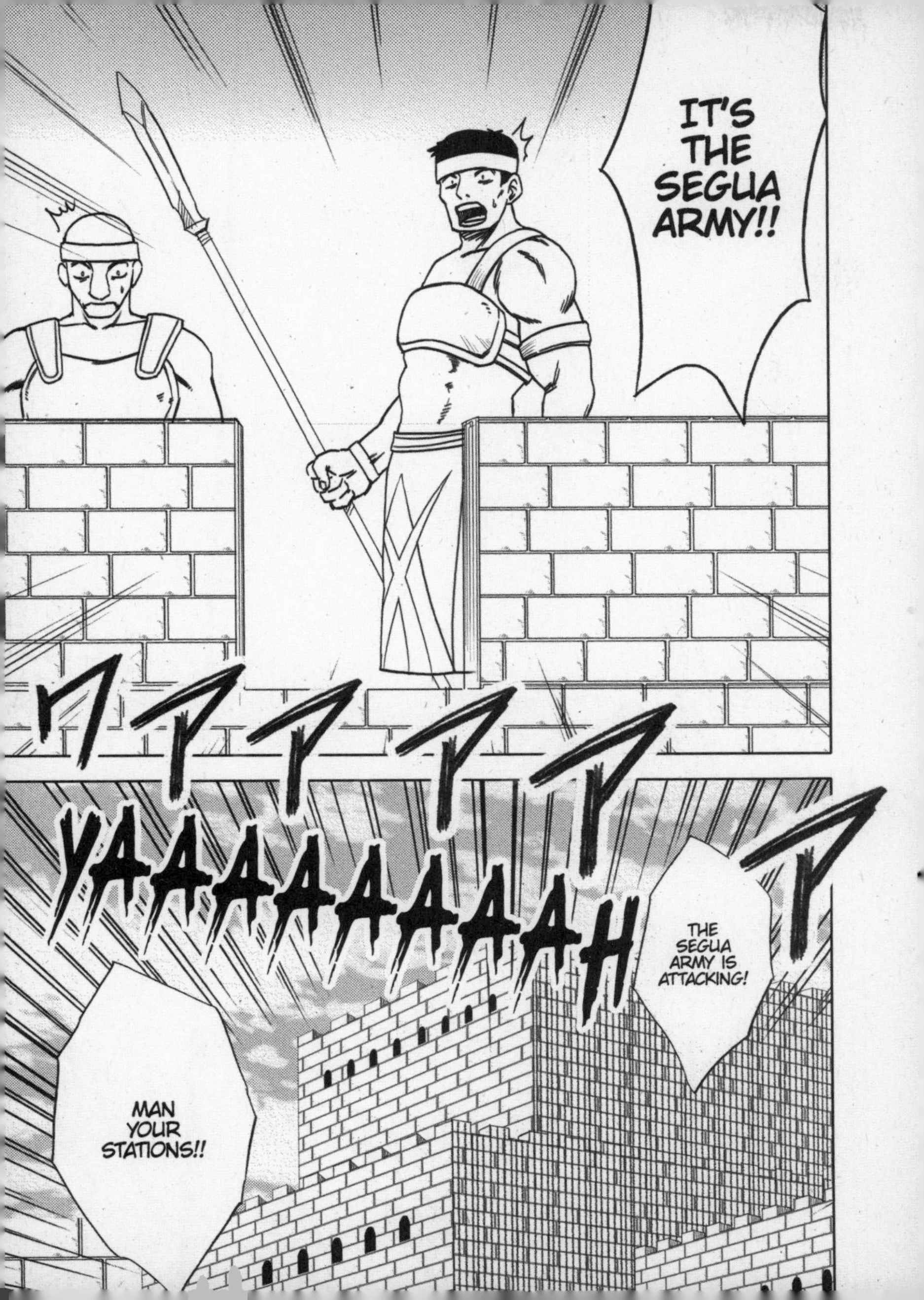
IT'S THE SEGUA ARMY!!
YAAAAAAAAAH
THE SEGUA ARMY IS ATTACKING!
MAN YOUR STATIONS!!

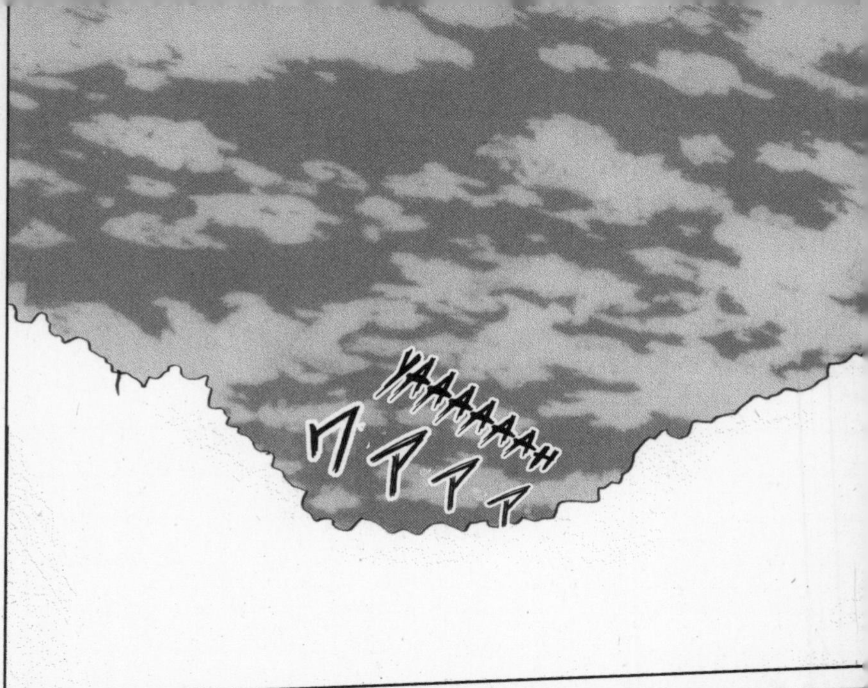
YAAAAAAAH
ワアァァ

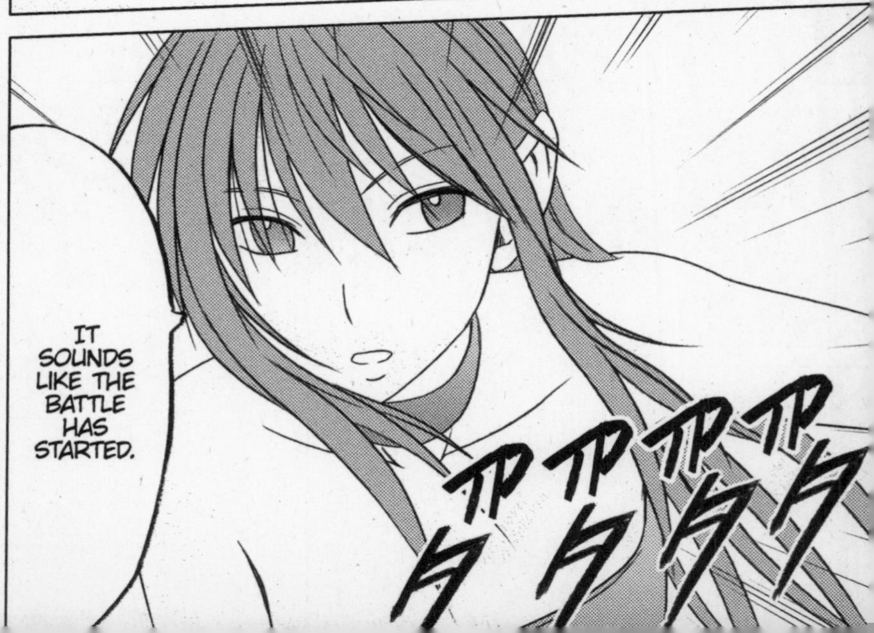
IT SOUNDS LIKE THE BATTLE HAS STARTED.
TP TP TP TP
タタタタ

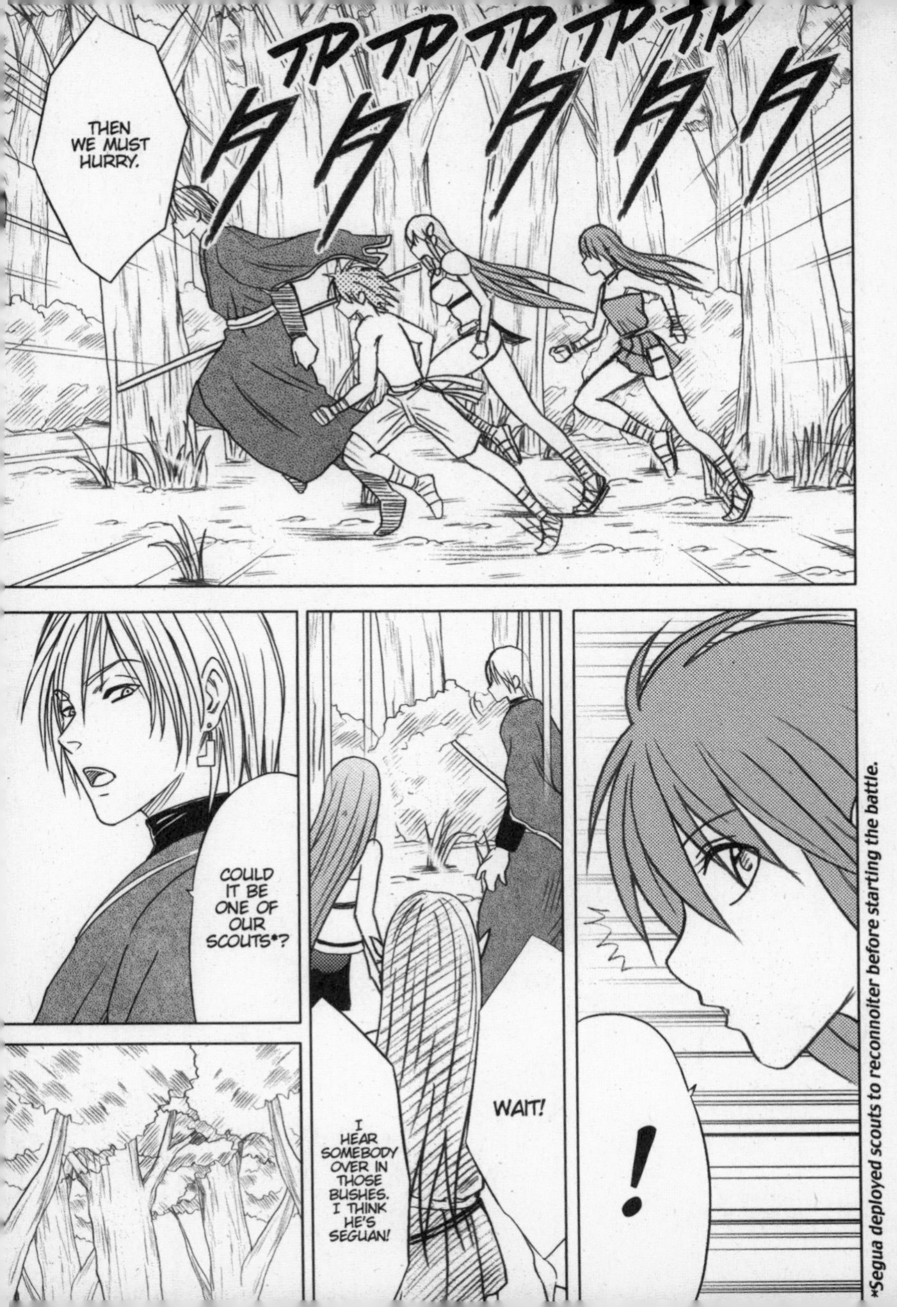
TP TP TP TP TK
タタタタタ
THEN WE MUST HURRY.
!
WAIT!
I HEAR SOMEBODY OVER IN THOSE BUSHES. I THINK HE'S SEGUAN!
COULD IT BE ONE OF OUR SCOUTS*?

*Segua deployed scouts to reconnoiter before starting the battle.

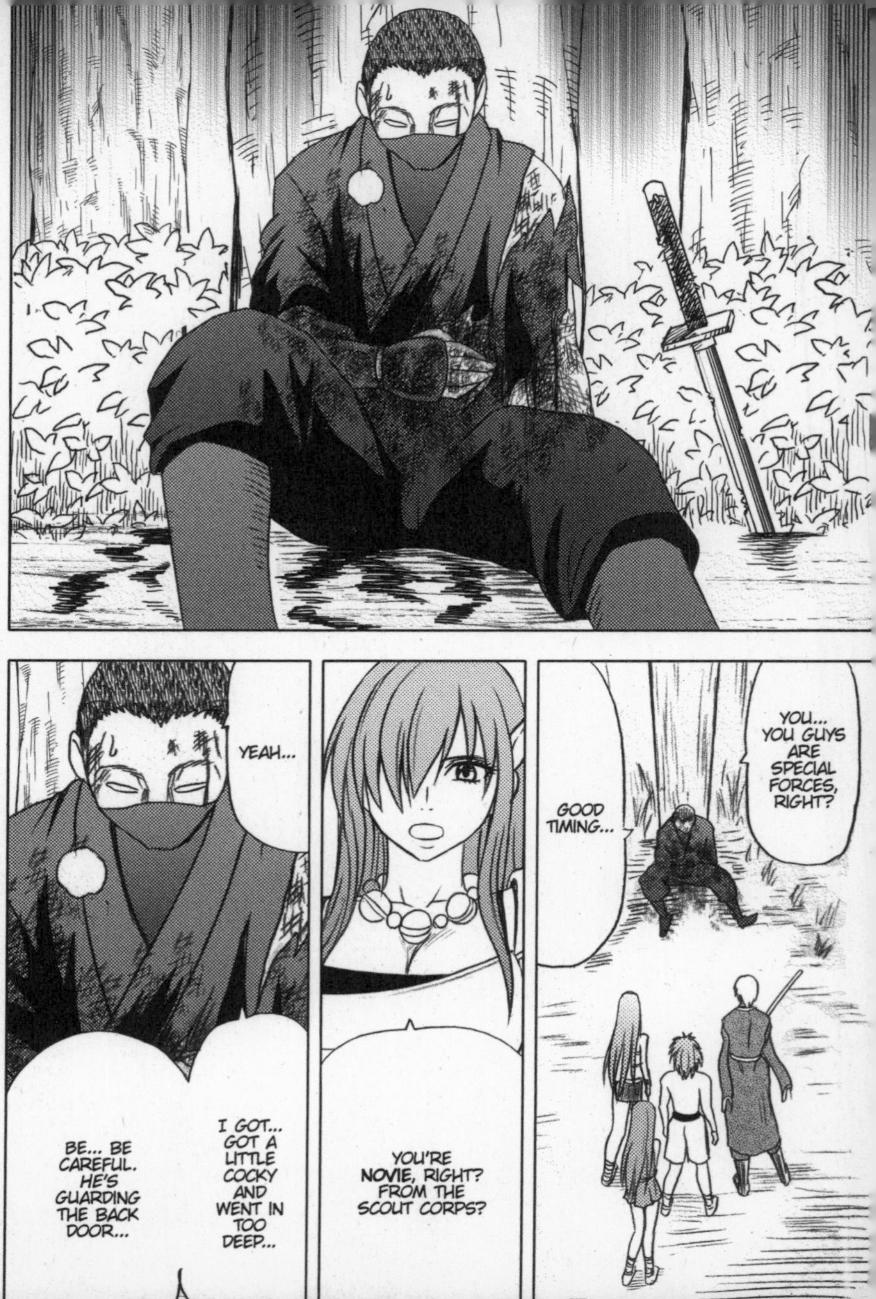
YOU... YOU GUYS ARE SPECIAL FORCES, RIGHT?
GOOD TIMING...
YOU'RE NOVIE, RIGHT? FROM THE SCOUT CORPS?
YEAH...
I GOT... GOT A LITTLE COCKY AND WENT IN TOO DEEP...
BE... BE CAREFUL. HE'S GUARDING THE BACK DOOR...

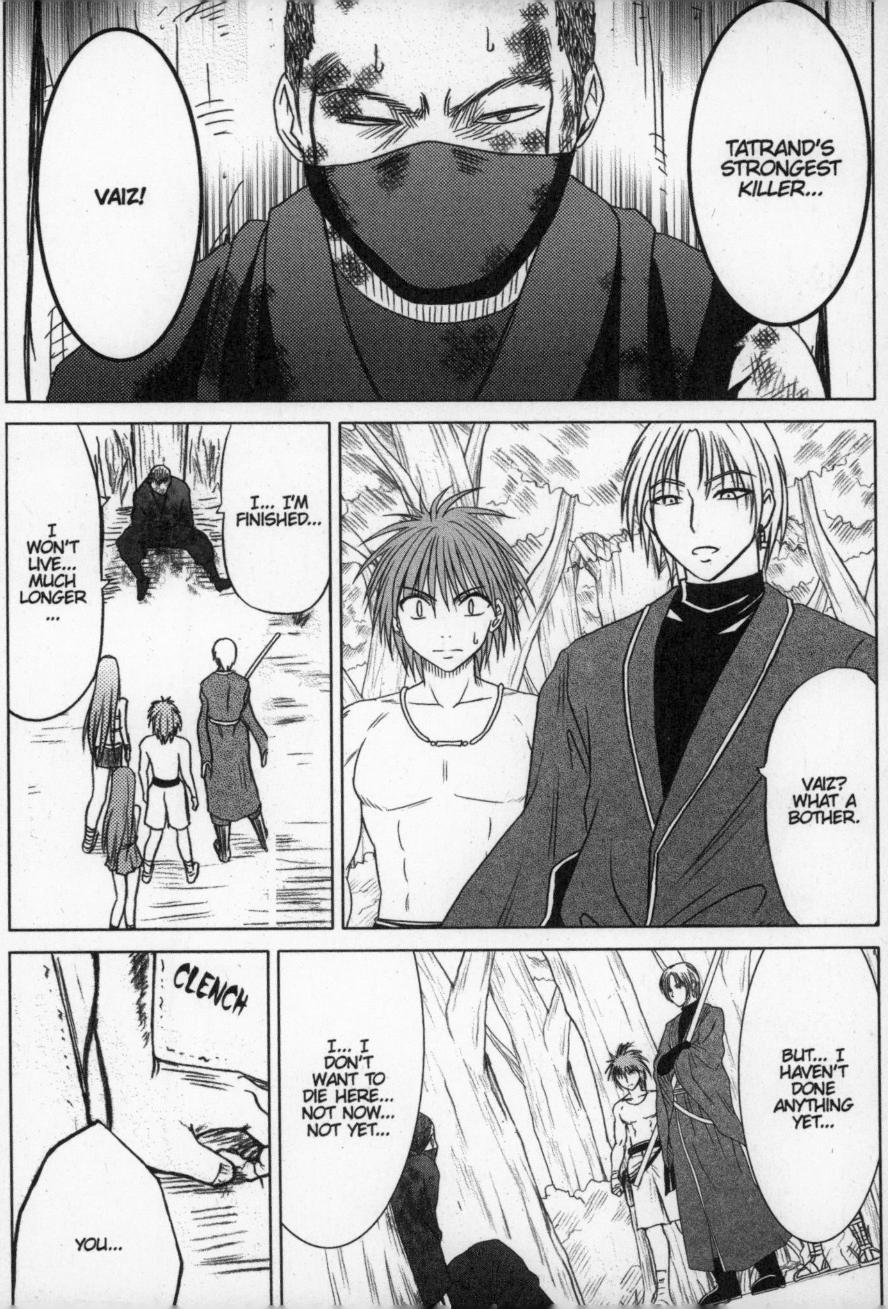
TATRAND'S STRONGEST KILLER...
VAIZ!
VAIZ? WHAT A BOTHER.
I... I'M FINISHED...
I WON'T LIVE... MUCH LONGER ...
BUT... I HAVEN'T DONE ANYTHING YET...
I... I DON'T WANT TO DIE HERE... NOT NOW... NOT YET...
CLENCH
YOU...

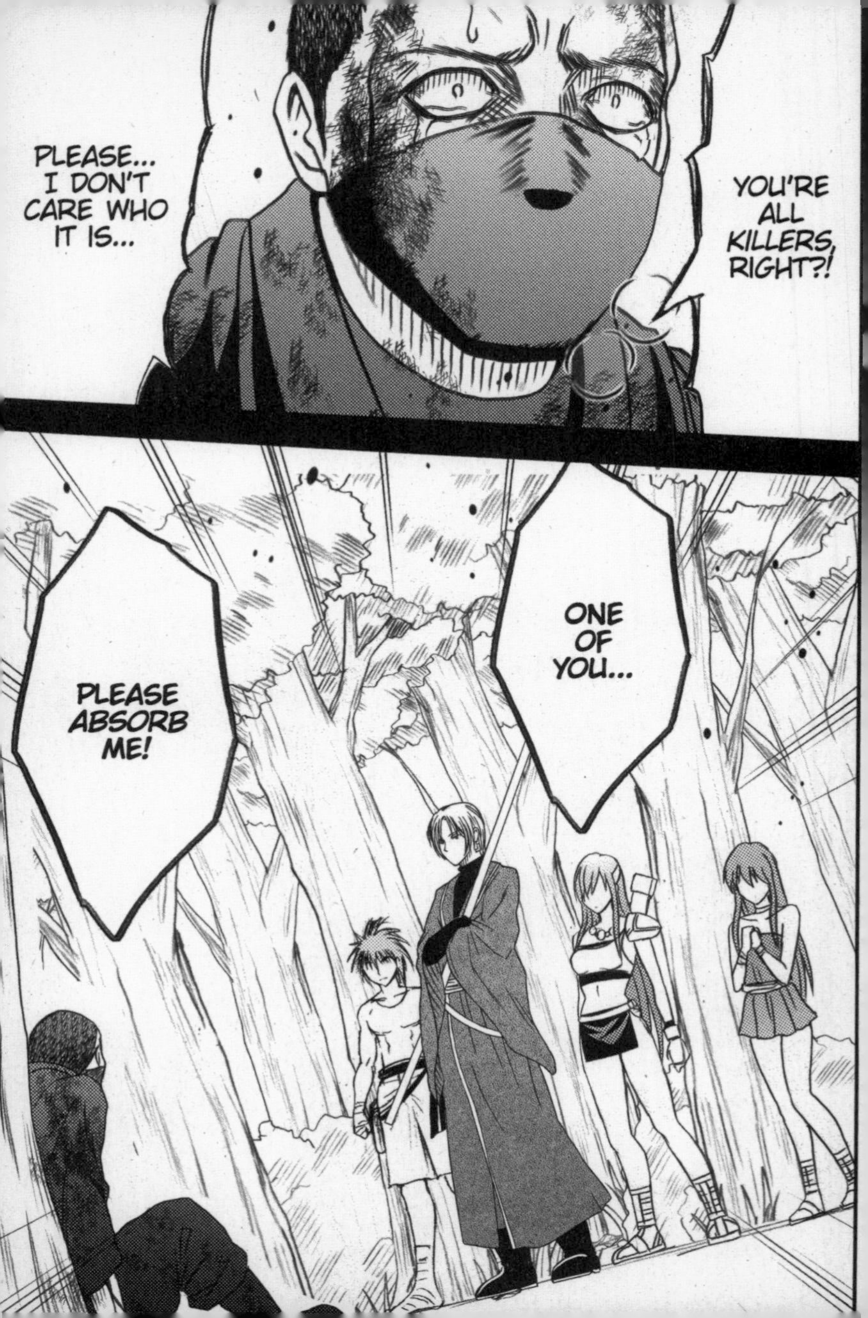
YOU'RE ALL KILLERS, RIGHT?!
PLEASE... I DON'T CARE WHO IT IS...
ONE OF YOU...
PLEASE ABSORB ME!

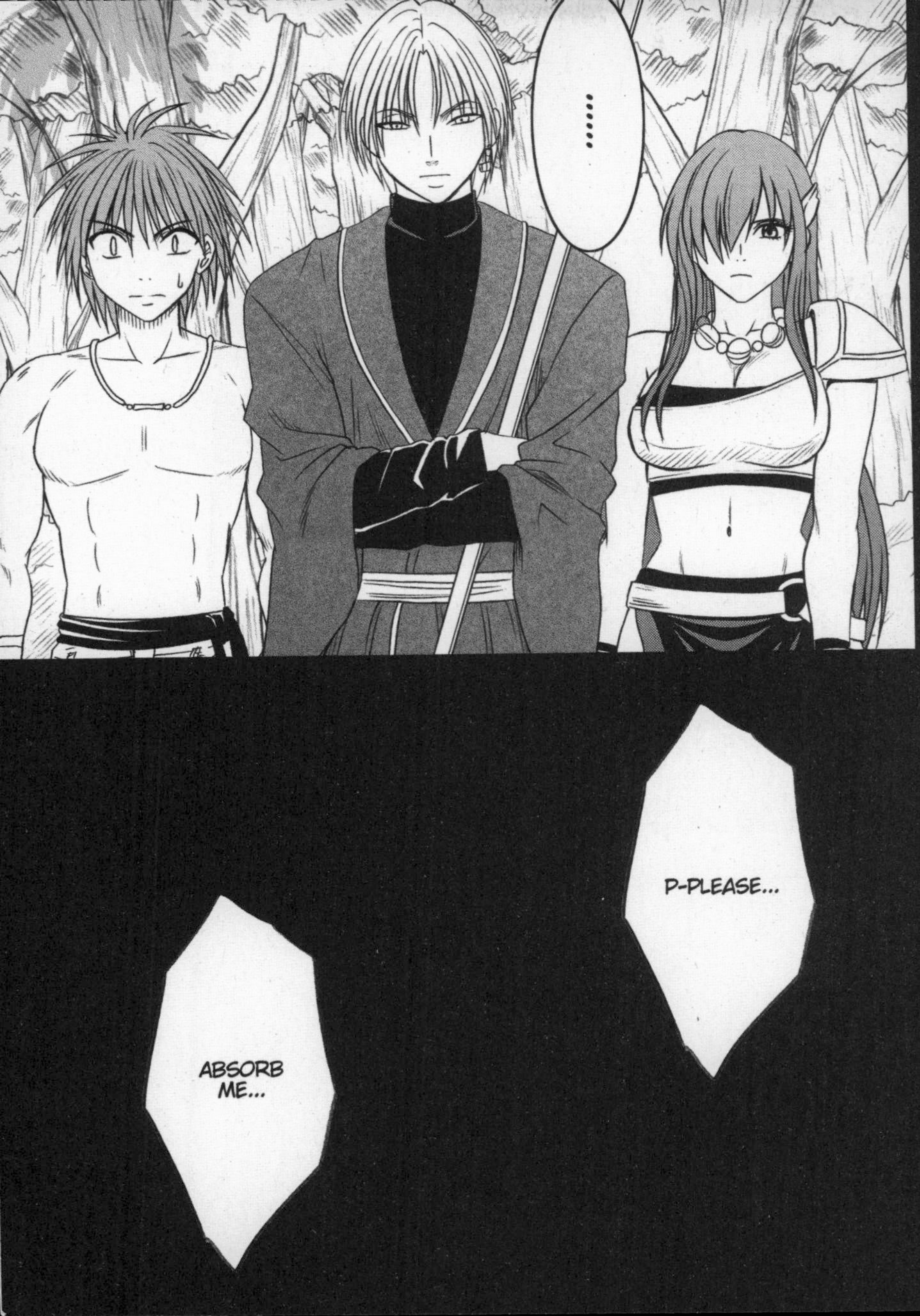
......
P-PLEASE...
ABSORB ME...

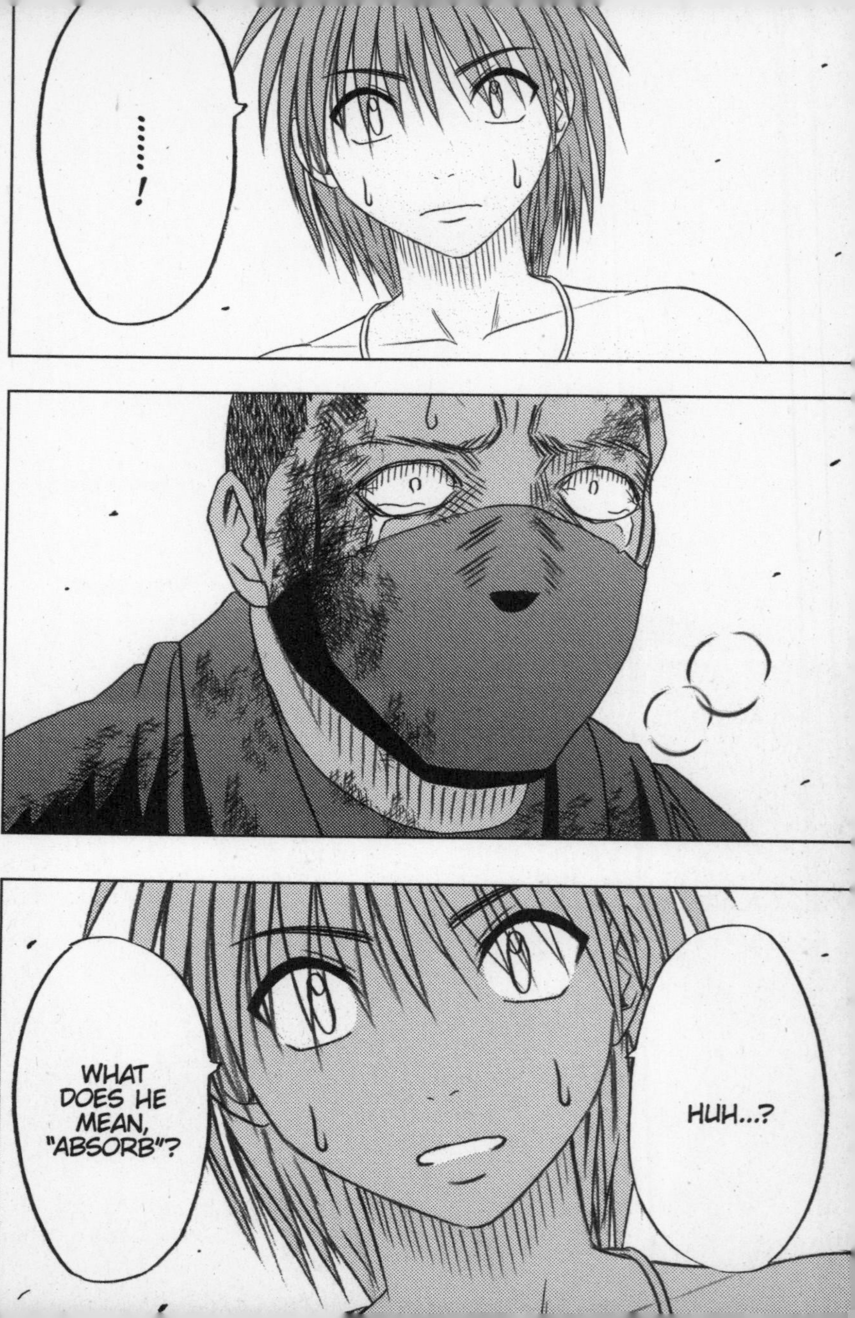
......!
HUH...?
WHAT DOES HE MEAN, "ABSORB"?

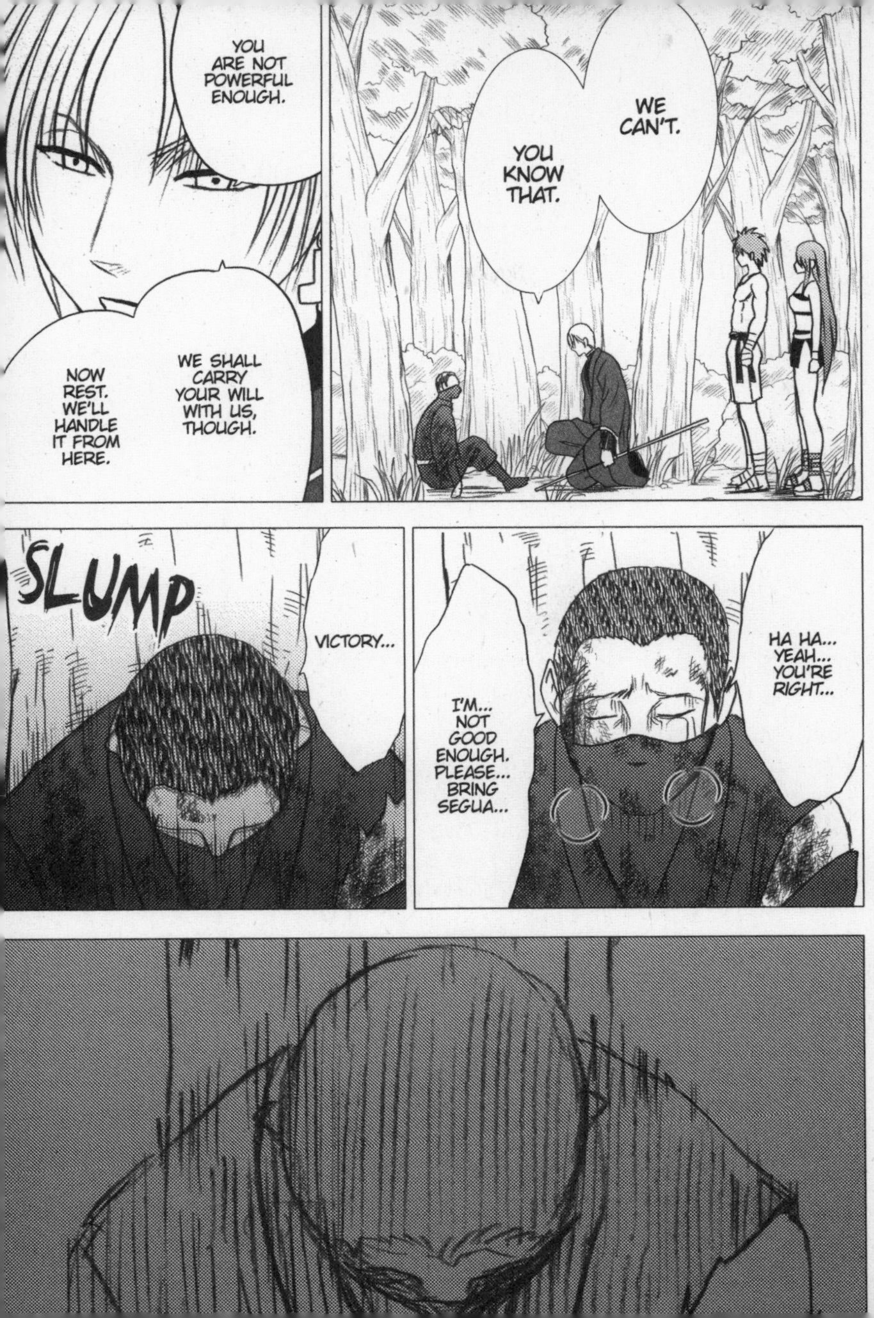
WE CAN'T.
YOU KNOW THAT.
YOU ARE NOT POWERFUL ENOUGH.
WE SHALL CARRY YOUR WILL WITH US, THOUGH.
NOW REST. WE'LL HANDLE IT FROM HERE.
HA HA... YEAH... YOU'RE RIGHT...
I'M... NOT GOOD ENOUGH. PLEASE... BRING SEGUA...
VICTORY...
SLUMP

. . . . .

I SKIPPED THAT PART...

AH, YES.

WHAT DID HE MEAN BY HE WANTED US TO "ABSORB" HIM?

WHAT WAS THAT ALL ABOUT?

. . . . .

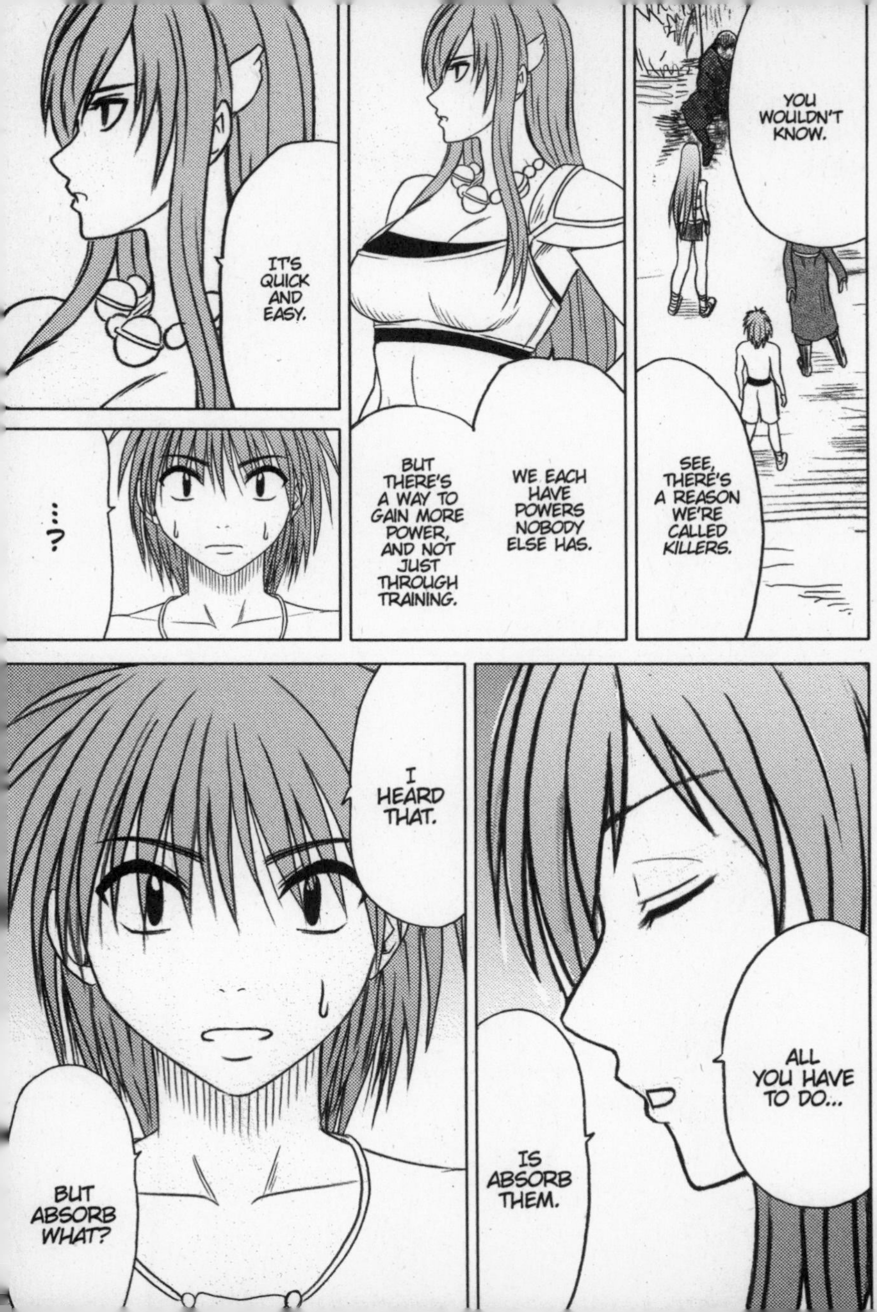
YOU WOULDN'T KNOW.
SEE, THERE'S A REASON WE'RE CALLED KILLERS.
WE EACH HAVE POWERS NOBODY ELSE HAS.
BUT THERE'S A WAY TO GAIN MORE POWER, AND NOT JUST THROUGH TRAINING.
IT'S QUICK AND EASY.
ALL YOU HAVE TO DO...
IS ABSORB THEM.
I HEARD THAT.
BUT ABSORB WHAT?

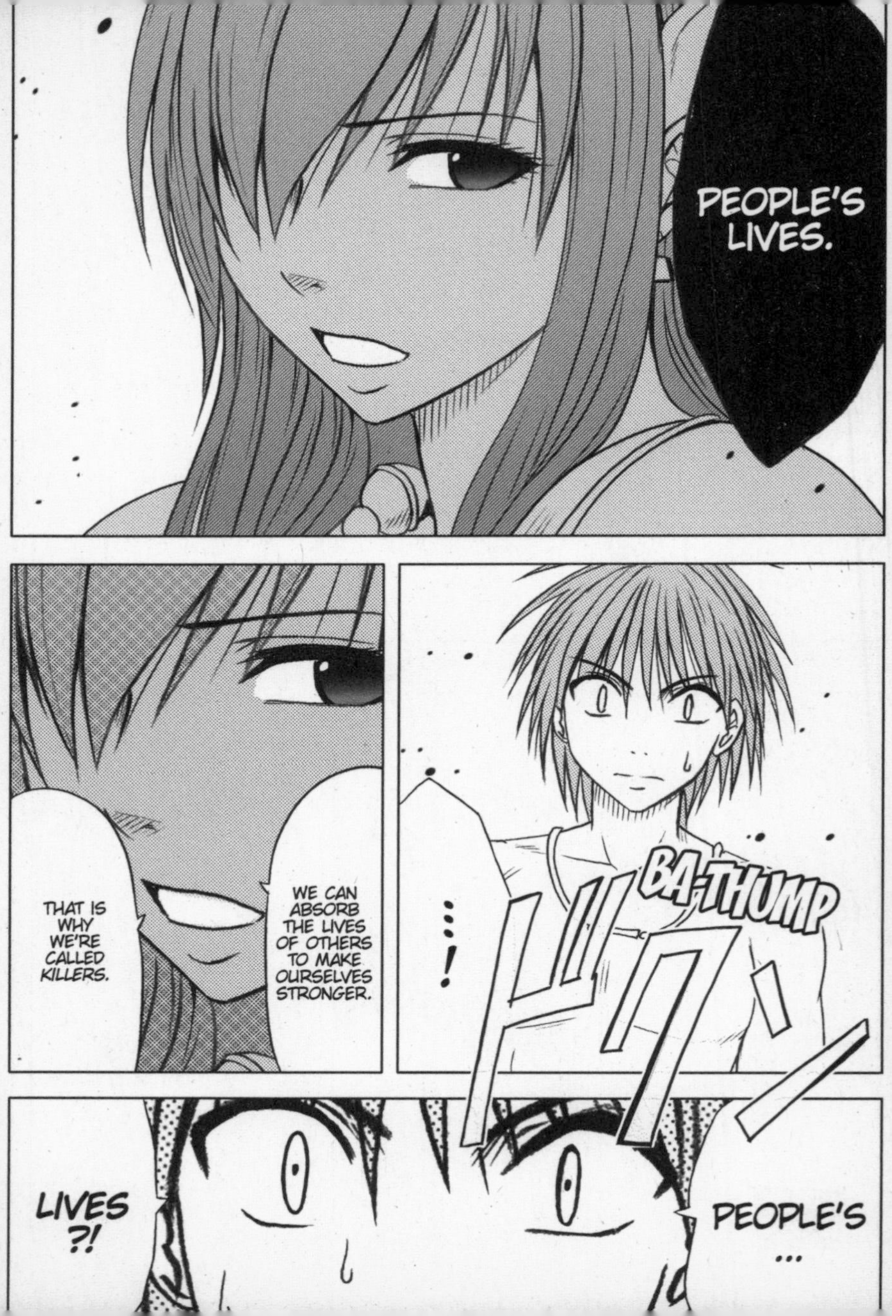
PEOPLE'S LIVES.
...!
BA-THUMP
WE CAN ABSORB THE LIVES OF OTHERS TO MAKE OURSELVES STRONGER.
THAT IS WHY WE'RE CALLED KILLERS.
PEOPLE'S ...
LIVES ?!

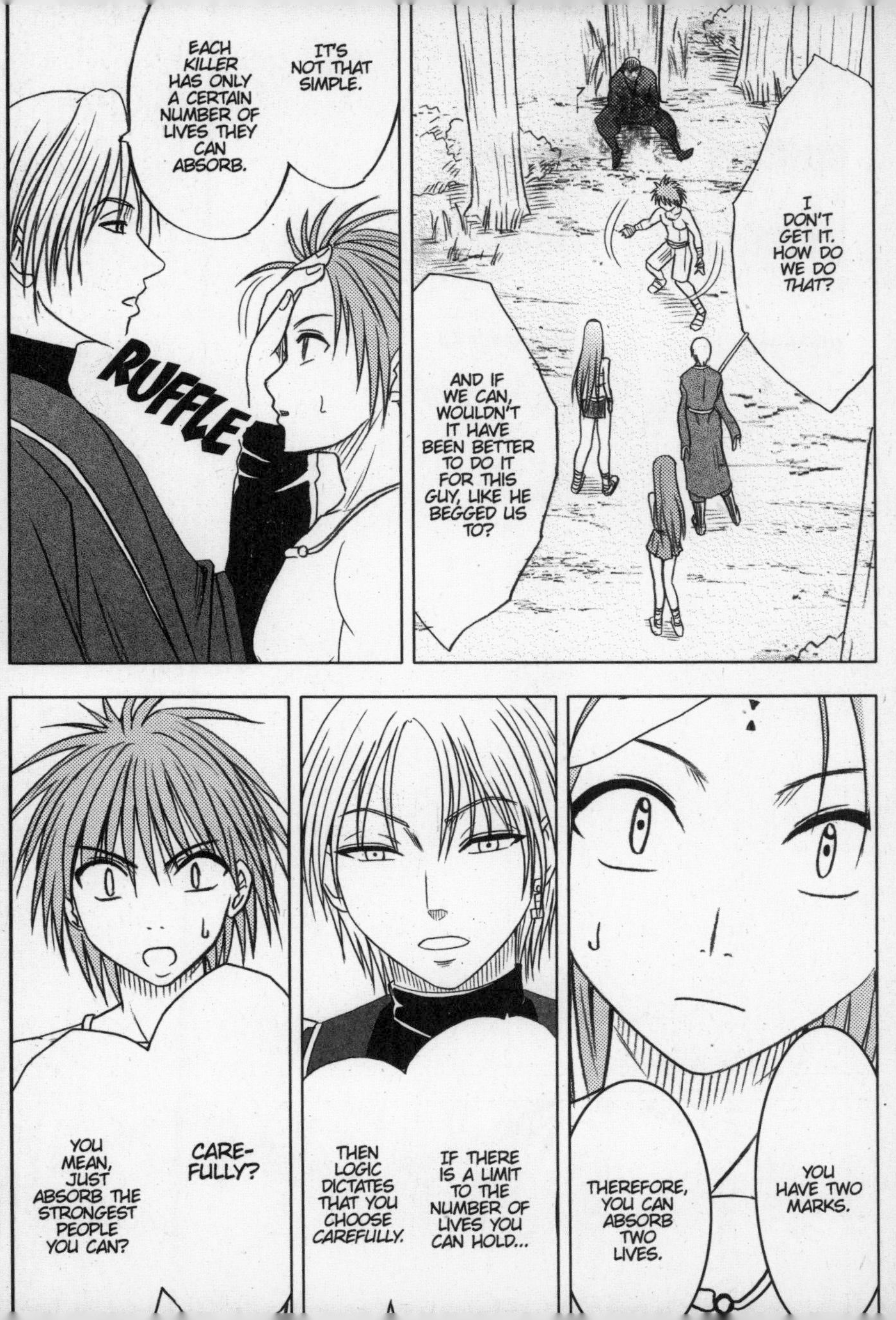
I DON'T GET IT. HOW DO WE DO THAT?
AND IF WE CAN, WOULDN'T IT HAVE BEEN BETTER TO DO IT FOR THIS GUY, LIKE HE BEGGED US TO?
IT'S NOT THAT SIMPLE.
EACH KILLER HAS ONLY A CERTAIN NUMBER OF LIVES THEY CAN ABSORB.
RUFFLE
YOU HAVE TWO MARKS.
THEREFORE, YOU CAN ABSORB TWO LIVES.
IF THERE IS A LIMIT TO THE NUMBER OF LIVES YOU CAN HOLD...
THEN LOGIC DICTATES THAT YOU CHOOSE CAREFULLY.
CARE-FULLY?
YOU MEAN, JUST ABSORB THE STRONGEST PEOPLE YOU CAN?

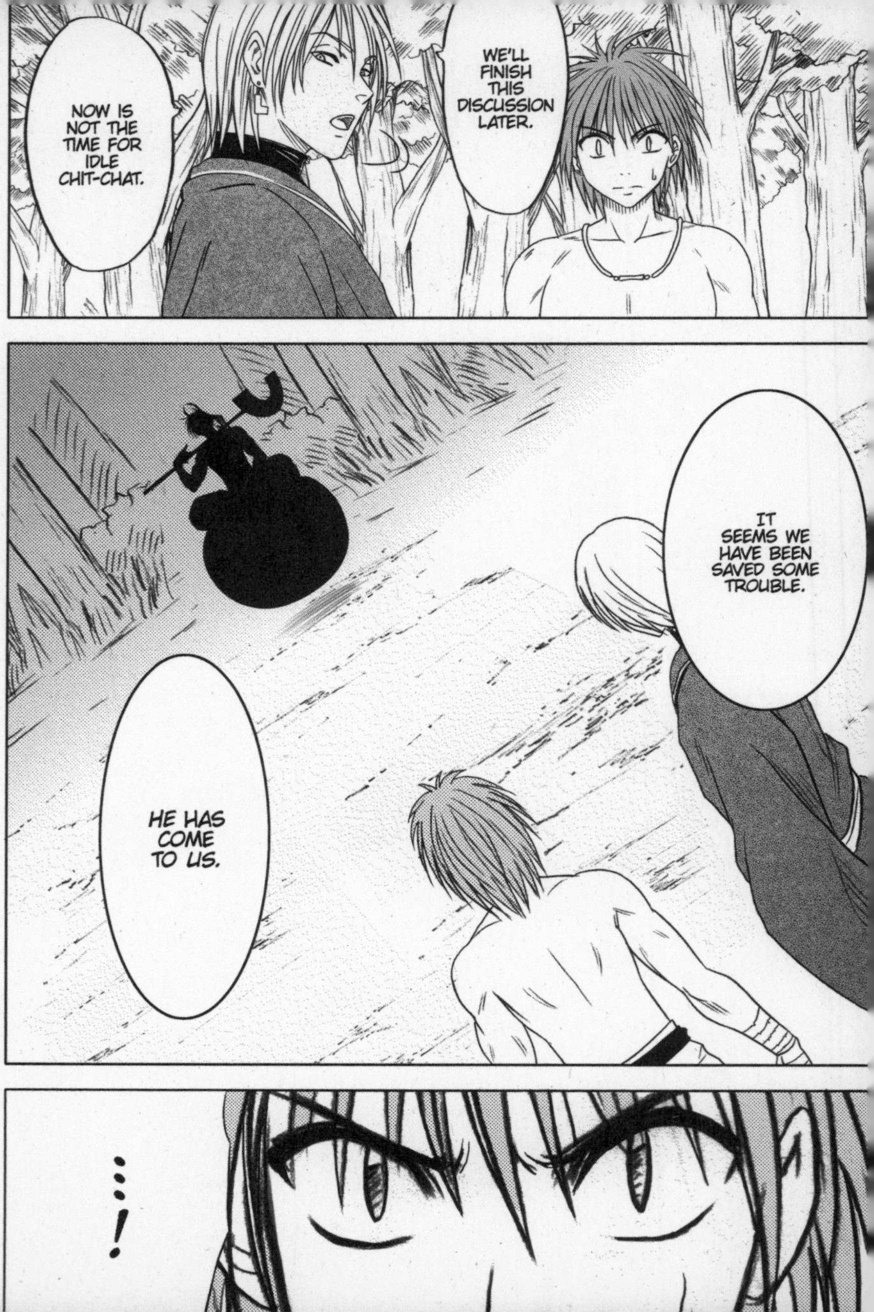
WE'LL FINISH THIS DISCUSSION LATER.
NOW IS NOT THE TIME FOR IDLE CHIT-CHAT.
IT SEEMS WE HAVE BEEN SAVED SOME TROUBLE.
HE HAS COME TO US.
...!

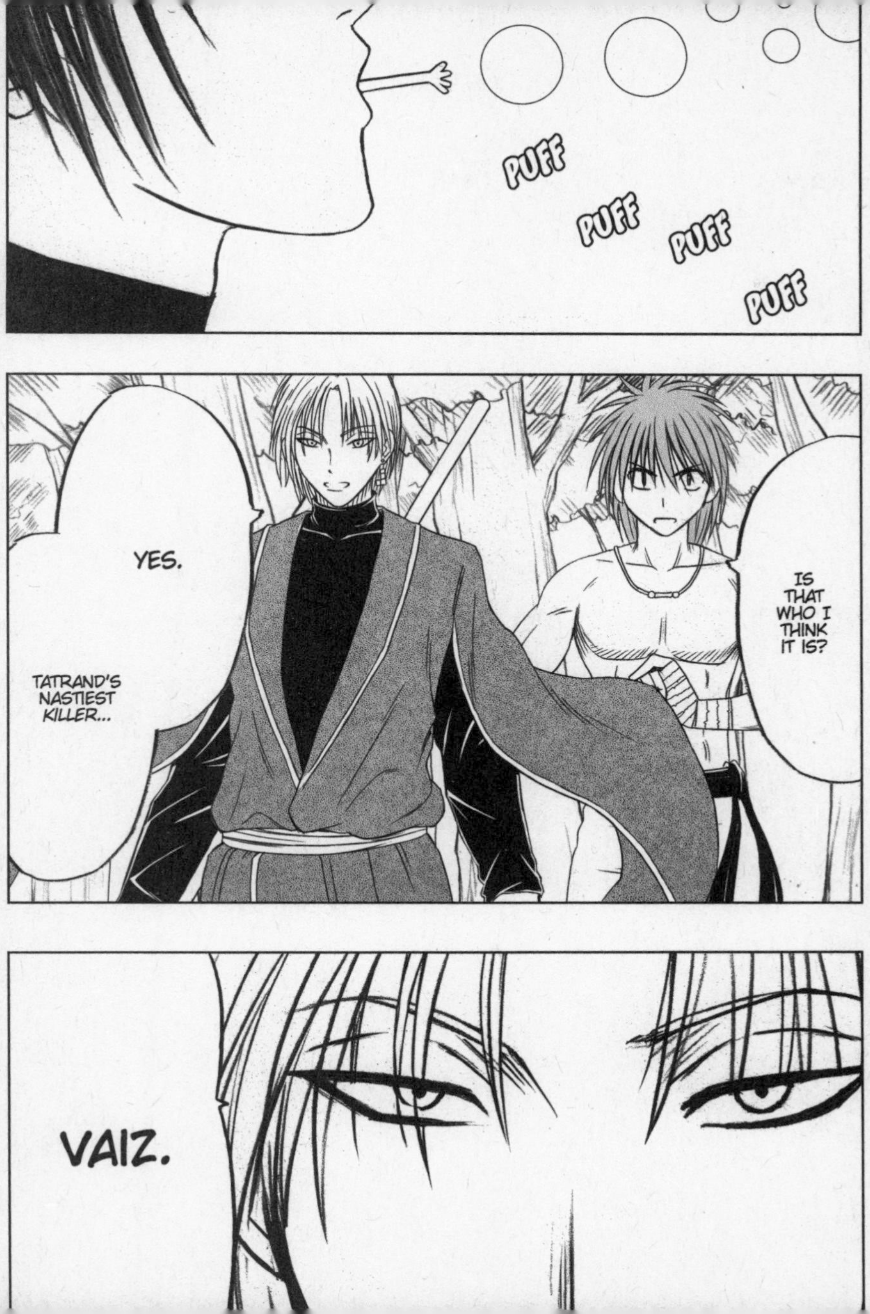
PUFF
PUFF
PUFF
PUFF
IS THAT WHO I THINK IT IS?
YES.
TATRAND'S NASTIEST KILLER...
VAIZ.

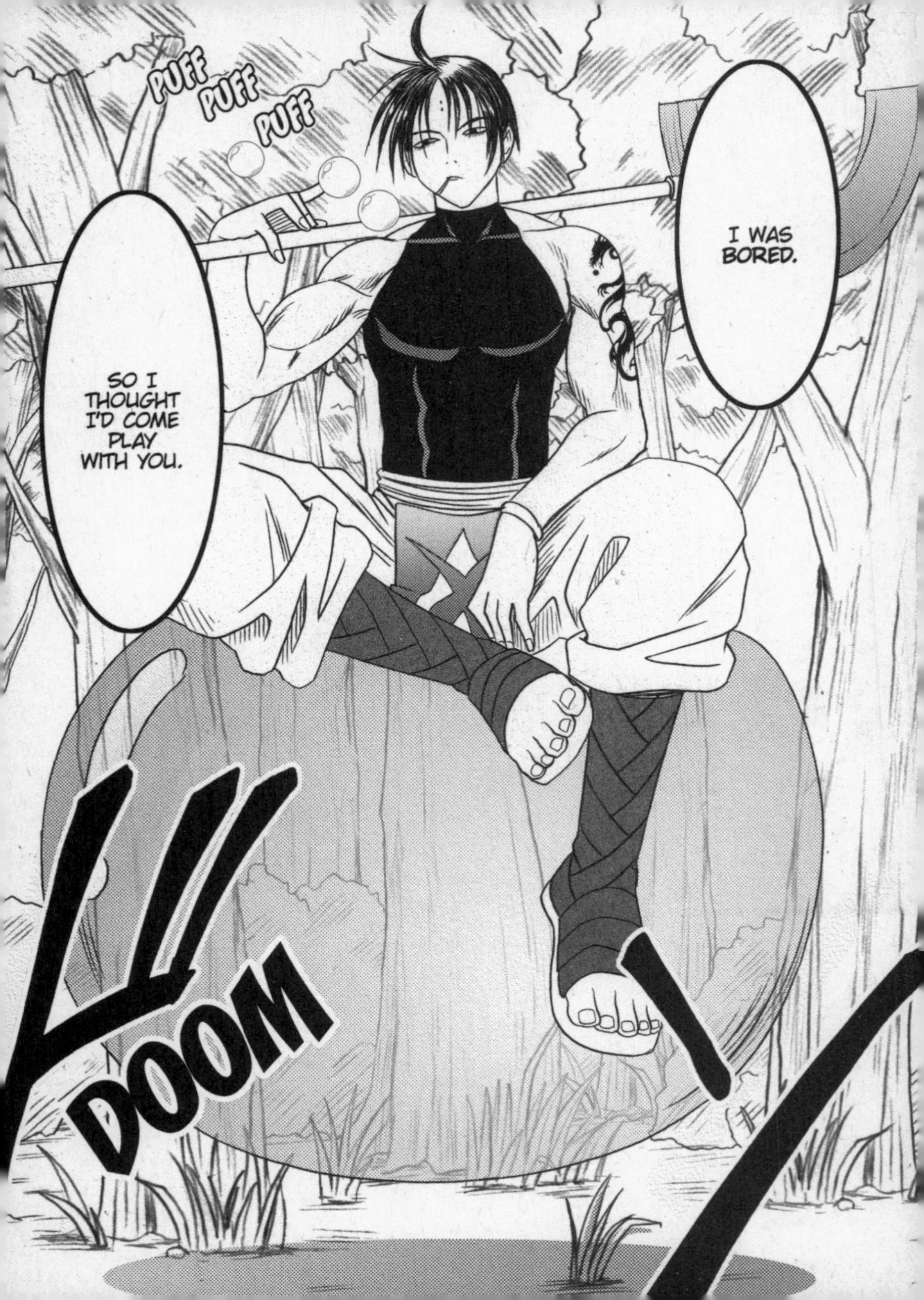
PUFF PUFF PUFF
I WAS BORED.
SO I THOUGHT I'D COME PLAY WITH YOU.
DOOM

CHAPTER 8

OUR POWERS COMBINED
Part 2

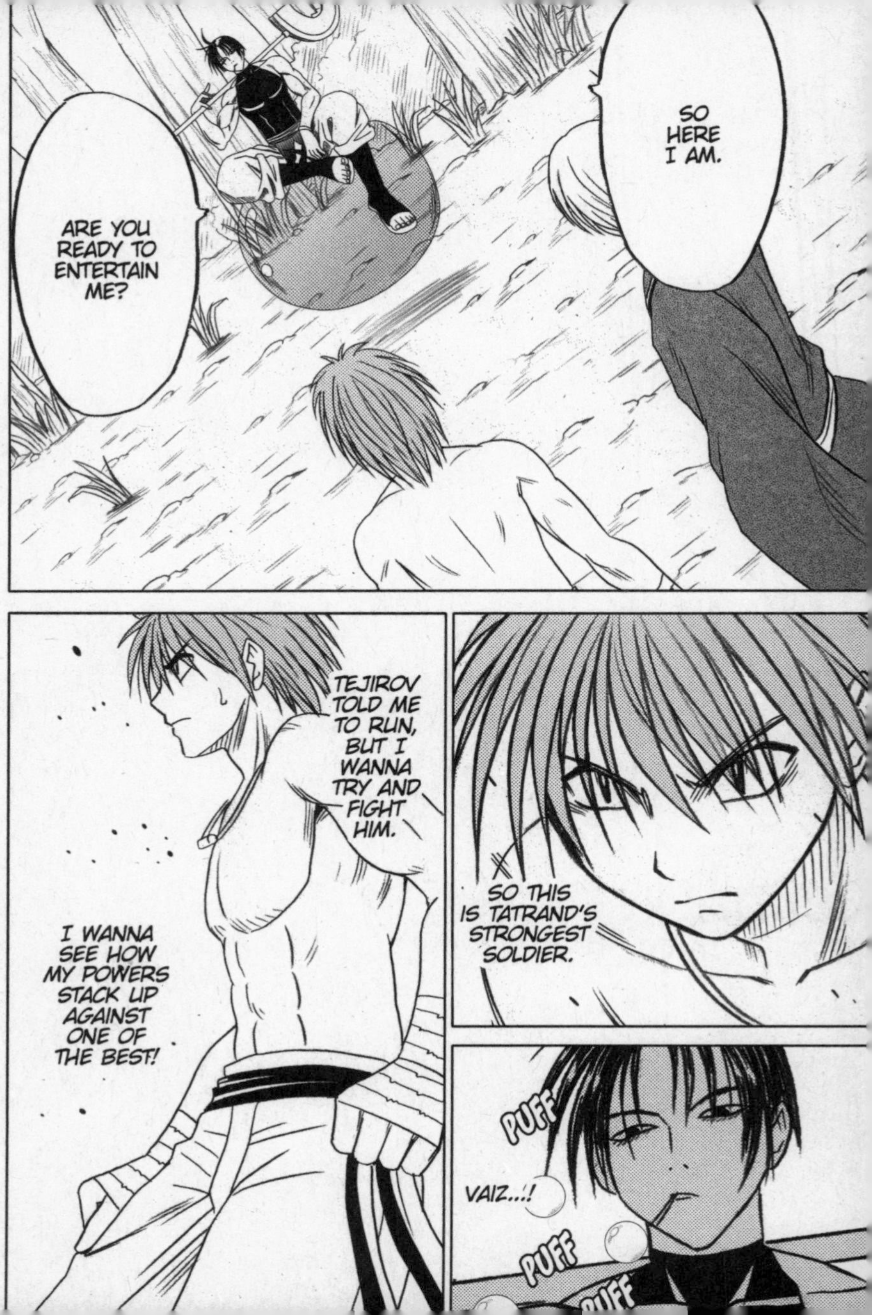
SO HERE I AM.
ARE YOU READY TO ENTERTAIN ME?
SO THIS IS TATRAND'S STRONGEST SOLDIER.
PUFF
VAIZ...!
PUFF
PUFF
TEJIROV TOLD ME TO RUN, BUT I WANNA TRY AND FIGHT HIM.
I WANNA SEE HOW MY POWERS STACK UP AGAINST ONE OF THE BEST!

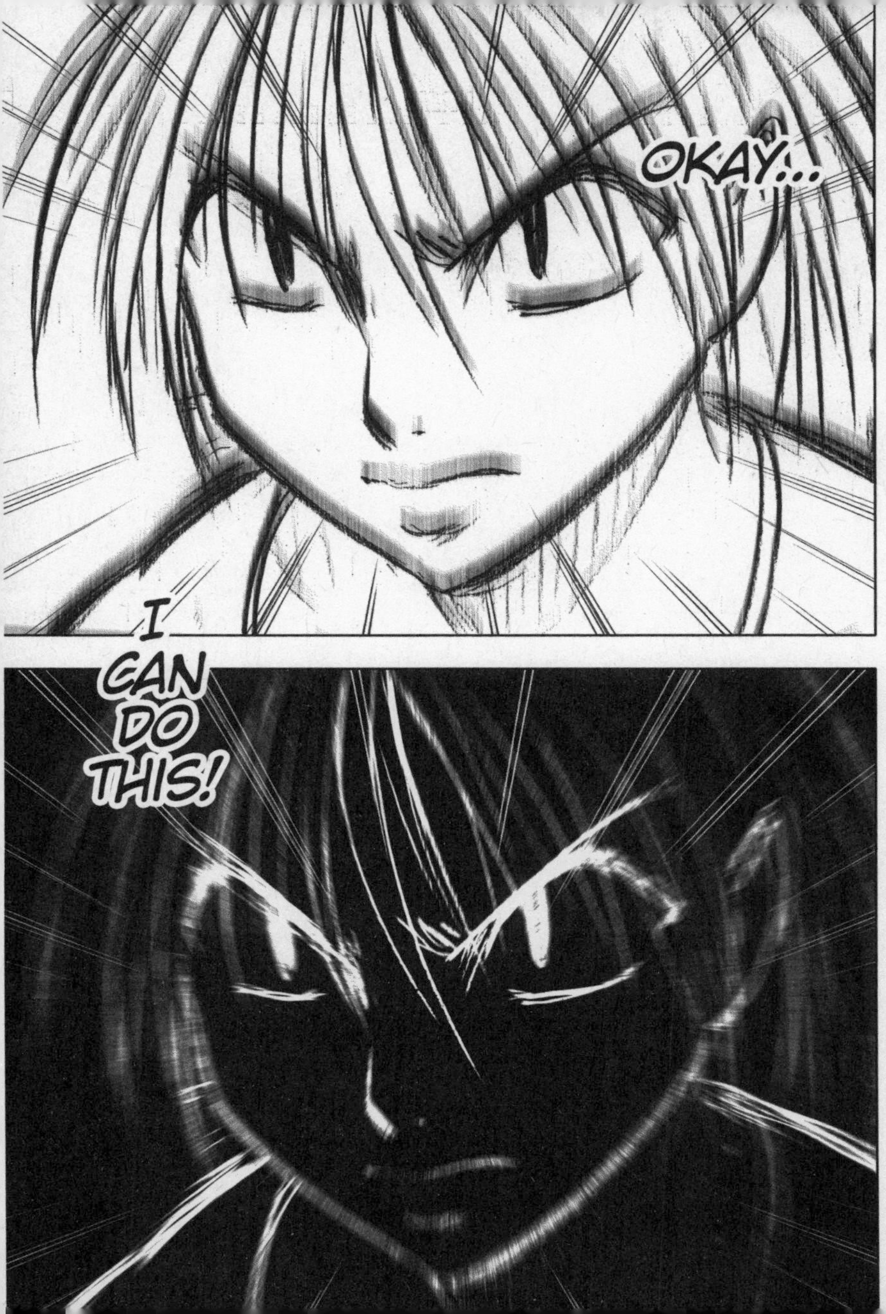
OKAY...
I CAN DO THIS!

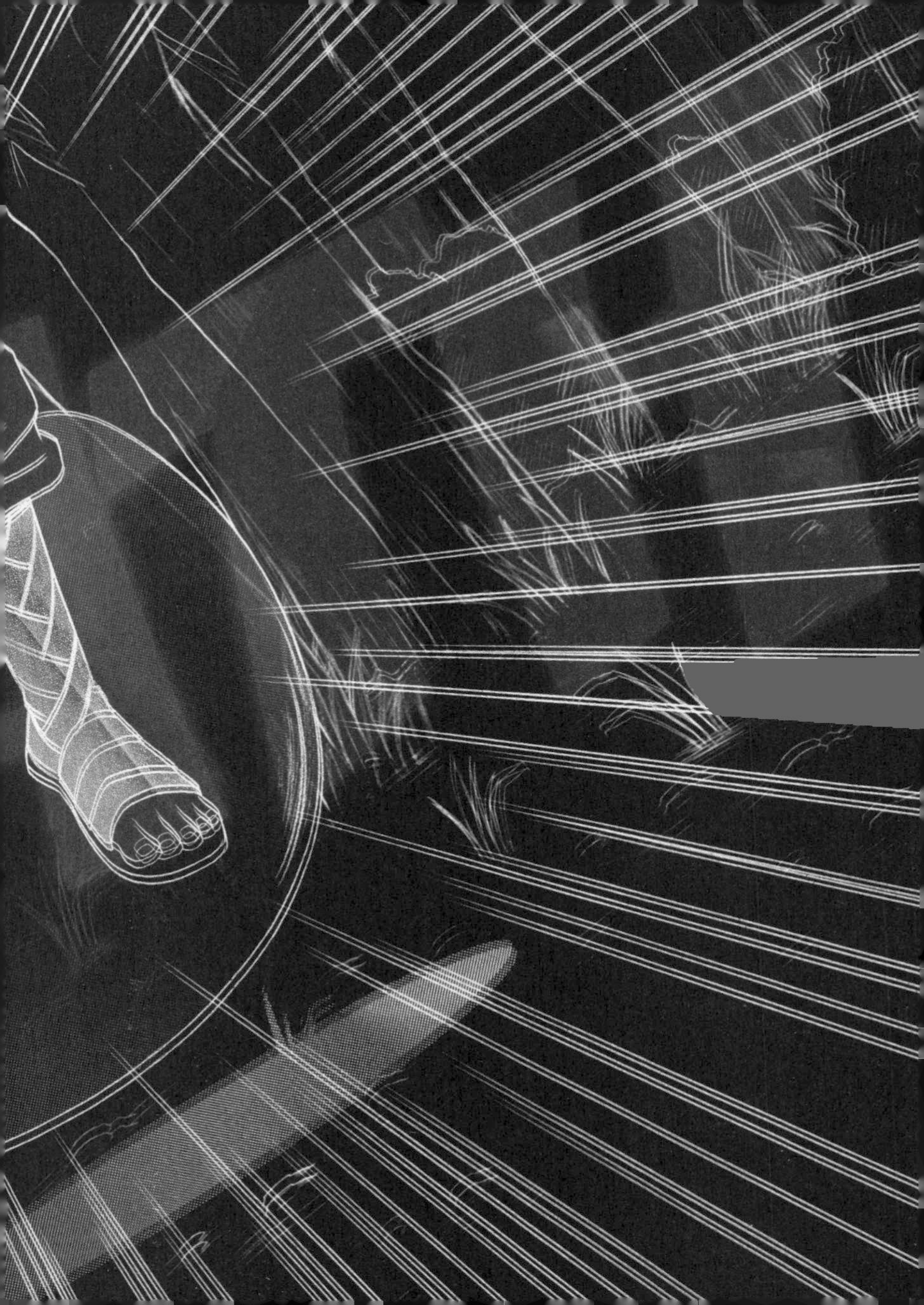

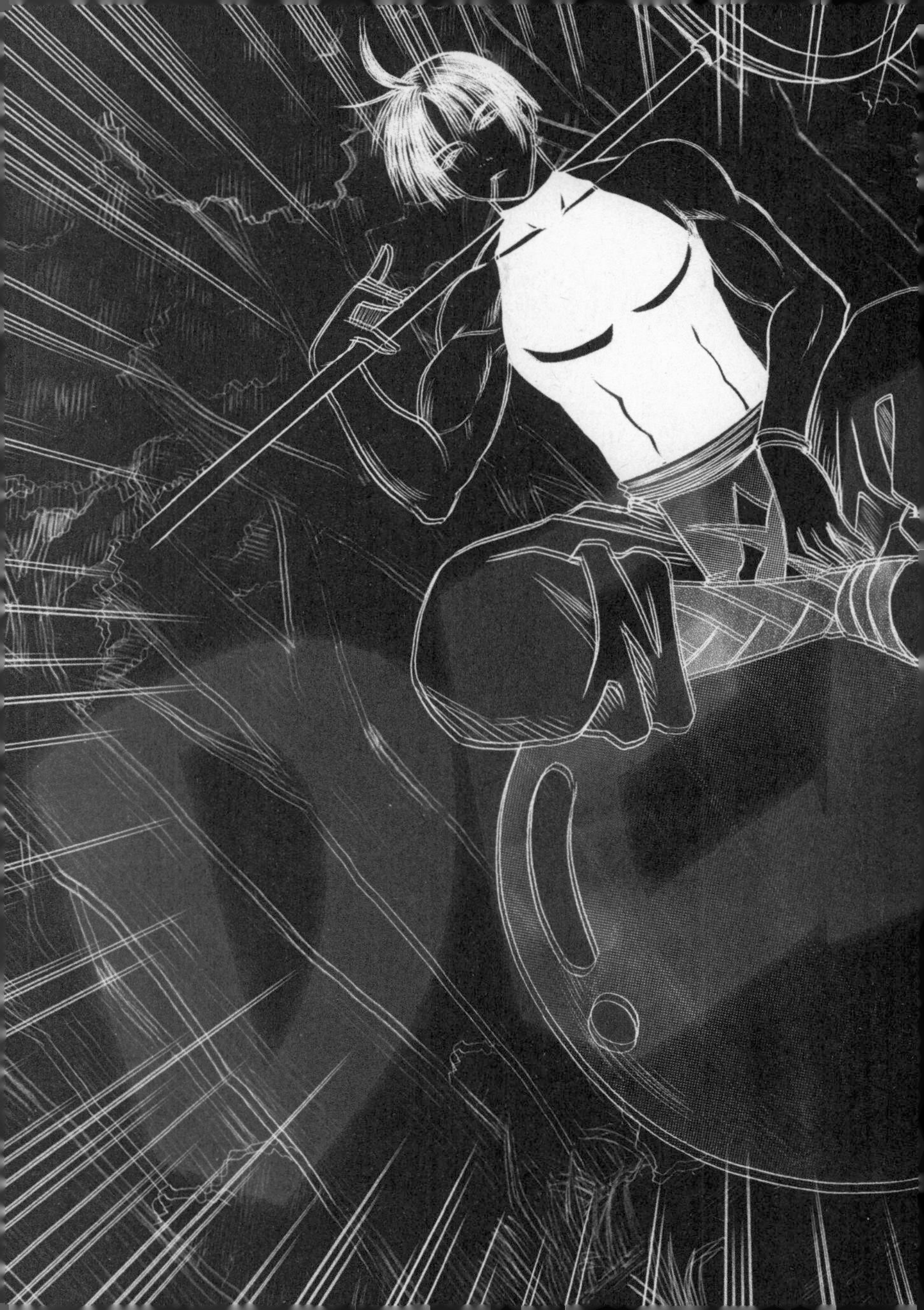

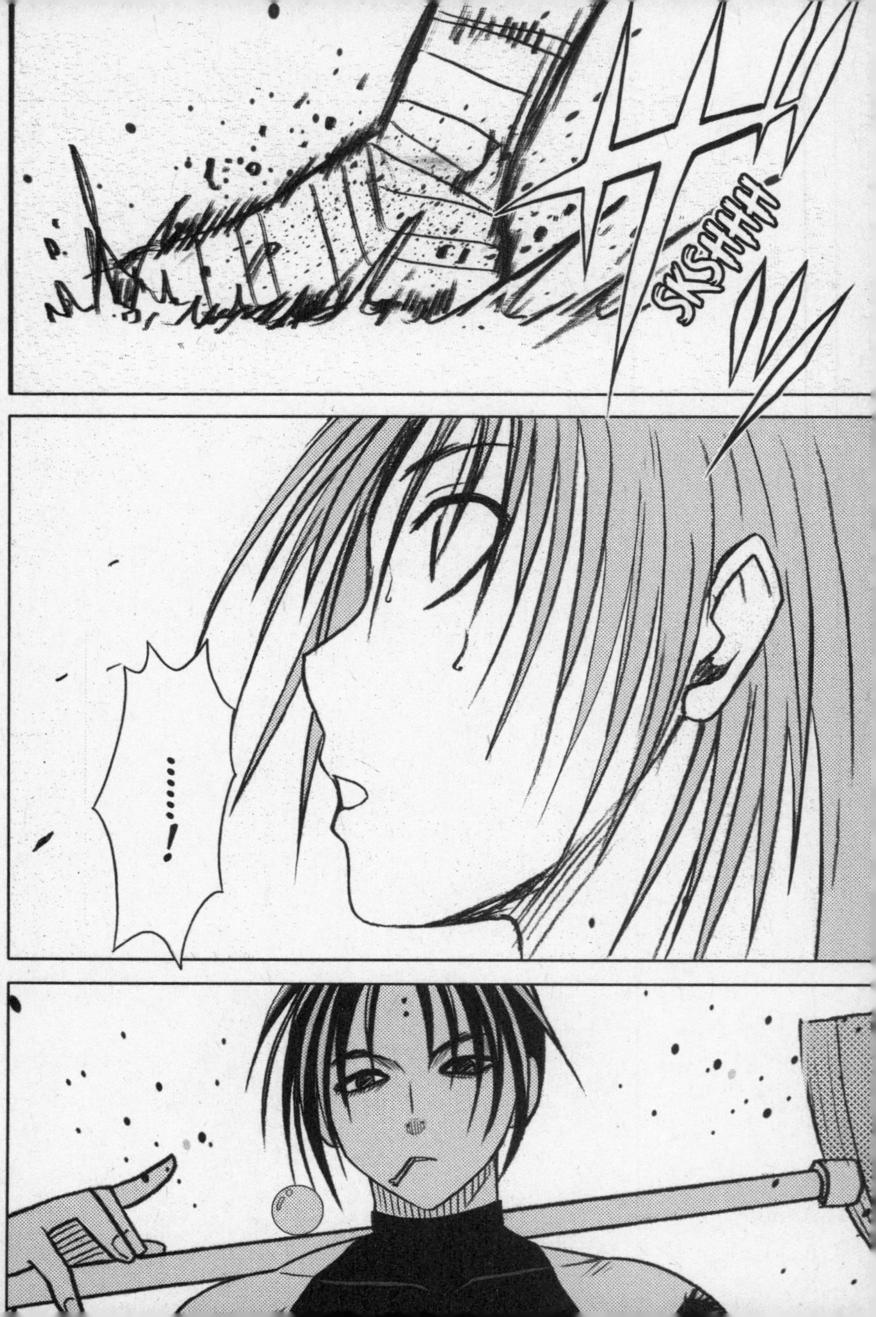
SKSHHHH
......!

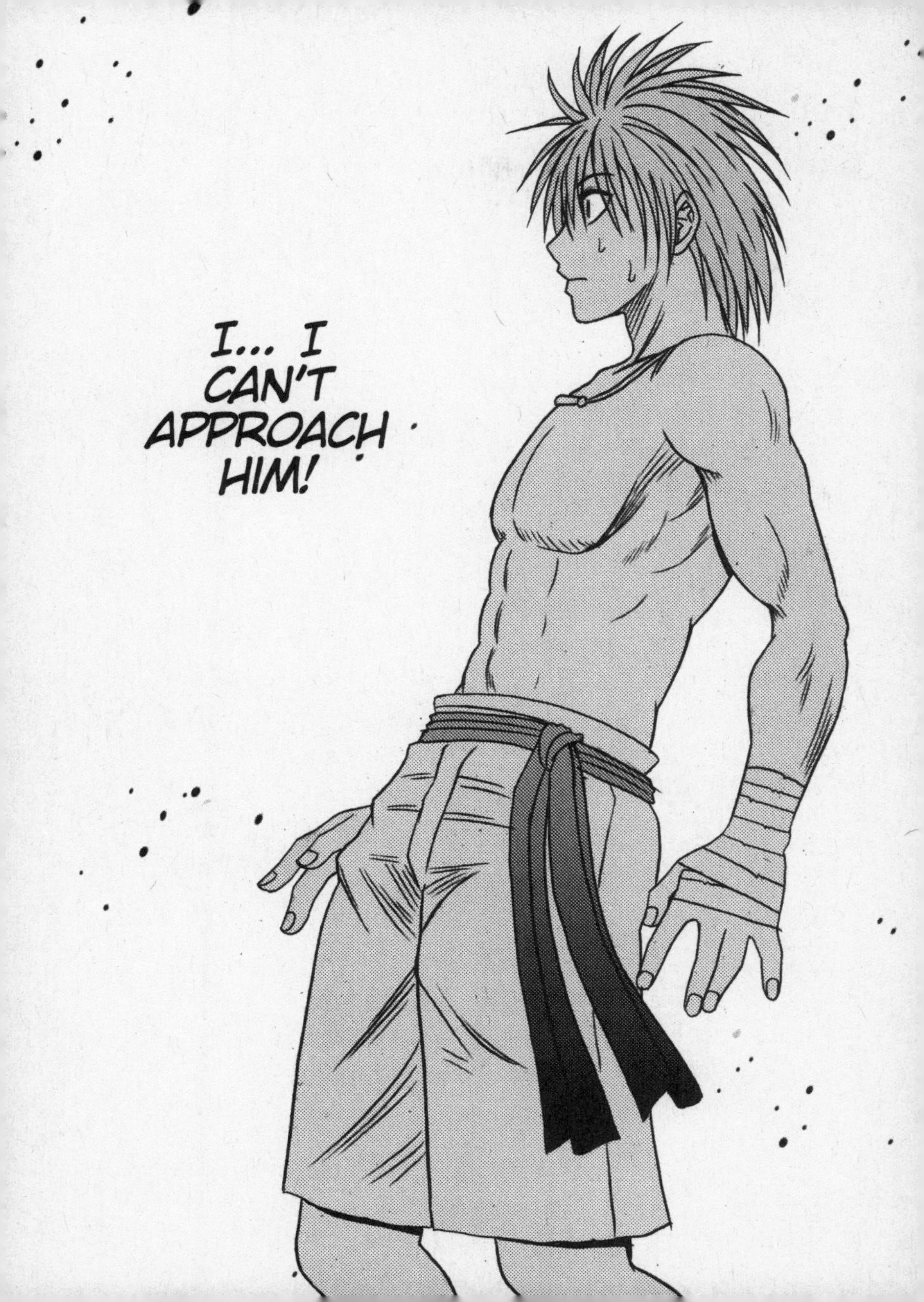
I... I CAN'T APPROACH HIM!

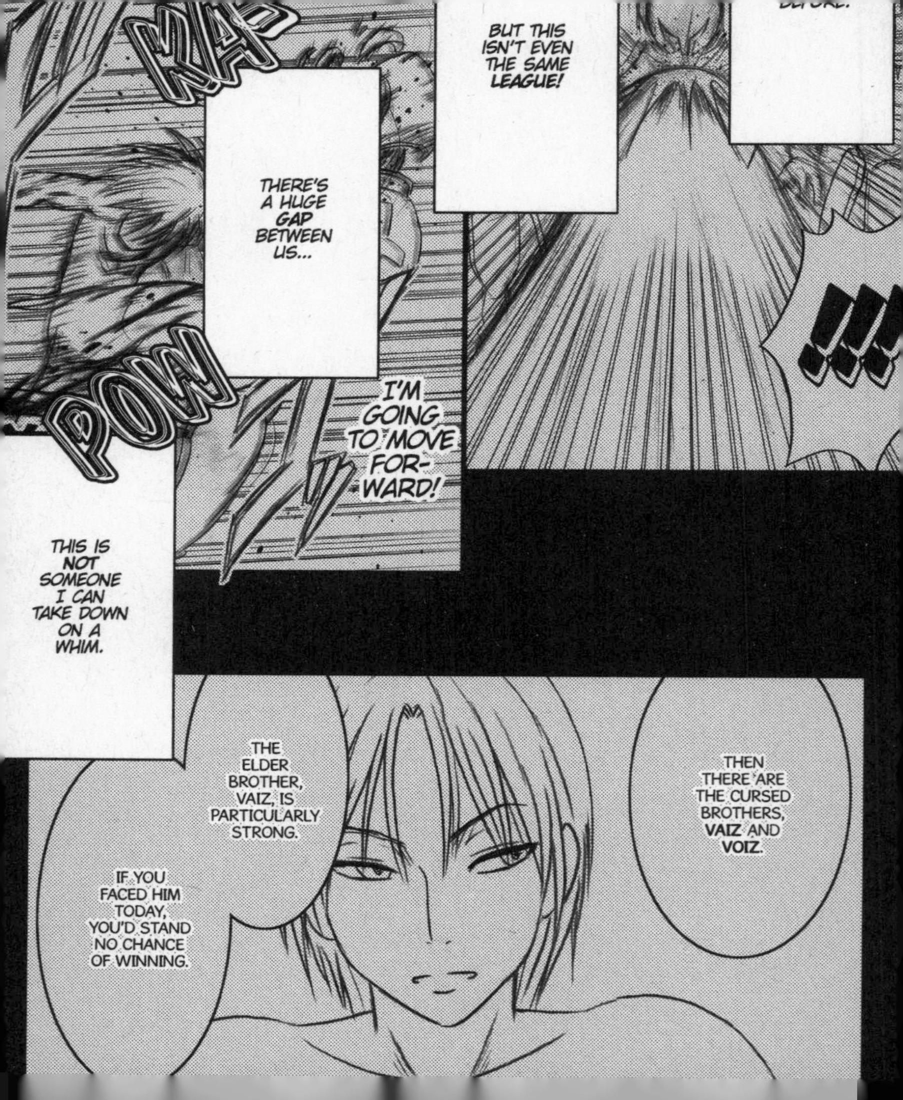
BUT THIS ISN'T EVEN THE SAME LEAGUE!
!!!
THERE'S A HUGE GAP BETWEEN US...
POW
I'M GOING TO MOVE FOR-WARD!
THIS IS NOT SOMEONE I CAN TAKE DOWN ON A WHIM.
THEN THERE ARE THE CURSED BROTHERS, VAIZ AND VOIZ.
THE ELDER BROTHER, VAIZ, IS PARTICULARLY STRONG.
IF YOU FACED HIM TODAY, YOU'D STAND NO CHANCE OF WINNING.

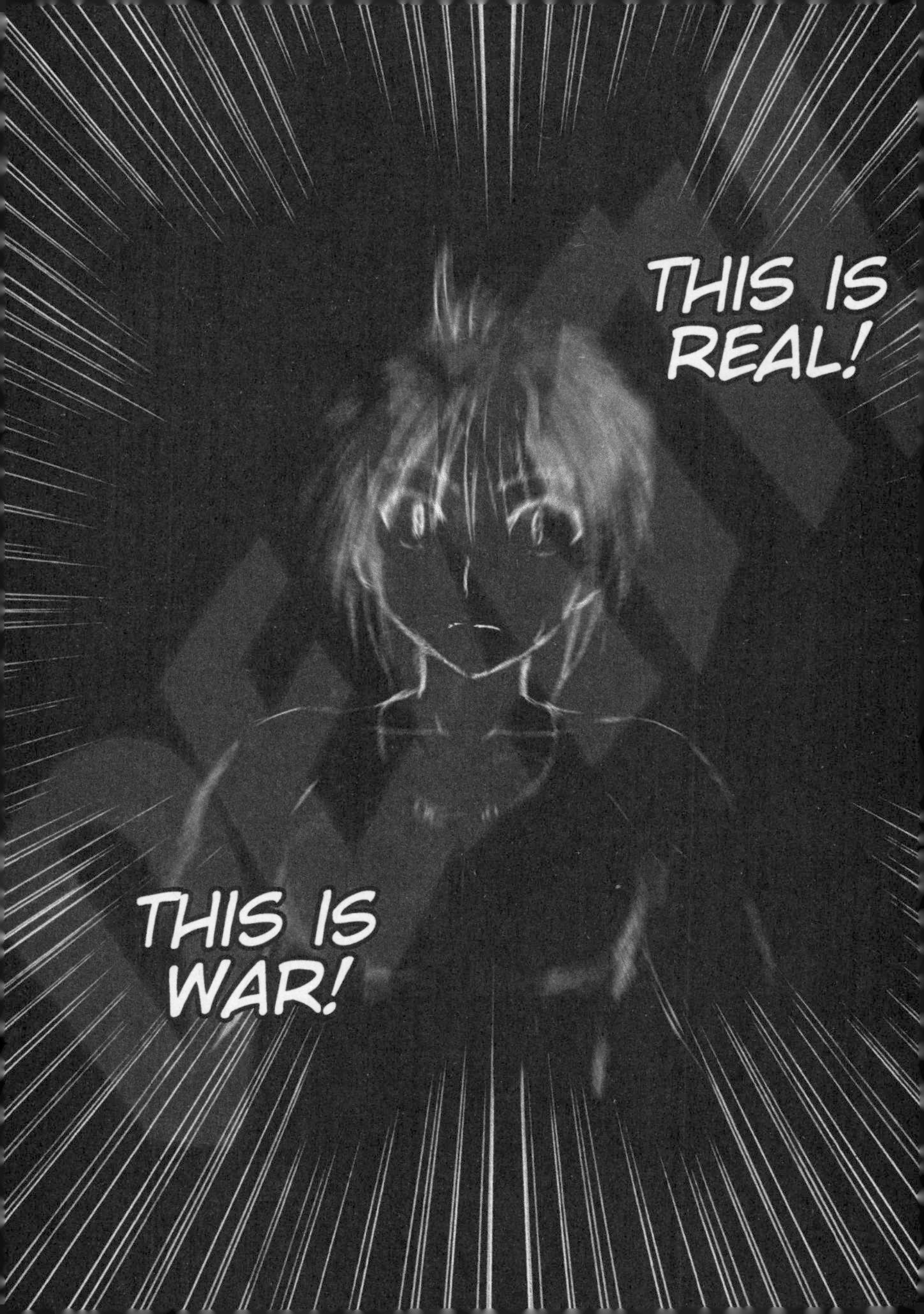
THIS IS REAL!
THIS IS WAR!

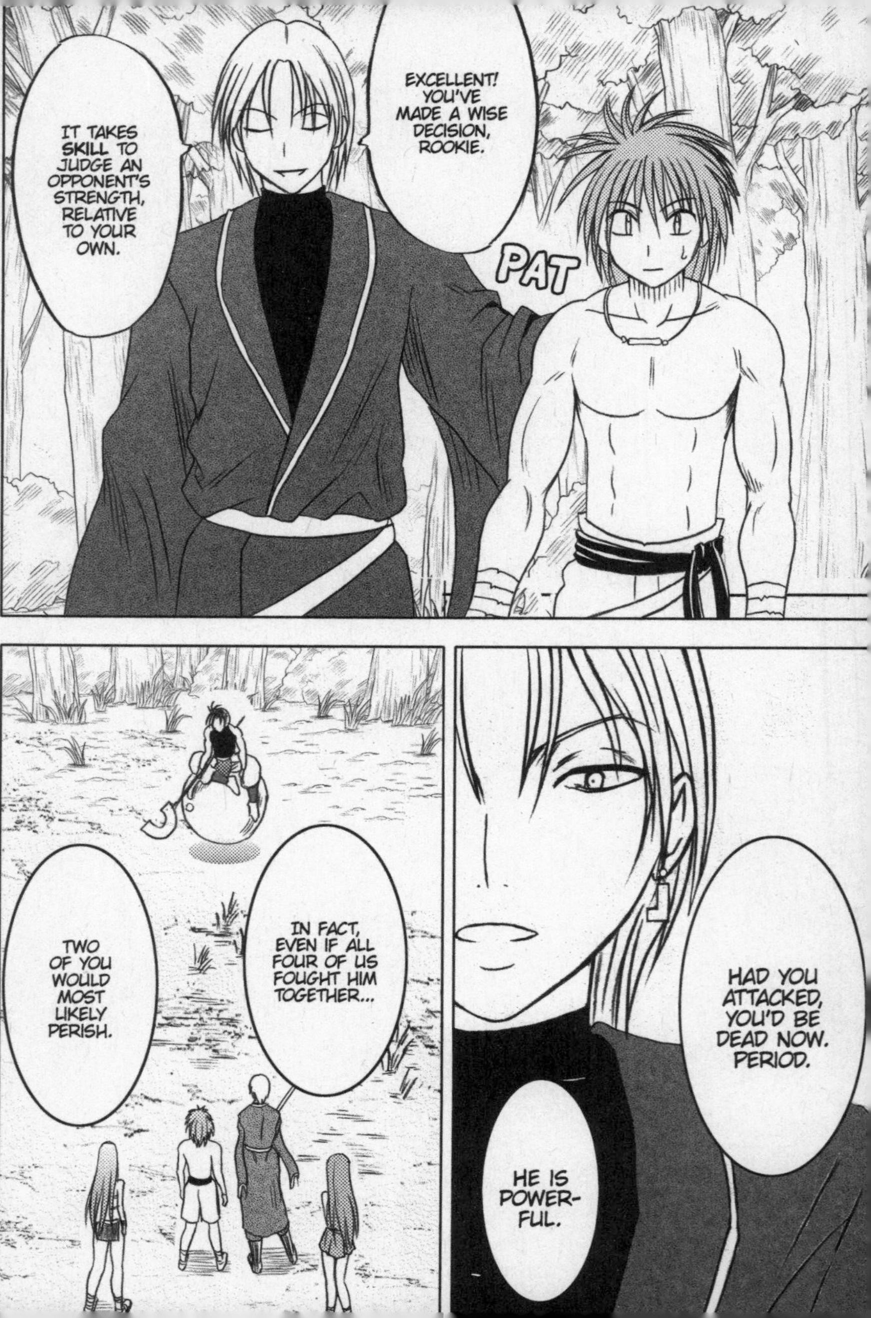
EXCELLENT! YOU'VE MADE A WISE DECISION, ROOKIE.
PAT
IT TAKES SKILL TO JUDGE AN OPPONENT'S STRENGTH, RELATIVE TO YOUR OWN.
HAD YOU ATTACKED, YOU'D BE DEAD NOW. PERIOD.
HE IS POWER-FUL.
IN FACT, EVEN IF ALL FOUR OF US FOUGHT HIM TOGETHER...
TWO OF YOU WOULD MOST LIKELY PERISH.

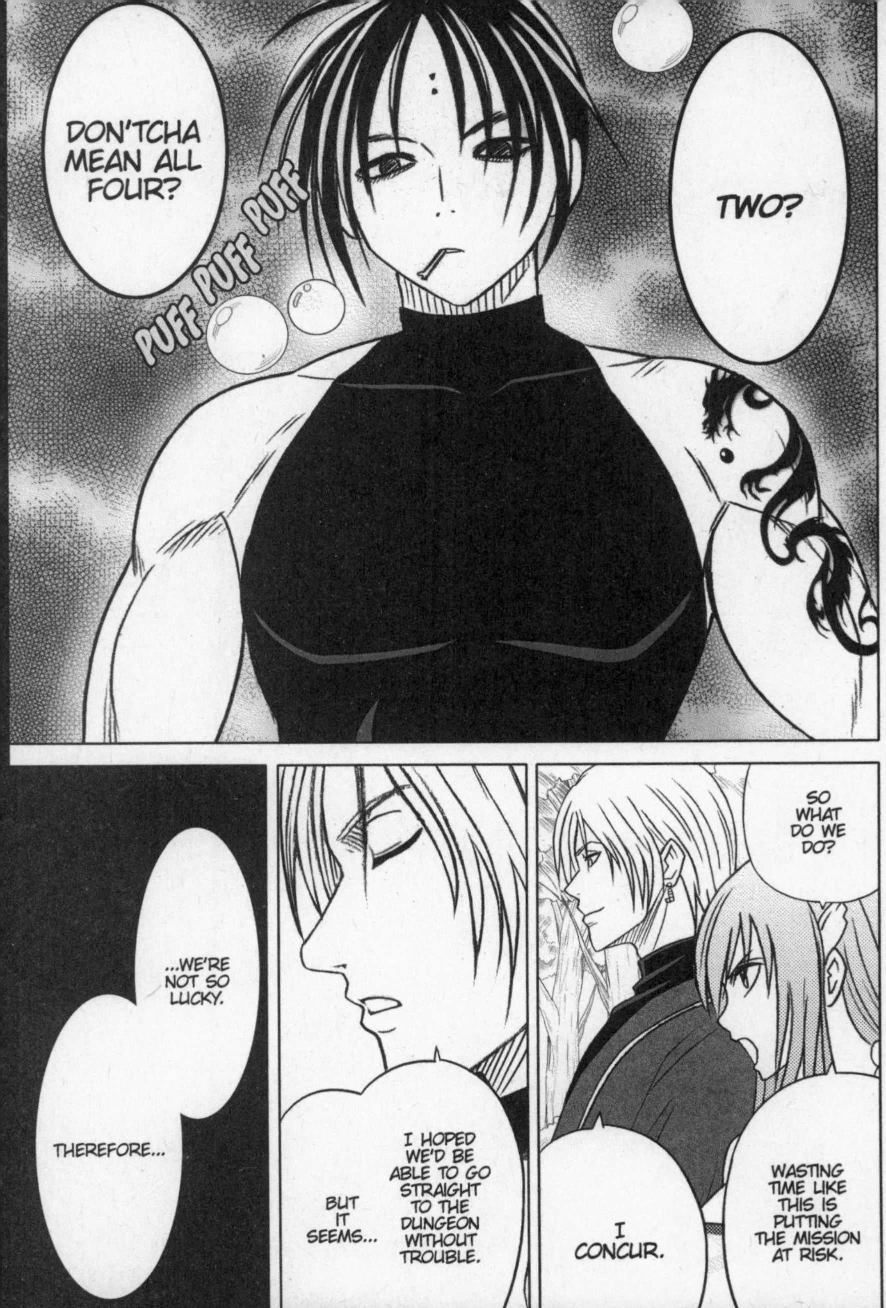
TWO?
DON'TCHA MEAN ALL FOUR?
PUFF PUFF PUFF
SO WHAT DO WE DO?
WASTING TIME LIKE THIS IS PUTTING THE MISSION AT RISK.
I CONCUR.
I HOPED WE'D BE ABLE TO GO STRAIGHT TO THE DUNGEON WITHOUT TROUBLE.
BUT IT SEEMS...
...WE'RE NOT SO LUCKY.
THEREFORE...

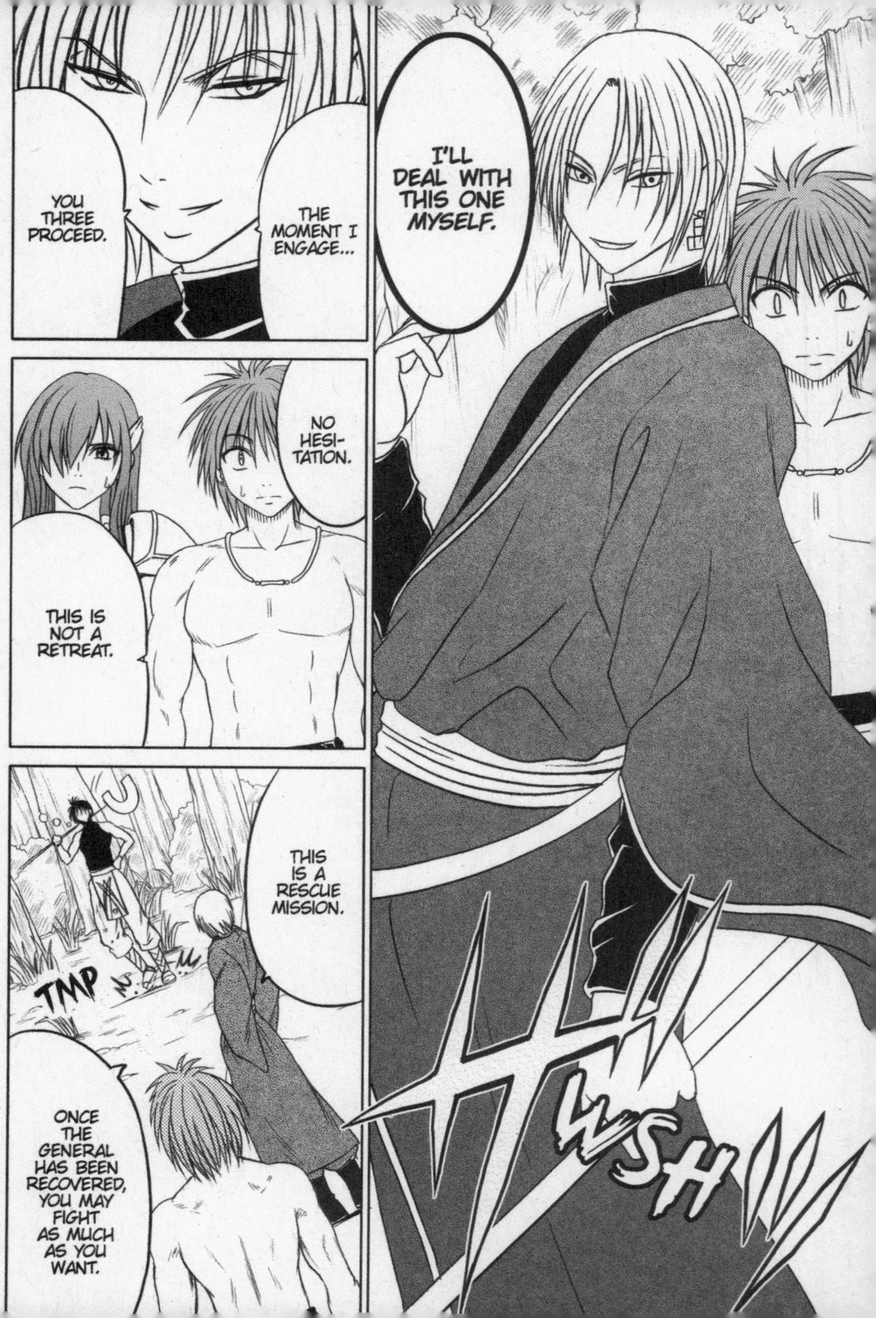
I'LL DEAL WITH THIS ONE MYSELF.
WSH
THE MOMENT I ENGAGE...
YOU THREE PROCEED.
NO HESI-TATION.
THIS IS NOT A RETREAT.
THIS IS A RESCUE MISSION.
TMP
ONCE THE GENERAL HAS BEEN RECOVERED, YOU MAY FIGHT AS MUCH AS YOU WANT.

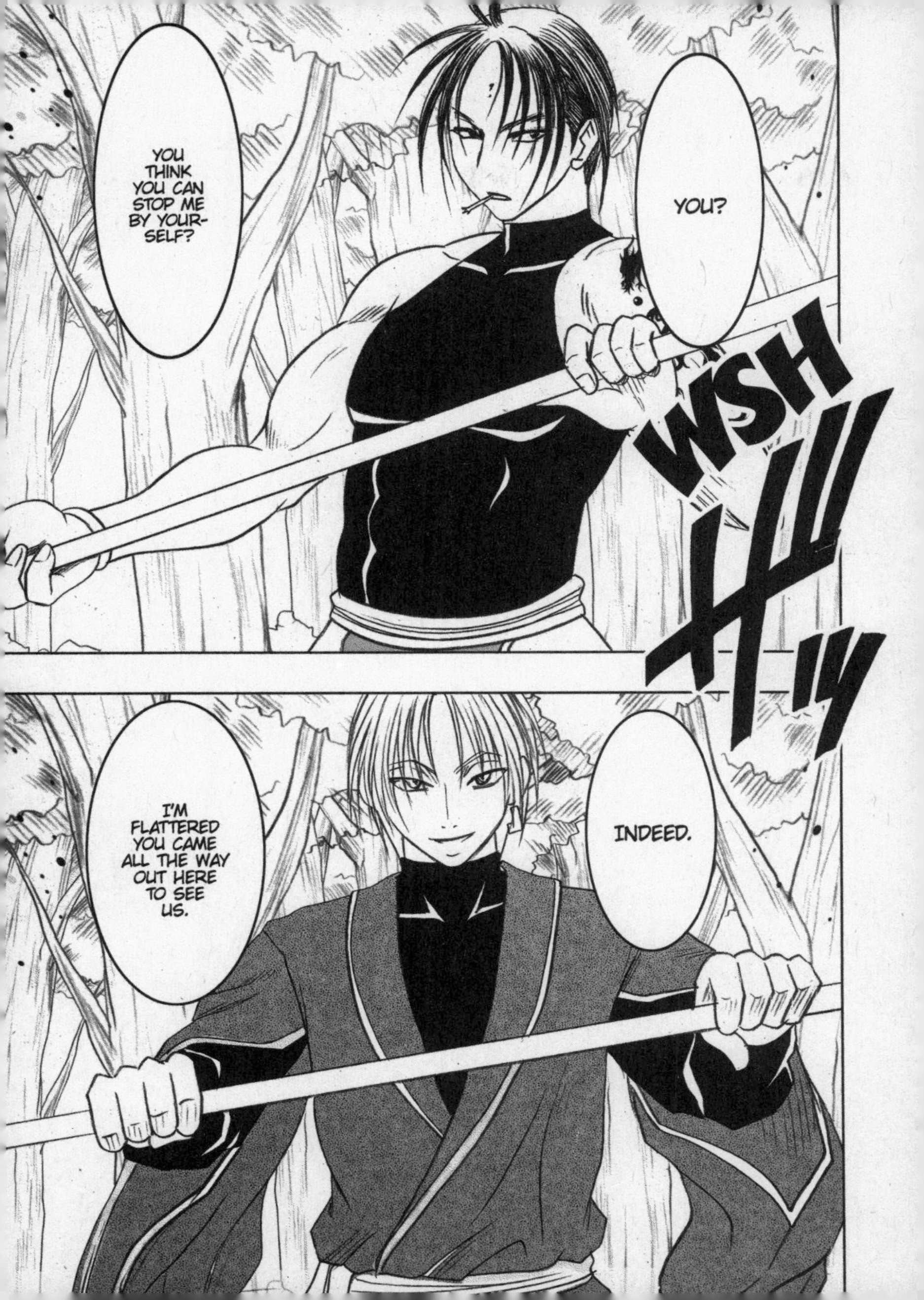
YOU?
YOU THINK YOU CAN STOP ME BY YOURSELF?
WSH
INDEED.
I'M FLATTERED YOU CAME ALL THE WAY OUT HERE TO SEE US.

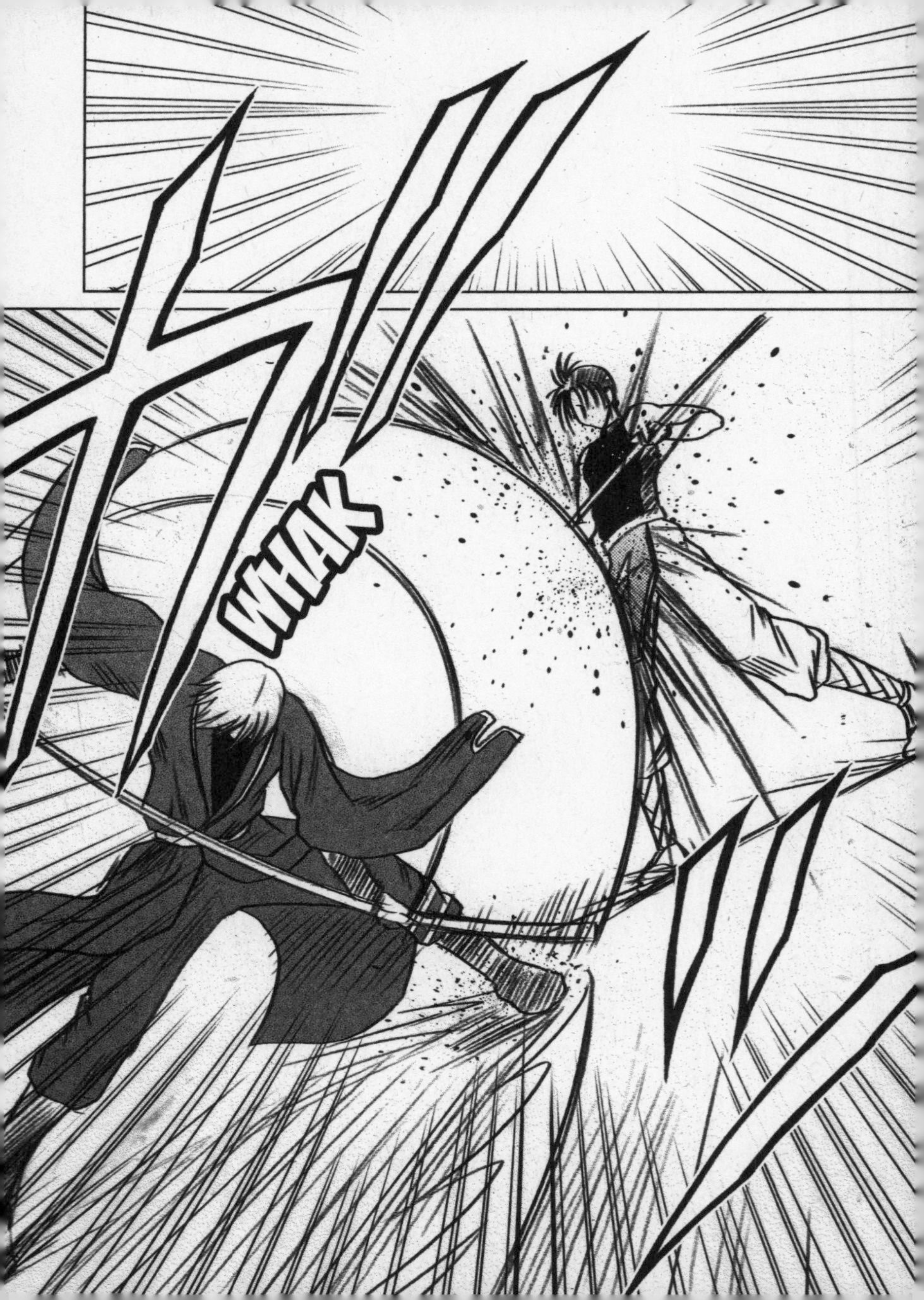
WHAK

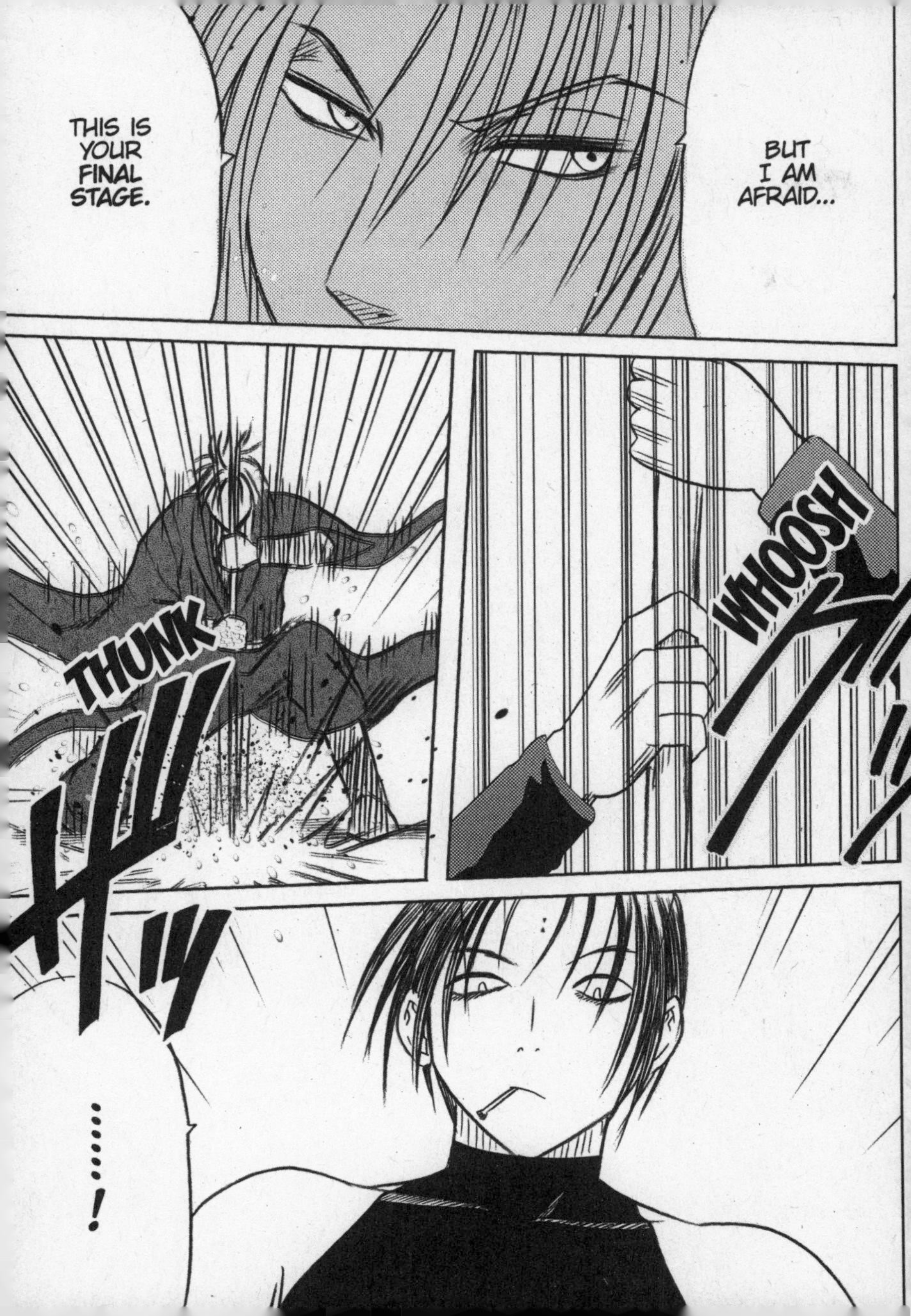
BUT I AM AFRAID...
THIS IS YOUR FINAL STAGE.
WHOOSH
THUNK
......!

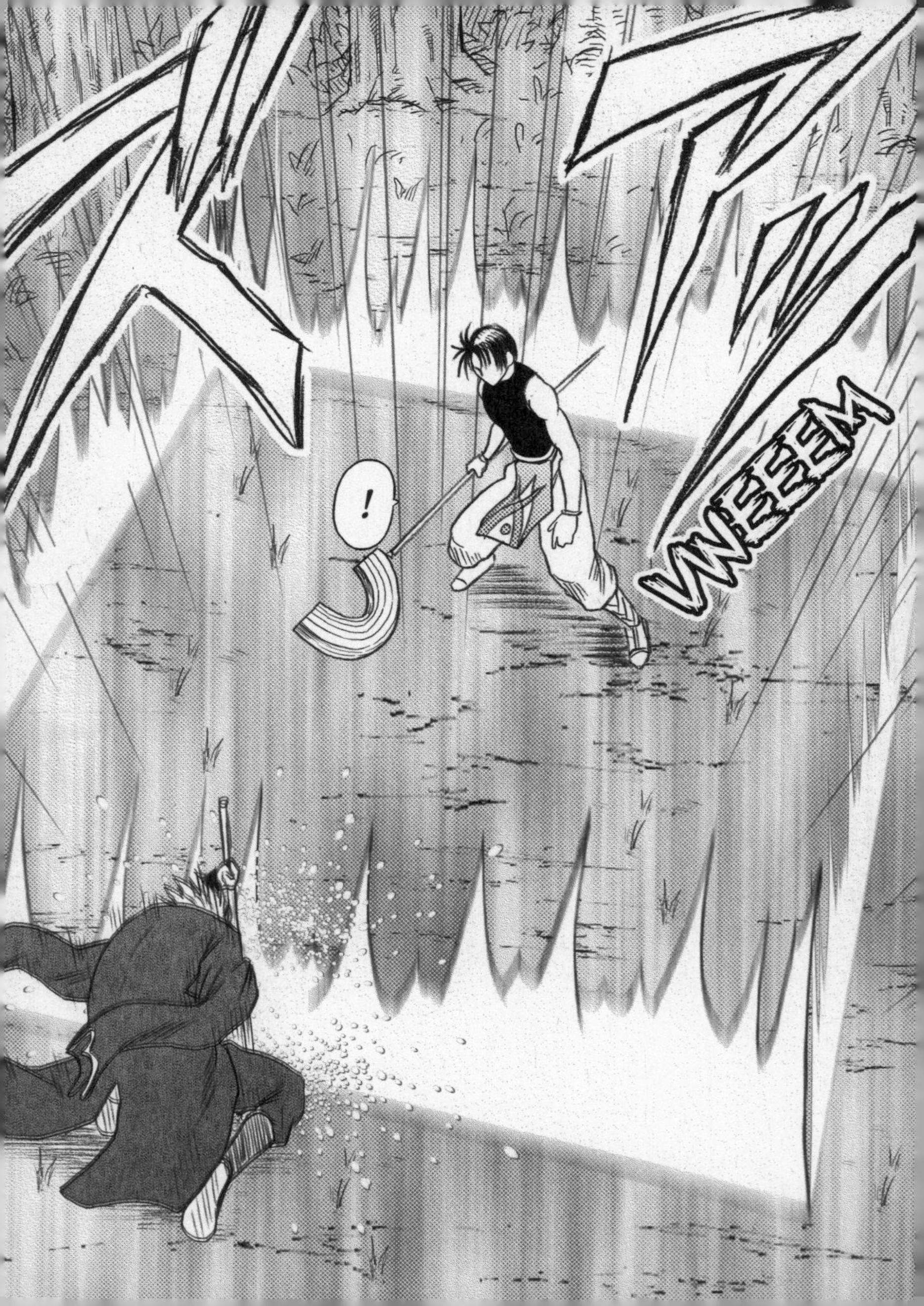
!
VWEEEM

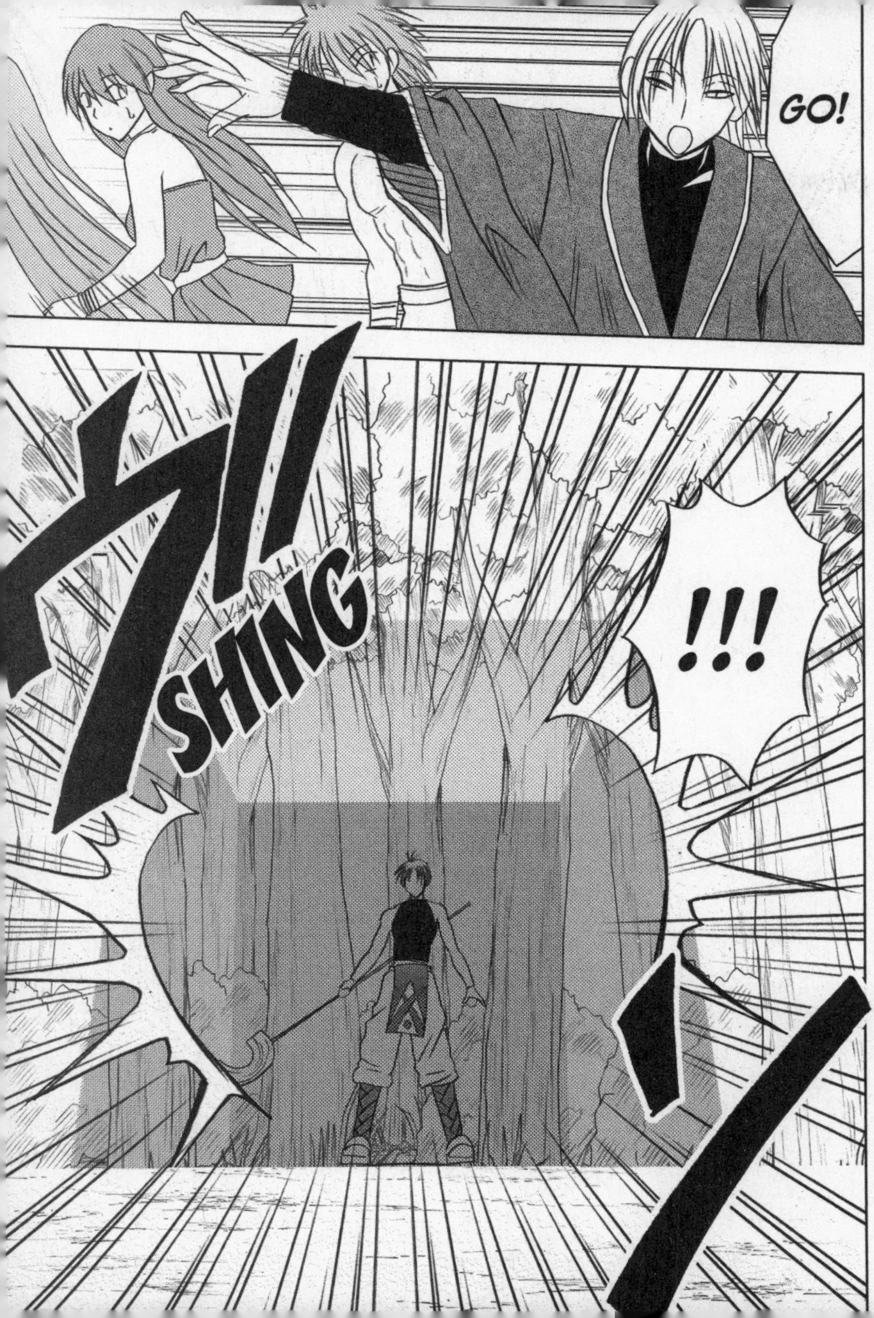
GO!
!!!
SHING

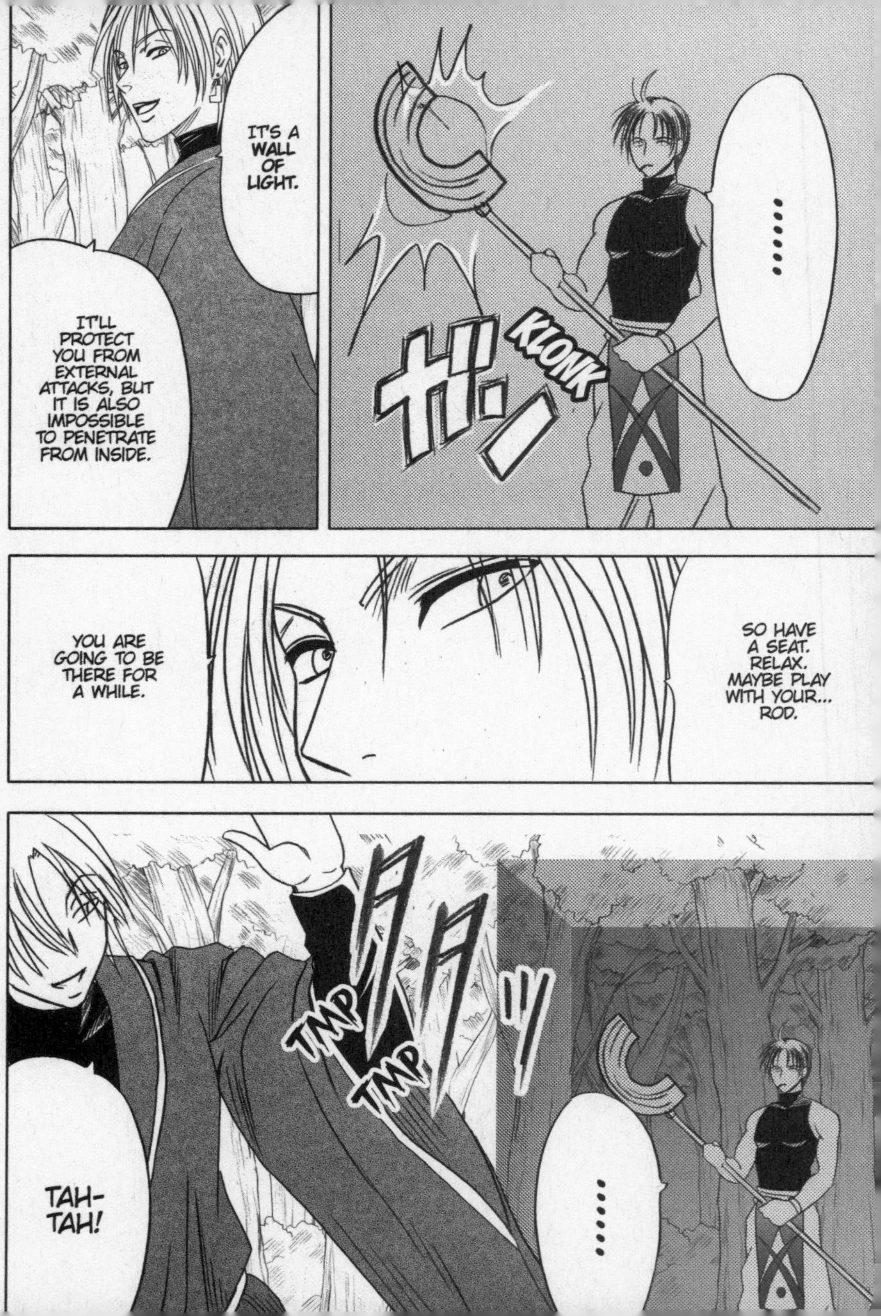
......
KLONK
IT'S A WALL OF LIGHT.
IT'LL PROTECT YOU FROM EXTERNAL ATTACKS, BUT IT IS ALSO IMPOSSIBLE TO PENETRATE FROM INSIDE.
SO HAVE A SEAT. RELAX. MAYBE PLAY WITH YOUR... ROD.
YOU ARE GOING TO BE THERE FOR A WHILE.
......
TMP
TMP
TAH-TAH!

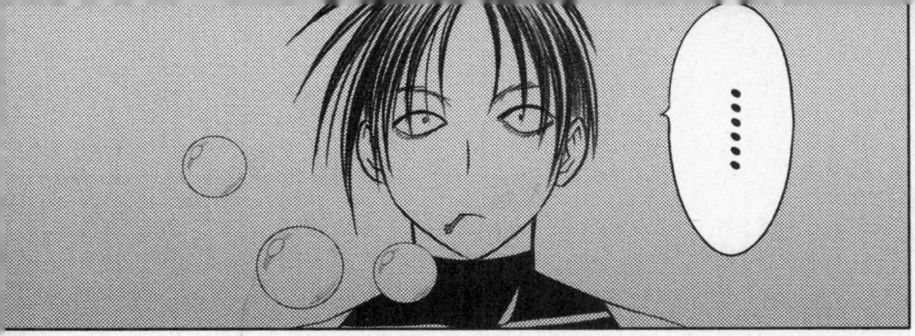
......
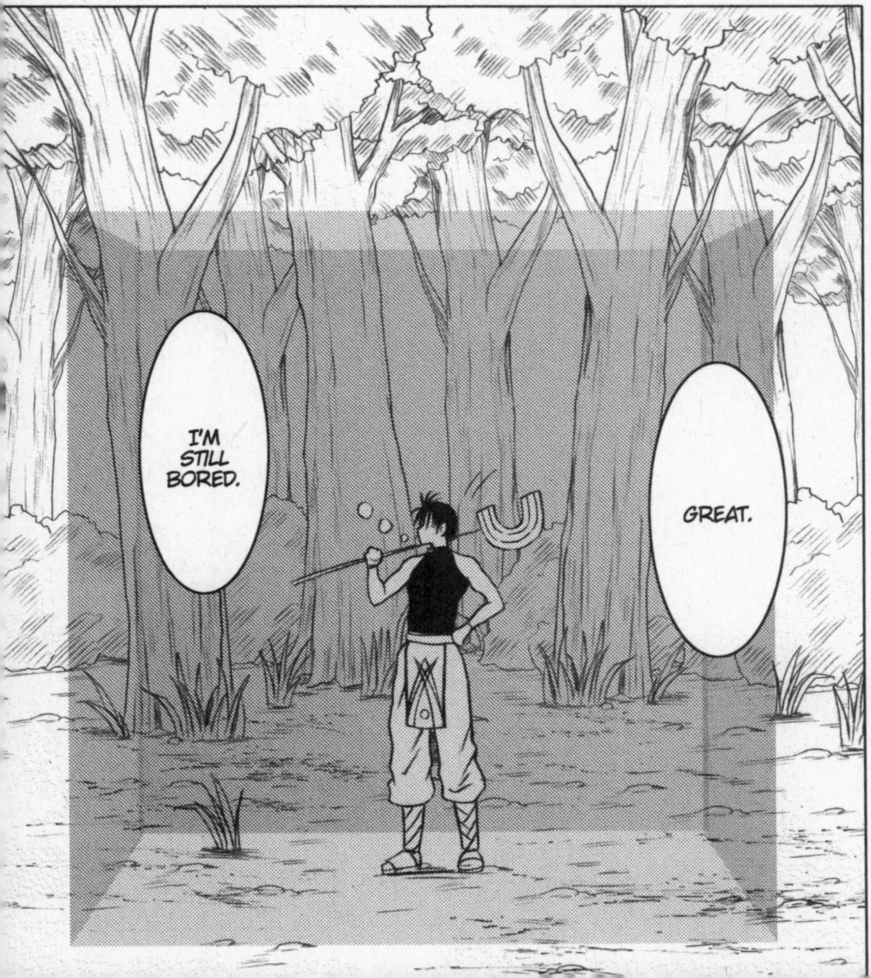
GREAT.
I'M STILL BORED.

Perusing Video Game History

ON THE EDGE OF THE BLUE WORLD

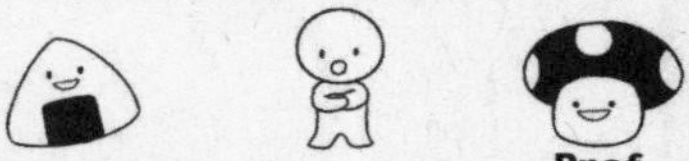

Dr. Onigiri Mr. Why Prof. Mushroom

Today's Topic

TAITO

Mr. Why: Okay, I've been wanting to ask this for a while, but Nintendo really put video games on the map in Japan, right?

Dr. Onigiri: I like to think it was Sega, actually.

Prof. Mushroom: Whoa, whoa! No makin' stuff up! Sure, Sega had a lot of success, but if we're talking about consoles only, then yes, it was Nintendo.

Mr. Why: Consoles only? What else is there?

Prof. Mushroom: Well, the first big video game hit in Japan was the arcade game *Space Invaders*, back in 1978. Without it, video games wouldn't be nearly the household name they are now.

Dr. Onigiri: In *Space Invaders*, the player piloted a ship at the bottom of the screen, and there were rows of "invaders" coming down from the top. You had to shoot at all the enemies, while dodging their fire. A simple game, it combined "dodging," "aiming" and "point scoring" together. *Space Invaders* is considered the origin of all shooter games, and everyone in Japan was hooked on it.

Prof. Mushroom: You got that right. They even made a version of the machine built into a table, so you could play it at cafés. Once they did that, you could walk into any café and see multiple people staring intently at the table, a towering stack of 100-yen coins by their elbows.

Mr. Why: Wow, was it really that big?

Dr. Onigiri: Big enough that it caused a shortage of 100-yen coins.

Mr. Why: Whoa.

Prof. Mushroom: It captured the nation's heart, that's for sure.

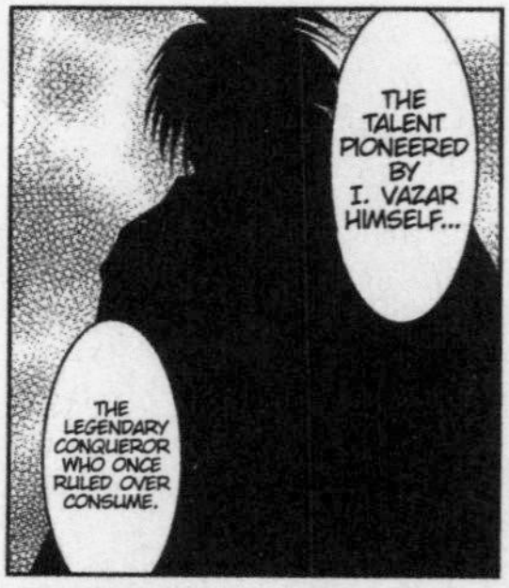
THE TALENT PIONEERED BY I. VAZAR HIMSELF...
THE LEGENDARY CONQUEROR WHO ONCE RULED OVER CONSUME.

Tatrand's I. Vazar is the founder of the Shooting technique.

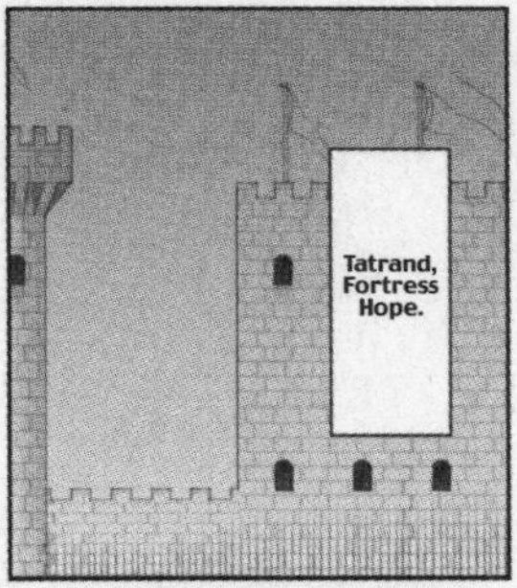
Tatrand, Fortress Hope.

Tatrand's Fortress Hope, where Segua's General Alex is being held captive. Will our heroes succeed?

Dr. Onigiri: Exactly. And thanks to that, Taito became a huge presence in the arcade game market. They produced a number of other killer arcade titles like *Elevator Action* and *KiKi KaiKai* (a.k.a. *Knight Boy* in the US and Europe, the forerunner to the *Pocky & Rocky* series).

Prof. Mushroom: Many of these games were ported onto consoles like the NES, and got real big there, too.

Dr. Onigiri: But when you talk about big Taito games, there are two titles you certainly can't forget.

Mr. Why: What, there's more?

Dr. Onigiri: You bet. First, there was the shooter game so massive it needed three screens lined up in a row: *Darius*. Then there was *Bubble Bobble*, an action game where you controlled two bubble-breathing lizard brothers, Bub and Bob. Bub in particular was so popular he eventually became Taito's mascot.

Prof. Mushroom: We'll dive a little more in-depth with those two games next time.

To Be Continued...

THE HISTORY OF TAITO

1953: Taito is founded

● Taito began as an importer and distributer of various items, including vending machines and vodka.

1973: *Elepong* released.

● It was the first coin-operated arcade game in Japan.

1978: *Space Invaders* released.

● Explosively popular in Japan.

1985: *Space Invaders & Chack'n Pop* released for NES.

● Two popular arcade games ported over to the NES home console.

1986: *Takeshi no Chosenjo (Takeshi's Challenge)* released.

● This infamously unique title generated a lot of attention.

1987: *Bubble Bobble* released for the FDS.*

● This was the first year Taito released games on the FDS.

1988: *Rainbow Islands* released.

● The sequel to *Bubble Bobble.*

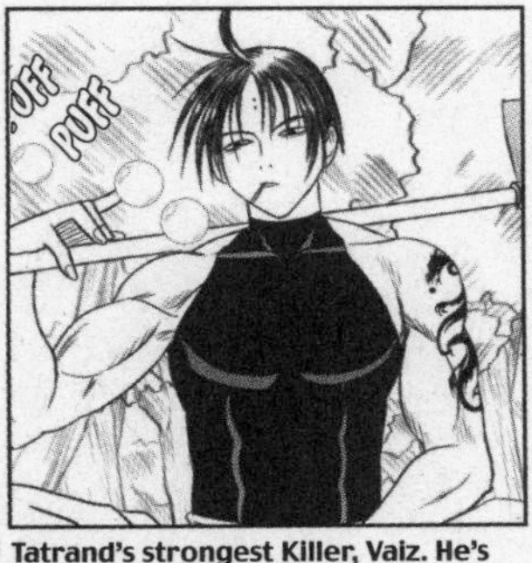

Tatrand's strongest Killer, Vaiz. He's always blowing bubbles.

***FDS = "Family Computer Disk System." It was a peripheral for the Famicom (the Japanese NES) which played games released on proprietary floppy disks, called Disk Cards.**

CHAPTER 9

GREAT THING

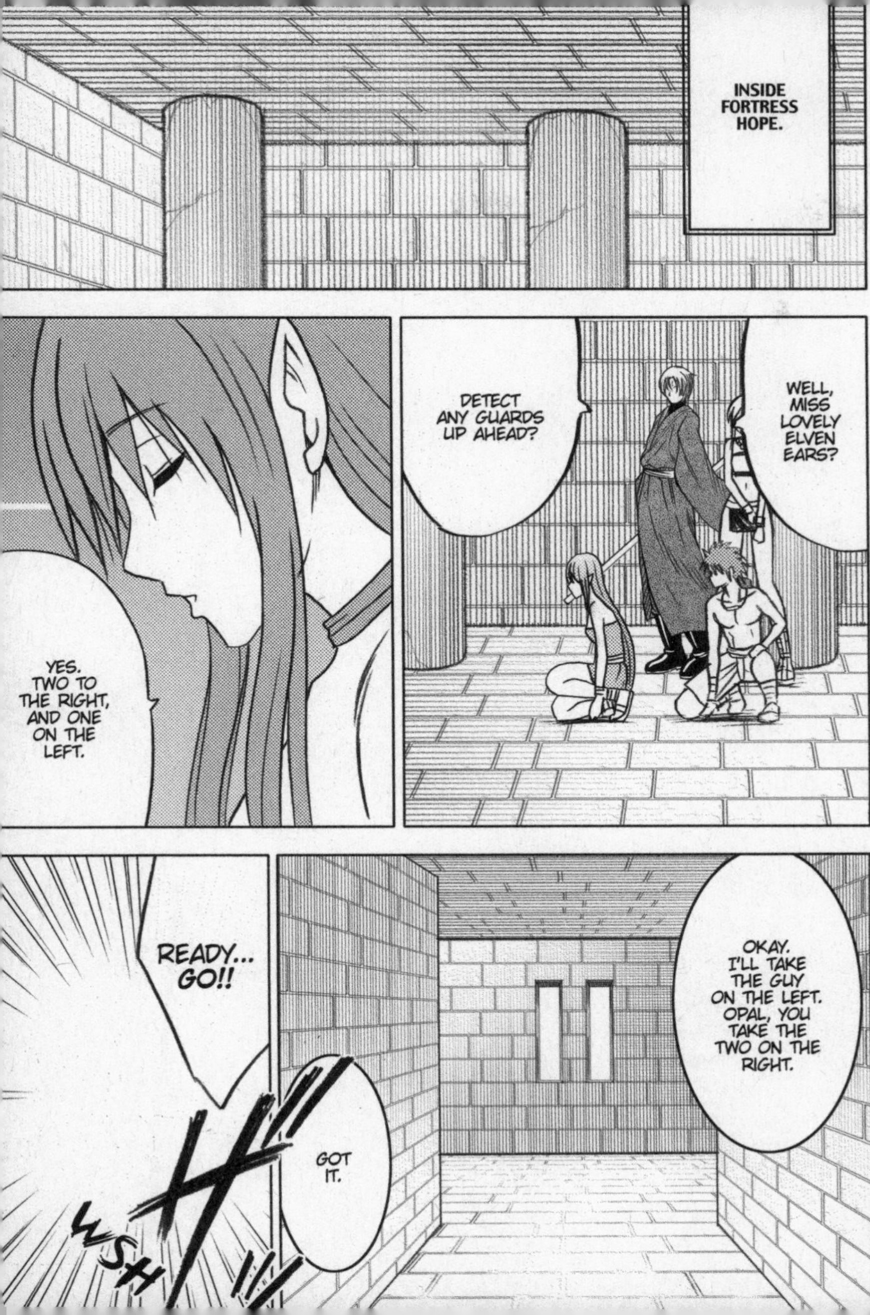
INSIDE FORTRESS HOPE.
WELL, MISS LOVELY ELVEN EARS?
DETECT ANY GUARDS UP AHEAD?
YES. TWO TO THE RIGHT, AND ONE ON THE LEFT.
OKAY. I'LL TAKE THE GUY ON THE LEFT. OPAL, YOU TAKE THE TWO ON THE RIGHT.
GOT IT.
READY... GO!!
WSH

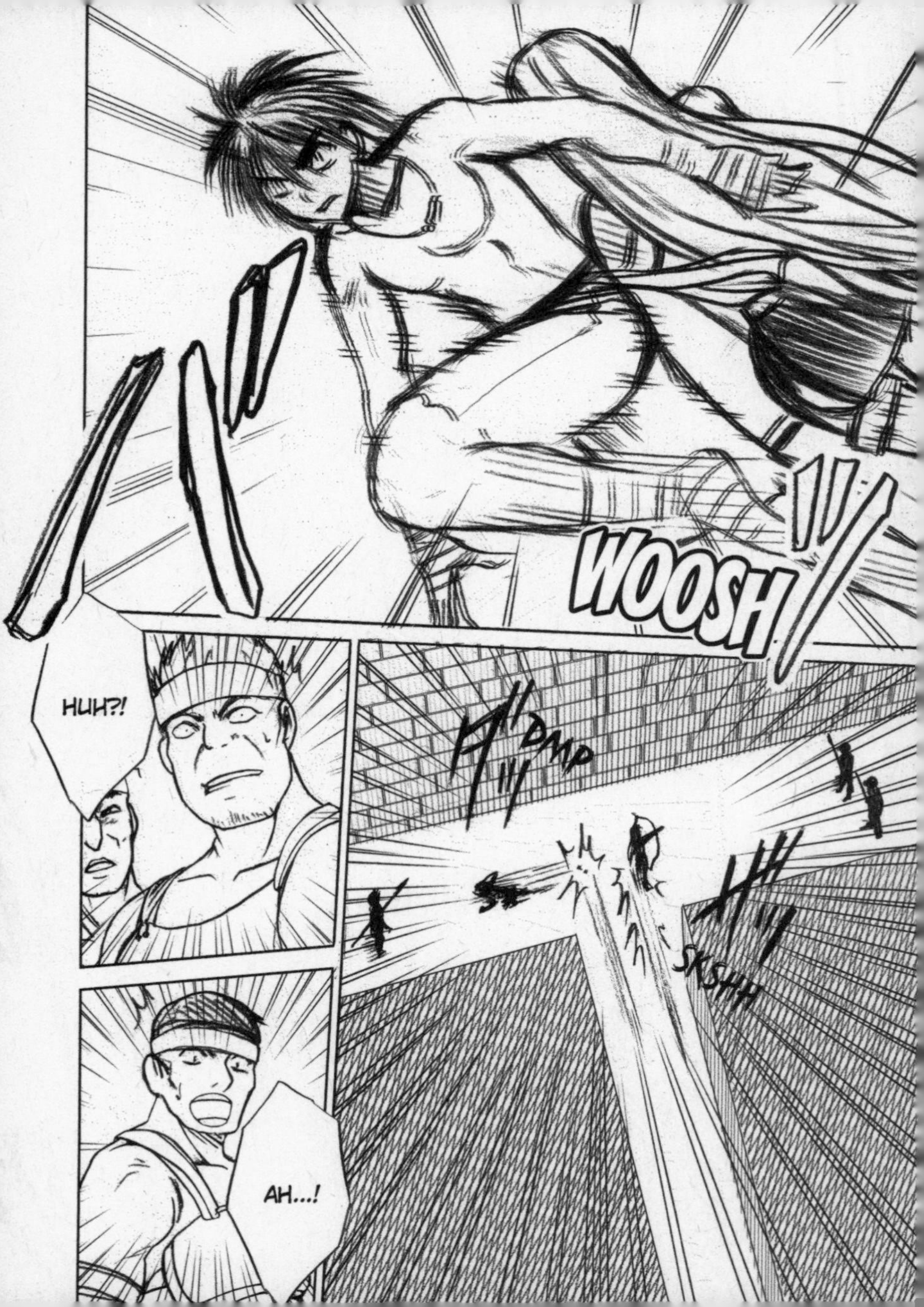
WOOSH
DMP
SKSHH
HUH?!
AH...!

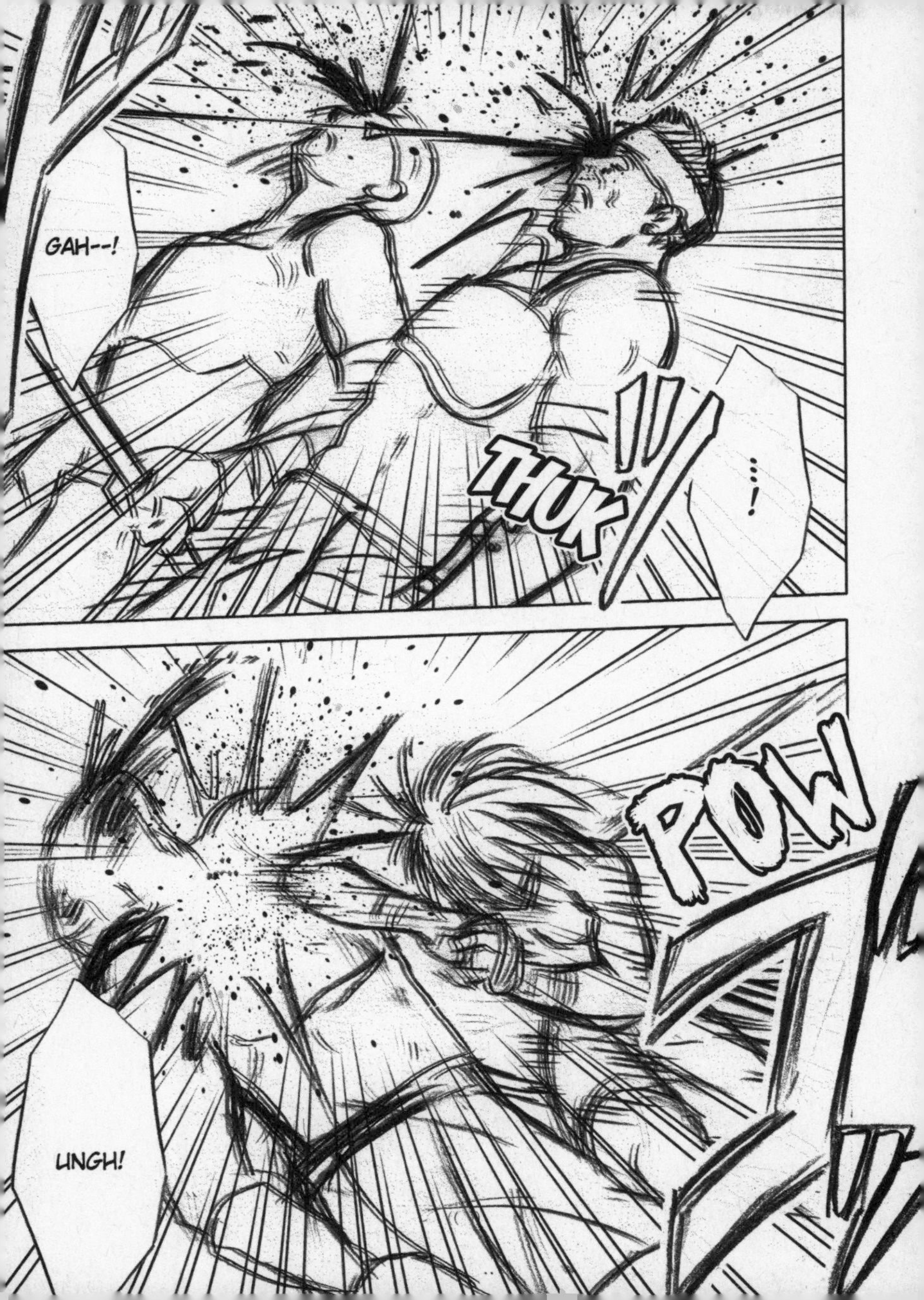
...!
THUK
GAH--!
POW
UNGH!

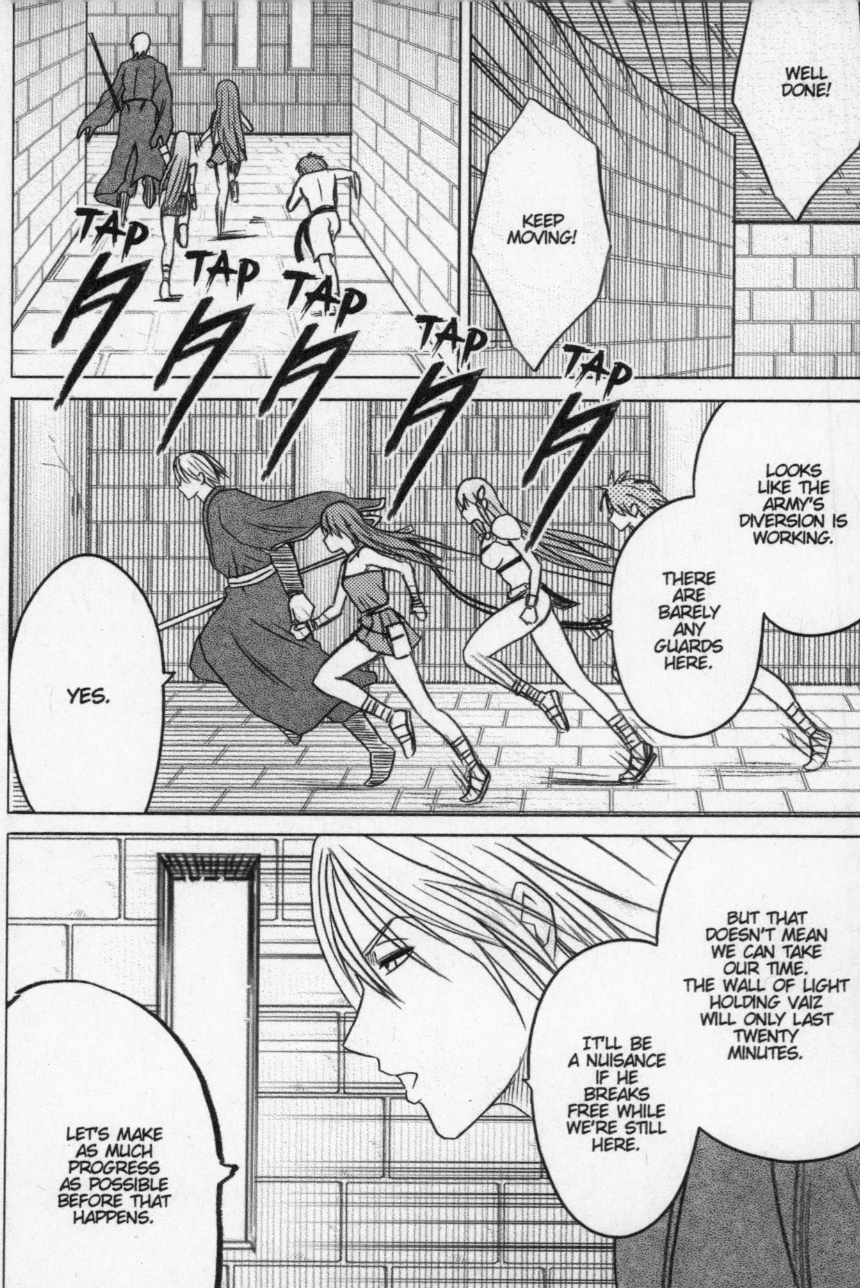
WELL DONE!
KEEP MOVING!
TAP
TAP
TAP
TAP
TAP
LOOKS LIKE THE ARMY'S DIVERSION IS WORKING.
THERE ARE BARELY ANY GUARDS HERE.
YES.
BUT THAT DOESN'T MEAN WE CAN TAKE OUR TIME. THE WALL OF LIGHT HOLDING VAIZ WILL ONLY LAST TWENTY MINUTES.
IT'LL BE A NUISANCE IF HE BREAKS FREE WHILE WE'RE STILL HERE.
LET'S MAKE AS MUCH PROGRESS AS POSSIBLE BEFORE THAT HAPPENS.

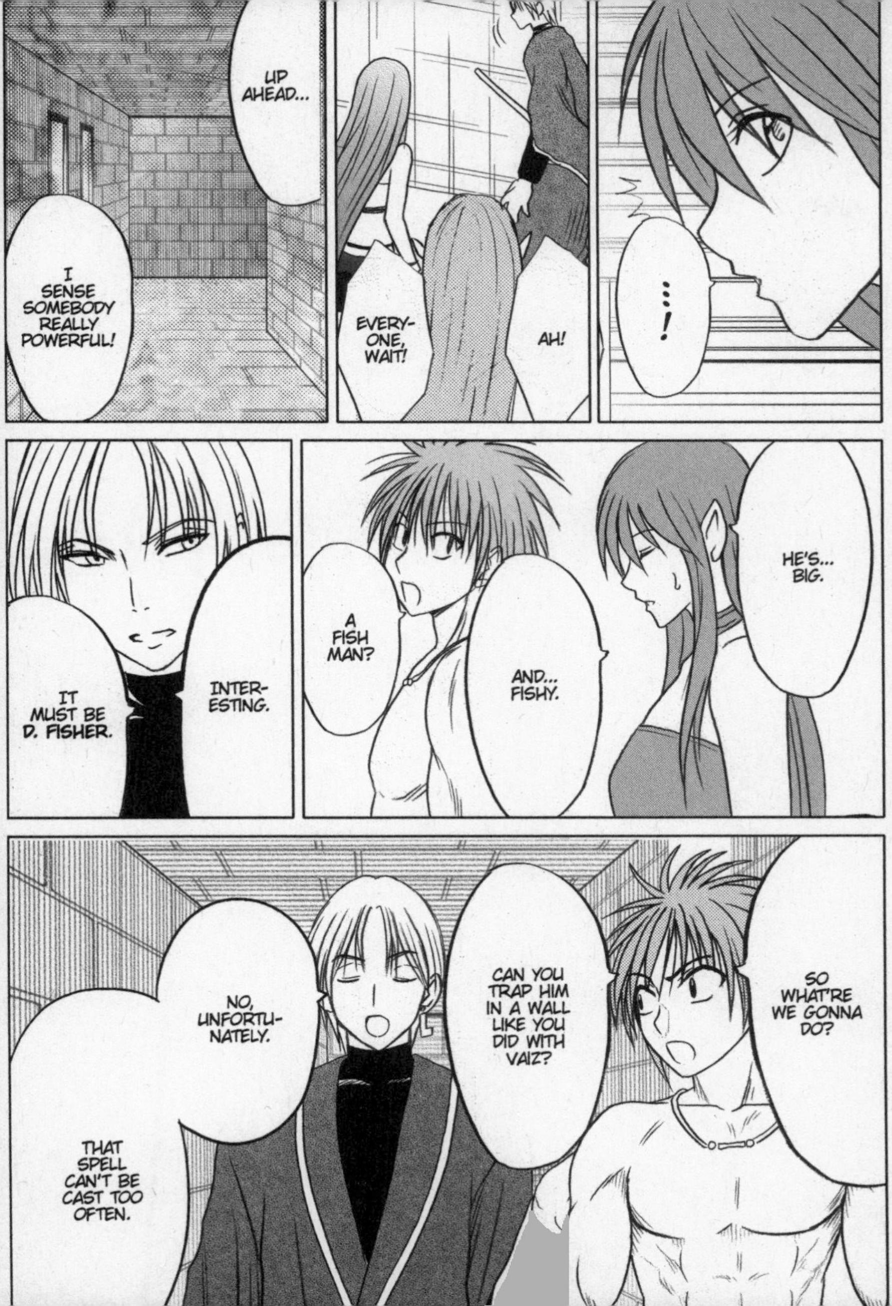
...!
AH!
EVERY-ONE, WAIT!
UP AHEAD...
I SENSE SOMEBODY REALLY POWERFUL!
HE'S... BIG.
AND... FISHY.
A FISH MAN?
INTER-ESTING.
IT MUST BE D. FISHER.
SO WHAT'RE WE GONNA DO?
CAN YOU TRAP HIM IN A WALL LIKE YOU DID WITH VAIZ?
NO, UNFORTU-NATELY.
THAT SPELL CAN'T BE CAST TOO OFTEN.

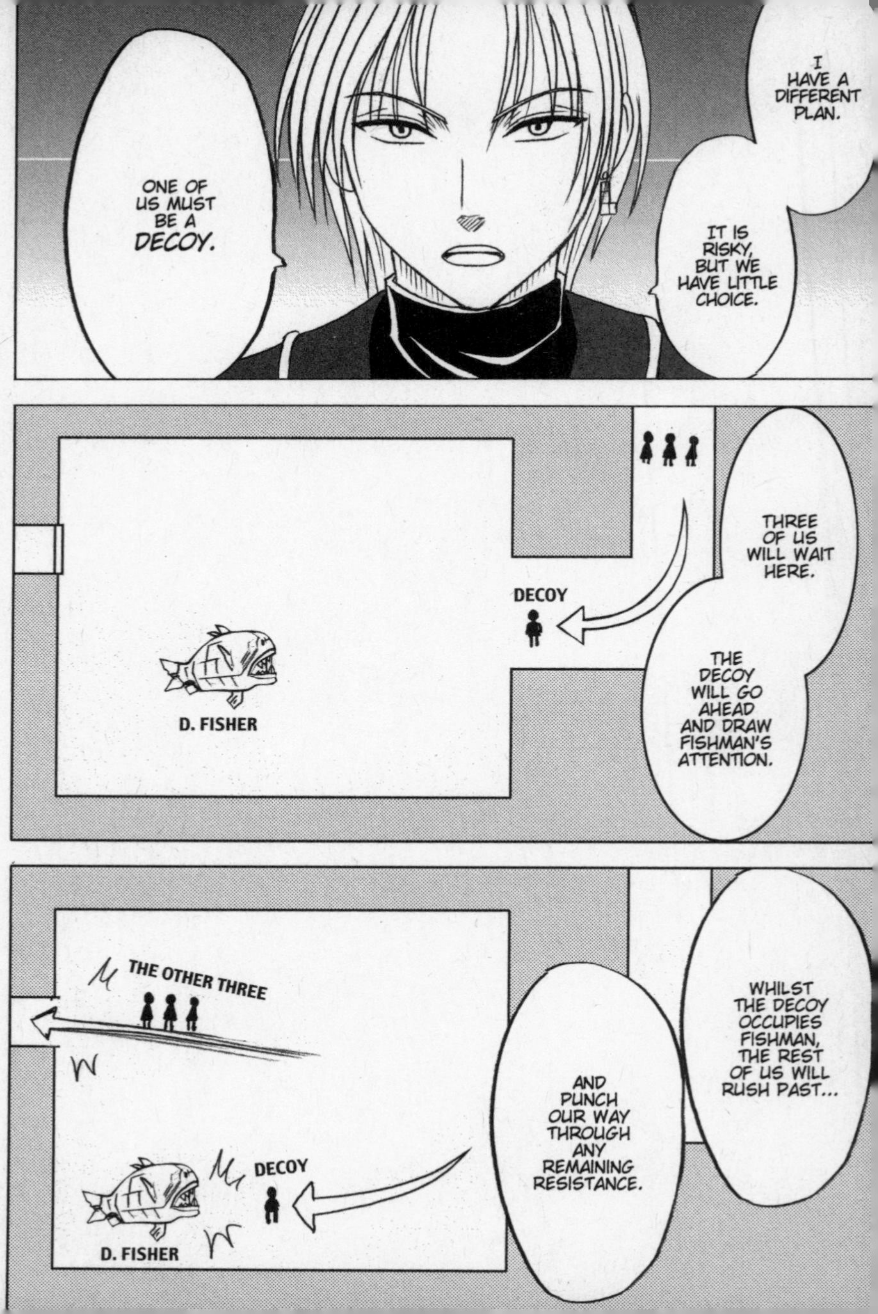
I HAVE A DIFFERENT PLAN.
IT IS RISKY, BUT WE HAVE LITTLE CHOICE.
ONE OF US MUST BE A DECOY.
THREE OF US WILL WAIT HERE.
THE DECOY WILL GO AHEAD AND DRAW FISHMAN'S ATTENTION.
DECOY
D. FISHER
WHILST THE DECOY OCCUPIES FISHMAN, THE REST OF US WILL RUSH PAST...
AND PUNCH OUR WAY THROUGH ANY REMAINING RESISTANCE.
THE OTHER THREE
DECOY
D. FISHER

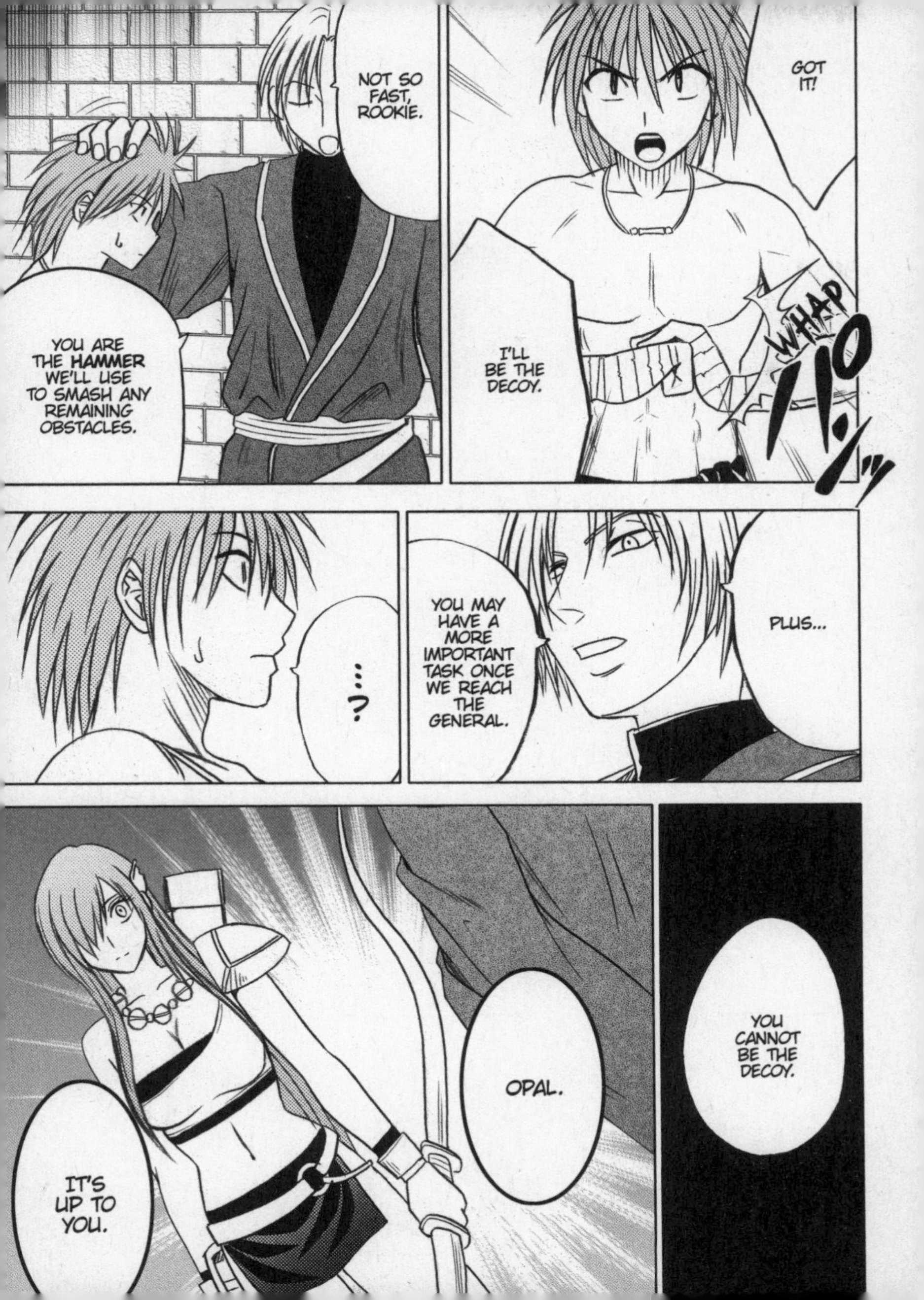
GOT IT!
I'LL BE THE DECOY.
WHAP
NOT SO FAST, ROOKIE.
YOU ARE THE **HAMMER** WE'LL USE TO SMASH ANY REMAINING OBSTACLES.
PLUS...
YOU MAY HAVE A MORE IMPORTANT TASK ONCE WE REACH THE GENERAL.
?...
YOU CANNOT BE THE DECOY.
OPAL.
IT'S UP TO YOU.

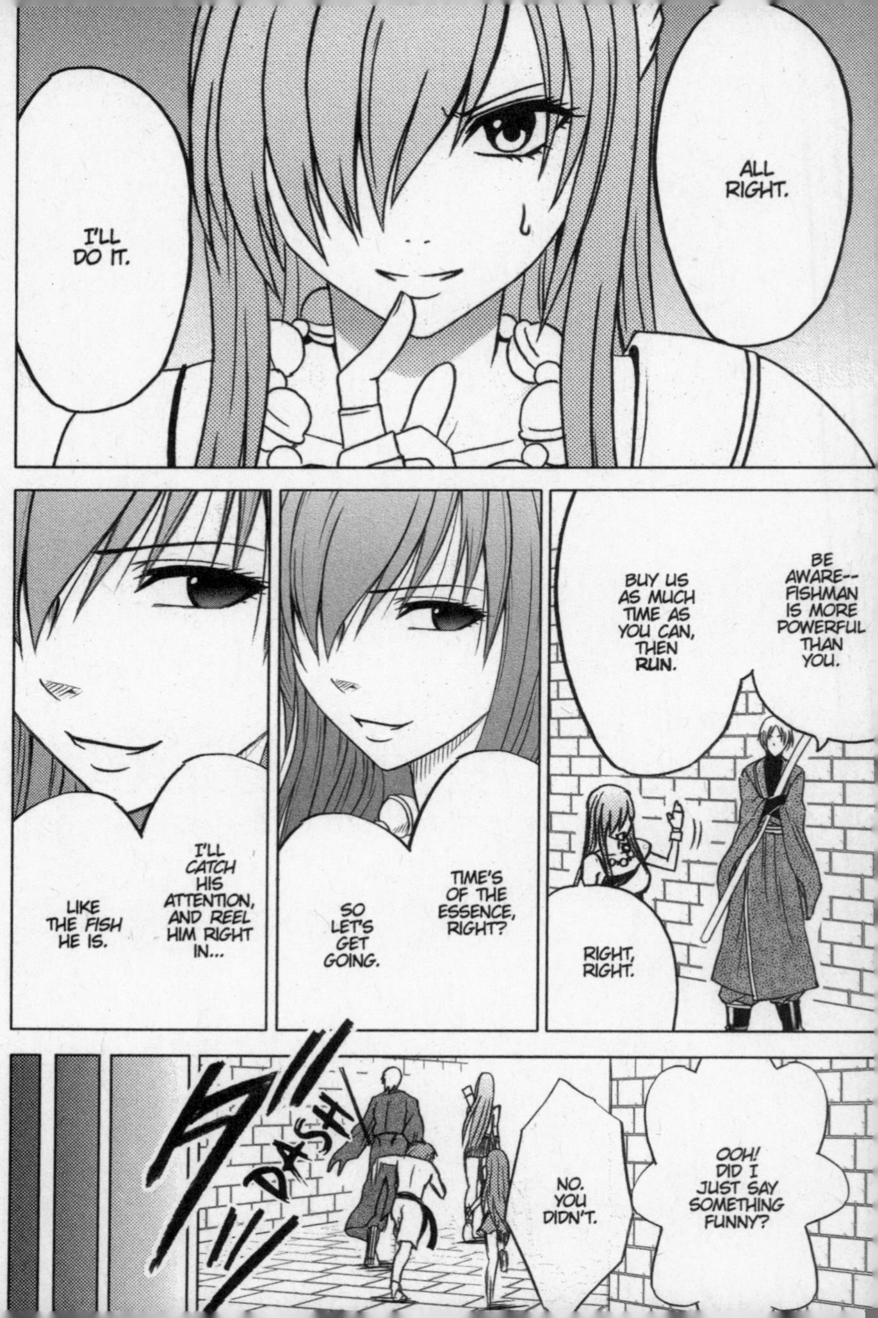
ALL RIGHT.
I'LL DO IT.
BE AWARE--FISHMAN IS MORE POWERFUL THAN YOU.
BUY US AS MUCH TIME AS YOU CAN, THEN RUN.
RIGHT, RIGHT.
TIME'S OF THE ESSENCE, RIGHT?
SO LET'S GET GOING.
I'LL CATCH HIS ATTENTION, AND REEL HIM RIGHT IN...
LIKE THE FISH HE IS.
OOH! DID I JUST SAY SOMETHING FUNNY?
NO. YOU DIDN'T.
DASH

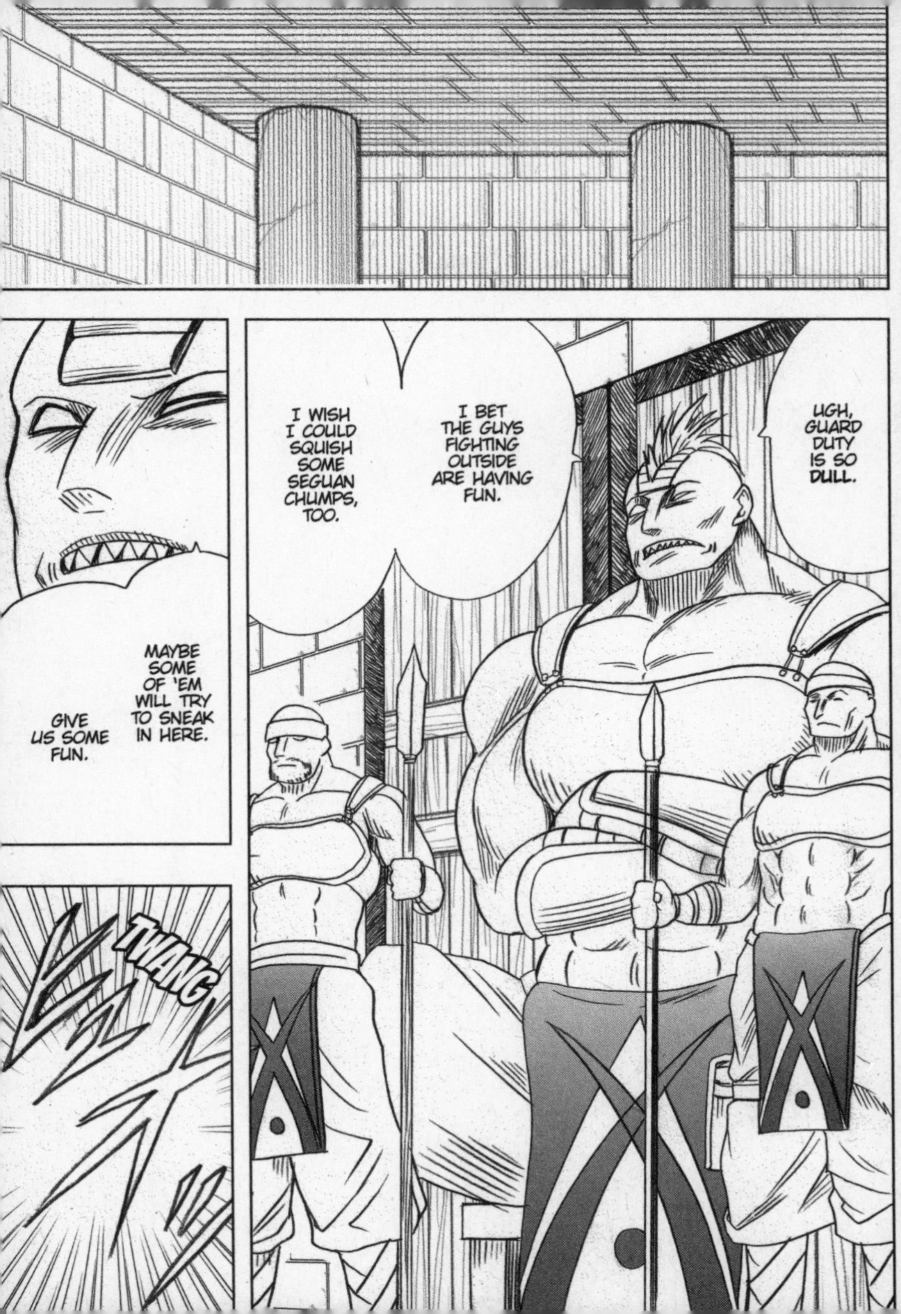
UGH, GUARD DUTY IS SO DULL.
I BET THE GUYS FIGHTING OUTSIDE ARE HAVING FUN.
I WISH I COULD SQUISH SOME SEGUAN CHUMPS, TOO.
MAYBE SOME OF 'EM WILL TRY TO SNEAK IN HERE.
GIVE US SOME FUN.
TWANG

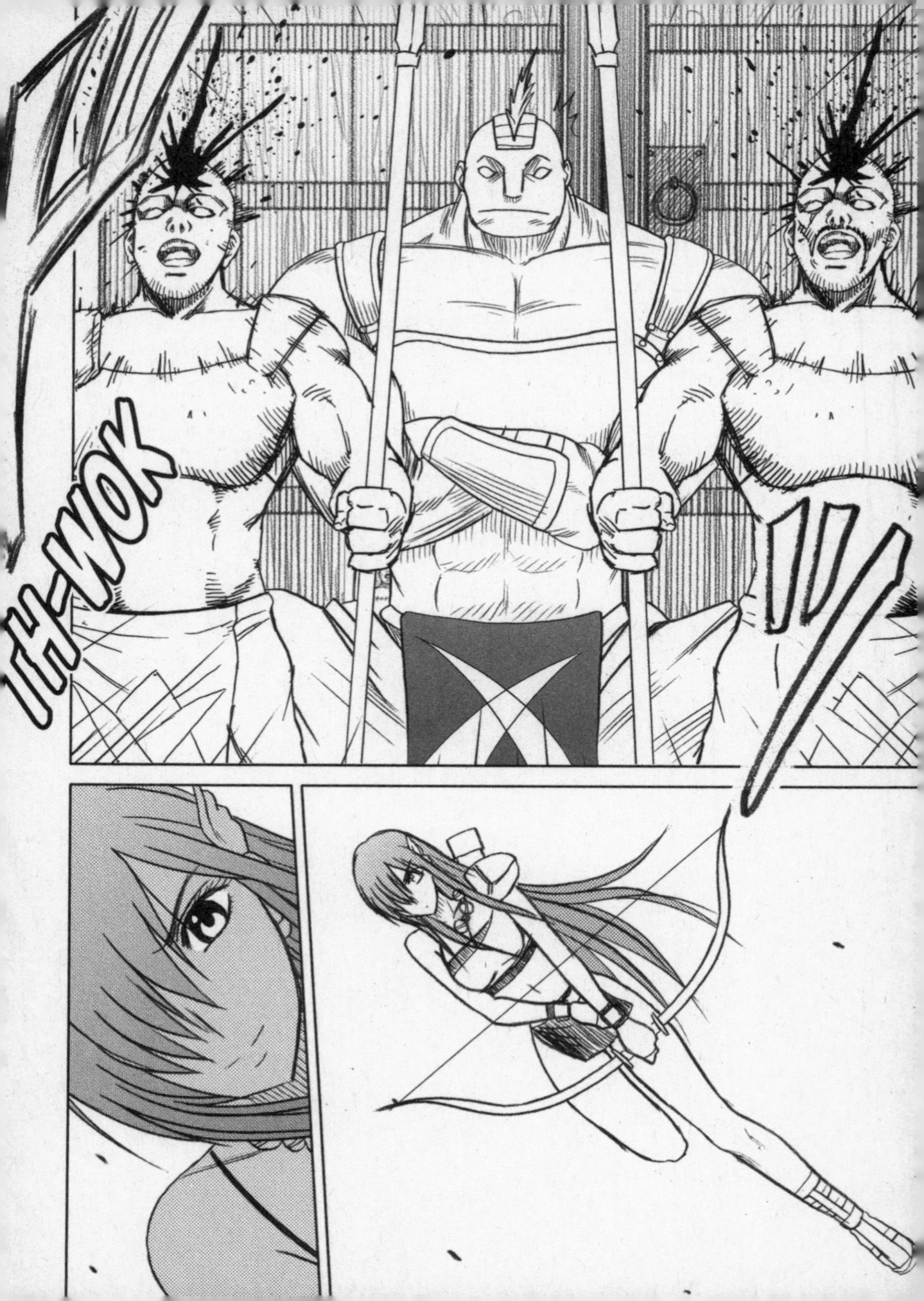
TH-WOK

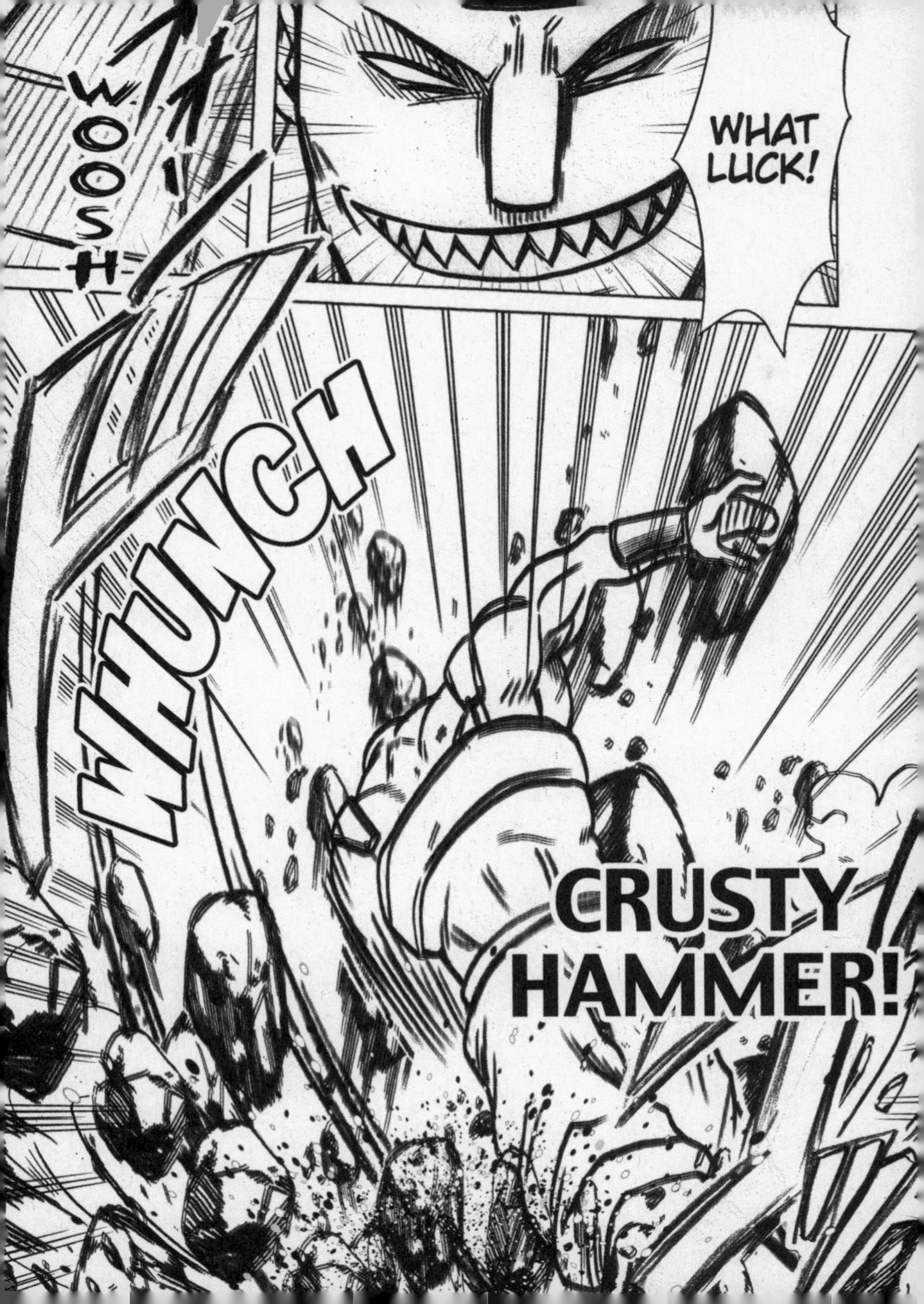
WHAT LUCK!
WOOSH
CRUSTY HAMMER!
WHUNCH

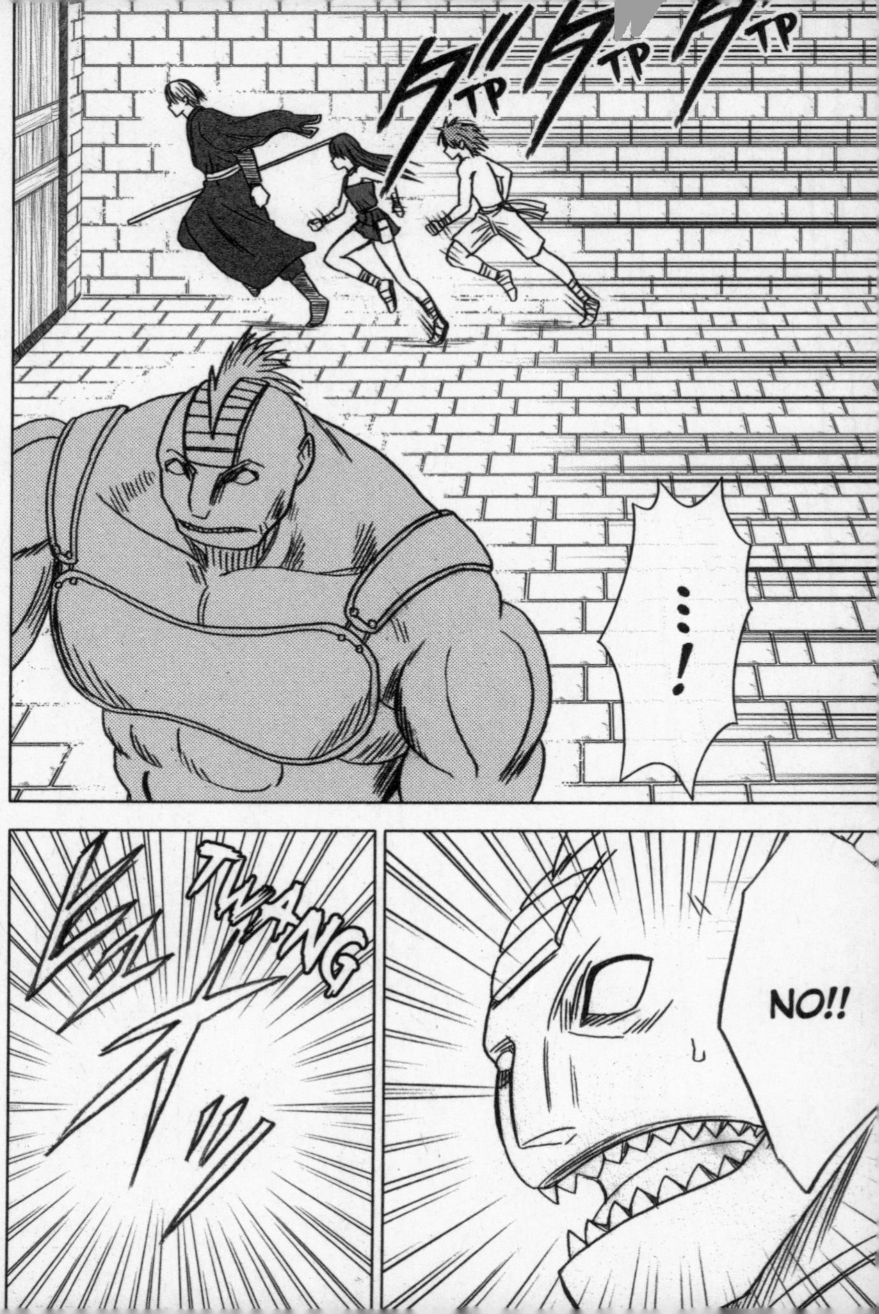
TP
TP
TP
TP
…!
NO!!
TWANG

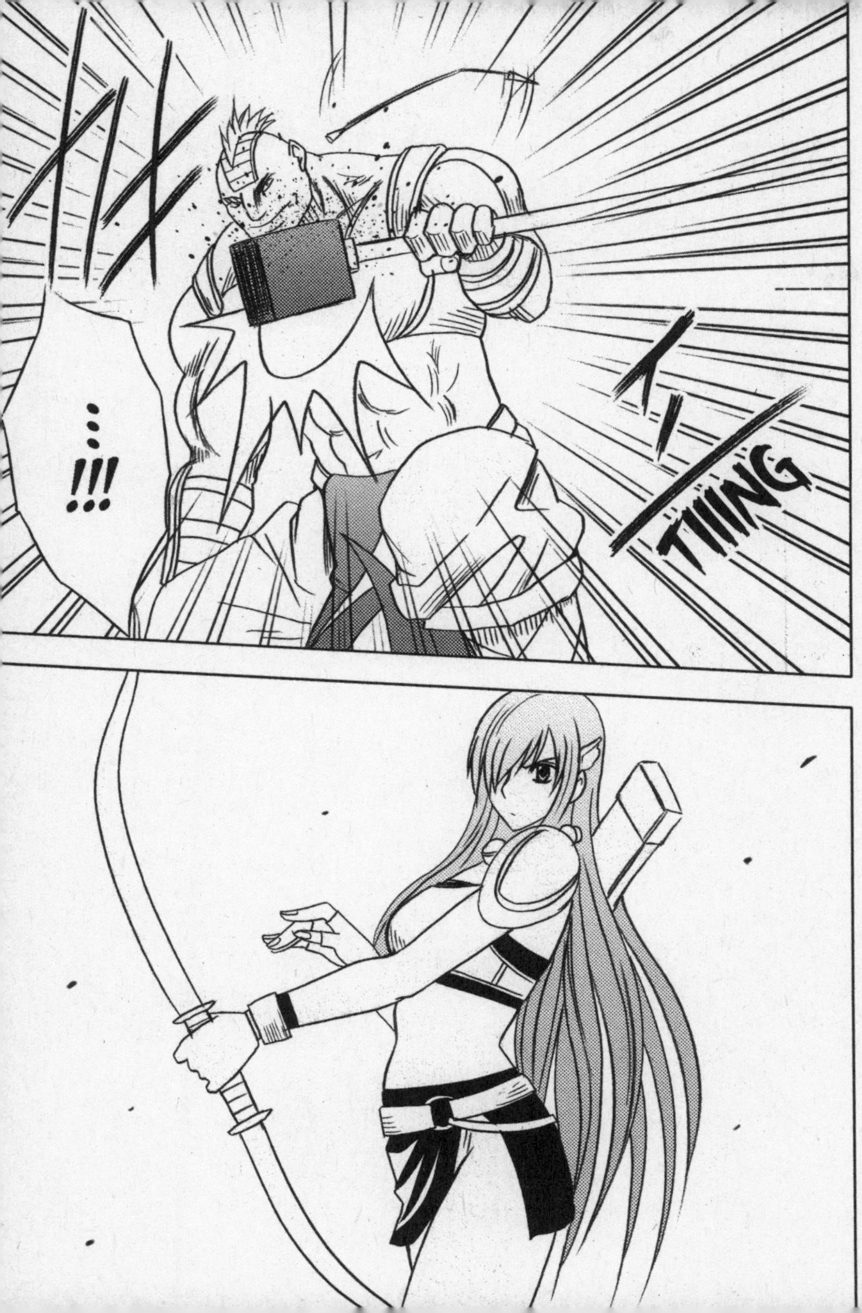
TIING
...!!!

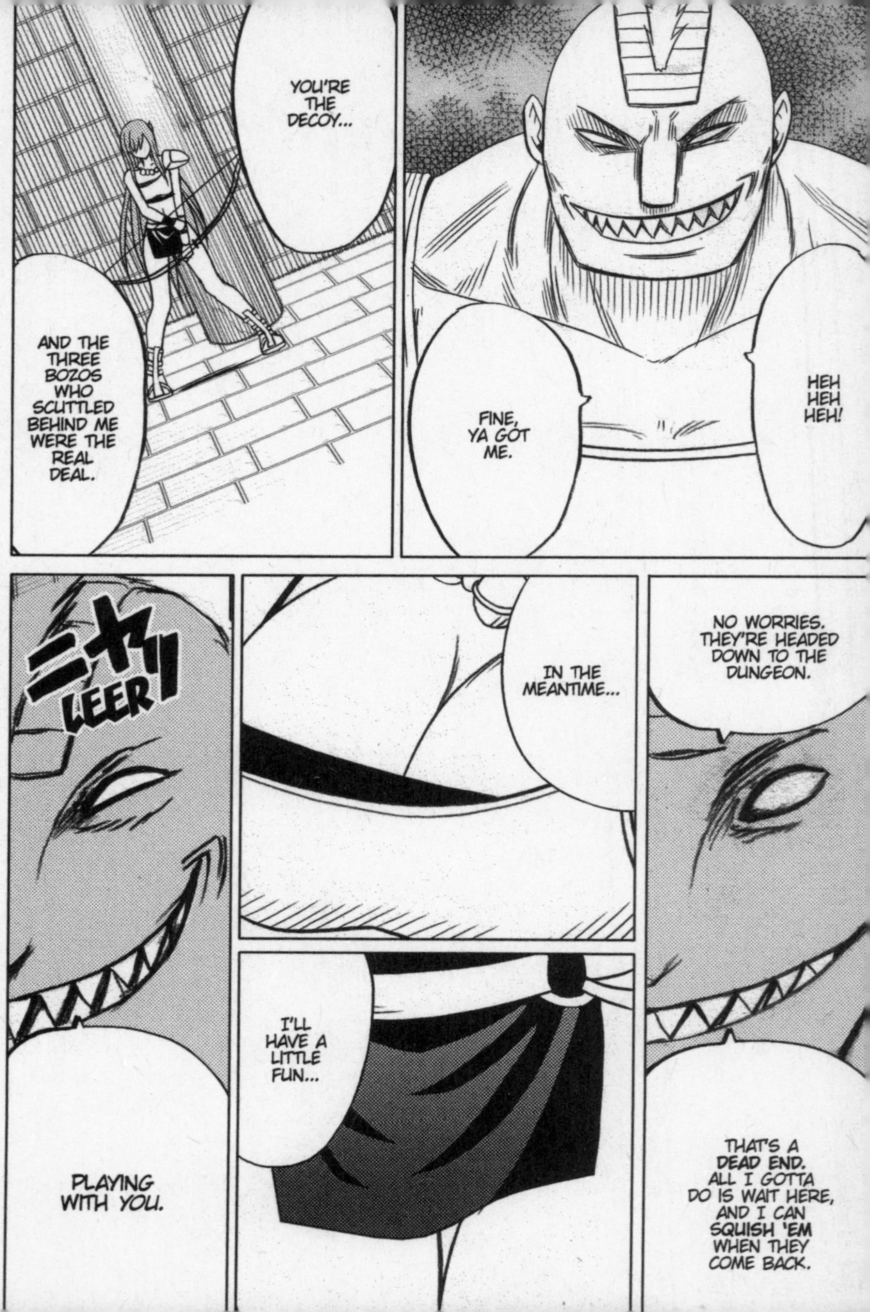
HEH HEH HEH!
FINE, YA GOT ME.
YOU'RE THE DECOY...
AND THE THREE BOZOS WHO SCUTTLED BEHIND ME WERE THE REAL DEAL.
NO WORRIES. THEY'RE HEADED DOWN TO THE DUNGEON.
THAT'S A DEAD END. ALL I GOTTA DO IS WAIT HERE, AND I CAN SQUISH 'EM WHEN THEY COME BACK.
IN THE MEANTIME...
I'LL HAVE A LITTLE FUN...
ニヤリ
LEER
PLAYING WITH YOU.

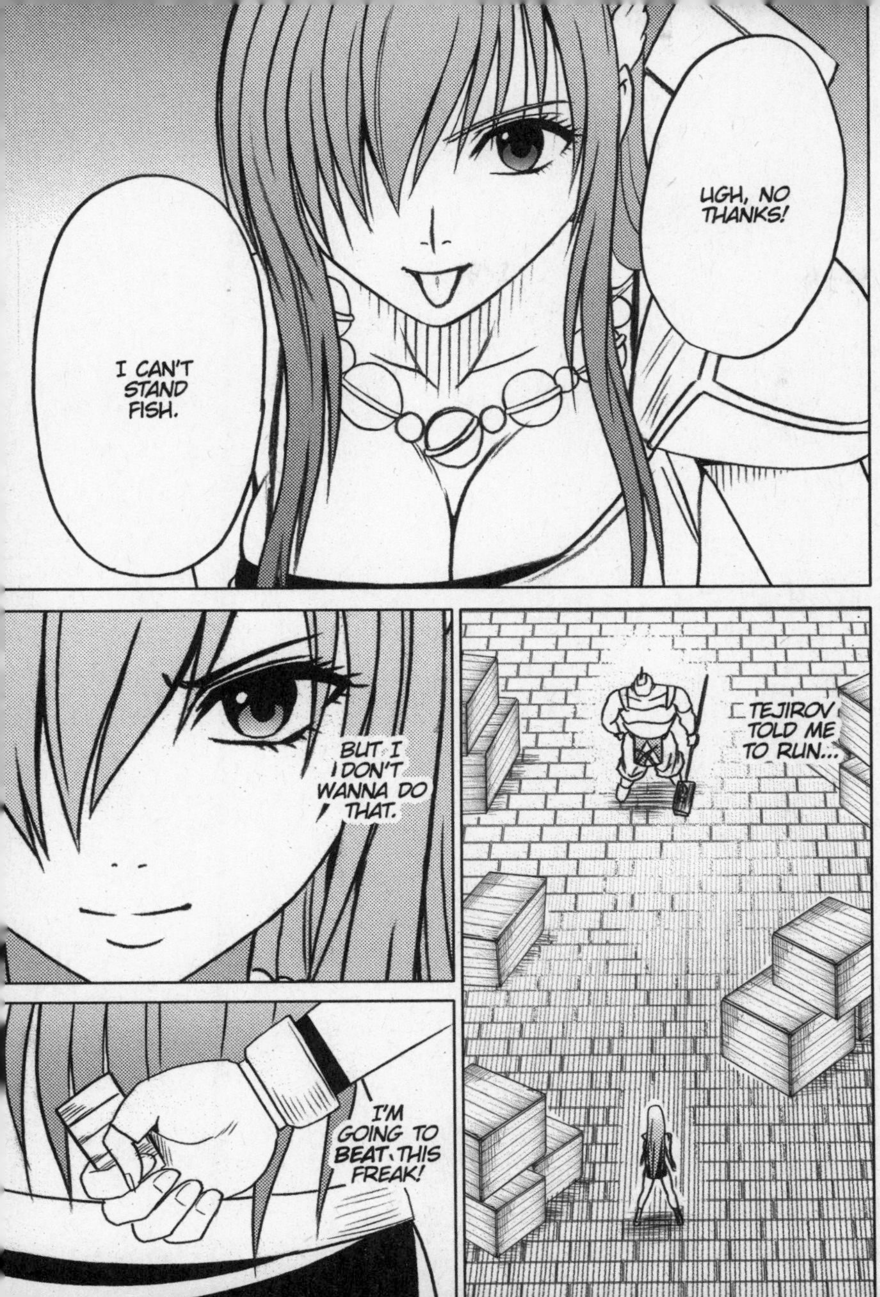
UGH, NO THANKS!
I CAN'T STAND FISH.
TEJIROV TOLD ME TO RUN...
BUT I DON'T WANNA DO THAT.
I'M GOING TO BEAT THIS FREAK!

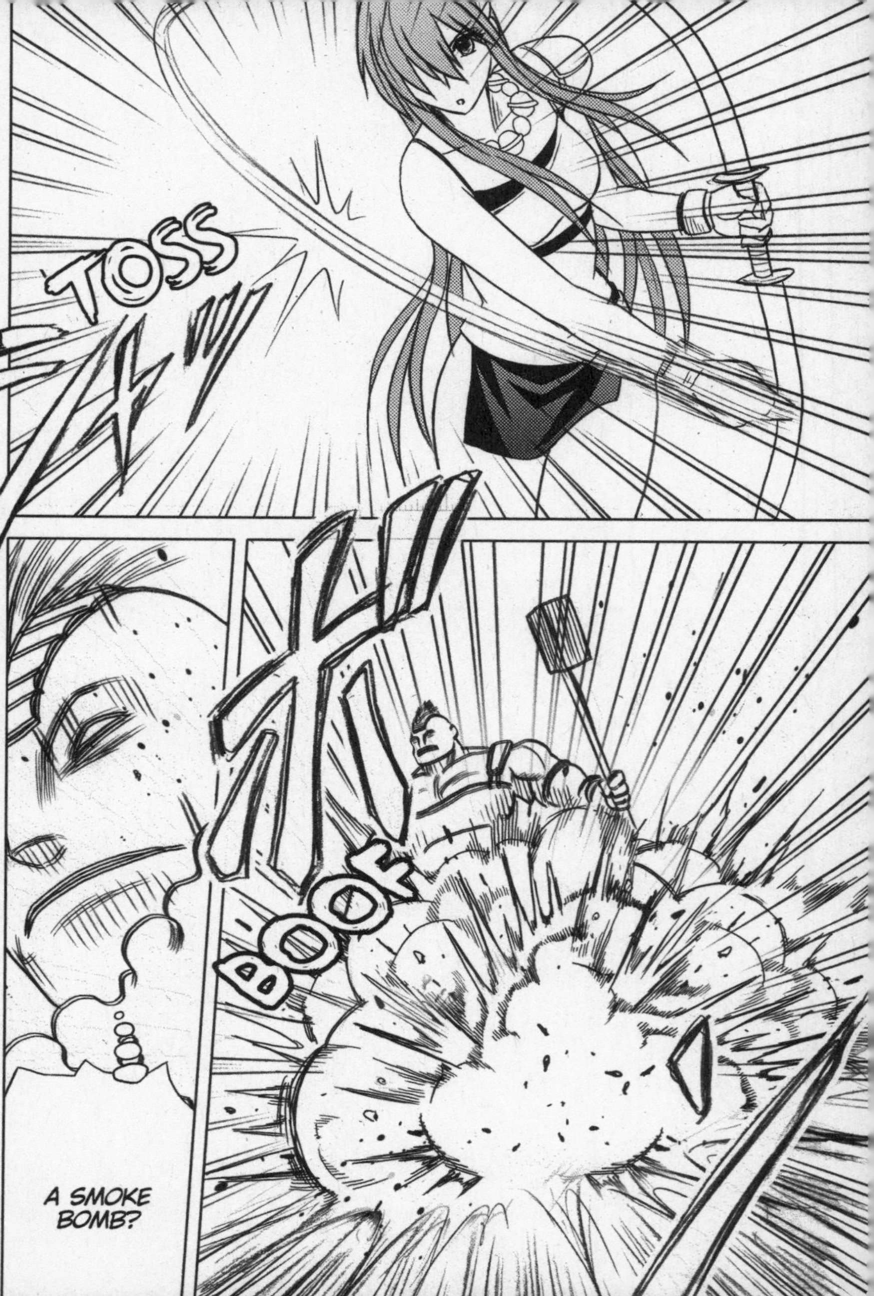
TOSS
BOOF
A SMOKE BOMB?

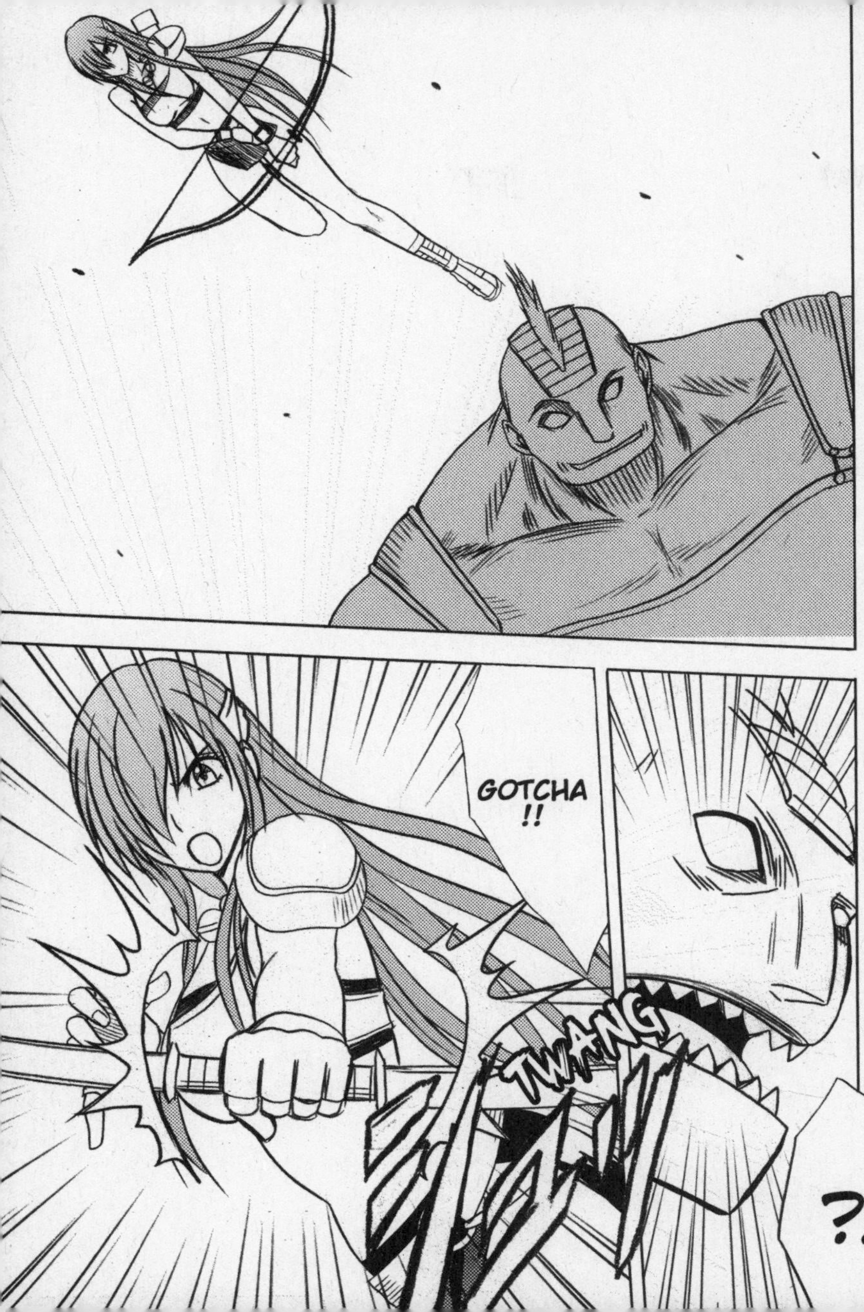
?!
GOTCHA !!
TWANG

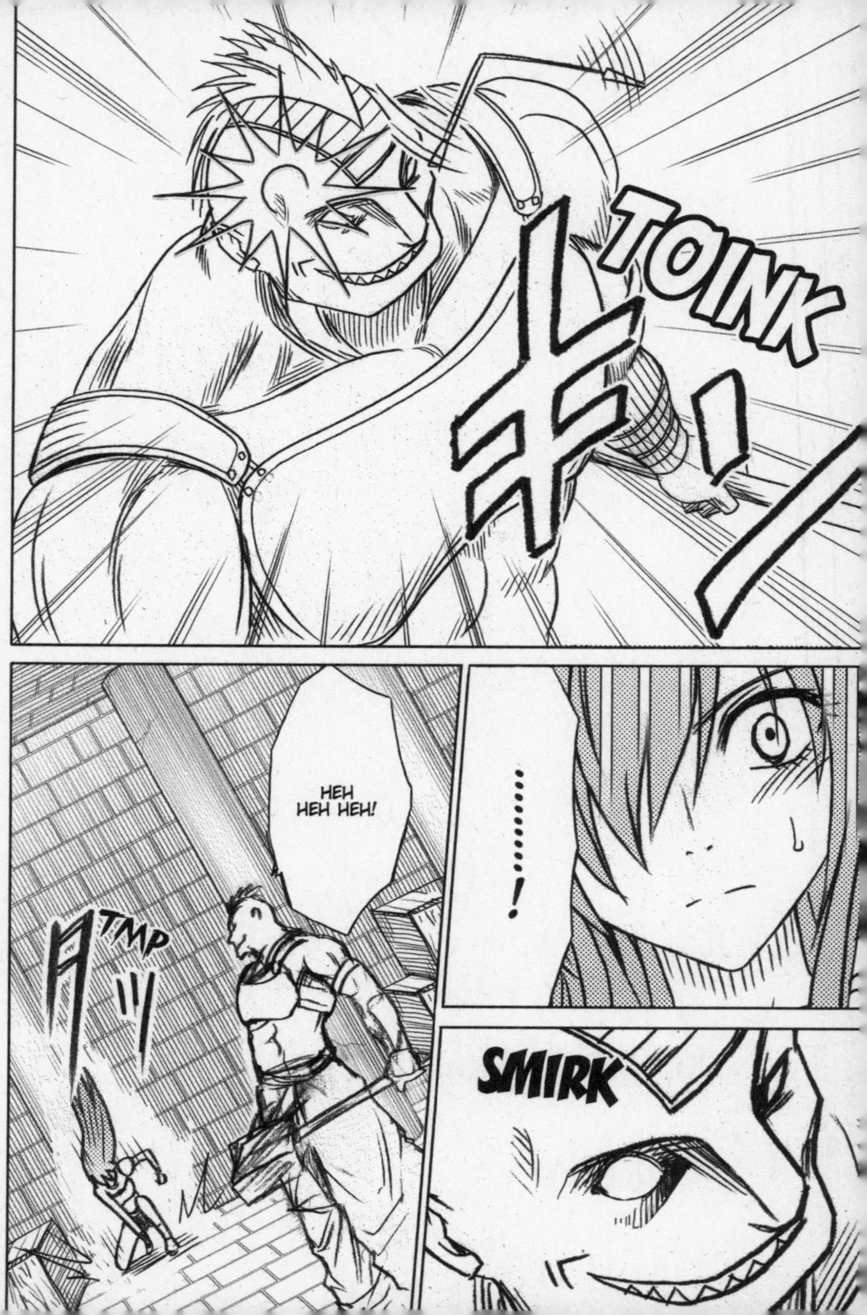
TOINK
......!
SMIRK
HEH HEH HEH!
TMP

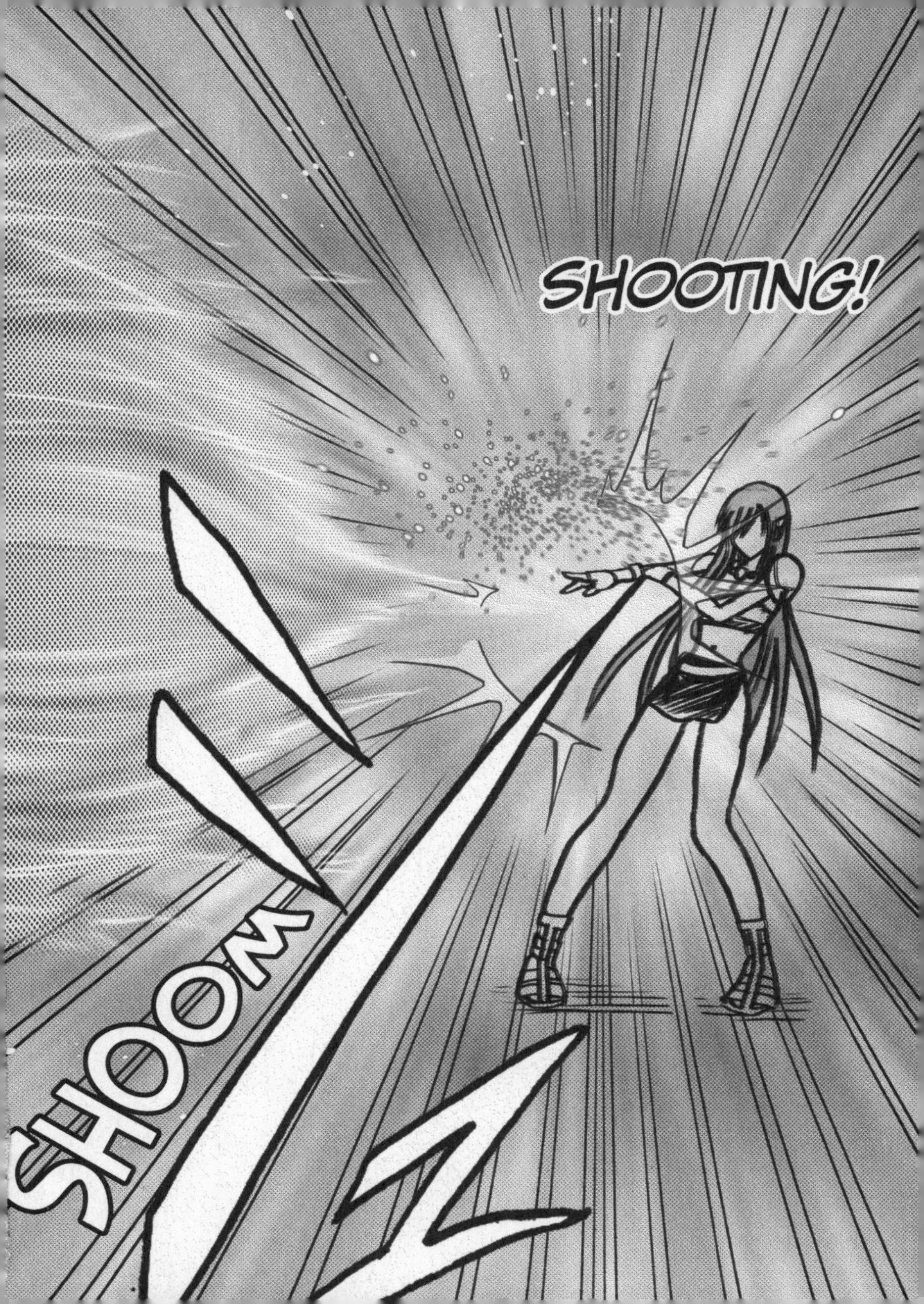
SHOOTING!
SHOOM

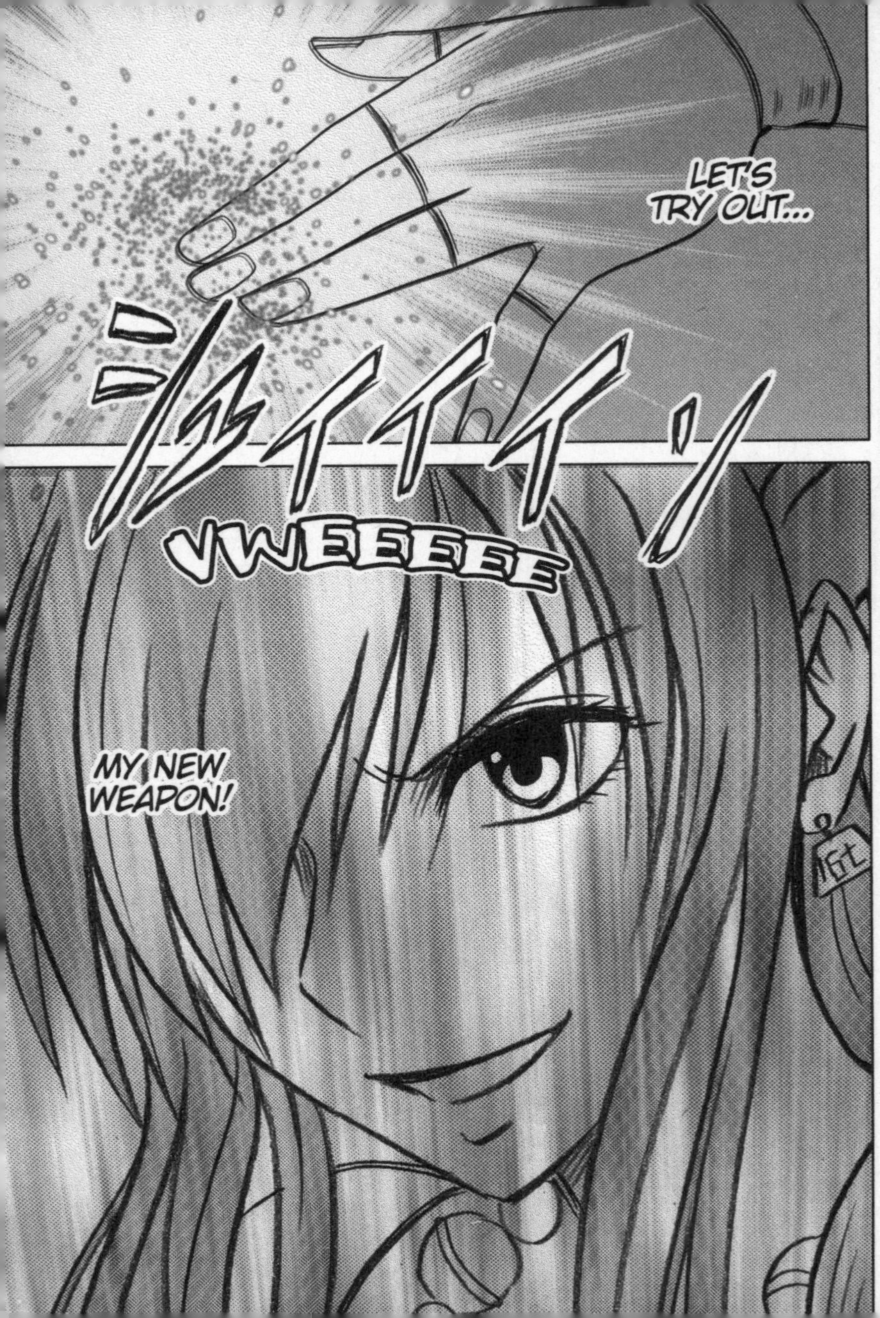
LET'S TRY OUT...
VWEEEEEE
MY NEW WEAPON!

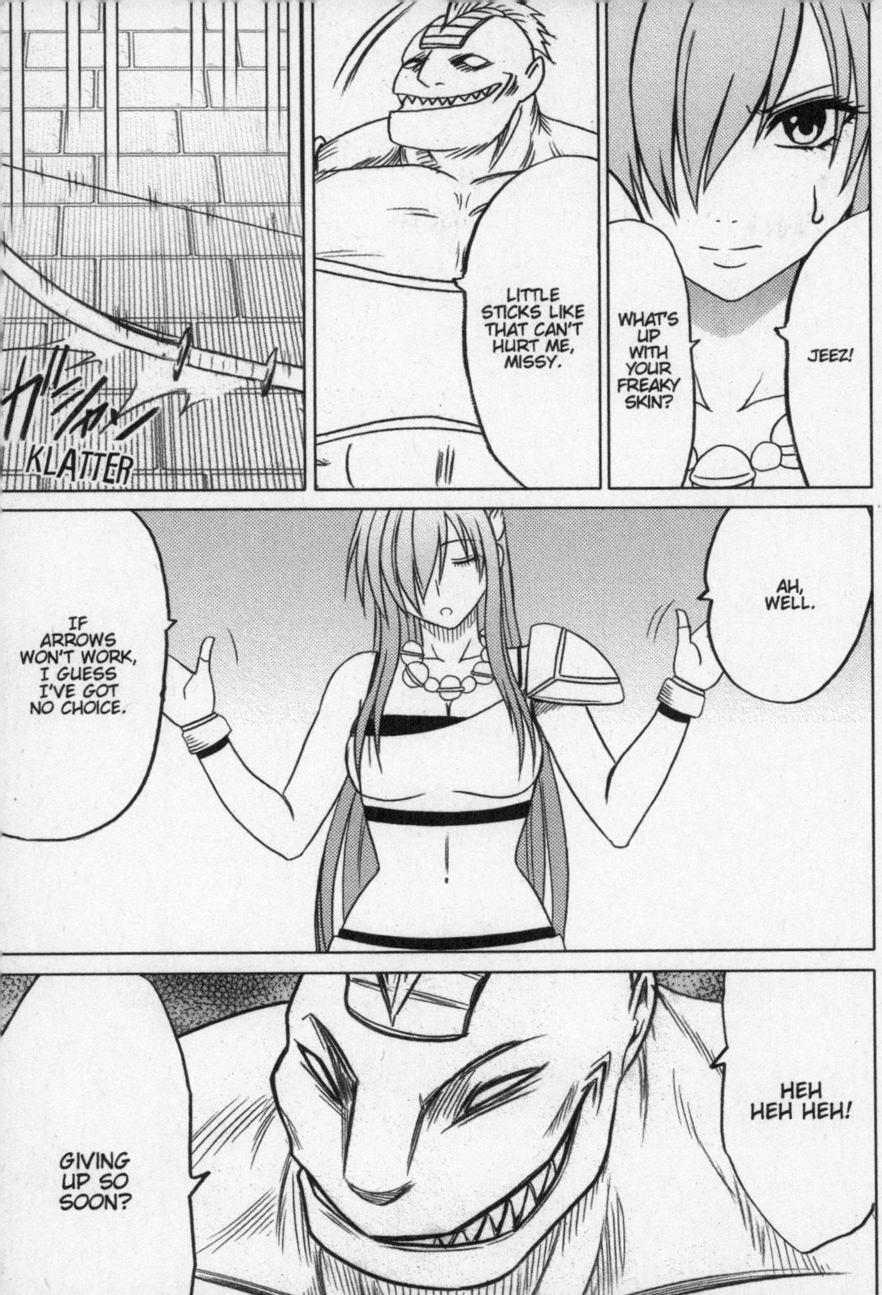
JEEZ!
WHAT'S UP WITH YOUR FREAKY SKIN?
LITTLE STICKS LIKE THAT CAN'T HURT ME, MISSY.
KLATTER
AH, WELL.
IF ARROWS WON'T WORK, I GUESS I'VE GOT NO CHOICE.
HEH HEH HEH!
GIVING UP SO SOON?

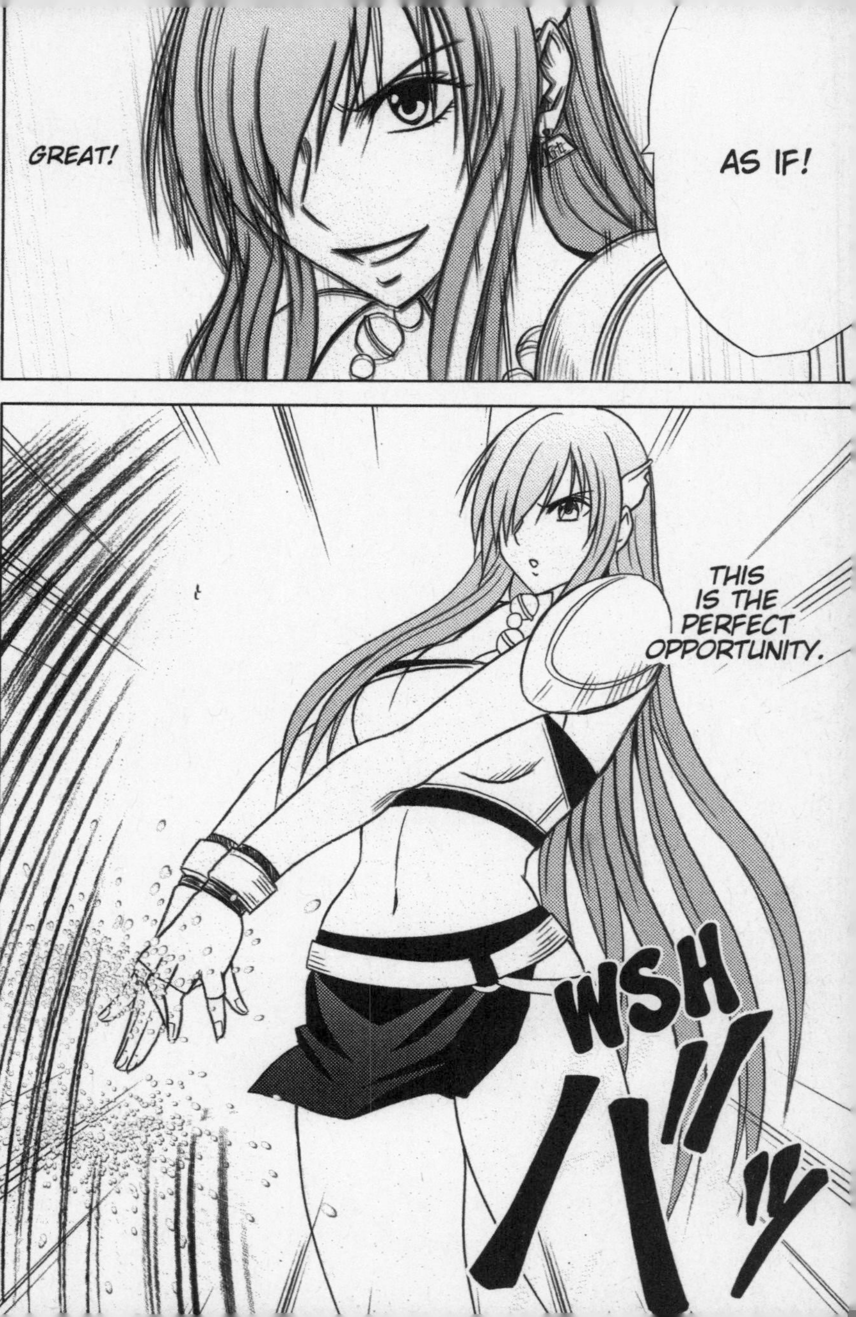
AS IF!
GREAT!
THIS IS THE PERFECT OPPORTUNITY.
WSH

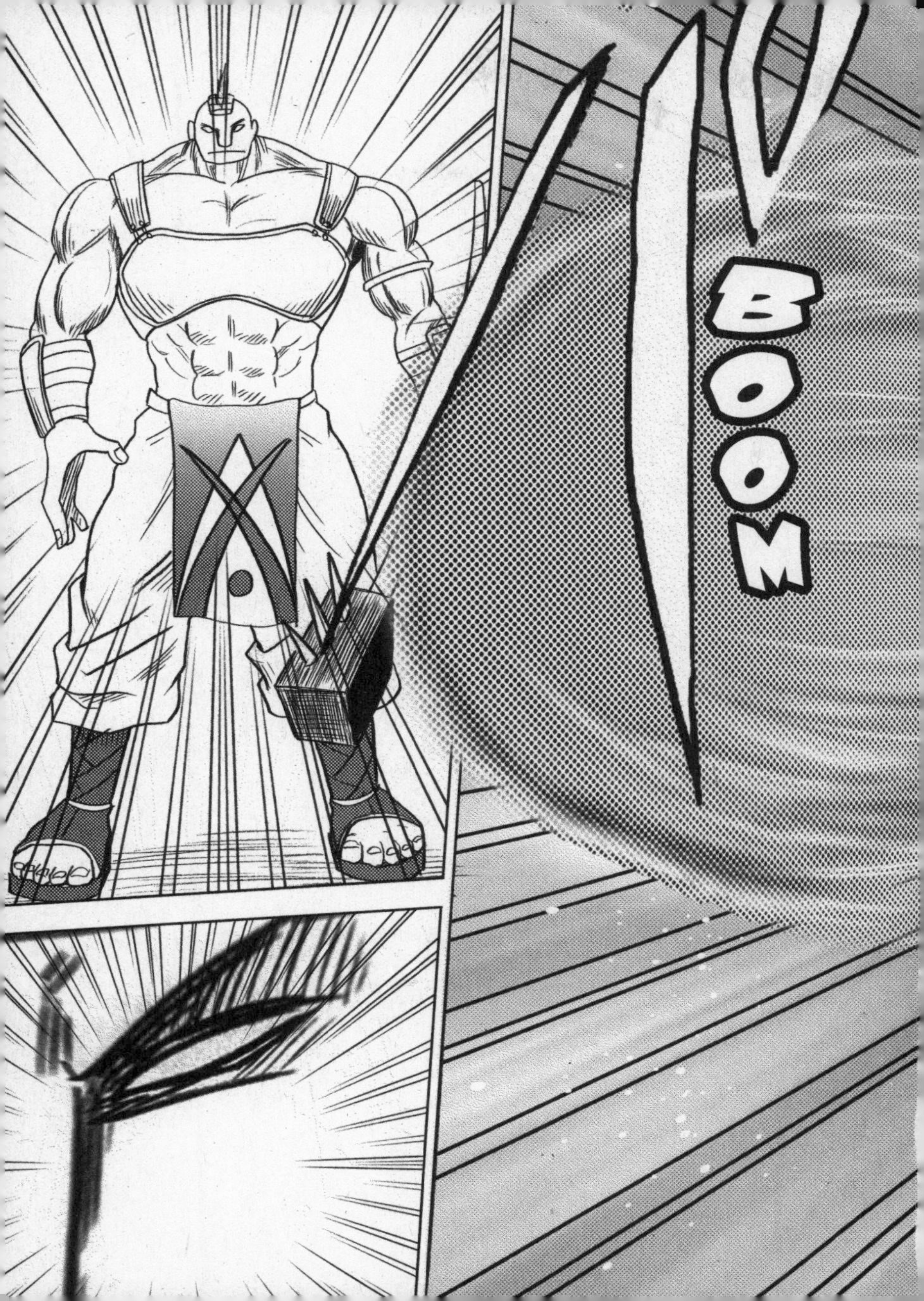
BOOM

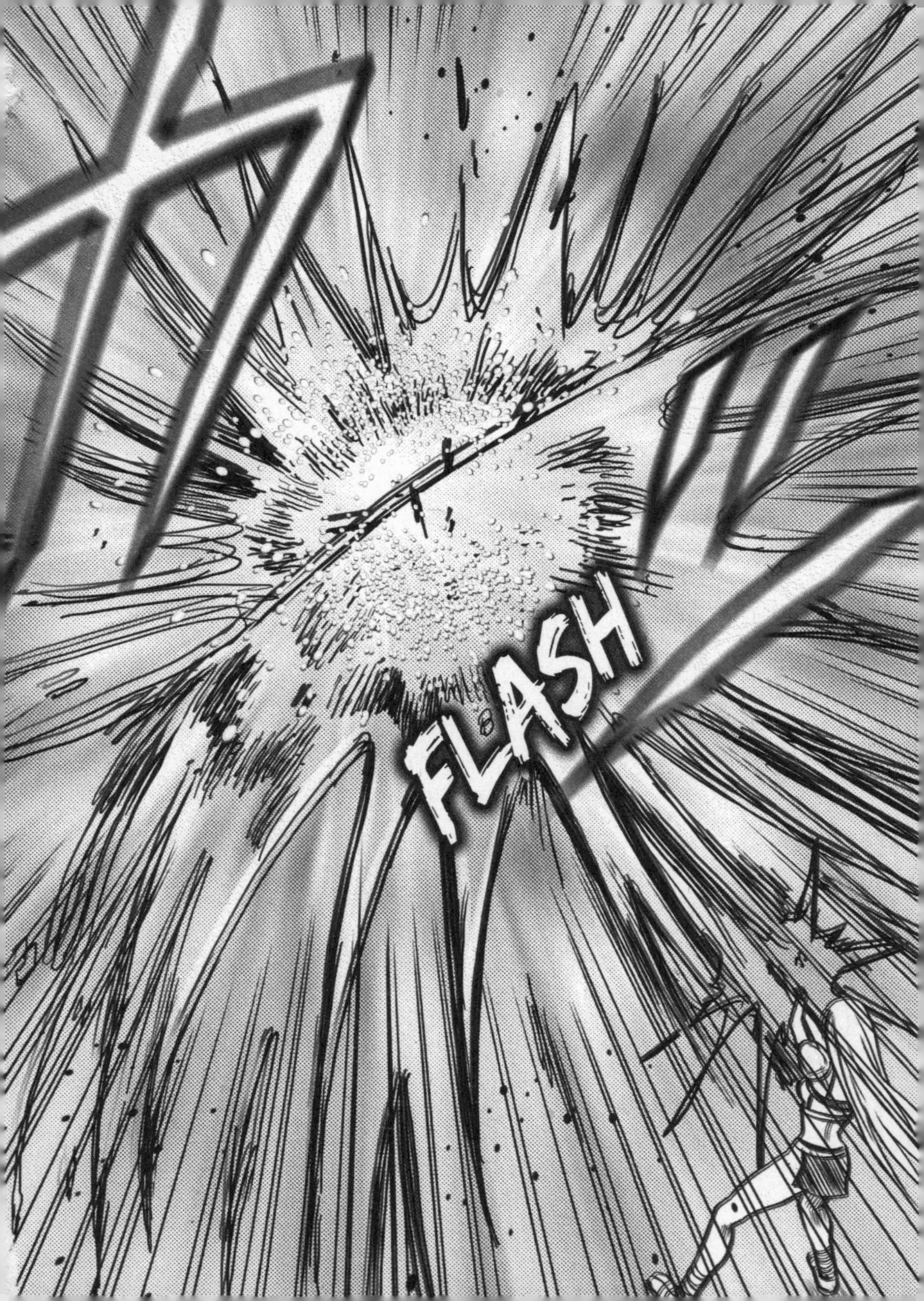
FLASH

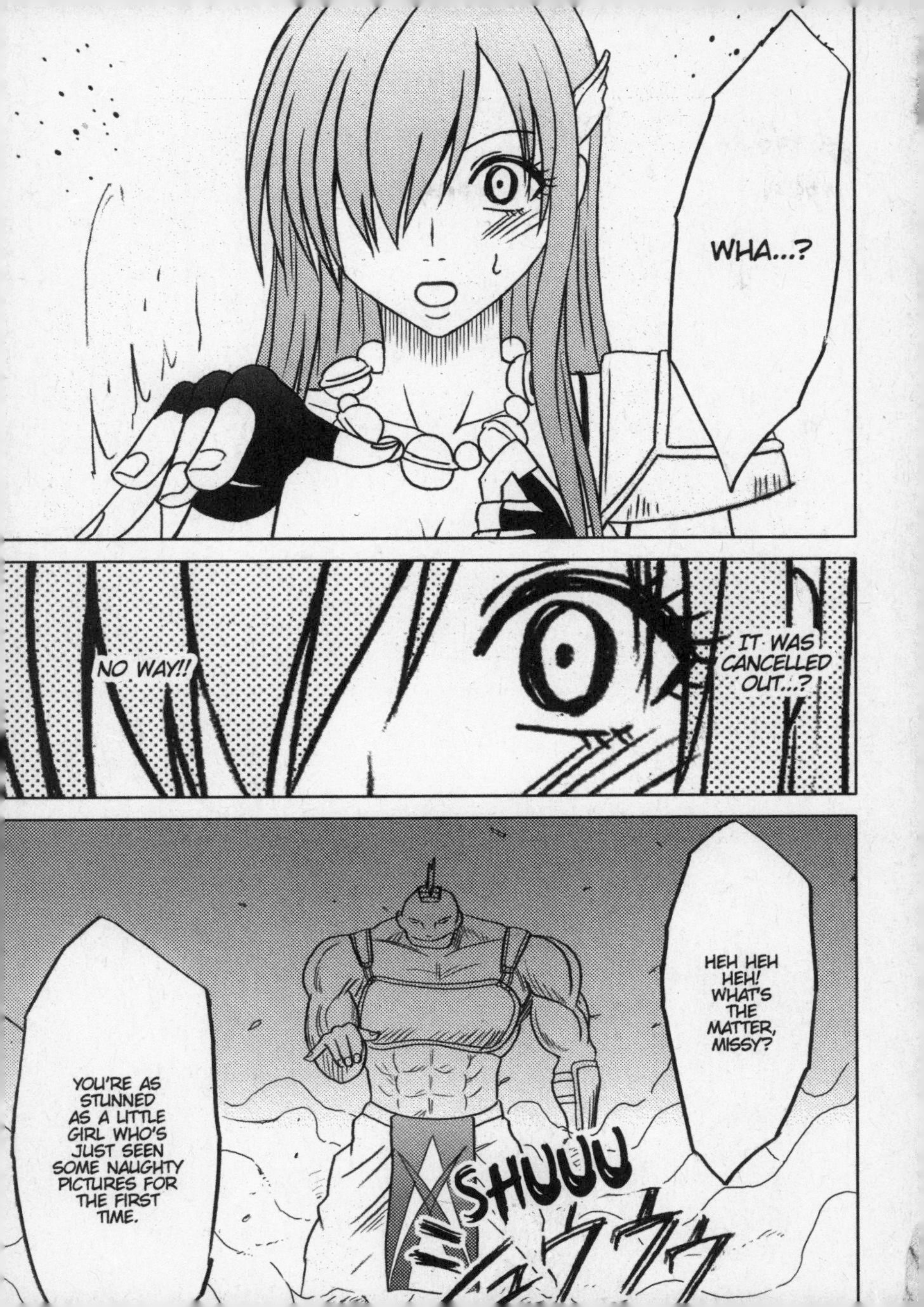
WHA...?
IT WAS CANCELLED OUT...?
NO WAY!!
HEH HEH HEH! WHAT'S THE MATTER, MISSY?
YOU'RE AS STUNNED AS A LITTLE GIRL WHO'S JUST SEEN SOME NAUGHTY PICTURES FOR THE FIRST TIME.
SHUUU

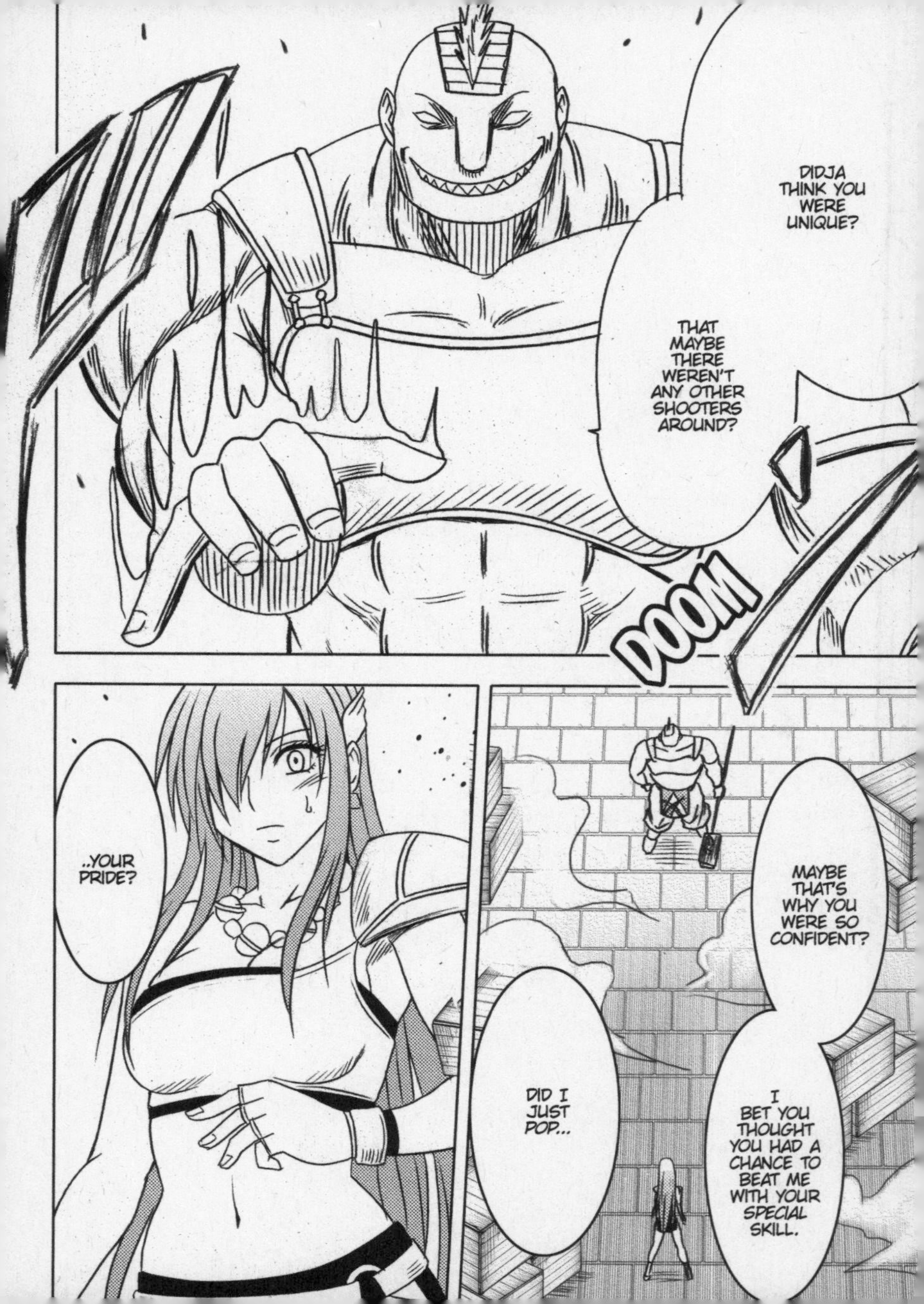
DIDJA THINK YOU WERE UNIQUE?
THAT MAYBE THERE WEREN'T ANY OTHER SHOOTERS AROUND?
DOOM
MAYBE THAT'S WHY YOU WERE SO CONFIDENT?
I BET YOU THOUGHT YOU HAD A CHANCE TO BEAT ME WITH YOUR SPECIAL SKILL.
DID I JUST POP...
..YOUR PRIDE?

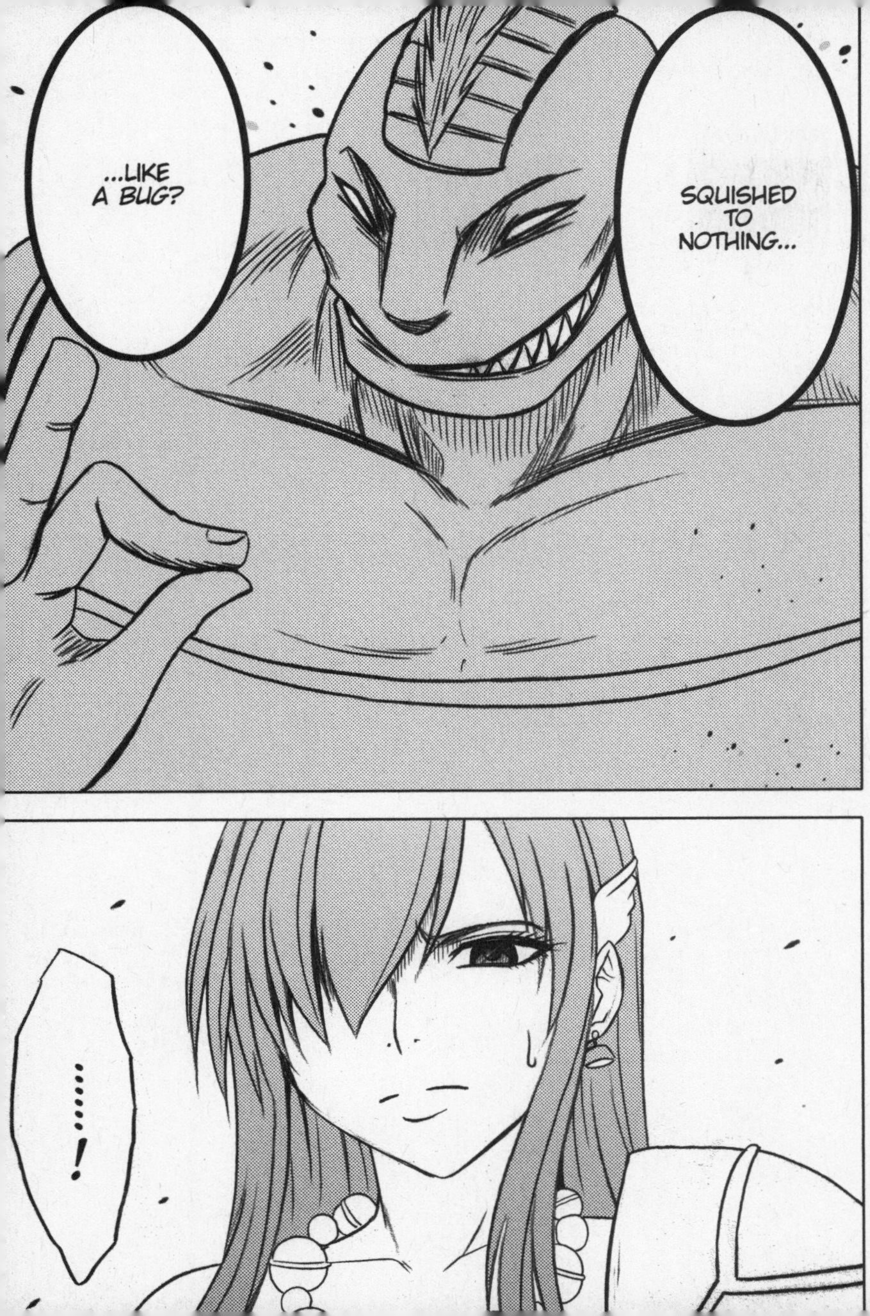
SQUISHED TO NOTHING...
...LIKE A BUG?
......!

Perusing Video Game History

ON THE EDGE OF THE BLUE WORLD

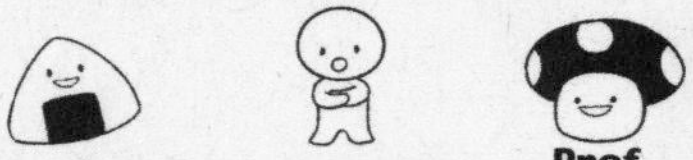

Dr. Onigiri — Mr. Why — Prof. Mushroom

Today's Topic

DARIUS

Mr. Why: Okay, was *Darius* really that incredible?

Prof. Mushroom: No, it was *even more* incredible.

Dr. Onigiri: *Darius*, a side-scrolling shooter, first appeared in arcades in 1987. The most groundbreaking aspect was that it scrolled across not one, but *three* screens lined up.

Mr. Why: So what was it like? Was it some kind of simulator, like those driving sims you find in drivers' ed?

Prof. Mushroom: No, it was way better than that. See, if you just line up three TVs next to each other, you're gonna get a gap between the screens, right? Think about the huge TV displays at electronics stores. It's kinda like that.

Mr. Why: Oh, I get it.

Dr. Onigiri: But the amazing thing about *Darius* was there was *no gap.*

Mr. Why: Wait, what? How?

Dr. Onigiri: Hidden mirrors. One showed the screen just as it was, and another showed the screen reflected in the mirror. Then, if you adjust those mirrors so that the reflections line right up, voila! You have made one big screen! Do that across all three monitors, and you have one giant screen across three separate cabinets!

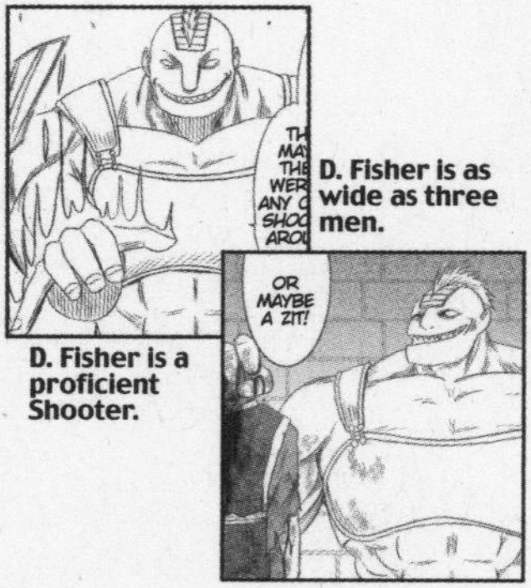
OR MAYBE A ZIT!

D. Fisher is as wide as three men.

D. Fisher is a proficient Shooter.

Prof. Mushroom: Back in the days before edgeless plasma TVs, that sort of thing took lots of effort. There had to be delicate programming, lots of fine adjustments, constant upkeep by the arcade staff and plenty of other work.

Dr. Onigiri: Definitely! Next time, I'll go into what the game is all about!

To Be Continued...

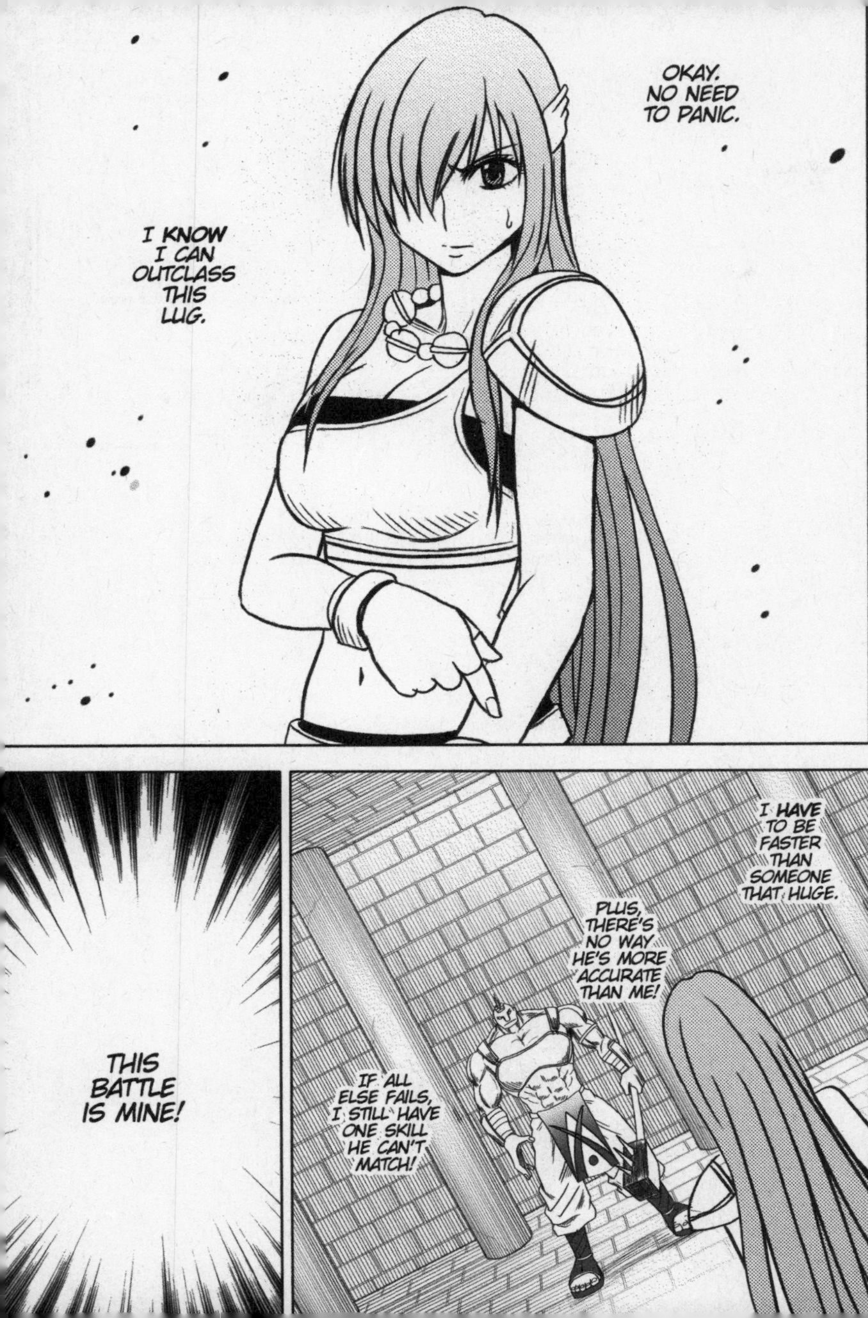
OKAY. NO NEED TO PANIC.
I KNOW I CAN OUTCLASS THIS LUG.
I HAVE TO BE FASTER THAN SOMEONE THAT HUGE.
PLUS, THERE'S NO WAY HE'S MORE ACCURATE THAN ME!
IF ALL ELSE FAILS, I STILL HAVE ONE SKILL HE CAN'T MATCH!
THIS BATTLE IS MINE!

CHAPTER 10

Z ZONE

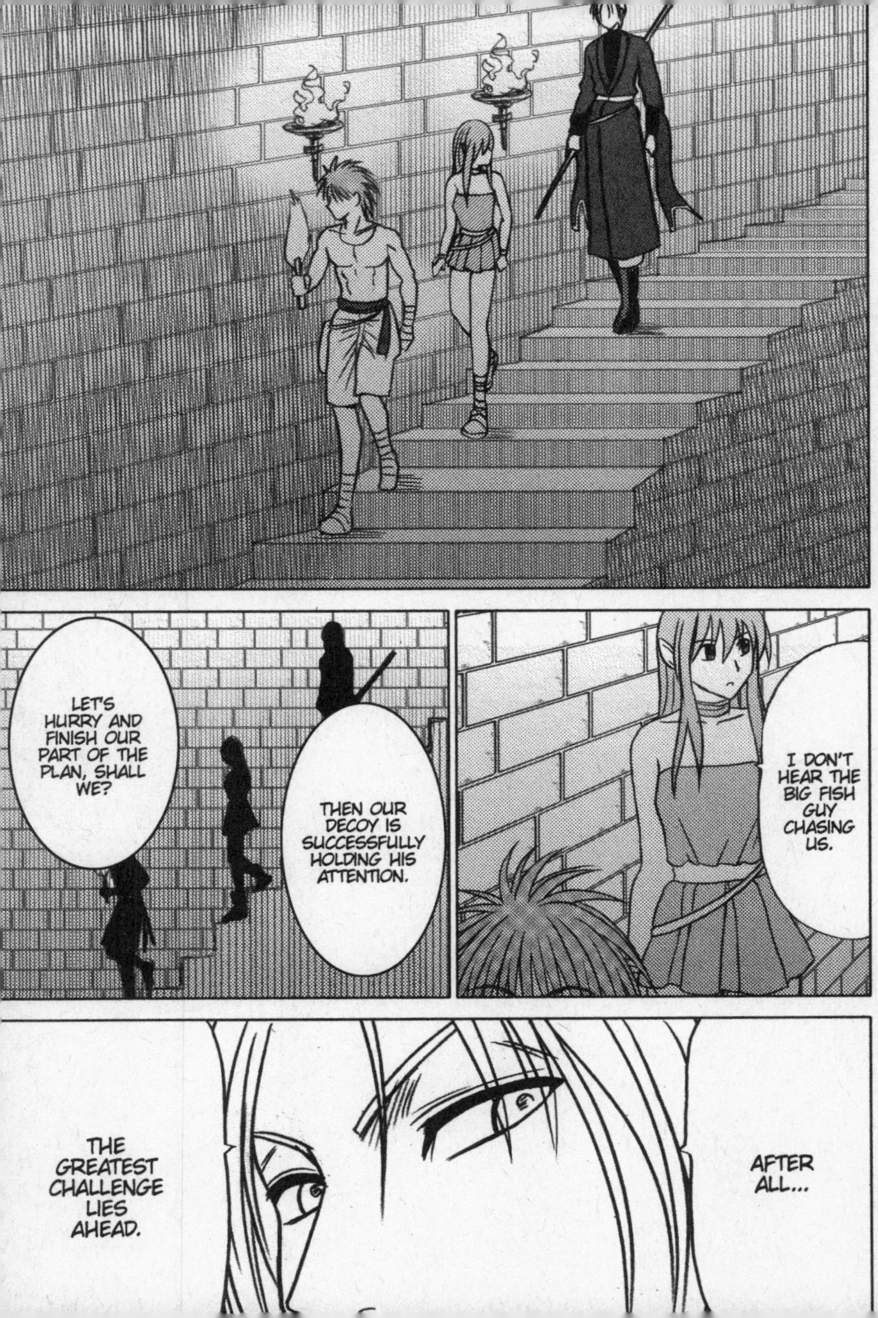
I DON'T HEAR THE BIG FISH GUY CHASING US.
THEN OUR DECOY IS SUCCESSFULLY HOLDING HIS ATTENTION.
LET'S HURRY AND FINISH OUR PART OF THE PLAN, SHALL WE?
AFTER ALL...
THE GREATEST CHALLENGE LIES AHEAD.

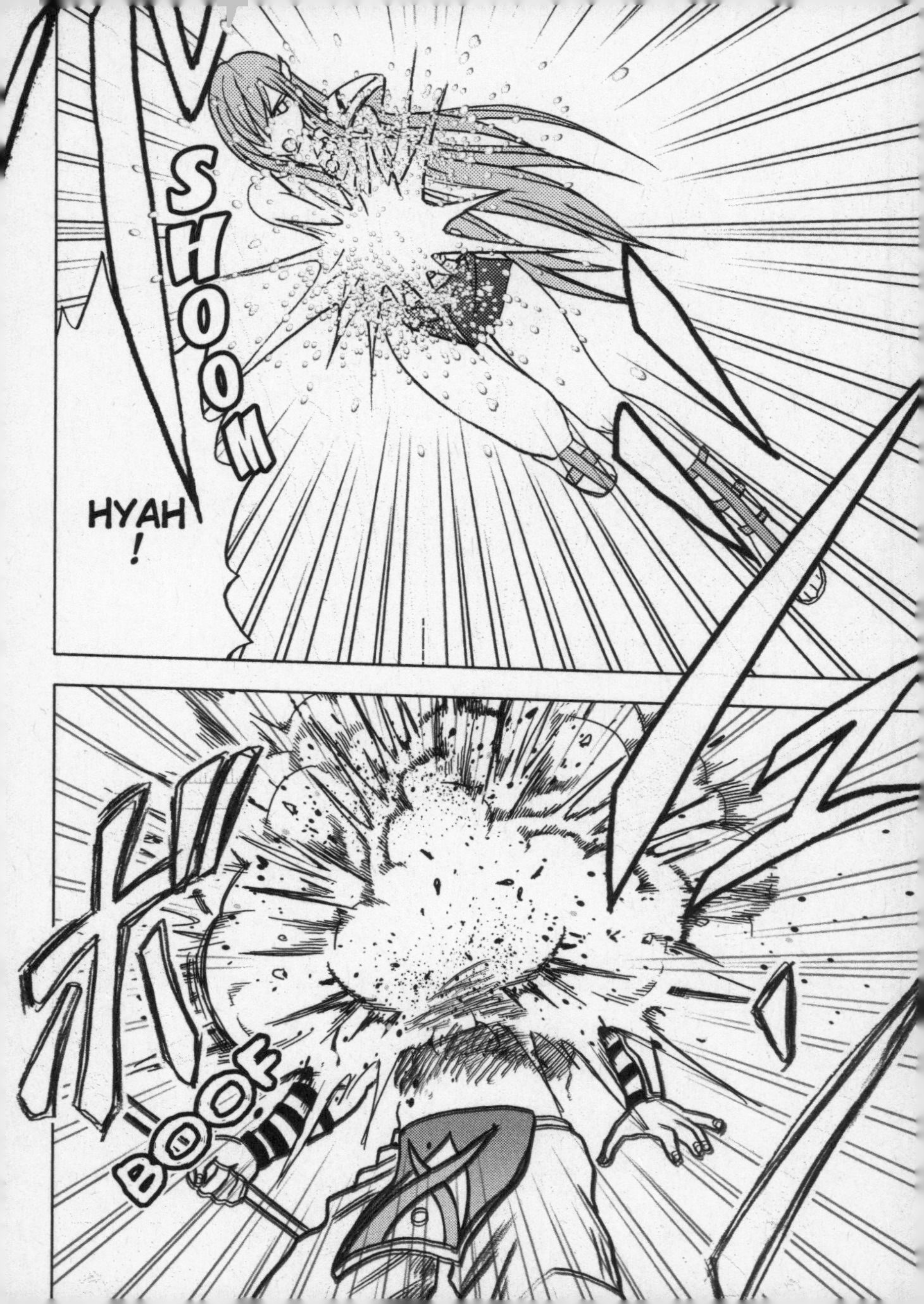
SHOOOM
HYAH!
BOOOF

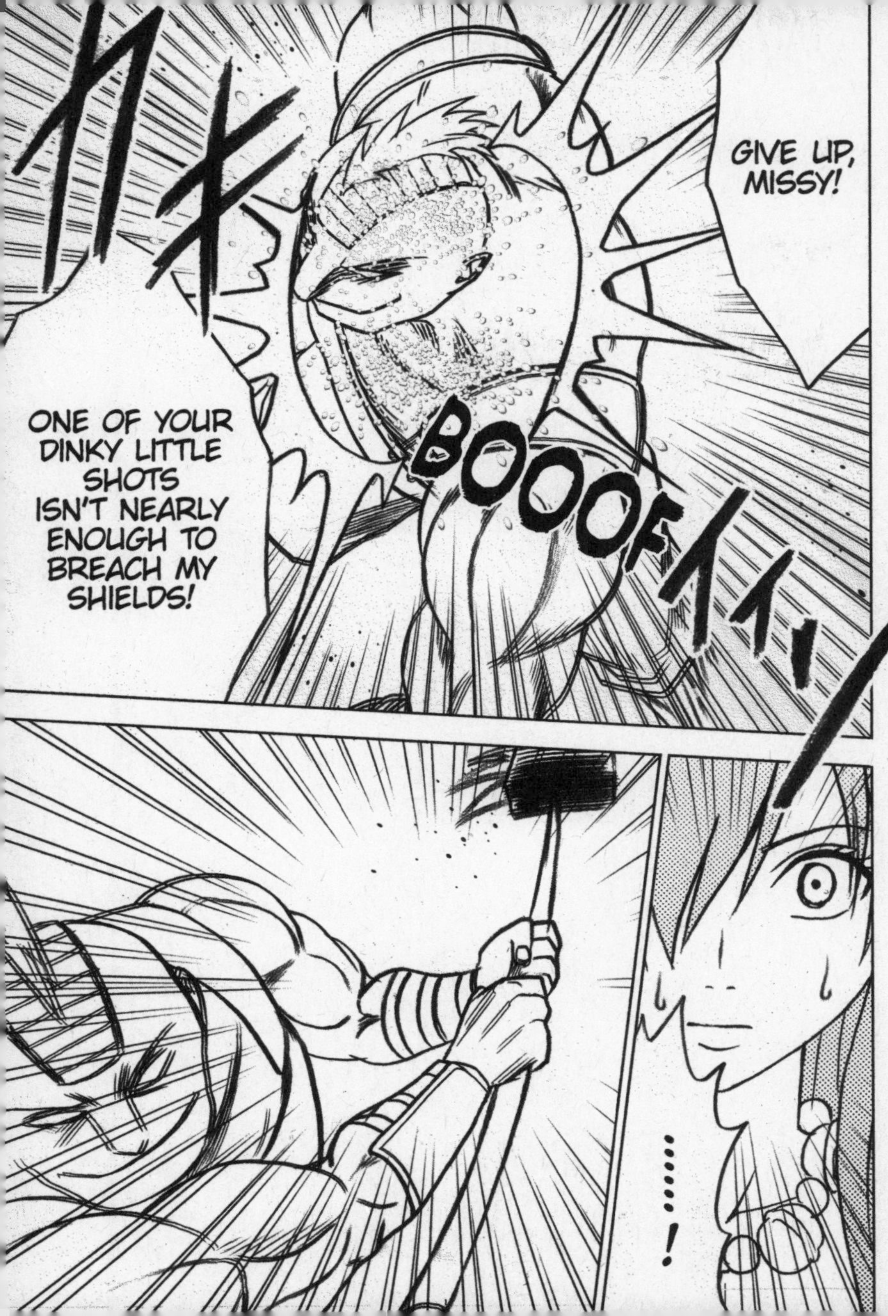
GIVE UP, MISSY!
BOOOF
ONE OF YOUR DINKY LITTLE SHOTS ISN'T NEARLY ENOUGH TO BREACH MY SHIELDS!
......!

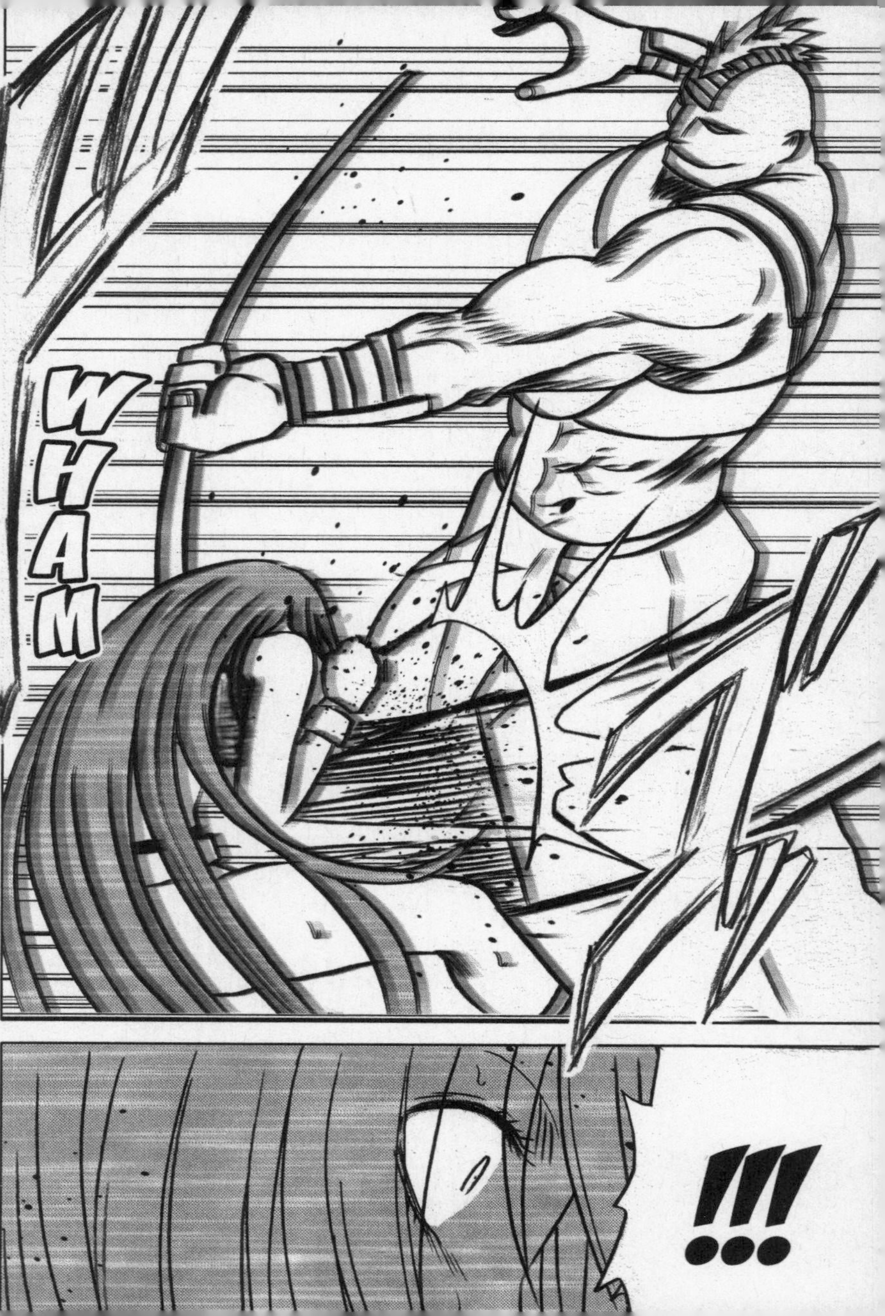
WHAM
!!!

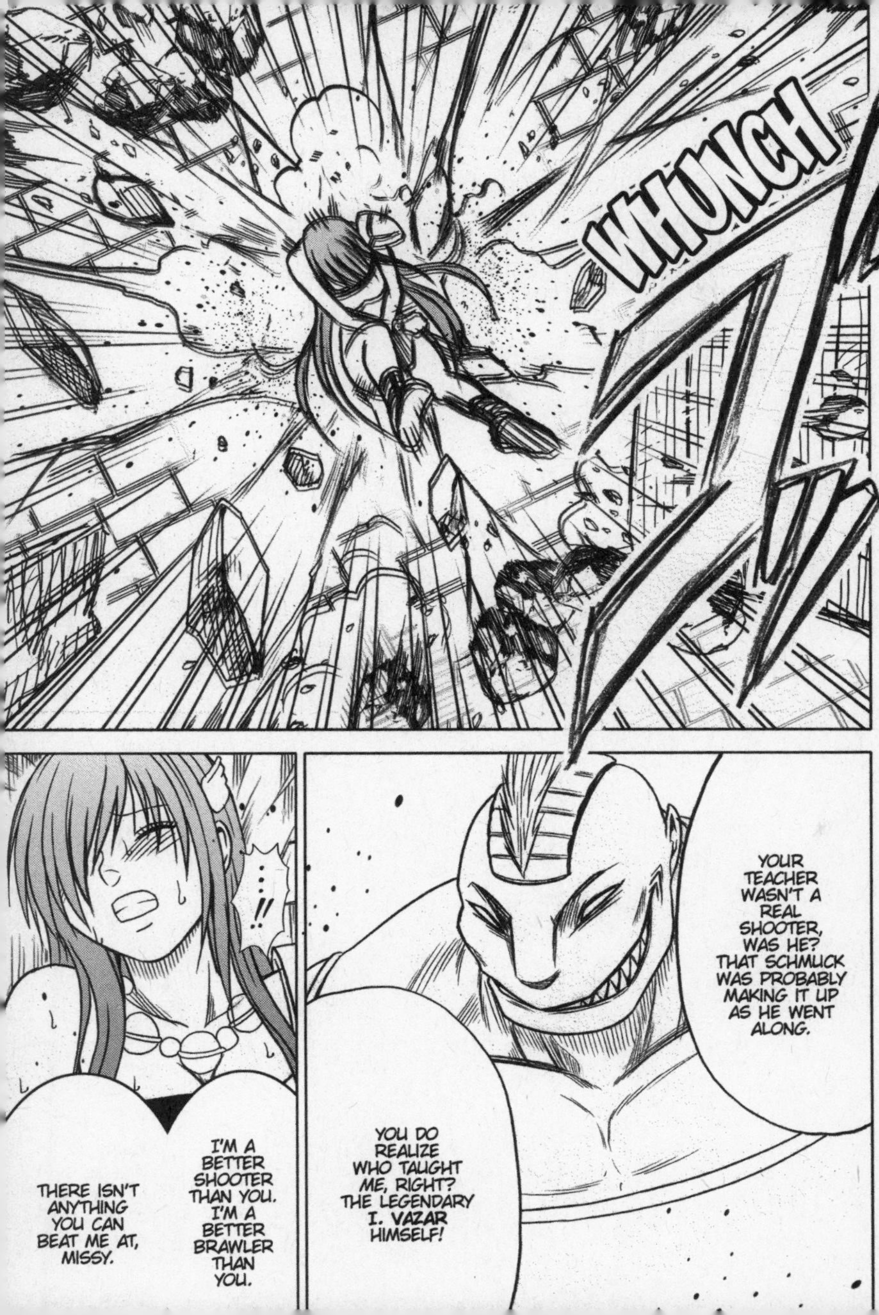
WHUNCH
YOUR TEACHER WASN'T A REAL SHOOTER, WAS HE? THAT SCHMUCK WAS PROBABLY MAKING IT UP AS HE WENT ALONG.
YOU DO REALIZE WHO TAUGHT ME, RIGHT? THE LEGENDARY **I. VAZAR** HIMSELF!
...!!
I'M A BETTER SHOOTER THAN YOU. I'M A BETTER BRAWLER THAN YOU.
THERE ISN'T ANYTHING YOU CAN BEAT ME AT, MISSY.

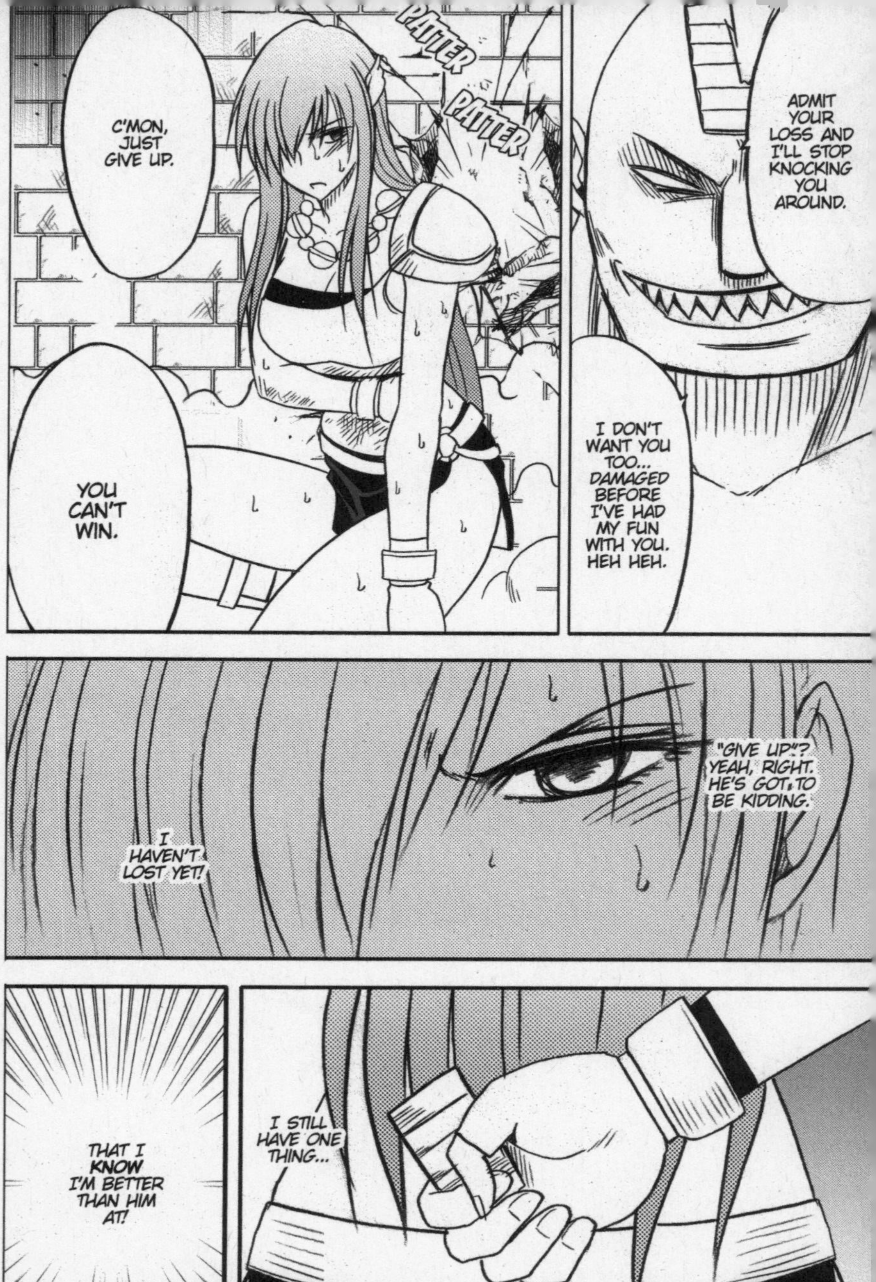
ADMIT YOUR LOSS AND I'LL STOP KNOCKING YOU AROUND.
I DON'T WANT YOU TOO... DAMAGED BEFORE I'VE HAD MY FUN WITH YOU. HEH HEH.
PATTER
PATTER
C'MON, JUST GIVE UP.
YOU CAN'T WIN.
"GIVE UP"? YEAH, RIGHT. HE'S GOT TO BE KIDDING.
I HAVEN'T LOST YET!
I STILL HAVE ONE THING...
THAT I KNOW I'M BETTER THAN HIM AT!

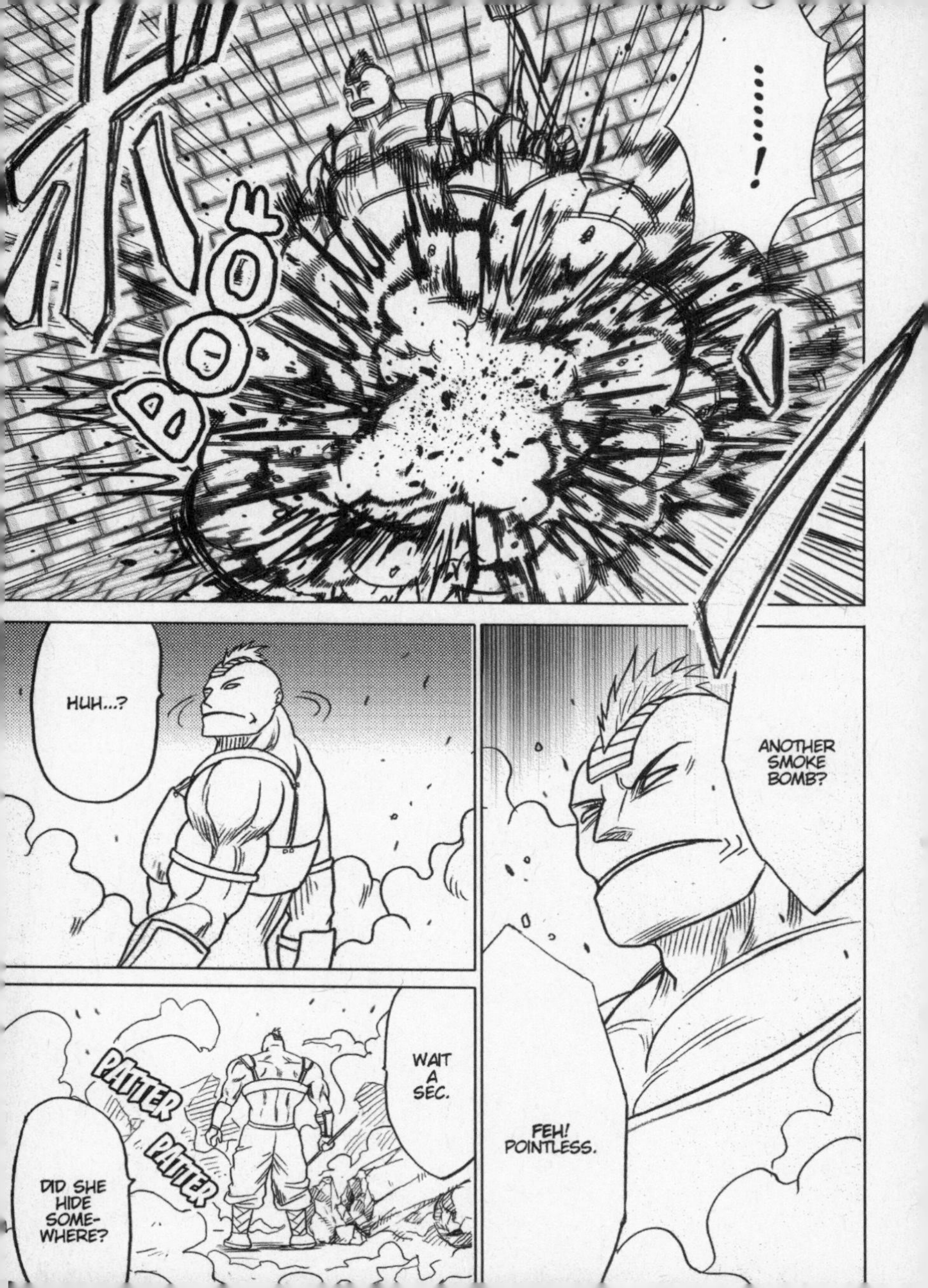
......!
BOOF
ANOTHER SMOKE BOMB?
FEH! POINTLESS.
HUH...?
WAIT A SEC.
PATTER PATTER
DID SHE HIDE SOME-WHERE?

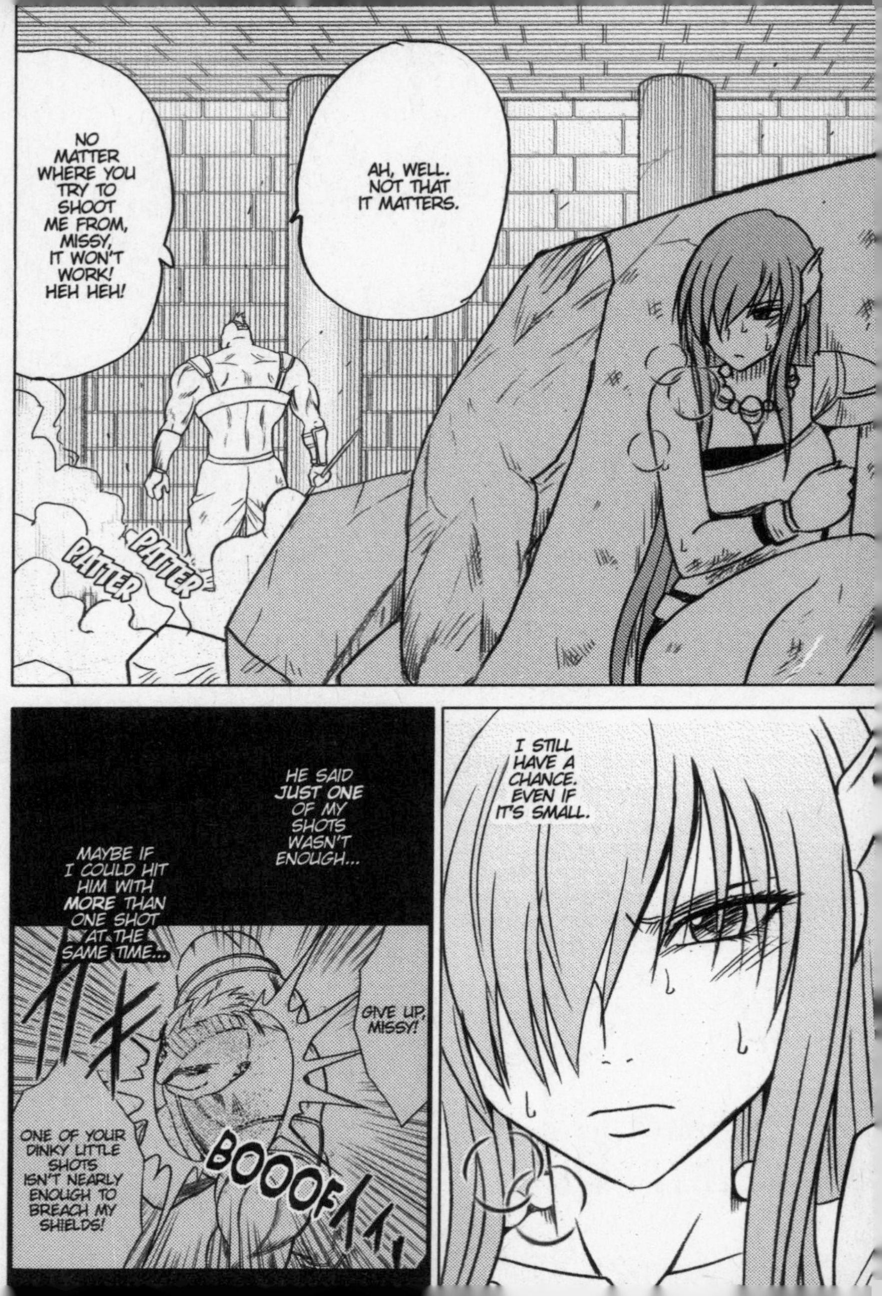
AH, WELL. NOT THAT IT MATTERS.
NO MATTER WHERE YOU TRY TO SHOOT ME FROM, MISSY, IT WON'T WORK! HEH HEH!
PATTER
PATTER
I STILL HAVE A CHANCE. EVEN IF IT'S SMALL.
HE SAID JUST ONE OF MY SHOTS WASN'T ENOUGH...
MAYBE IF I COULD HIT HIM WITH MORE THAN ONE SHOT AT THE SAME TIME...
GIVE UP, MISSY!
ONE OF YOUR DINKY LITTLE SHOTS ISN'T NEARLY ENOUGH TO BREACH MY SHIELDS!
BOOOF

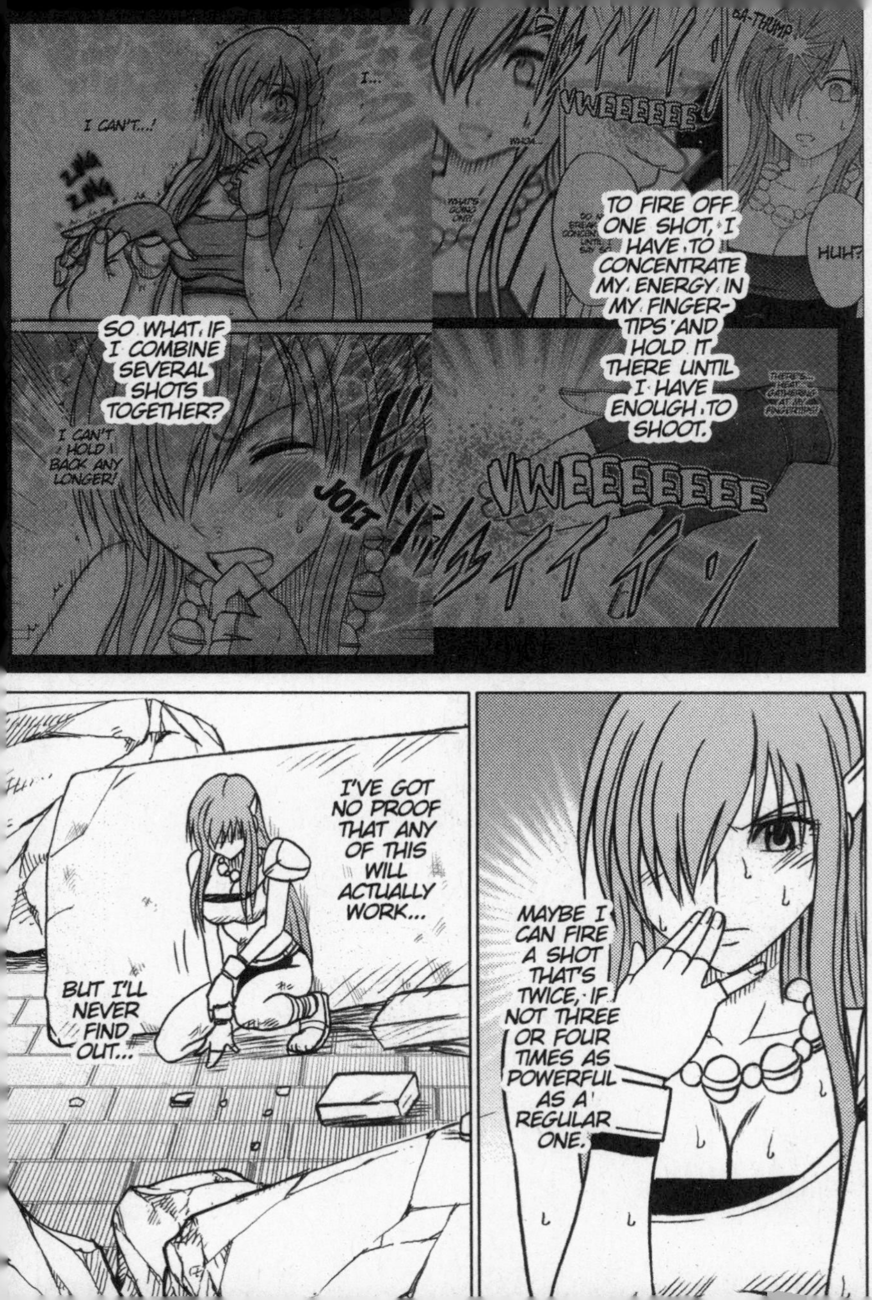
BA-THUMP
HUH?
VWEEEEEE
WHAT'S GOING ON!?
I...
I CAN'T...!
TO FIRE OFF ONE SHOT, I HAVE TO CONCENTRATE MY ENERGY IN MY FINGER-TIPS AND HOLD IT THERE UNTIL I HAVE ENOUGH TO SHOOT.
THERE'S... HEAT GATHERING AT MY FINGERTIPS!
VWEEEEEEE
SO WHAT IF I COMBINE SEVERAL SHOTS TOGETHER?
I CAN'T HOLD BACK ANY LONGER!
JOLT
MAYBE I CAN FIRE A SHOT THAT'S TWICE, IF NOT THREE OR FOUR TIMES AS POWERFUL AS A REGULAR ONE.
I'VE GOT NO PROOF THAT ANY OF THIS WILL ACTUALLY WORK...
BUT I'LL NEVER FIND OUT...

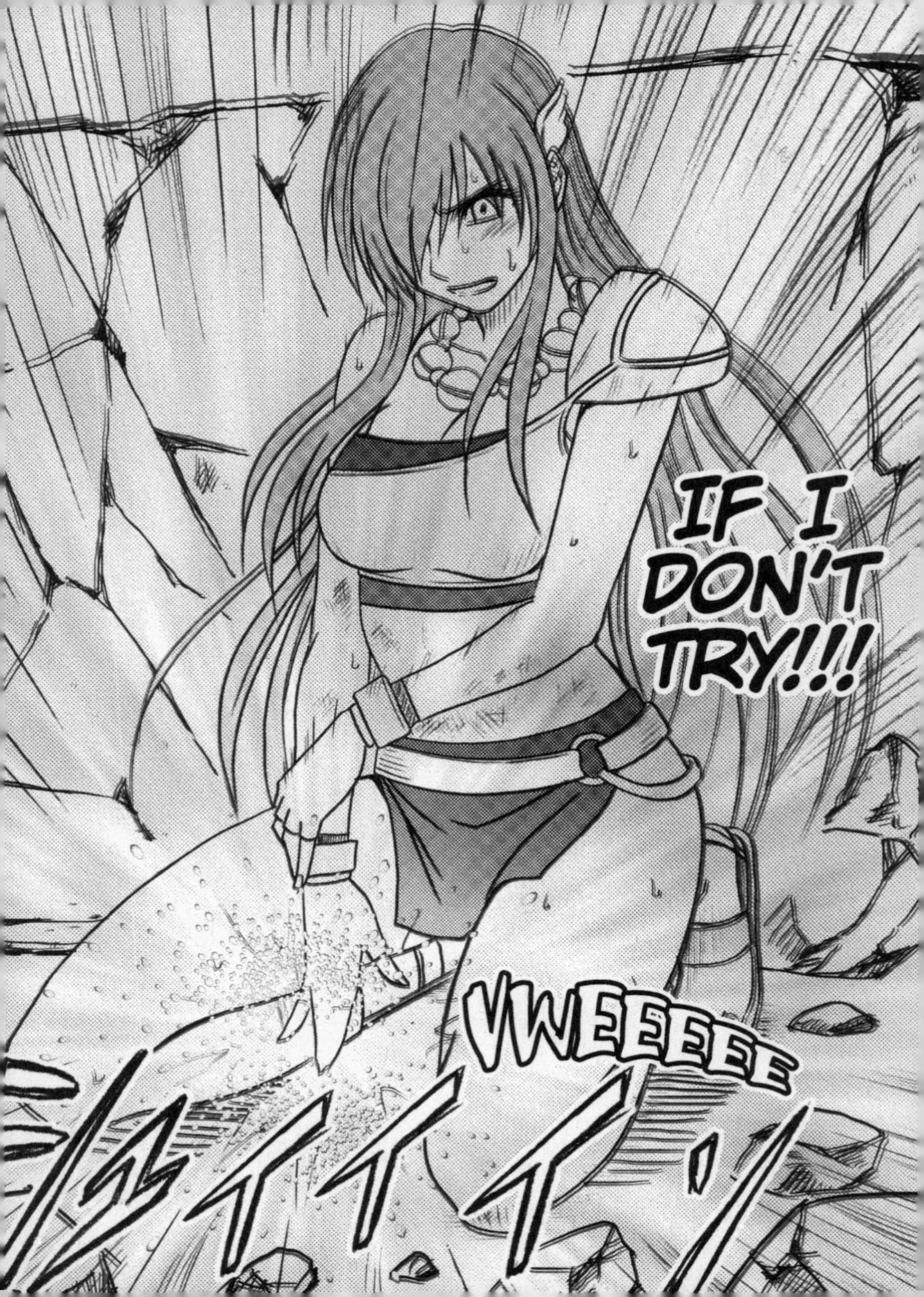
IF I DON'T TRY!!!
VWEEEEE

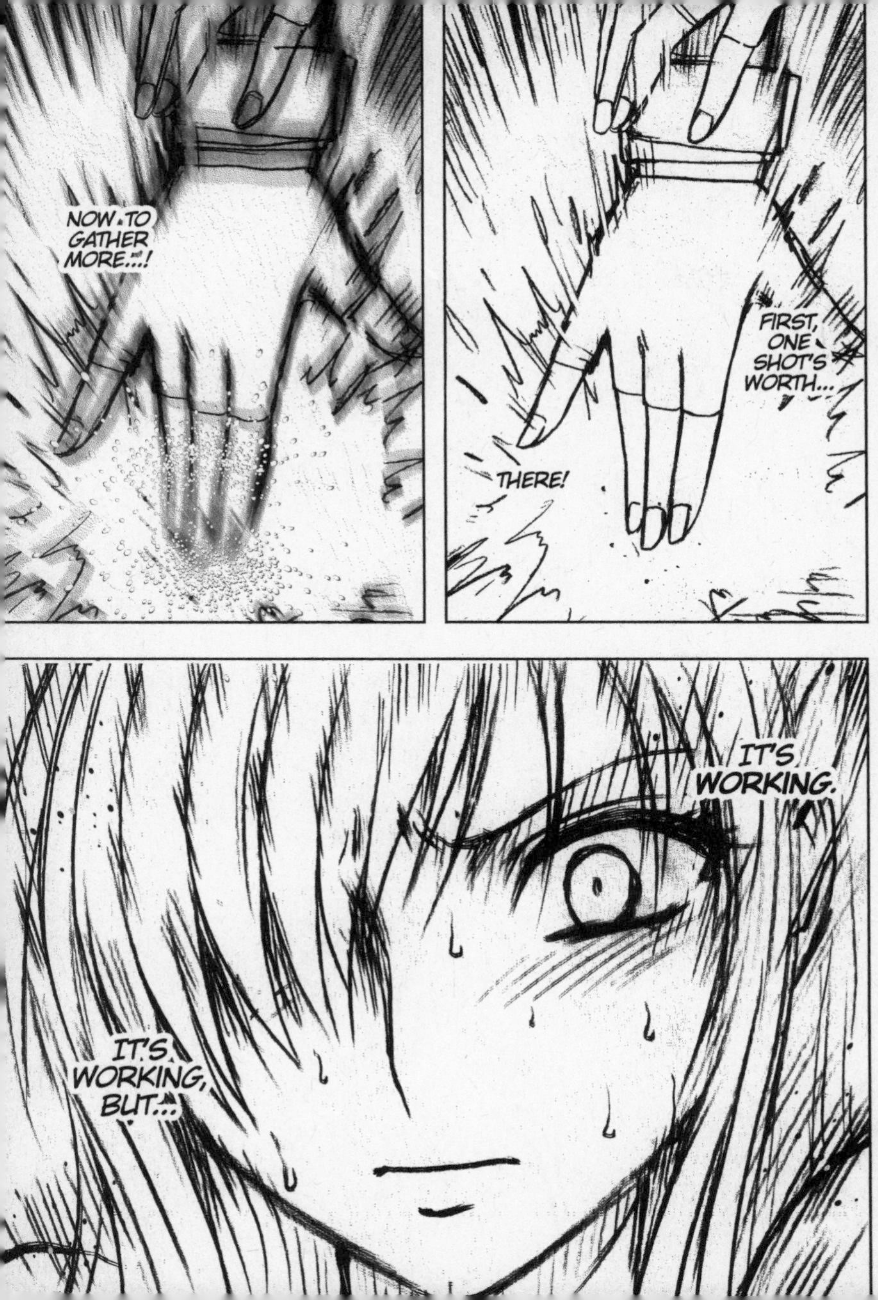
FIRST, ONE SHOT'S WORTH...
THERE!
NOW TO GATHER MORE...!
IT'S WORKING.
IT'S WORKING, BUT...

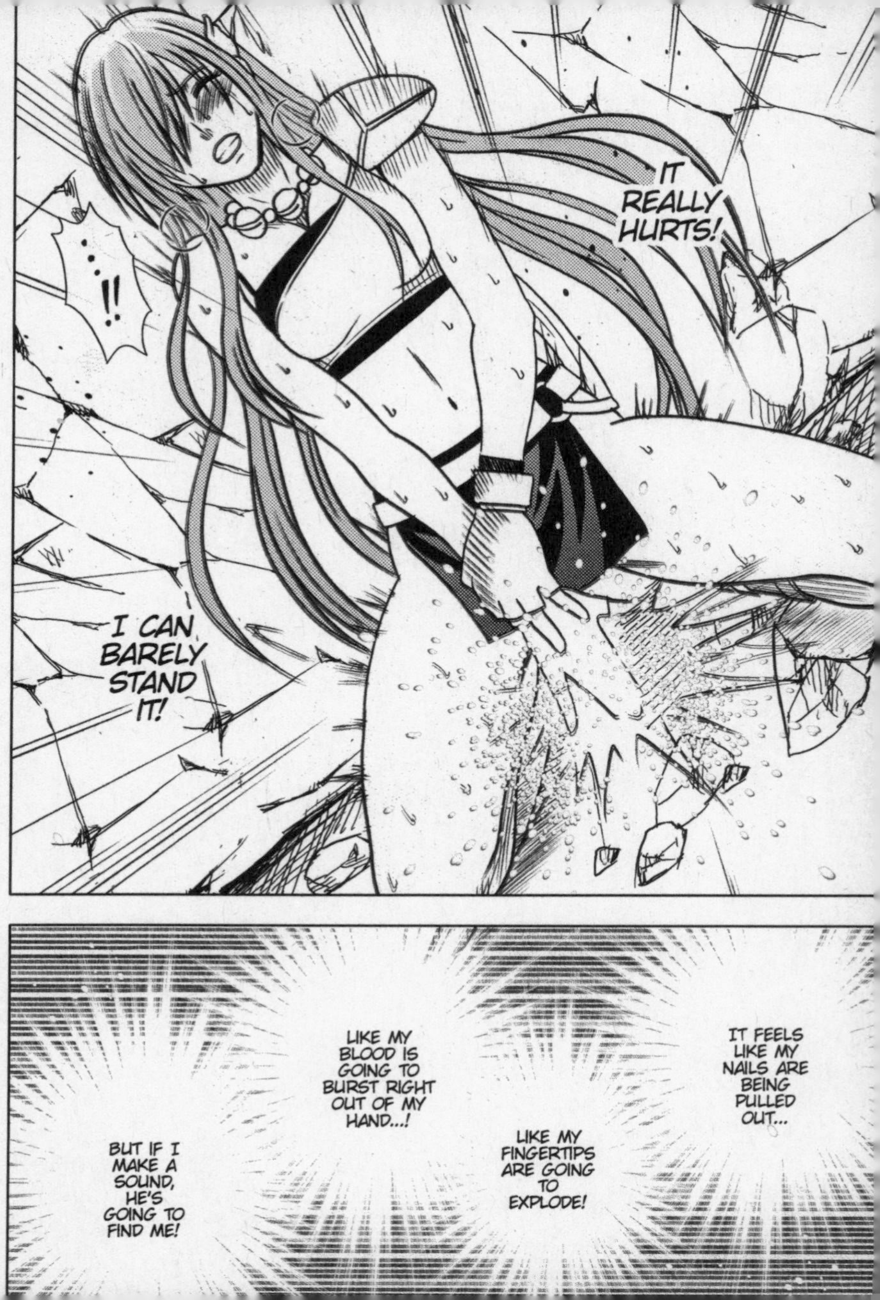
IT REALLY HURTS!
...!!
I CAN BARELY STAND IT!
IT FEELS LIKE MY NAILS ARE BEING PULLED OUT...
LIKE MY BLOOD IS GOING TO BURST RIGHT OUT OF MY HAND...!
LIKE MY FINGERTIPS ARE GOING TO EXPLODE!
BUT IF I MAKE A SOUND, HE'S GOING TO FIND ME!

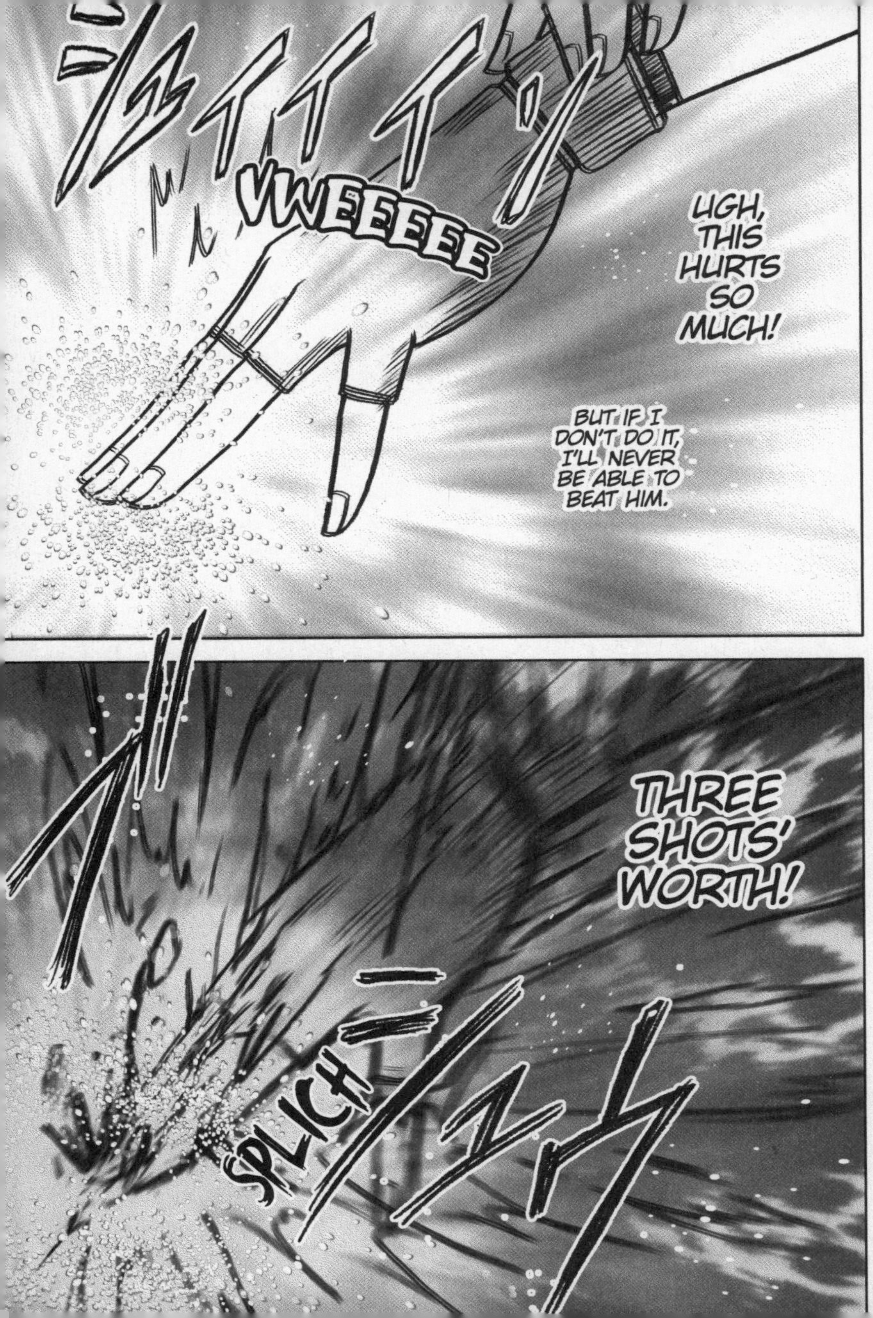
VWEEEEEE
UGH, THIS HURTS SO MUCH!
BUT IF I DON'T DO IT, I'LL NEVER BE ABLE TO BEAT HIM.
THREE SHOTS' WORTH!
SPLICH

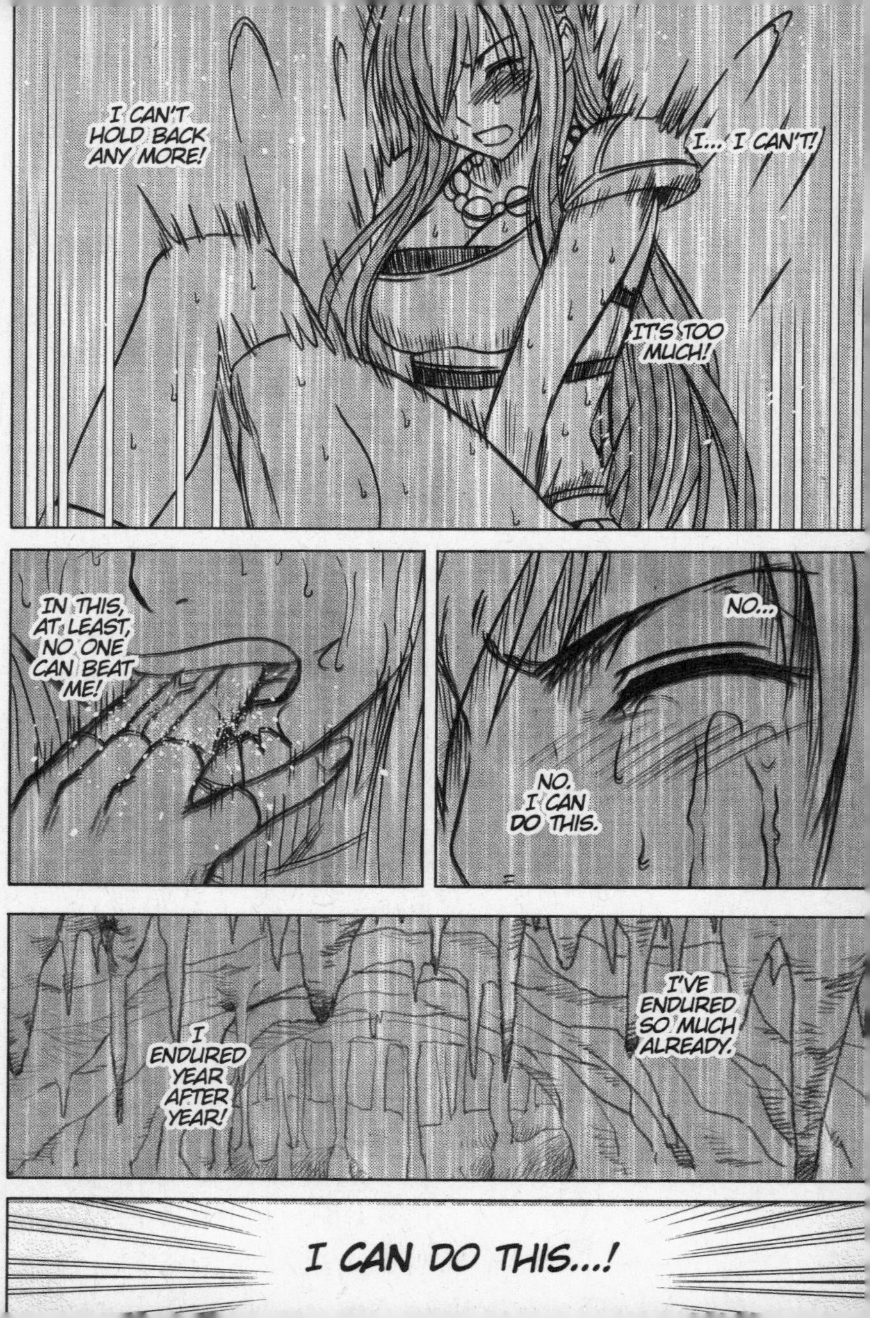
I... I CAN'T!
I CAN'T HOLD BACK ANY MORE!
IT'S TOO MUCH!
NO...
NO. I CAN DO THIS.
IN THIS, AT LEAST, NO ONE CAN BEAT ME!
I'VE ENDURED SO MUCH ALREADY.
I ENDURED YEAR AFTER YEAR!
I CAN DO THIS...!

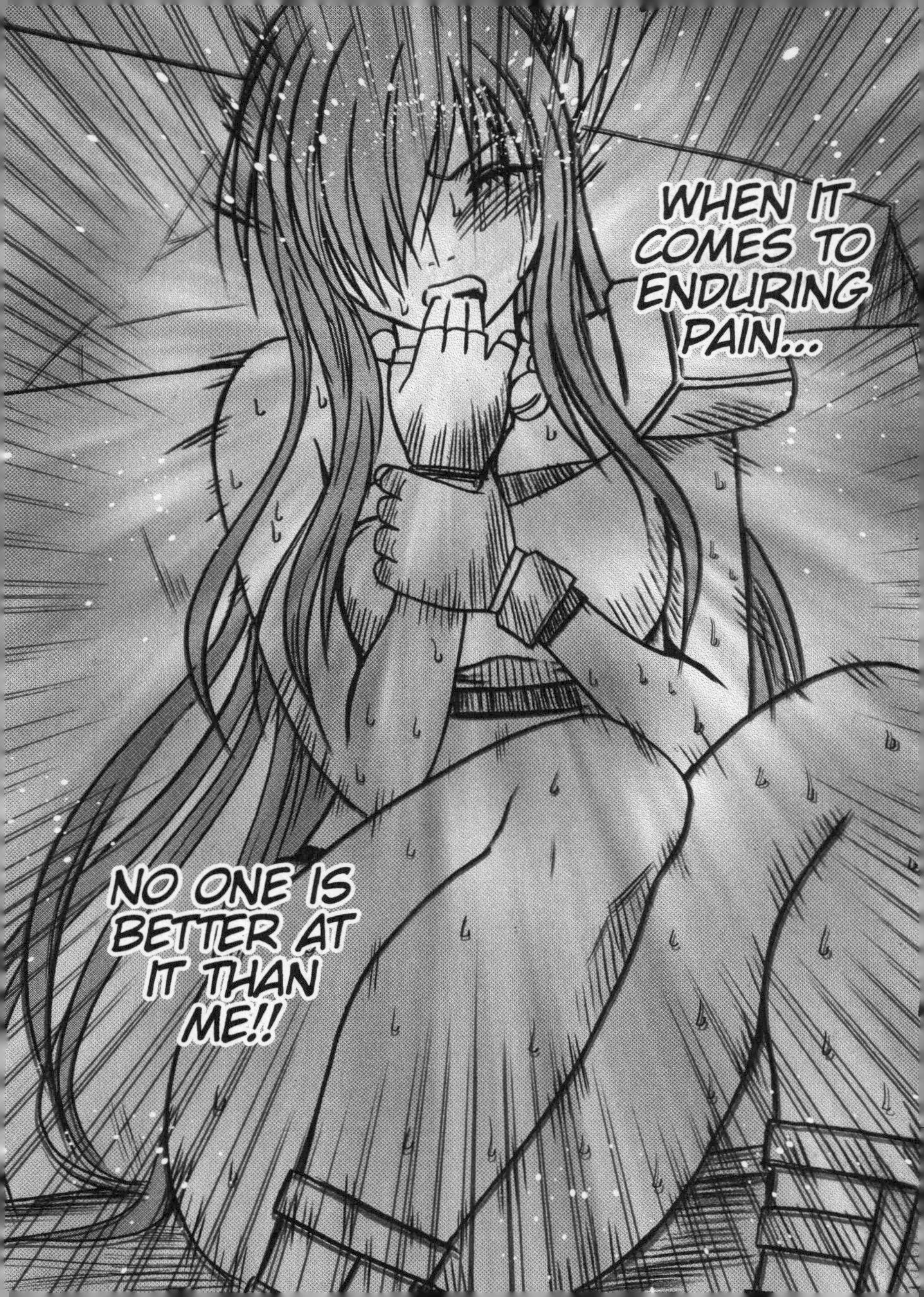
WHEN IT COMES TO ENDURING PAIN...
NO ONE IS BETTER AT IT THAN ME!!

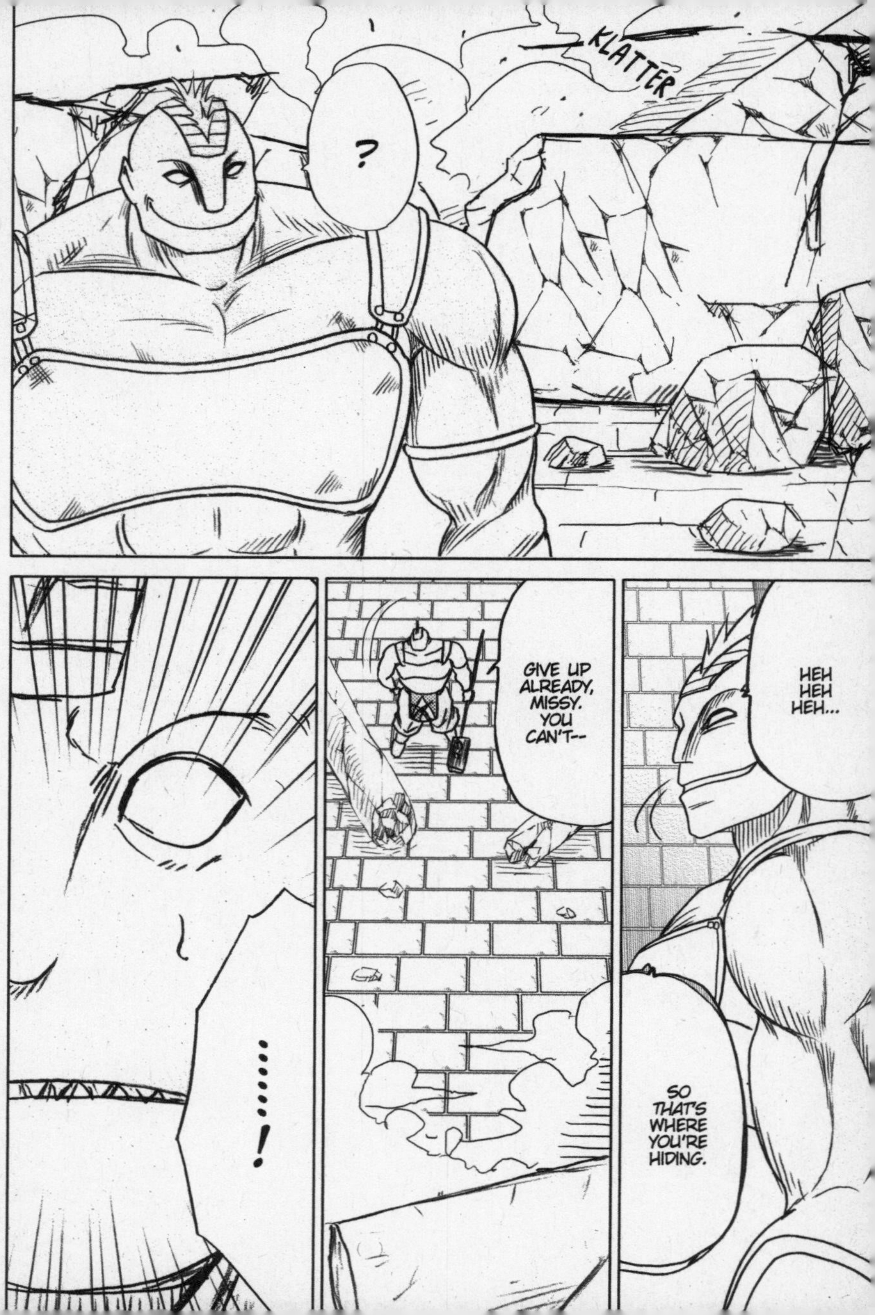
KLATTER
?
HEH HEH HEH...
SO THAT'S WHERE YOU'RE HIDING.
GIVE UP ALREADY, MISSY. YOU CAN'T--
......!

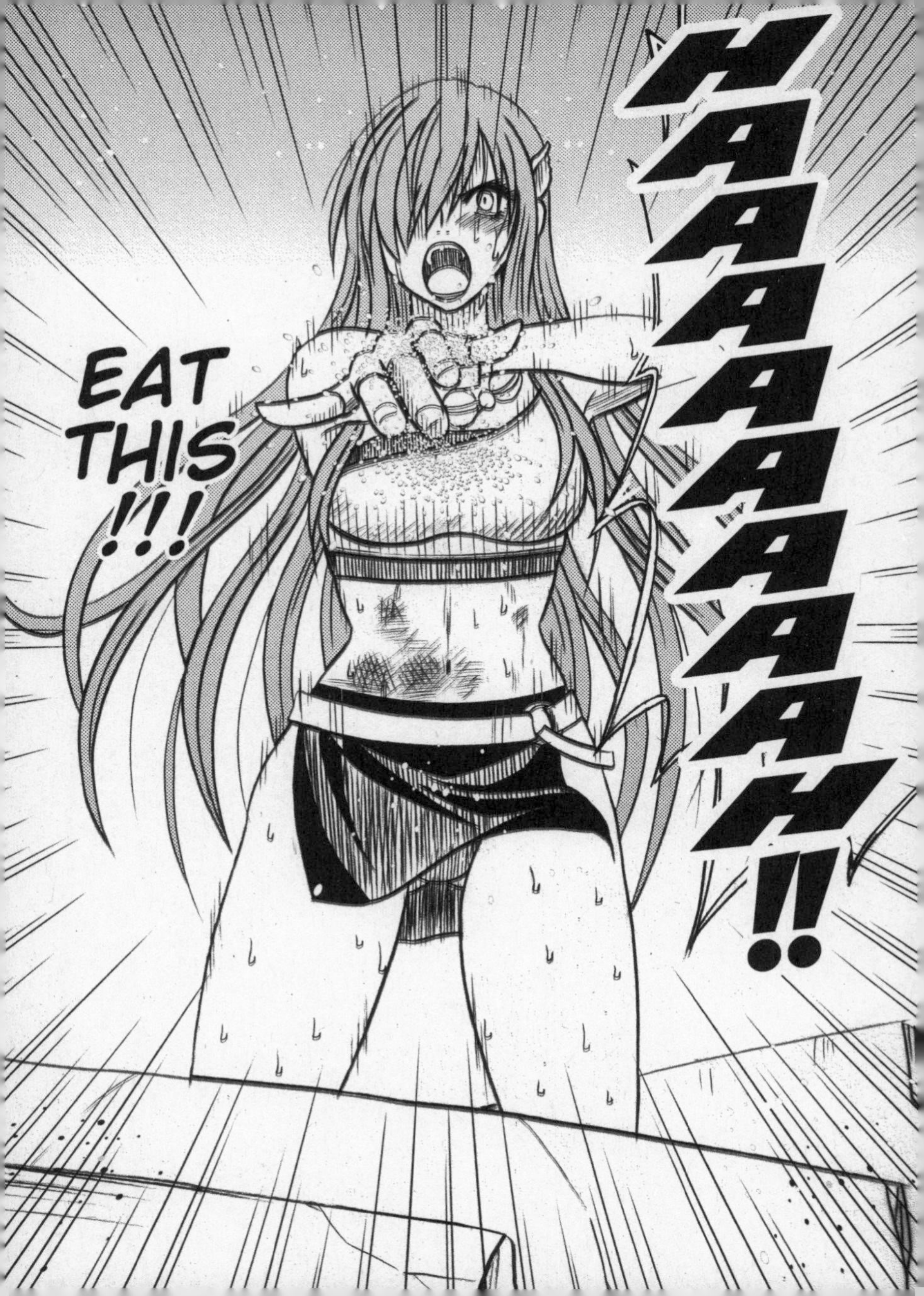

HAAAAAAAH!!
EAT THIS!!!

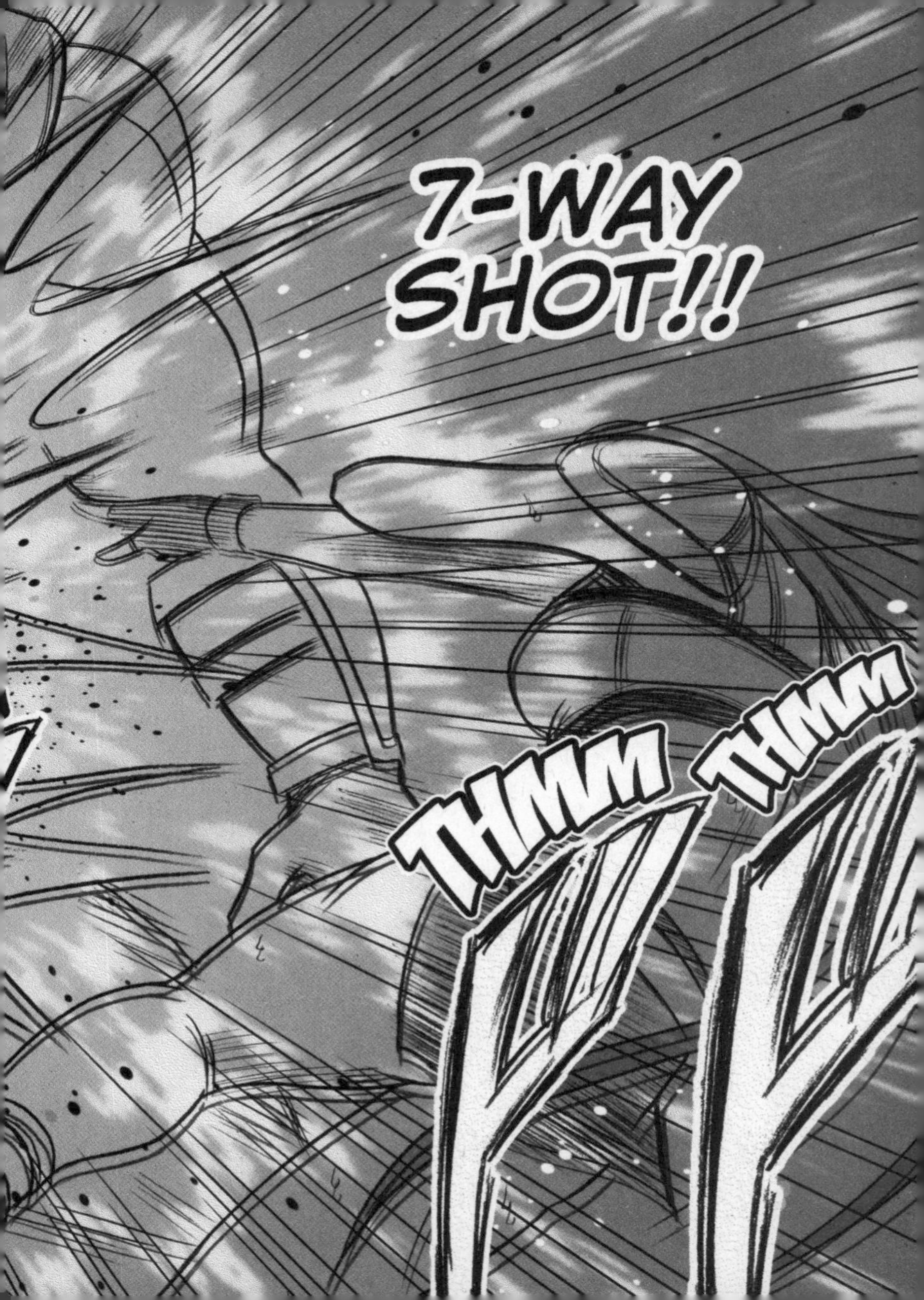
7-WAY SHOT!!
THMM
THMM

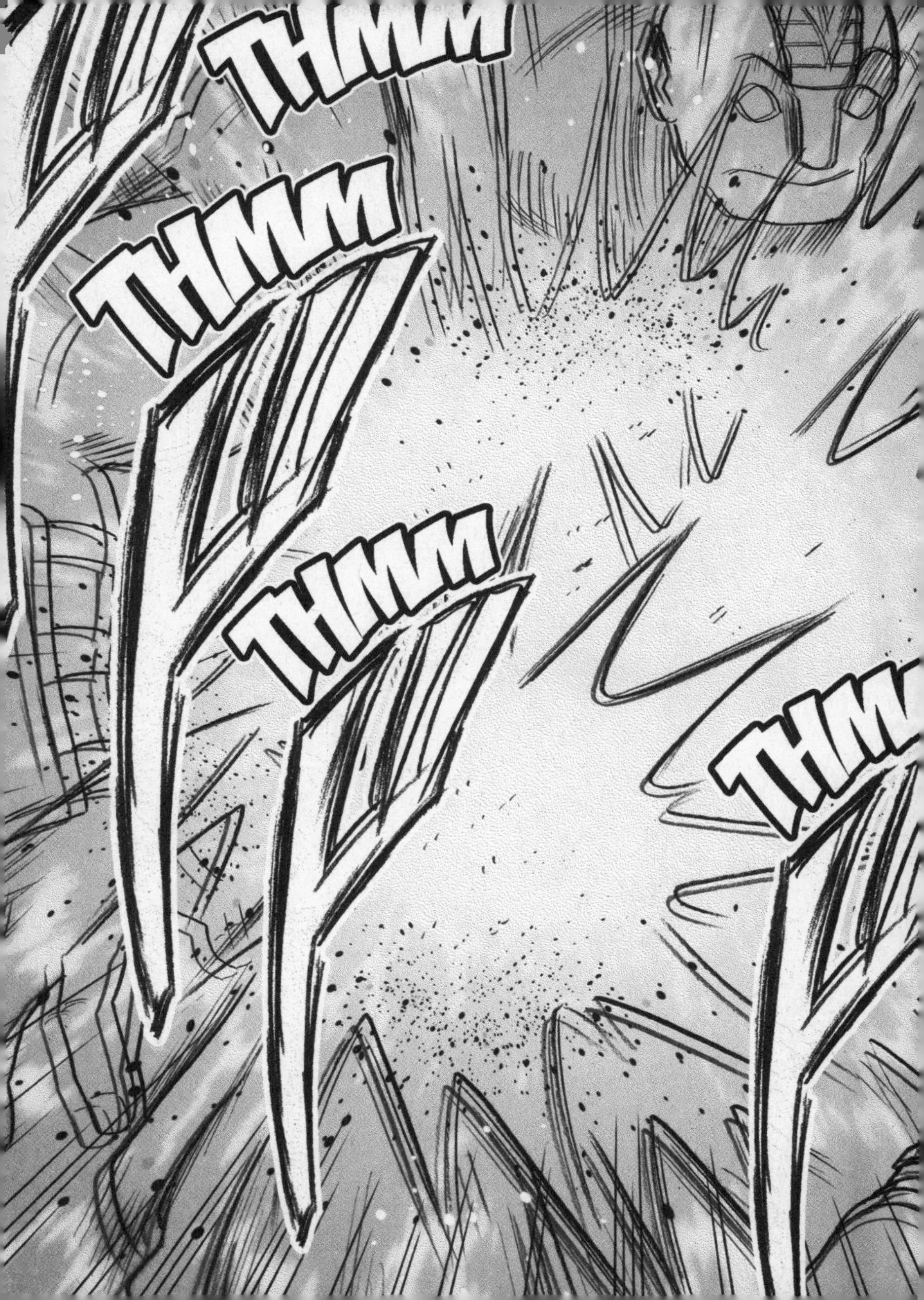
THMM
THMM
THMM
THM

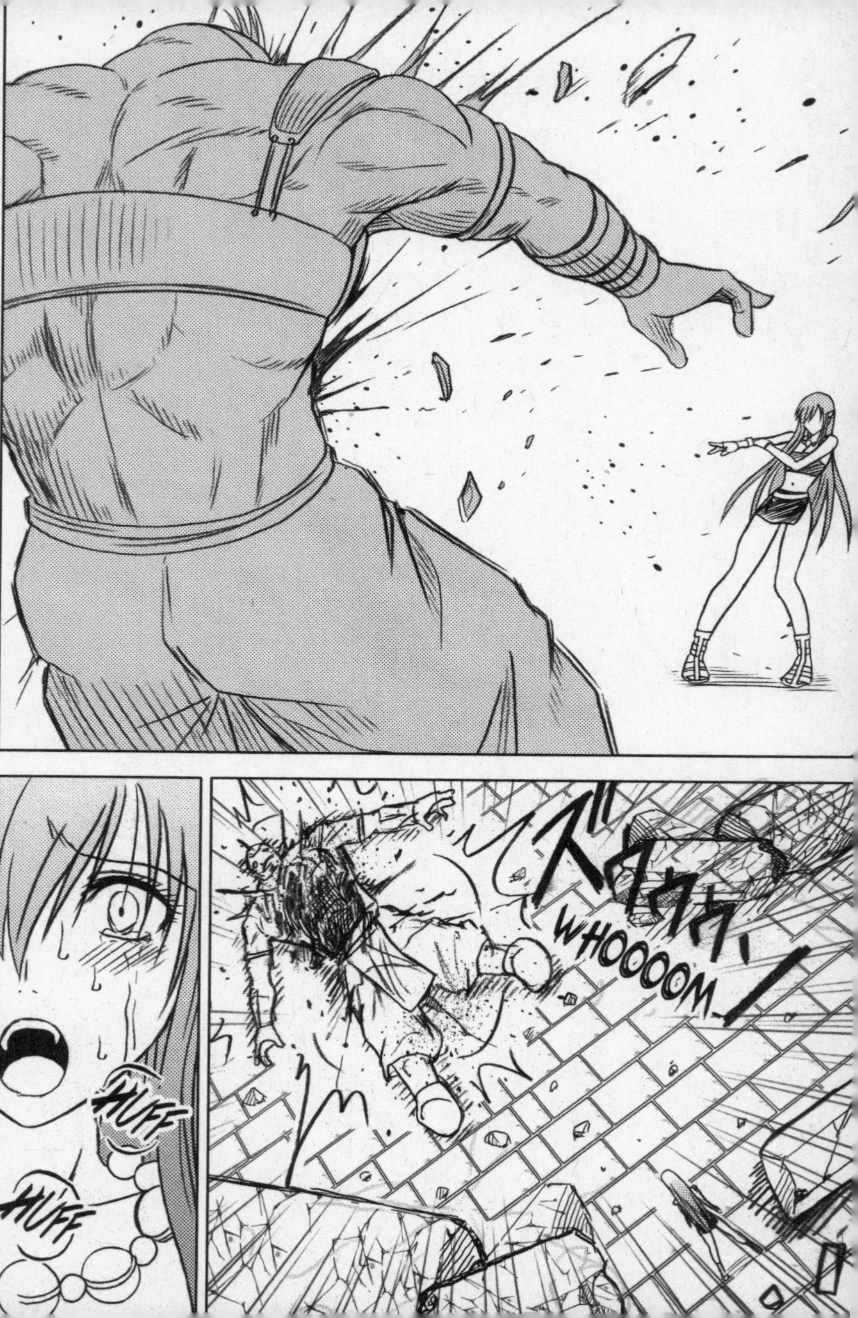
WHOOOOM
HUFF
HUFF

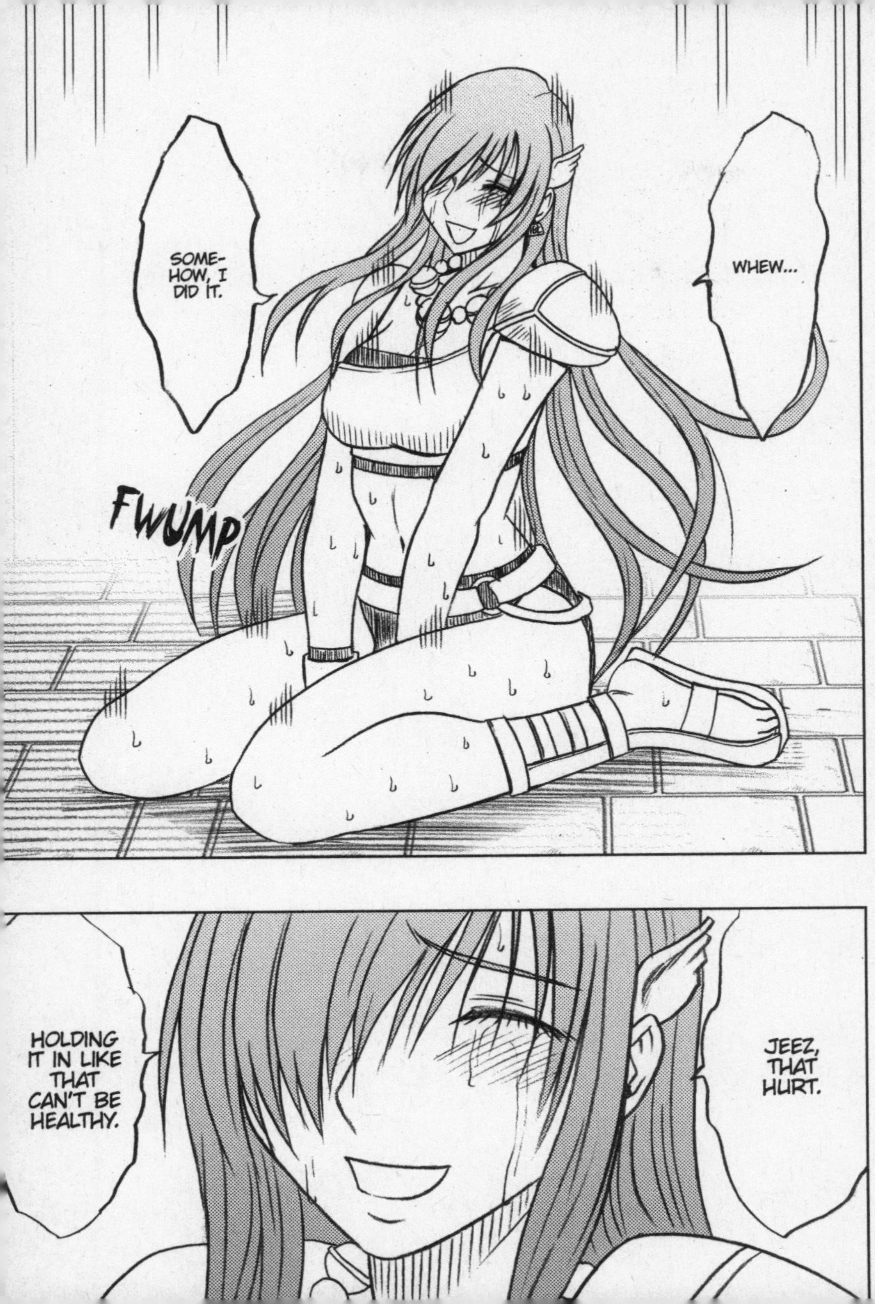
WHEW...
SOME-HOW, I DID IT.
FWUMP
JEEZ, THAT HURT.
HOLDING IT IN LIKE THAT CAN'T BE HEALTHY.

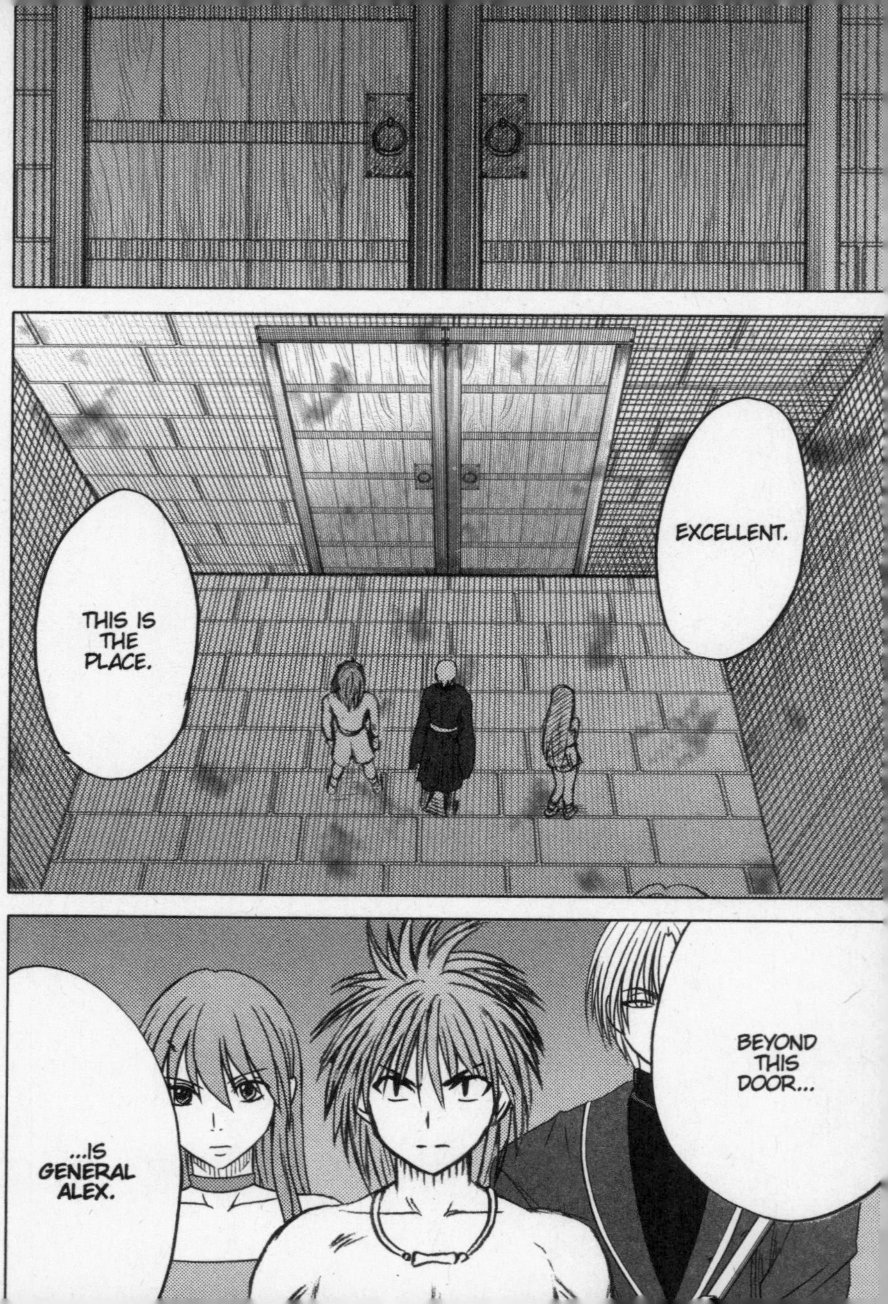
EXCELLENT.
THIS IS THE PLACE.
BEYOND THIS DOOR...
...IS GENERAL ALEX.

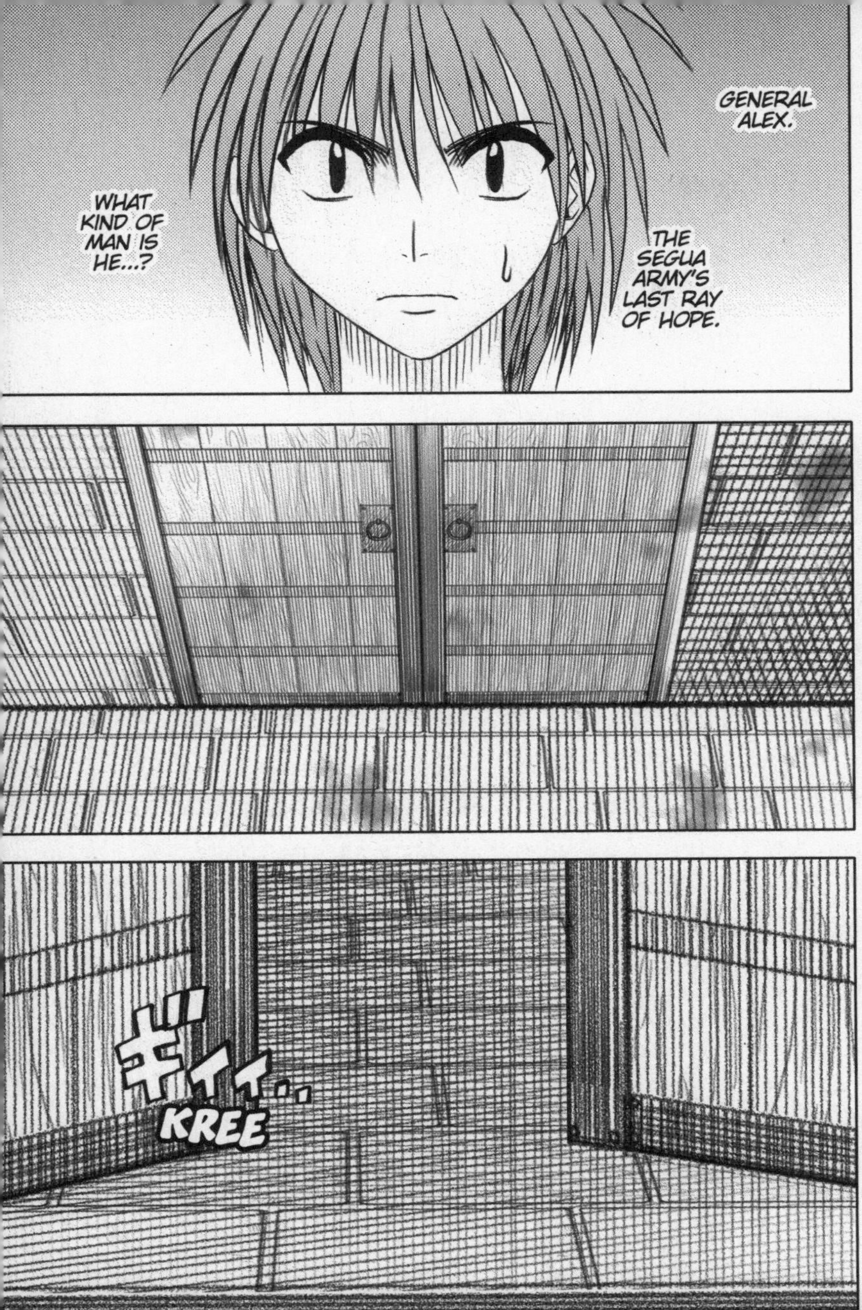
GENERAL ALEX.
THE SEGUA ARMY'S LAST RAY OF HOPE.
WHAT KIND OF MAN IS HE...?
ギィィ..
KREE

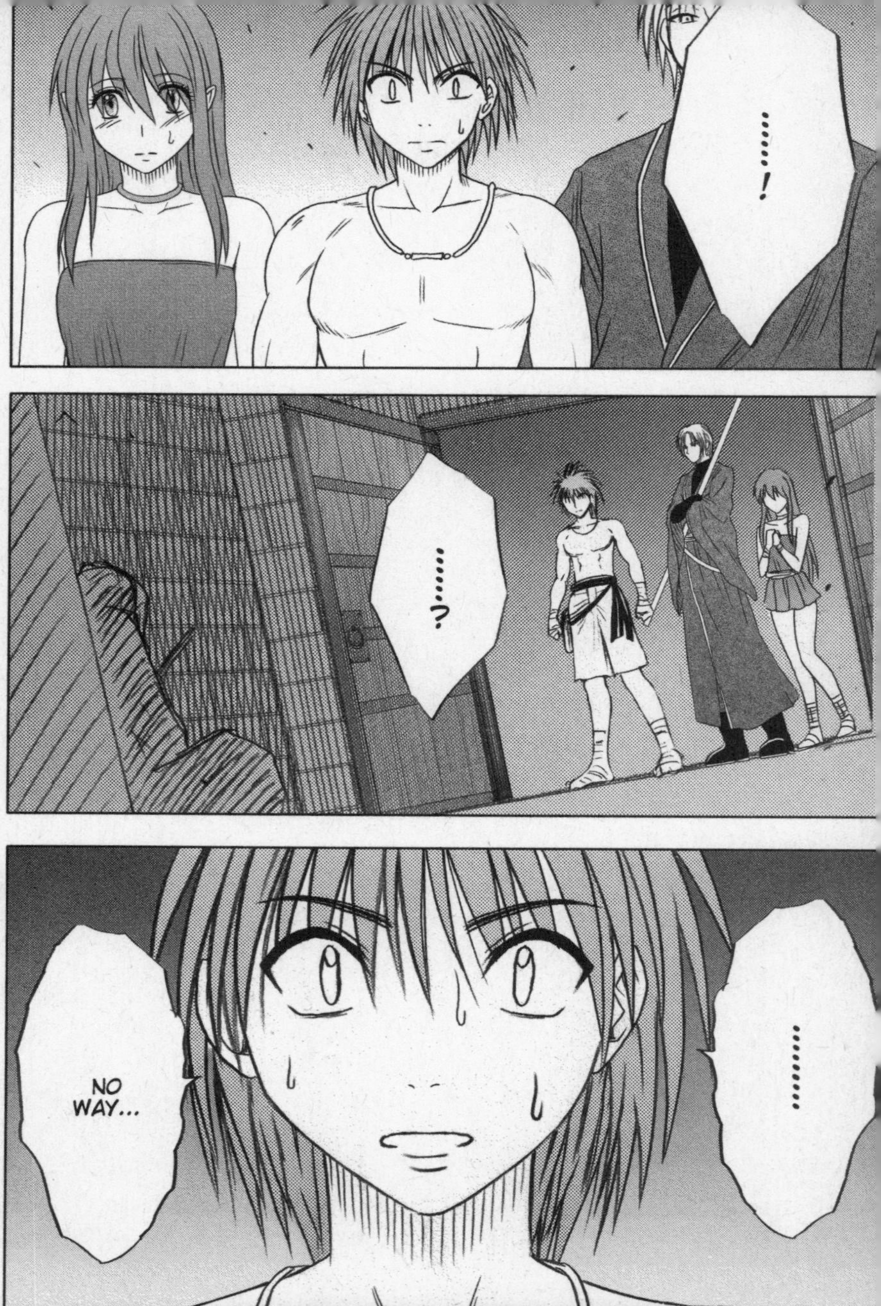
......!
......っ
......
NO WAY...

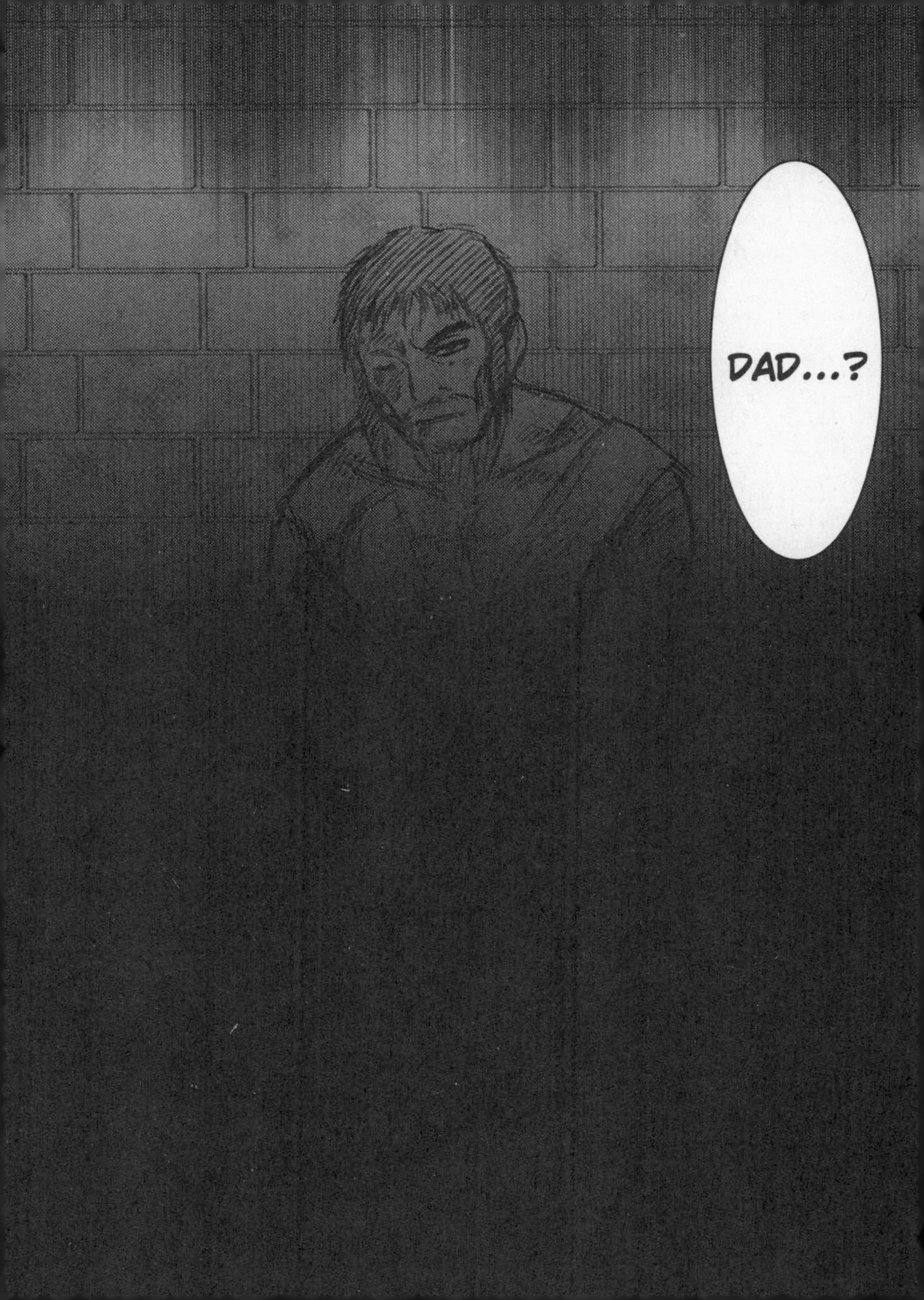
DAD...?

Perusing Video Game History

ON THE EDGE OF THE BLUE WORLD

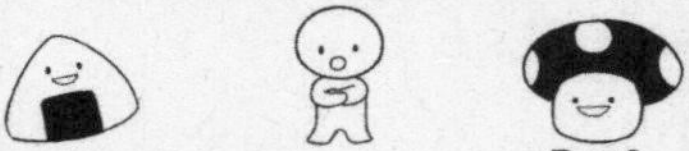

Dr. Onigiri Mr. Why Prof. Mushroom

Today's Topic

DARIUS: PART 2

Mr. Why: Okay, so I get how they put the three screens together. Now, what kind of game is *Darius*?

Prof. Mushroom: Like *Fantasy Zone*, it's a side-scrolling shooter, where you pilot your ship, the Silver Hawk, and shoot down incoming enemy ships.

Dr. Onigiri: The fun part of it is that all the enemy bosses are all variations on some kind of ocean creature.

Mr. Why: What, they're all fish?

Prof. Mushroom: Yep! Angler fish, blowfish, shrimp, squid, crabs, whales... Playing it made me want sushi something fierce, let me tell you.

Dr. Onigiri: There was a seahorse too, right?

Prof. Mushroom: Yeah. Some other fun ones are the coelacanth and piranhas.

Dr. Onigiri: Then there was the boss from *Darius Gaiden* that was modeled after a mantis shrimp. His "Crusty Hammer" attack was brutal! More than one player has been frustrated to tears by him. I mean, no matter how many force fields you had, they weren't enough.

Prof. Mushroom: The game was also unique due to its branching level design. To make it easy, they even labeled each area with a letter of the alphabet. So the first one would be Zone A.

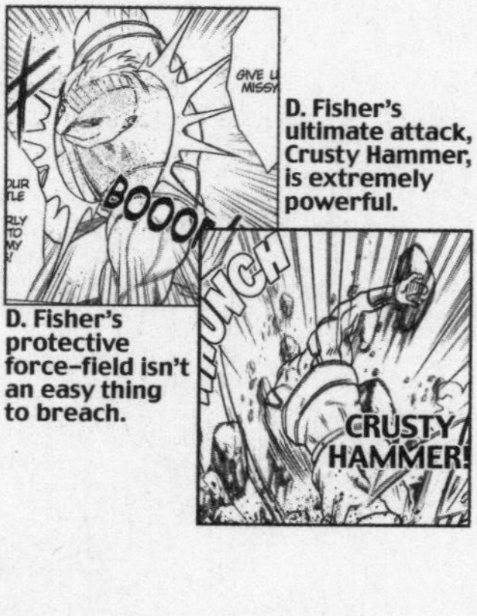
CRUSTY HAMMER!

D. Fisher's ultimate attack, Crusty Hammer, is extremely powerful.

D. Fisher's protective force-field isn't an easy thing to breach.

Mr. Why: Oh! So then the last one would be Zone Z, right?

Prof. Mushroom: Right! Well, mostly. Sometimes you could end with other zones. But the giant whale boss in Zone Z, "Great Thing," was a real nasty fight. I had a hard time beating him.

To Be Continued...

WORLD WAR BLUE

CHARACTER INTRODUCTION

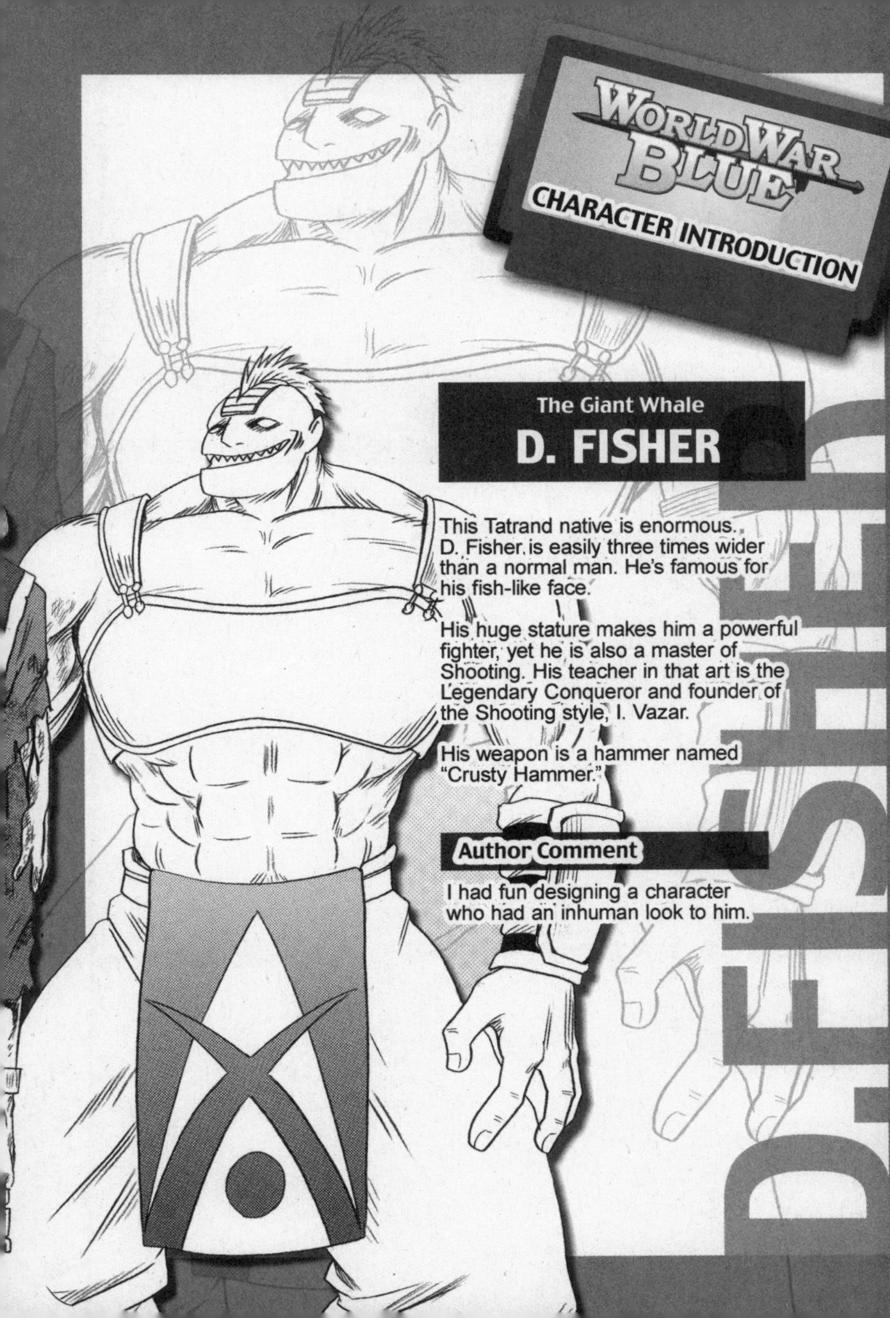

The Giant Whale

D. FISHER

This Tatrand native is enormous. D. Fisher is easily three times wider than a normal man. He's famous for his fish-like face.

His huge stature makes him a powerful fighter, yet he is also a master of Shooting. His teacher in that art is the Legendary Conqueror and founder of the Shooting style, I. Vazar.

His weapon is a hammer named "Crusty Hammer."

Author Comment

I had fun designing a character who had an inhuman look to him.

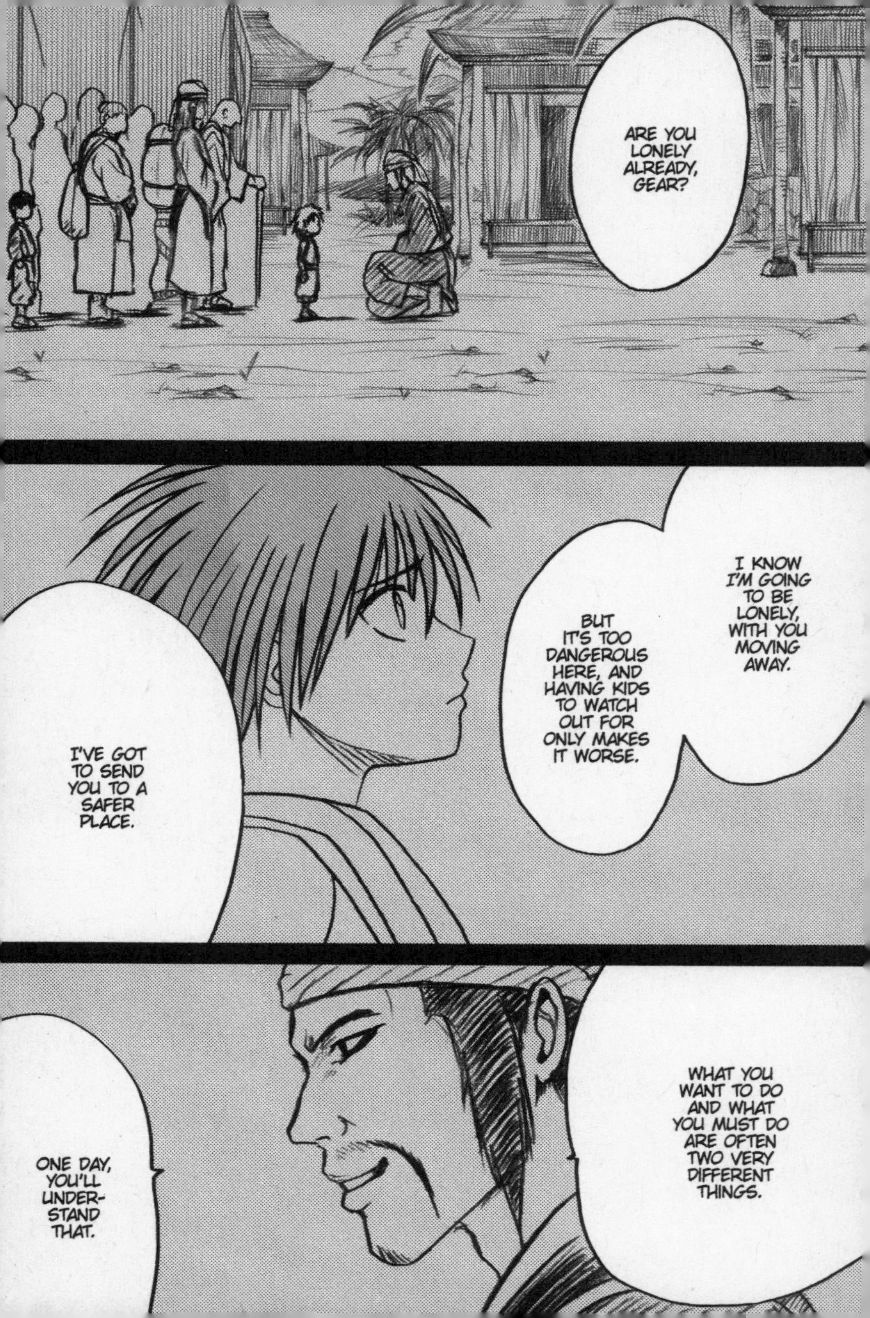
ARE YOU LONELY ALREADY, GEAR?
I KNOW I'M GOING TO BE LONELY, WITH YOU MOVING AWAY.
BUT IT'S TOO DANGEROUS HERE, AND HAVING KIDS TO WATCH OUT FOR ONLY MAKES IT WORSE.
I'VE GOT TO SEND YOU TO A SAFER PLACE.
WHAT YOU WANT TO DO AND WHAT YOU MUST DO ARE OFTEN TWO VERY DIFFERENT THINGS.
ONE DAY, YOU'LL UNDER-STAND THAT.

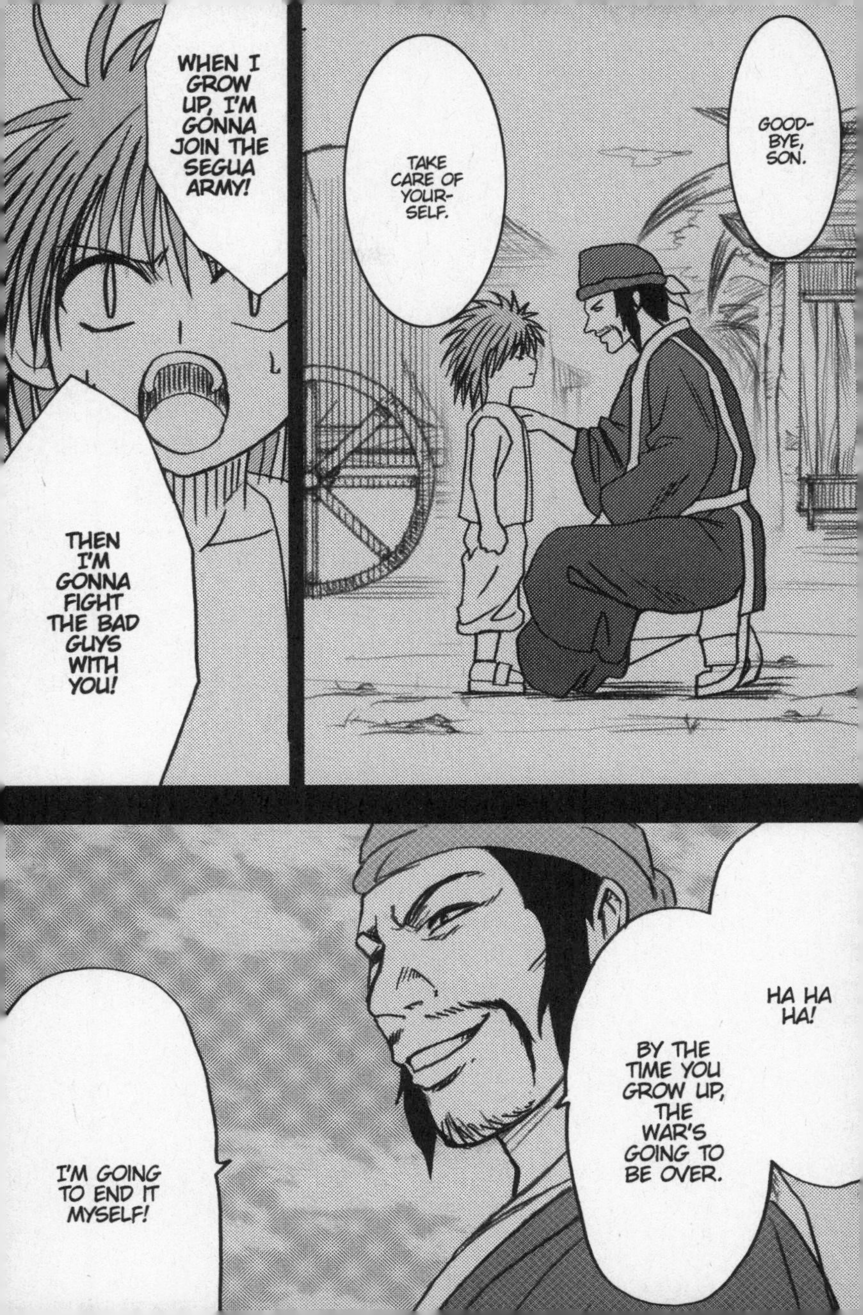
GOOD-BYE, SON.
TAKE CARE OF YOURSELF.
WHEN I GROW UP, I'M GONNA JOIN THE SEGUA ARMY!
THEN I'M GONNA FIGHT THE BAD GUYS WITH YOU!
HA HA HA!
BY THE TIME YOU GROW UP, THE WAR'S GOING TO BE OVER.
I'M GOING TO END IT MYSELF!

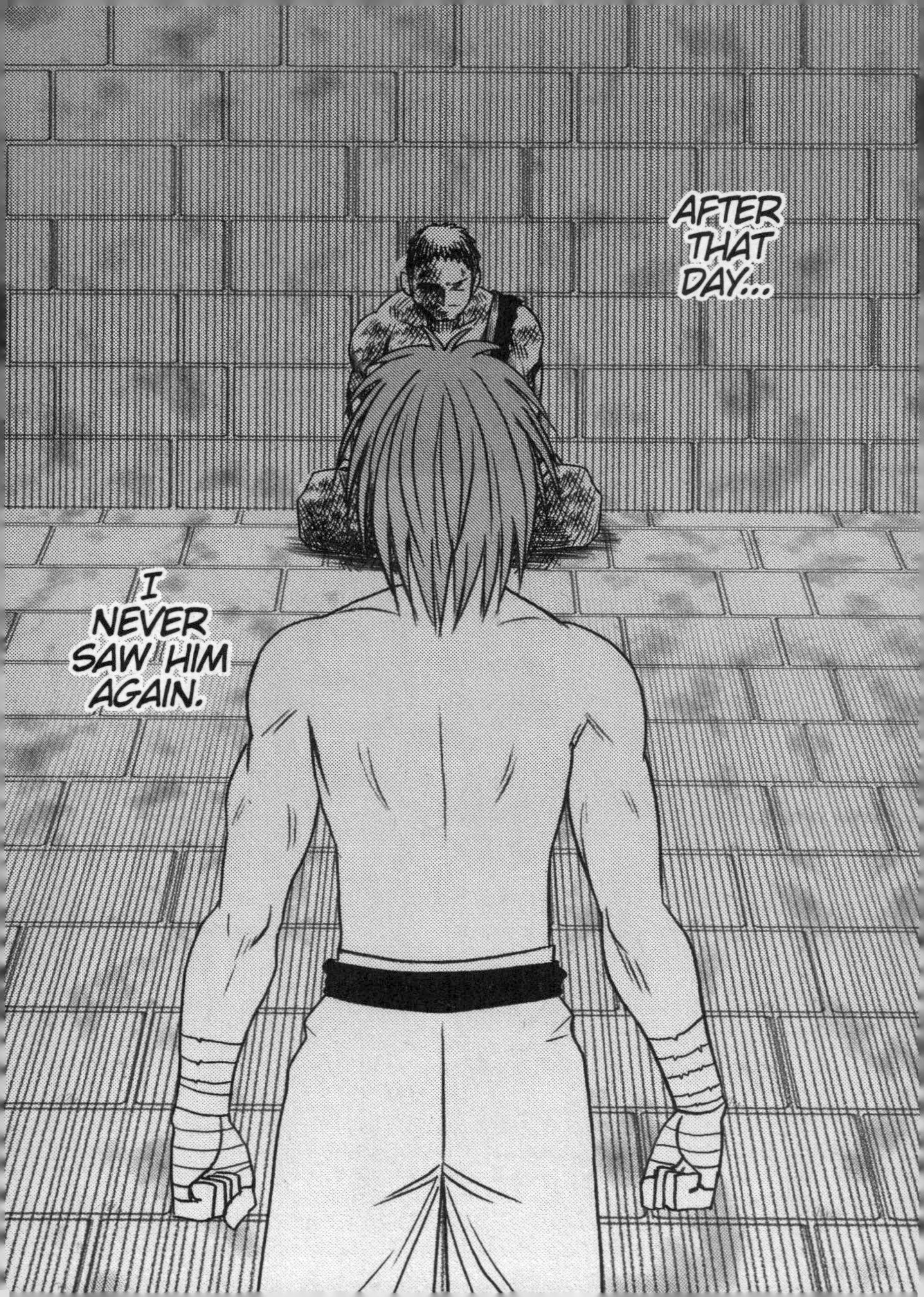
AFTER THAT DAY...
I NEVER SAW HIM AGAIN.

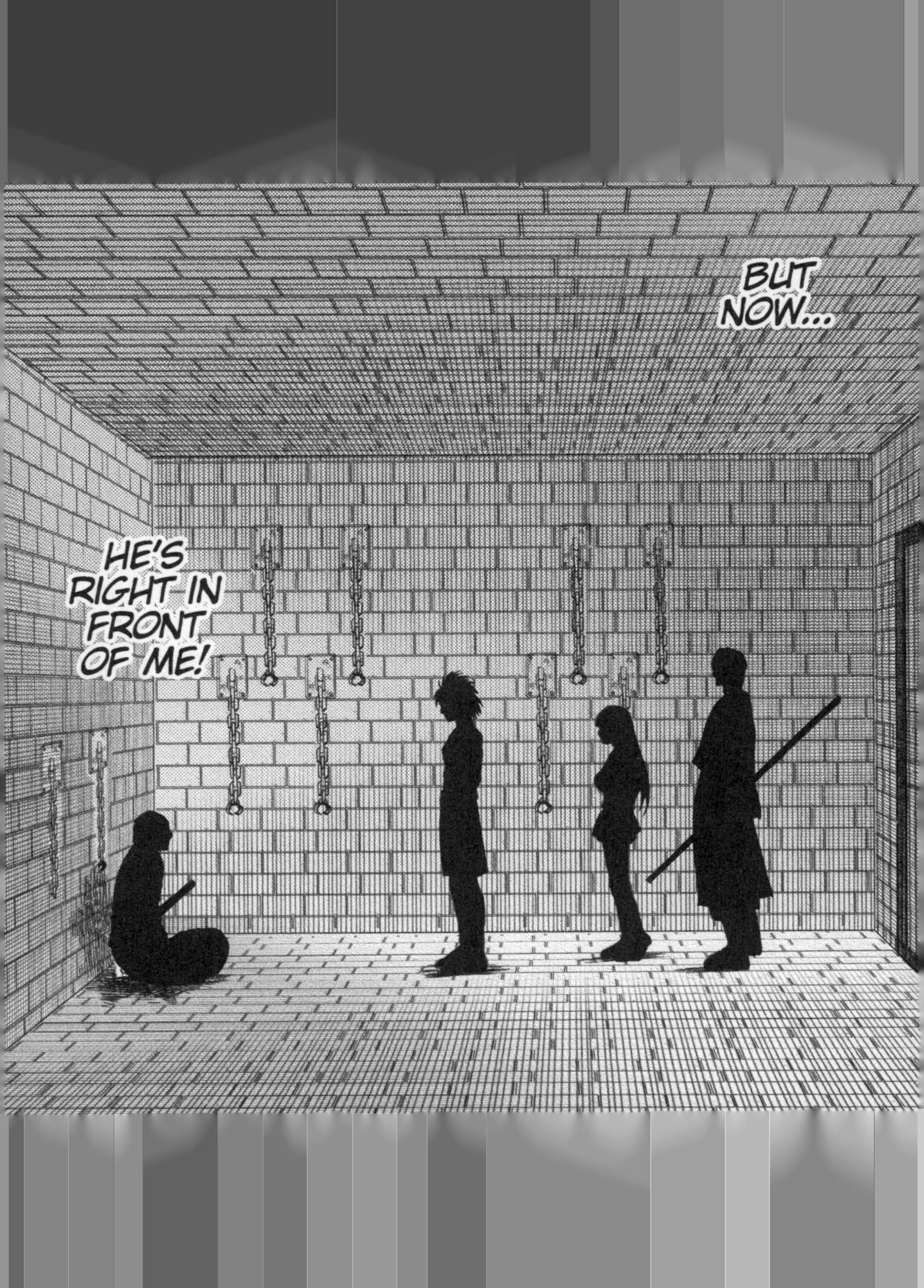
BUT NOW...
HE'S RIGHT IN FRONT OF ME!

CHAPTER 11

LOST STAR

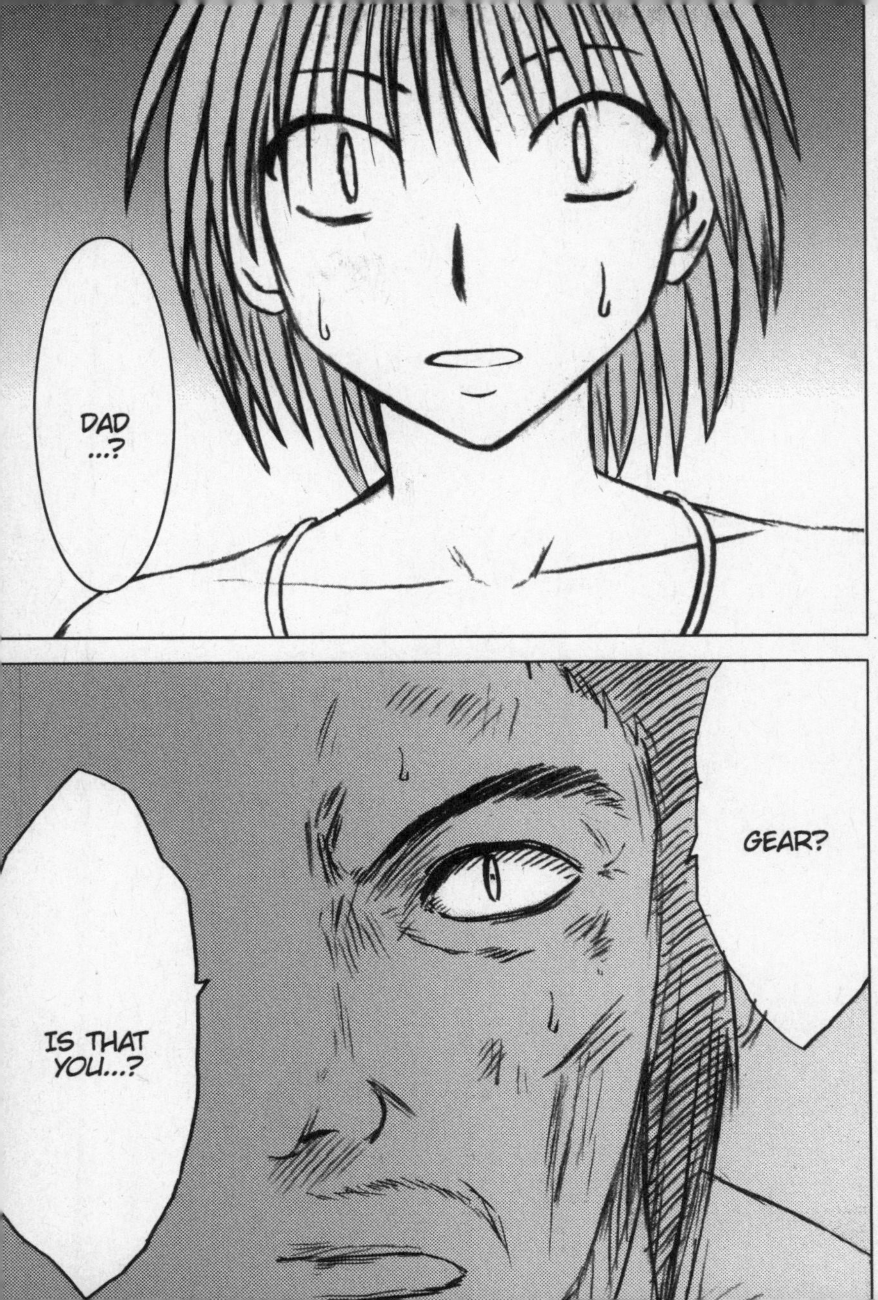
DAD ...?
GEAR?
IS THAT YOU...?

YOU'RE... ALIVE.

I THOUGHT, WHEN I HEARD ABOUT THE ATTACK...

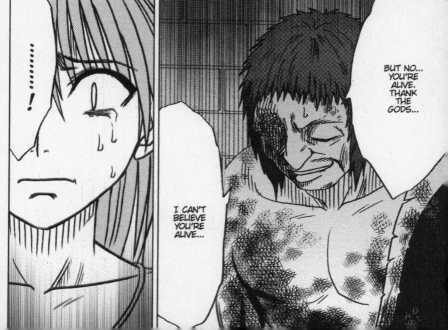

BUT NO... YOU'RE ALIVE. THANK THE GODS...

I CAN'T BELIEVE YOU'RE ALIVE...

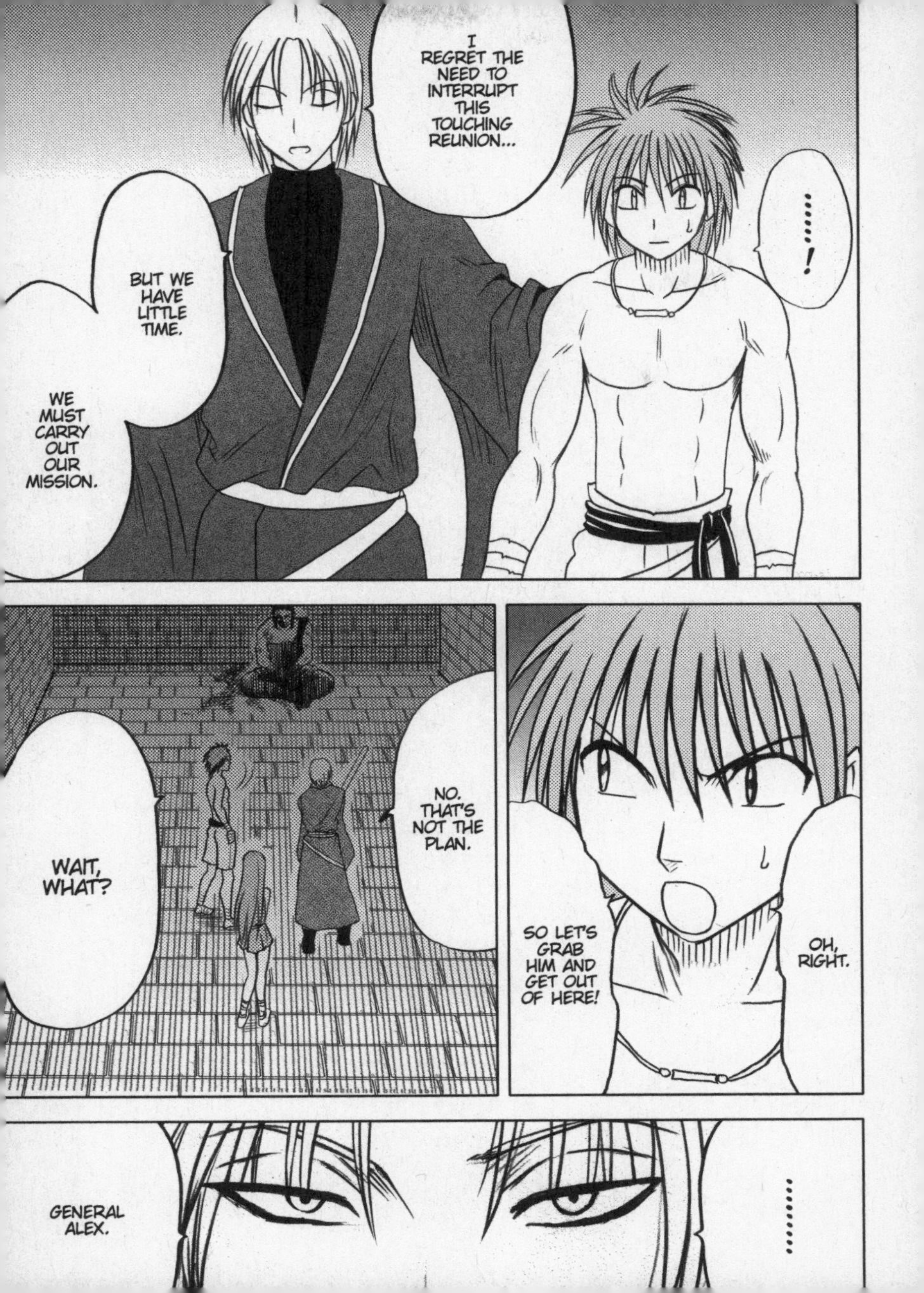
I REGRET THE NEED TO INTERRUPT THIS TOUCHING REUNION...
.....!
BUT WE HAVE LITTLE TIME.
WE MUST CARRY OUT OUR MISSION.
OH, RIGHT.
SO LET'S GRAB HIM AND GET OUT OF HERE!
NO. THAT'S NOT THE PLAN.
WAIT, WHAT?
....
GENERAL ALEX.

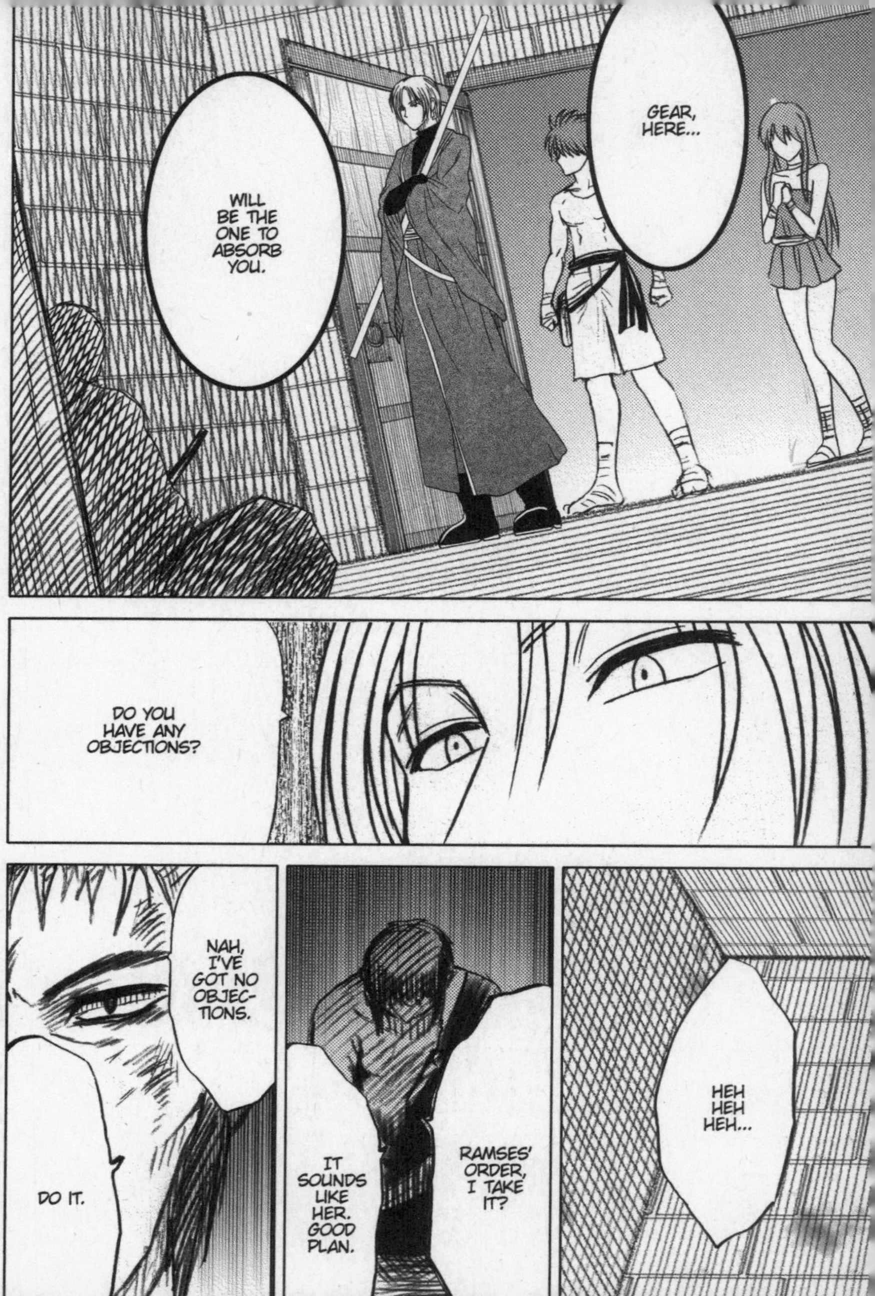
GEAR, HERE...
WILL BE THE ONE TO ABSORB YOU.
DO YOU HAVE ANY OBJECTIONS?
HEH HEH HEH...
RAMSES' ORDER, I TAKE IT?
IT SOUNDS LIKE HER. GOOD PLAN.
NAH, I'VE GOT NO OBJECTIONS.
DO IT.

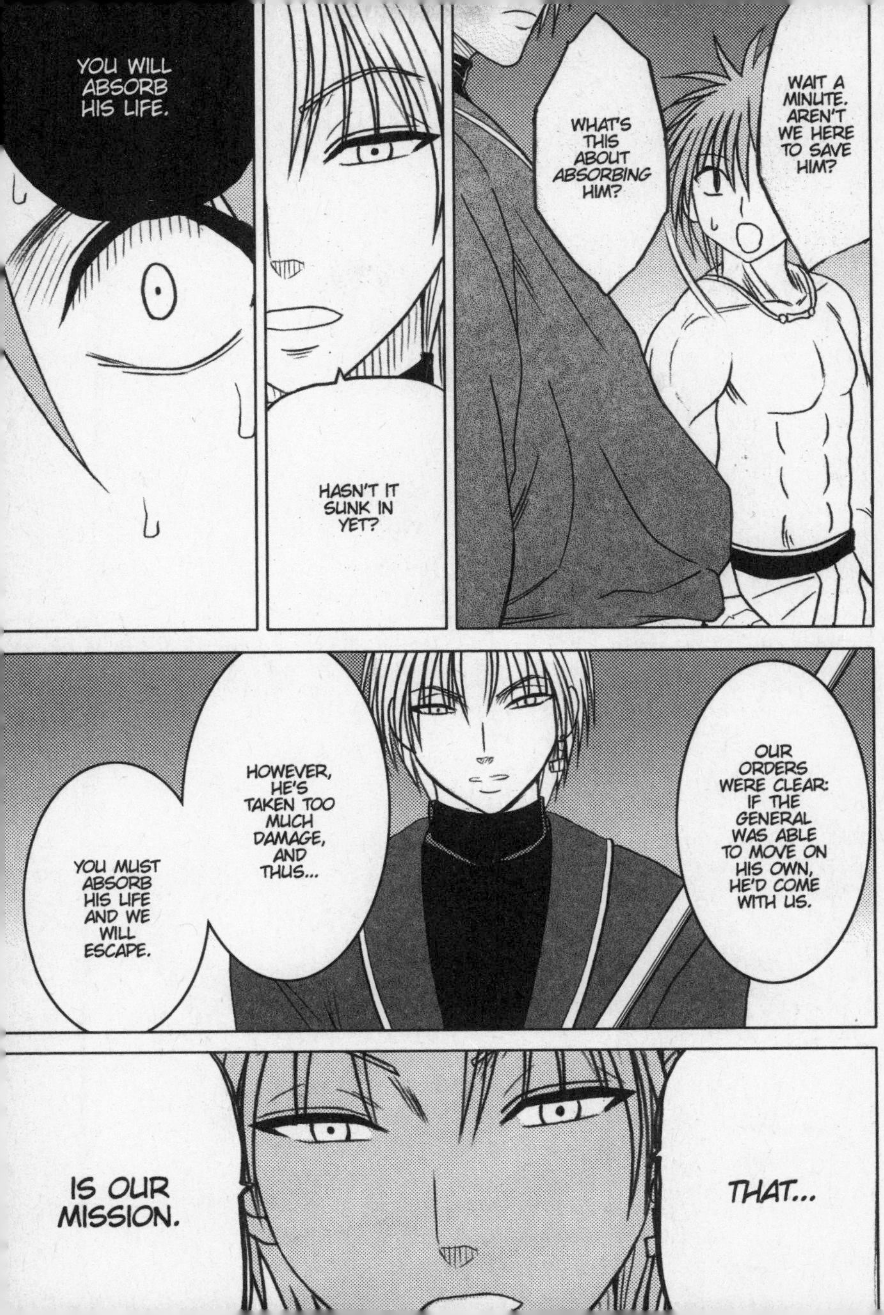
WAIT A MINUTE. AREN'T WE HERE TO SAVE HIM?
WHAT'S THIS ABOUT ABSORBING HIM?
HASN'T IT SUNK IN YET?
YOU WILL ABSORB HIS LIFE.
OUR ORDERS WERE CLEAR: IF THE GENERAL WAS ABLE TO MOVE ON HIS OWN, HE'D COME WITH US.
HOWEVER, HE'S TAKEN TOO MUCH DAMAGE, AND THUS...
YOU MUST ABSORB HIS LIFE AND WE WILL ESCAPE.
THAT...
IS OUR MISSION.

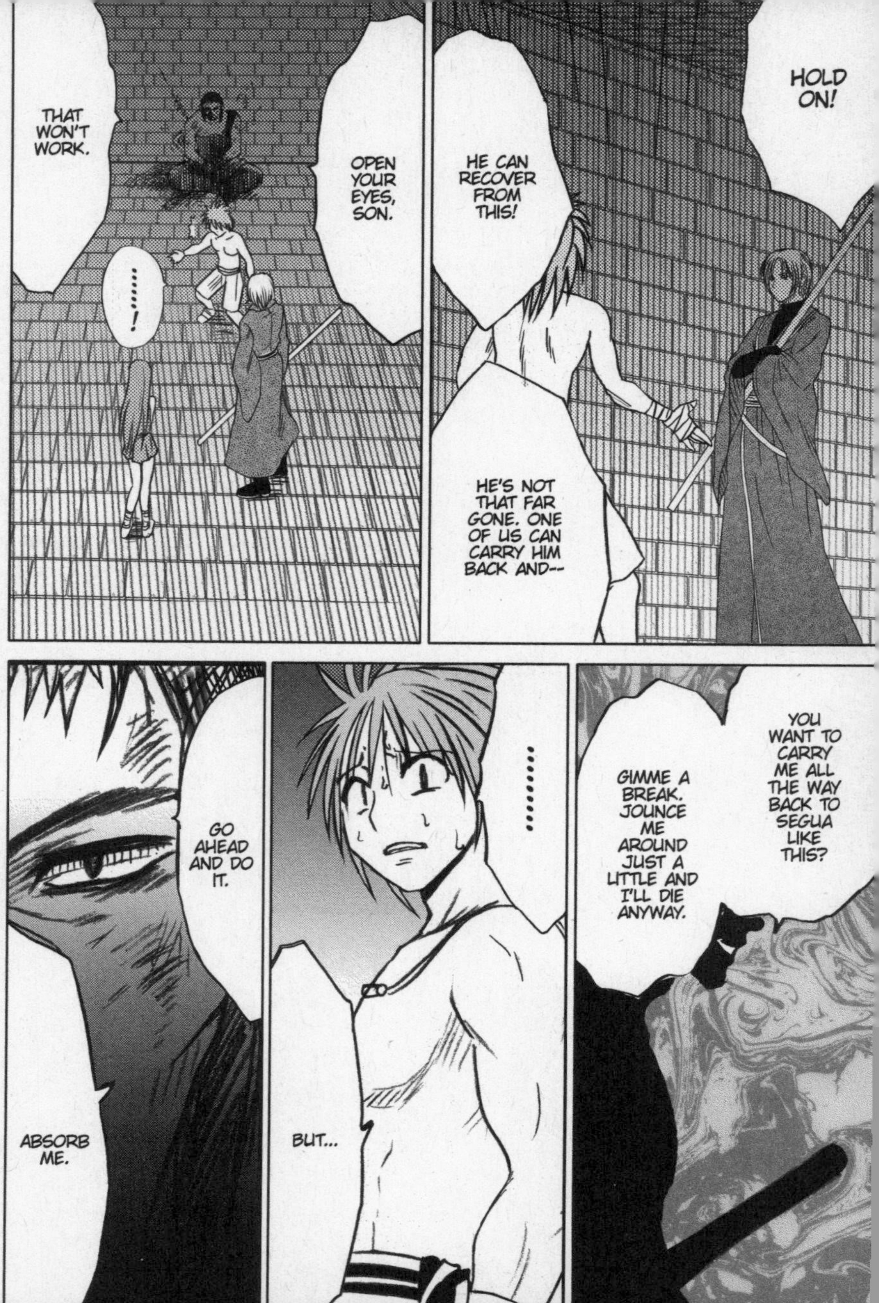
HOLD ON!
HE CAN RECOVER FROM THIS!
HE'S NOT THAT FAR GONE. ONE OF US CAN CARRY HIM BACK AND--
OPEN YOUR EYES, SON.
THAT WON'T WORK.
......!
YOU WANT TO CARRY ME ALL THE WAY BACK TO SEGUA LIKE THIS?
GIMME A BREAK. JOUNCE ME AROUND JUST A LITTLE AND I'LL DIE ANYWAY.
....
BUT...
GO AHEAD AND DO IT.
ABSORB ME.

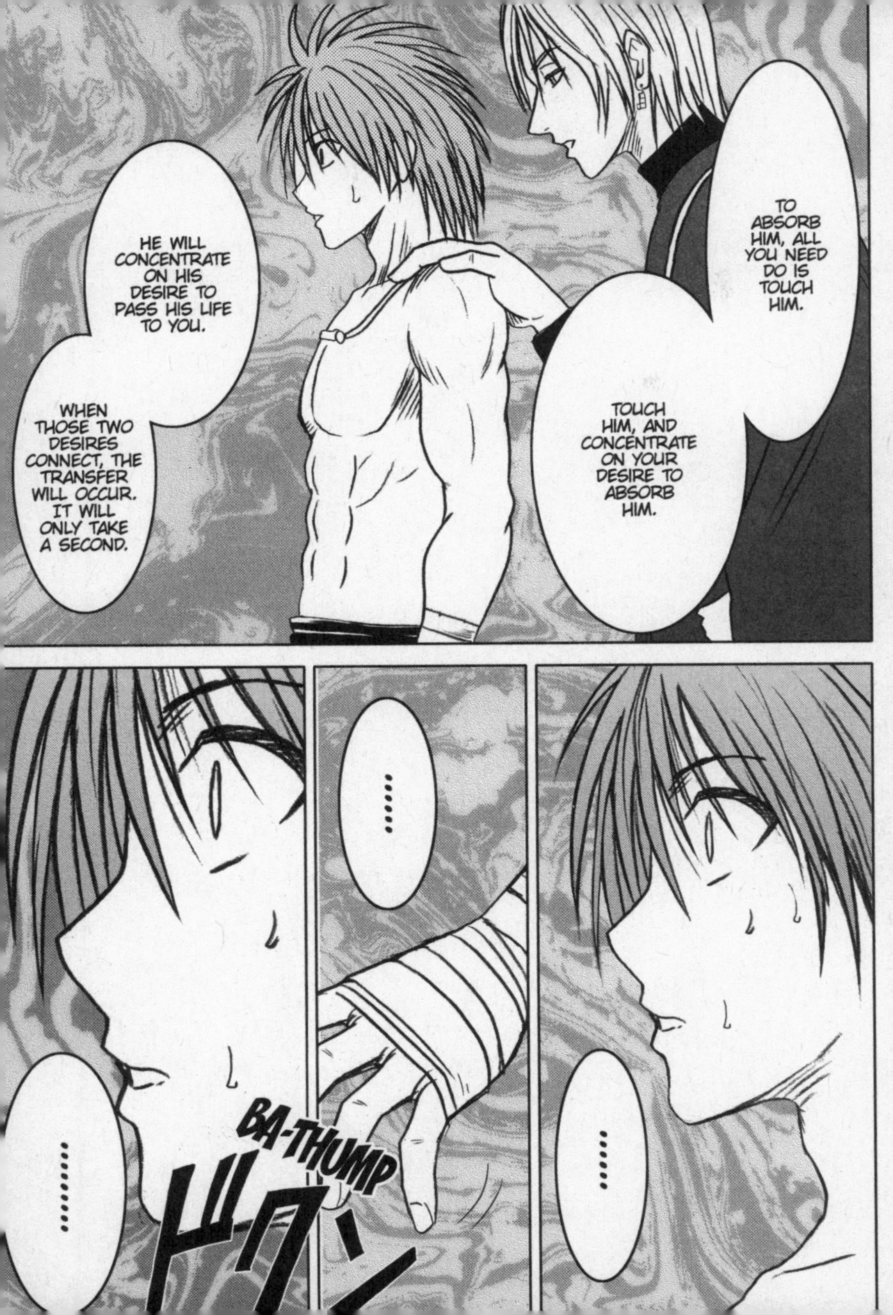
TO ABSORB HIM, ALL YOU NEED DO IS TOUCH HIM.
TOUCH HIM, AND CONCENTRATE ON YOUR DESIRE TO ABSORB HIM.
HE WILL CONCENTRATE ON HIS DESIRE TO PASS HIS LIFE TO YOU.
WHEN THOSE TWO DESIRES CONNECT, THE TRANSFER WILL OCCUR. IT WILL ONLY TAKE A SECOND.
......
......
......
BA-THUMP
ドクン

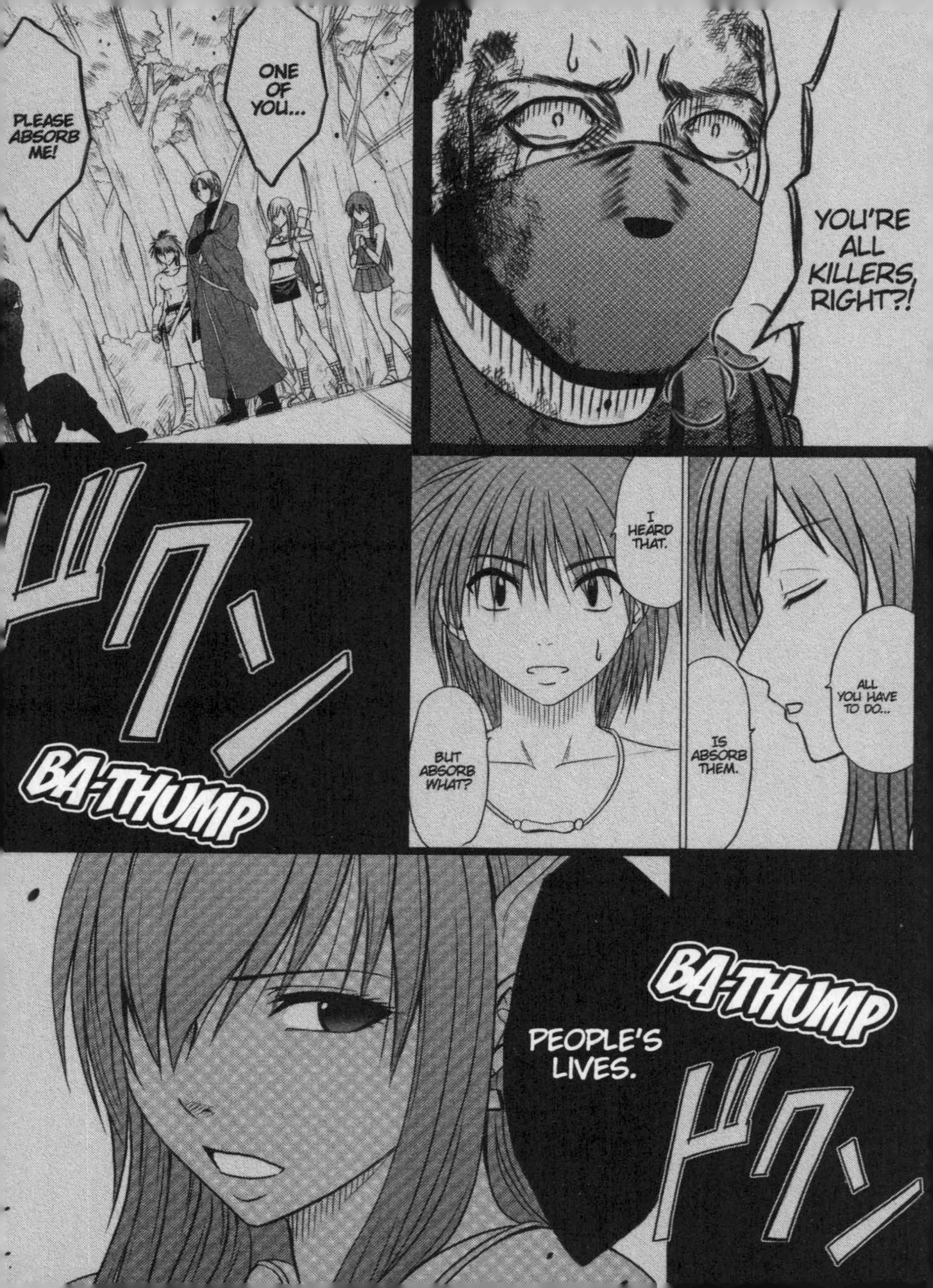
YOU'RE ALL KILLERS, RIGHT?!
ONE OF YOU...
PLEASE ABSORB ME!
ALL YOU HAVE TO DO...
IS ABSORB THEM.
I HEARD THAT.
BUT ABSORB WHAT?
BA-THUMP
BA-THUMP
PEOPLE'S LIVES.

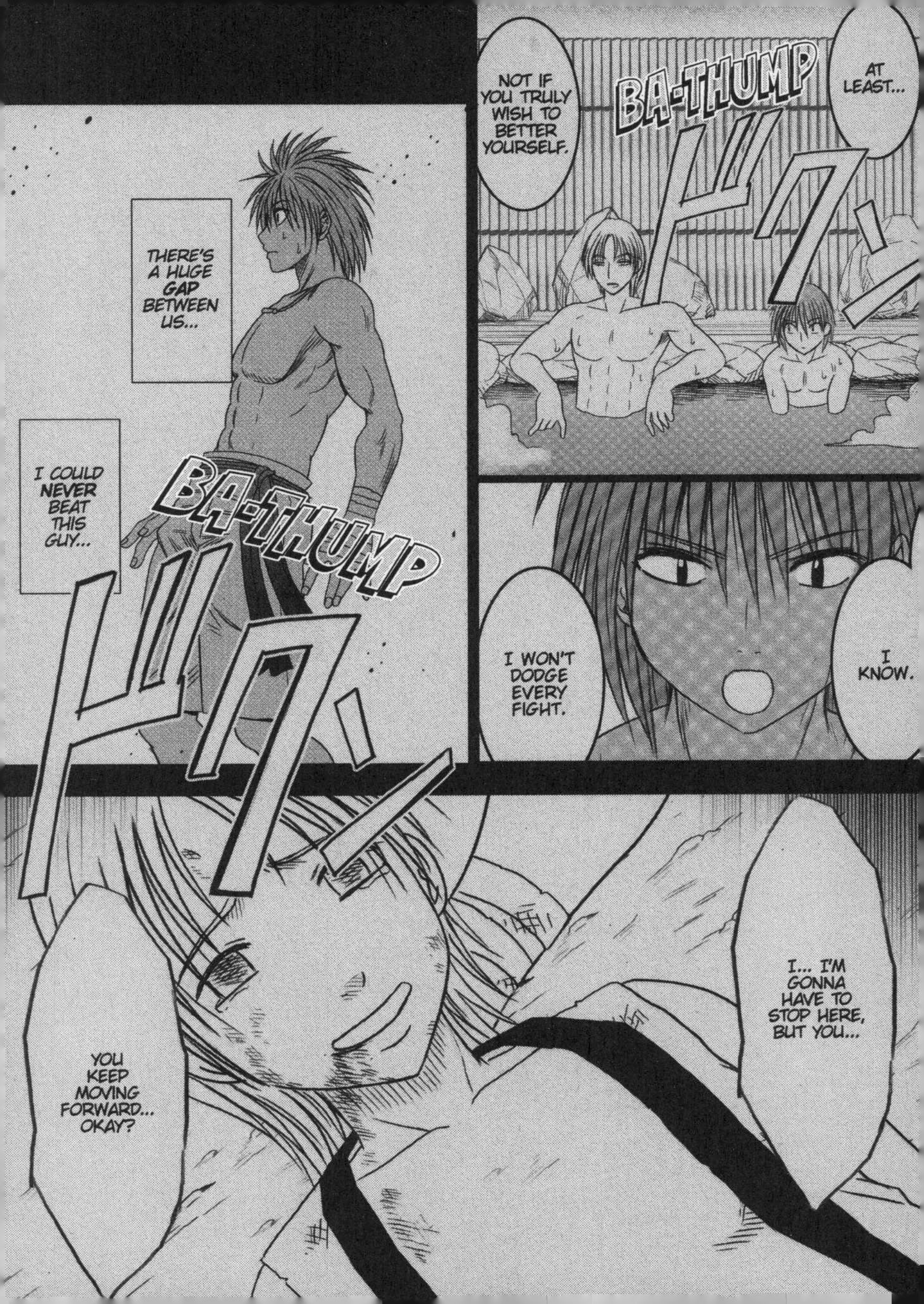
AT LEAST...
BA-THUMP
NOT IF YOU TRULY WISH TO BETTER YOURSELF.
I KNOW.
I WON'T DODGE EVERY FIGHT.
THERE'S A HUGE GAP BETWEEN US...
I COULD NEVER BEAT THIS GUY...
BA-THUMP
I... I'M GONNA HAVE TO STOP HERE, BUT YOU...
YOU KEEP MOVING FORWARD... OKAY?

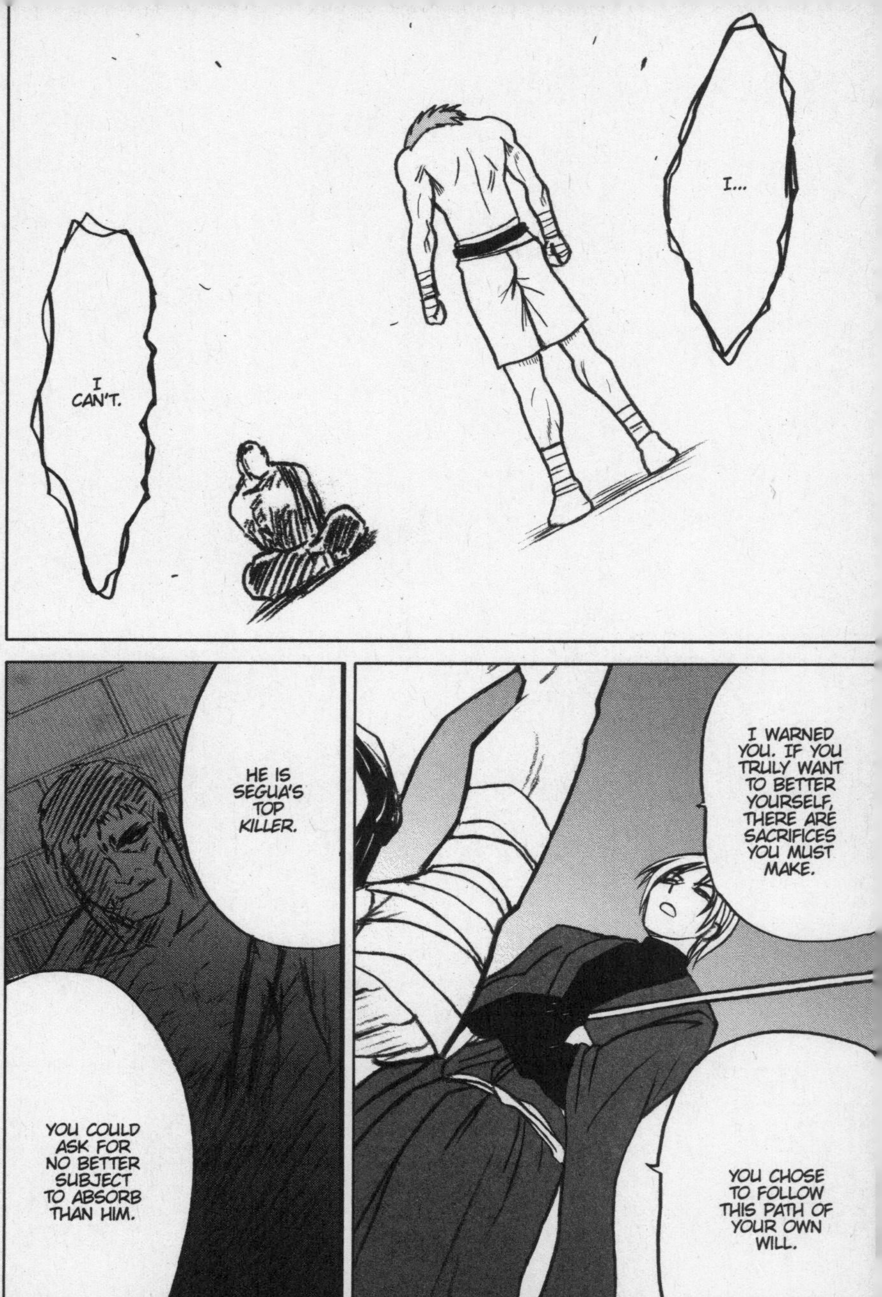
I...
I CAN'T.
I WARNED YOU. IF YOU TRULY WANT TO BETTER YOURSELF, THERE ARE SACRIFICES YOU MUST MAKE.
YOU CHOSE TO FOLLOW THIS PATH OF YOUR OWN WILL.
HE IS SEGUA'S TOP KILLER.
YOU COULD ASK FOR NO BETTER SUBJECT TO ABSORB THAN HIM.

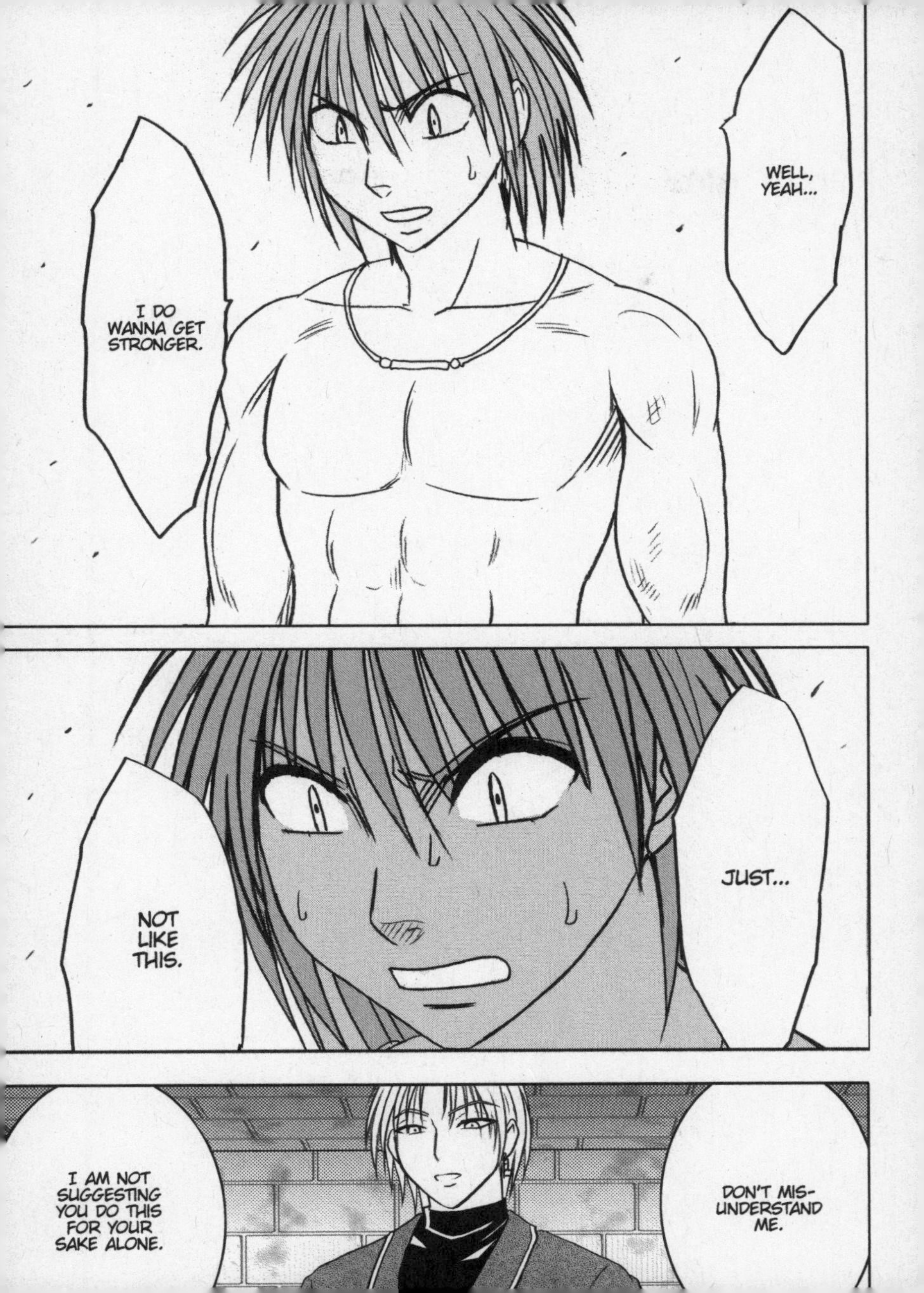
WELL, YEAH...
I DO WANNA GET STRONGER.
JUST...
NOT LIKE THIS.
DON'T MIS-UNDERSTAND ME.
I AM NOT SUGGESTING YOU DO THIS FOR YOUR SAKE ALONE.

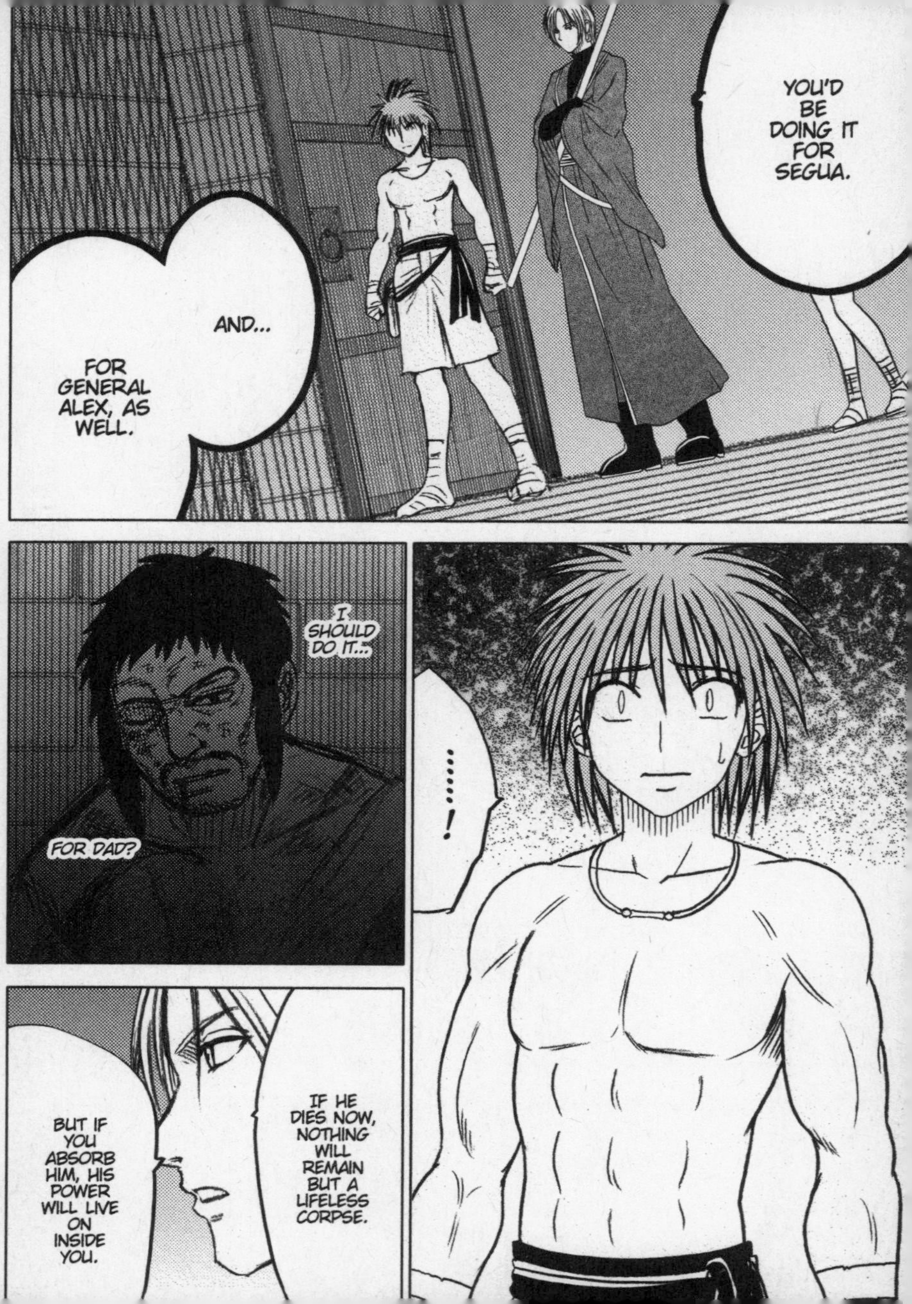
YOU'D BE DOING IT FOR SEGUA.
AND... FOR GENERAL ALEX, AS WELL.
......!
I SHOULD DO IT...
FOR DAD?
IF HE DIES NOW, NOTHING WILL REMAIN BUT A LIFELESS CORPSE.
BUT IF YOU ABSORB HIM, HIS POWER WILL LIVE ON INSIDE YOU.

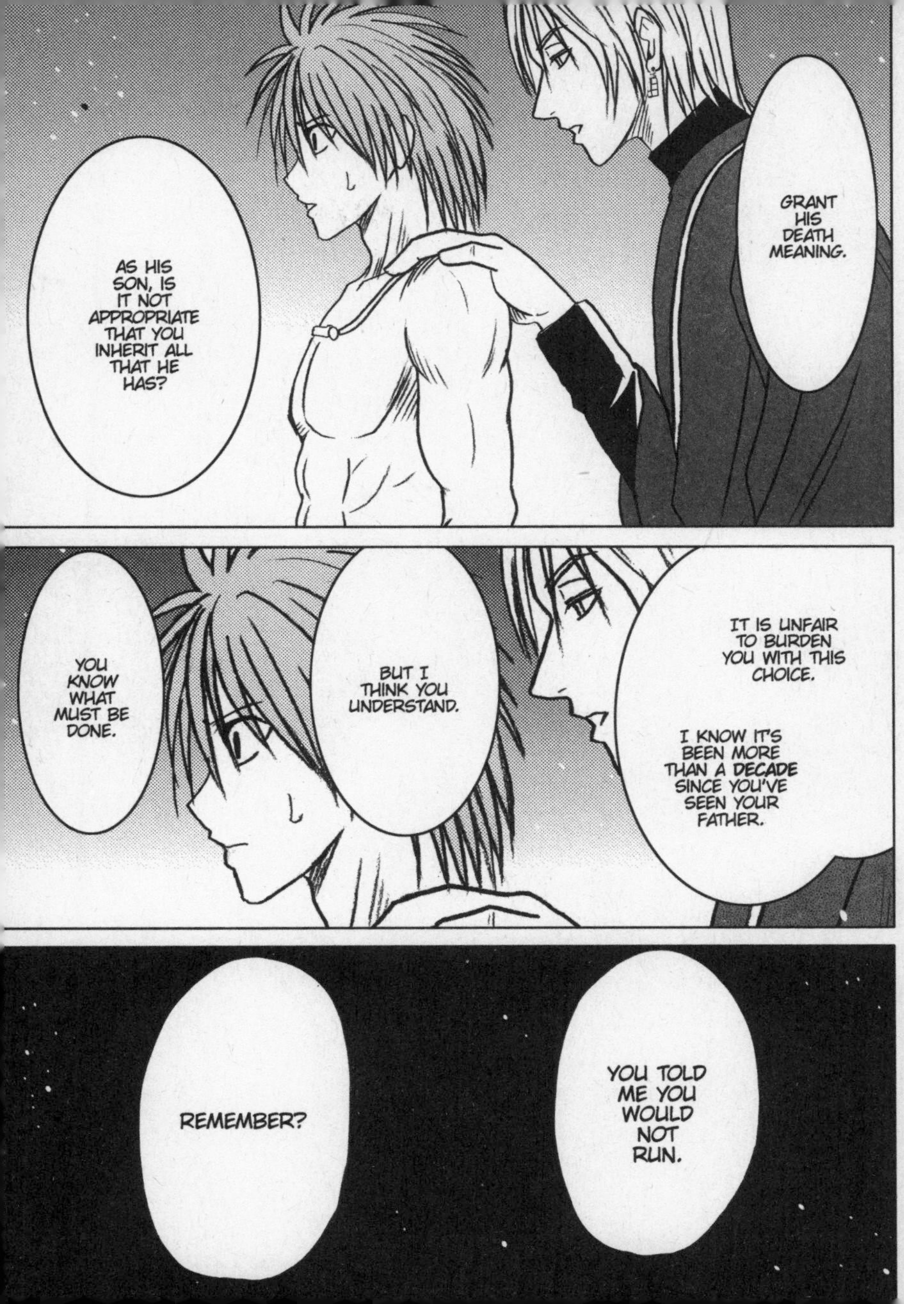
GRANT HIS DEATH MEANING.
AS HIS SON, IS IT NOT APPROPRIATE THAT YOU INHERIT ALL THAT HE HAS?
IT IS UNFAIR TO BURDEN YOU WITH THIS CHOICE.
I KNOW IT'S BEEN MORE THAN A DECADE SINCE YOU'VE SEEN YOUR FATHER.
BUT I THINK YOU UNDERSTAND.
YOU KNOW WHAT MUST BE DONE.
YOU TOLD ME YOU WOULD NOT RUN.
REMEMBER?

FOR SEGUA.

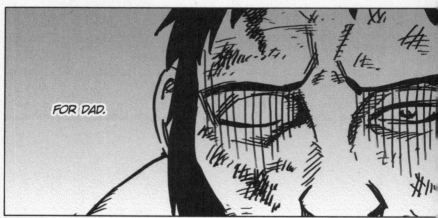

FOR DAD.

THERE ARE
TIMES WHEN YOU
HAVE TO SET
YOUR FEELINGS
ASIDE...

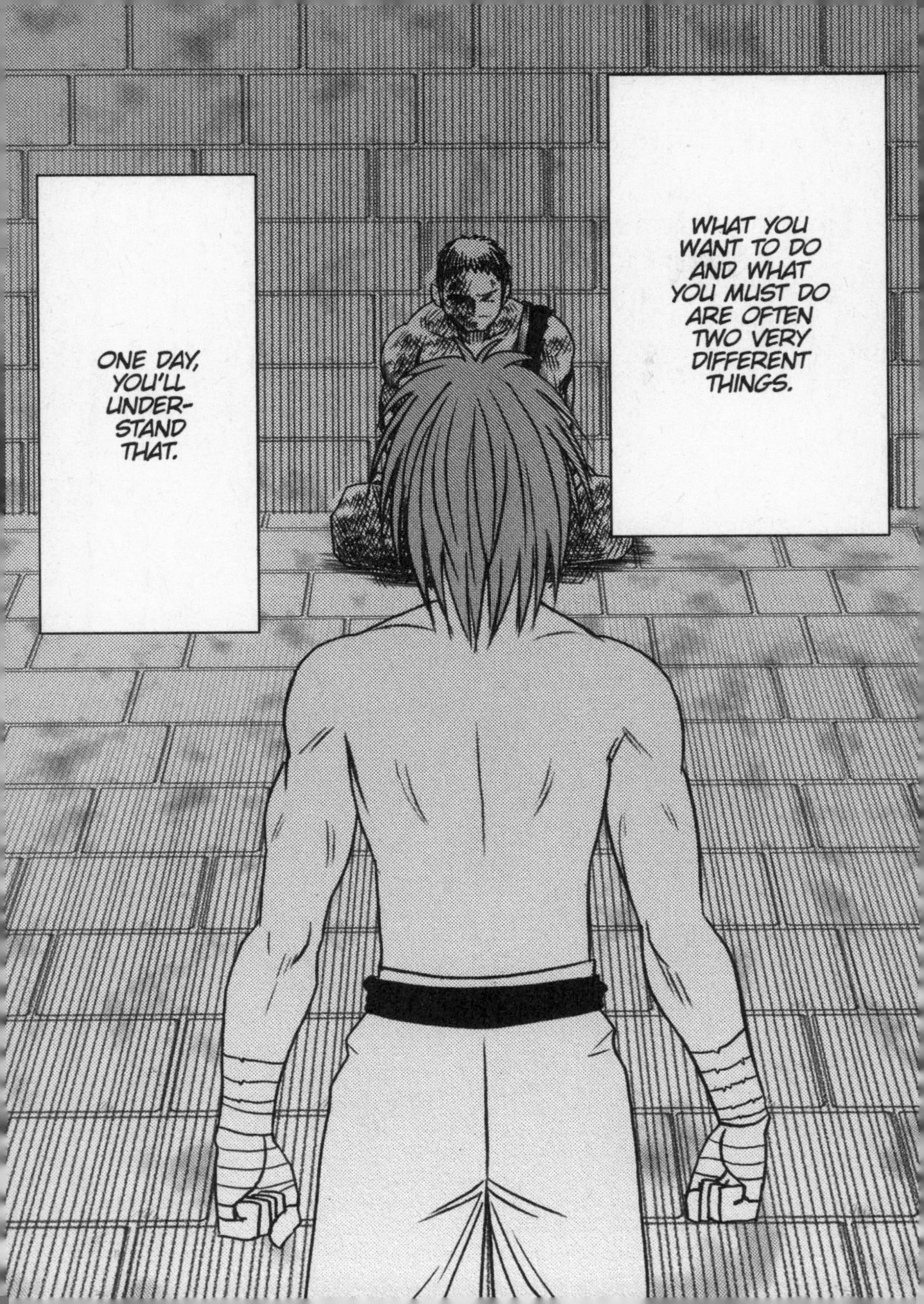
WHAT YOU WANT TO DO AND WHAT YOU MUST DO ARE OFTEN TWO VERY DIFFERENT THINGS.
ONE DAY, YOU'LL UNDER-STAND THAT.

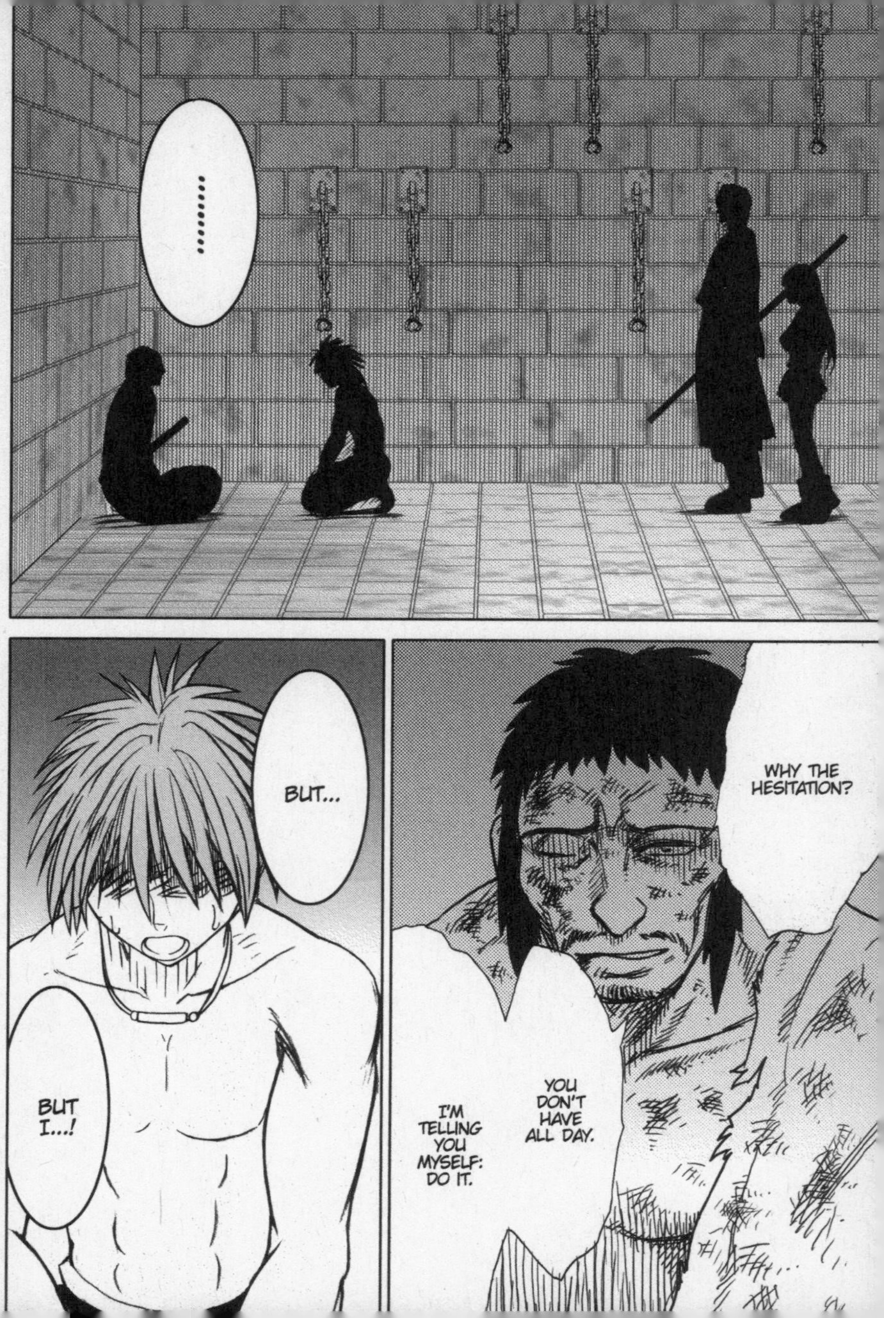
......
WHY THE HESITATION?
YOU DON'T HAVE ALL DAY.
I'M TELLING YOU MYSELF: DO IT.
BUT...
BUT I...!

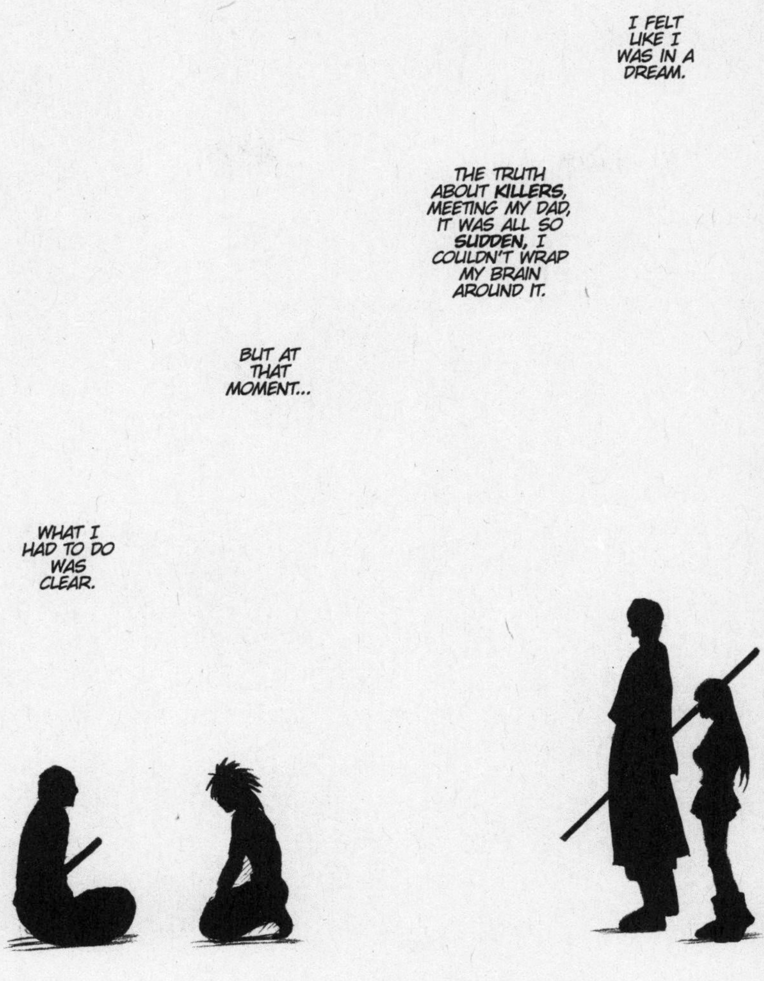
I FELT LIKE I WAS IN A DREAM.
THE TRUTH ABOUT **KILLERS**, MEETING MY DAD, IT WAS ALL SO **SUDDEN**, I COULDN'T WRAP MY BRAIN AROUND IT.
BUT AT THAT MOMENT...
WHAT I HAD TO DO WAS CLEAR.

I'M SO RELIEVED... TO FIND OUT YOU'RE STILL ALIVE.

HA HA...

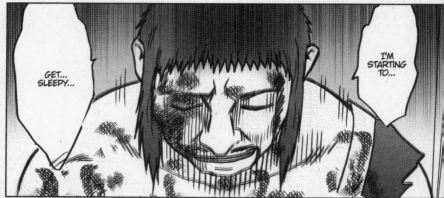

GET... SLEEPY...

I'M STARTING TO...

ド'シ'ヤ
GRAB

DAD ?!

......!

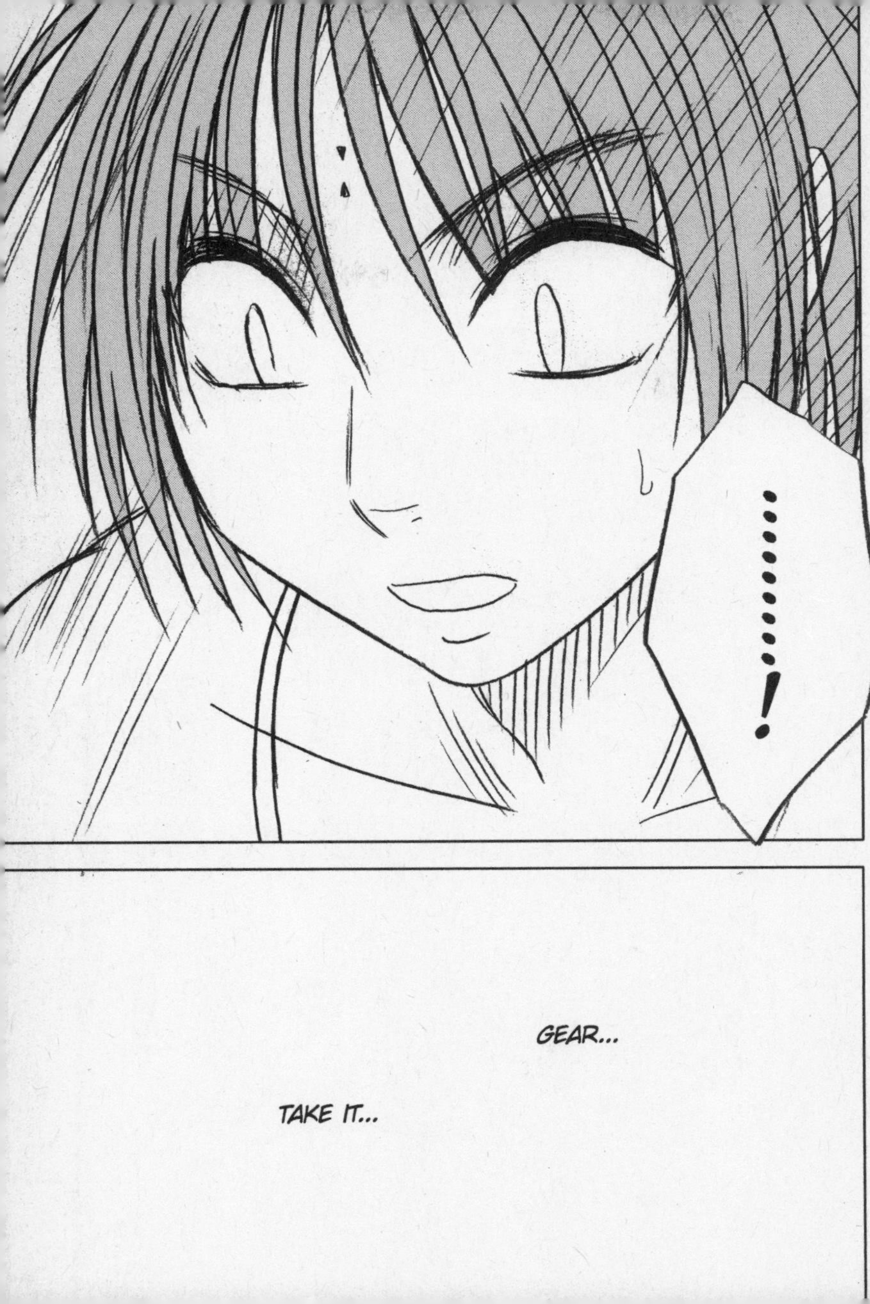
......!
GEAR...
TAKE IT...

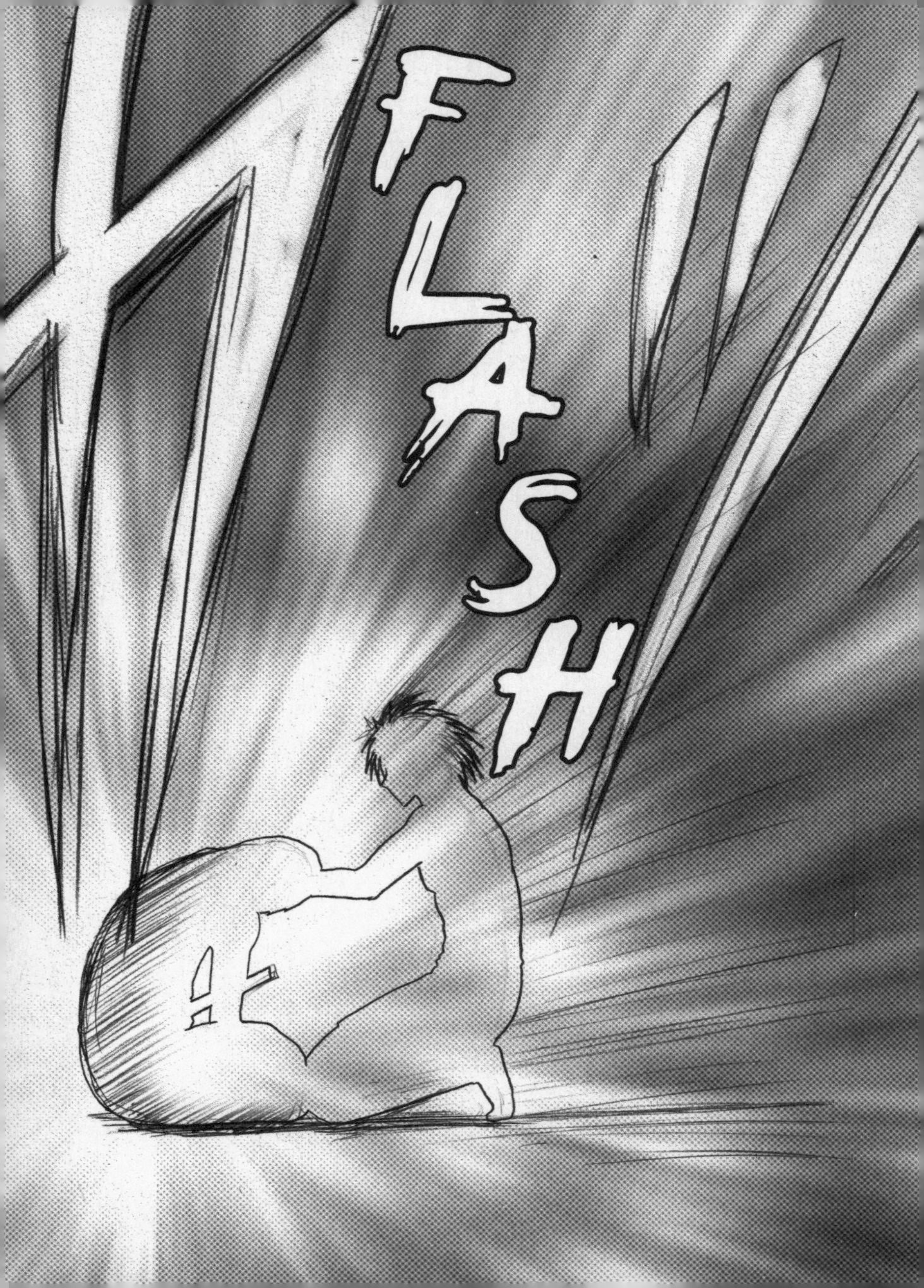
FLASH
!!

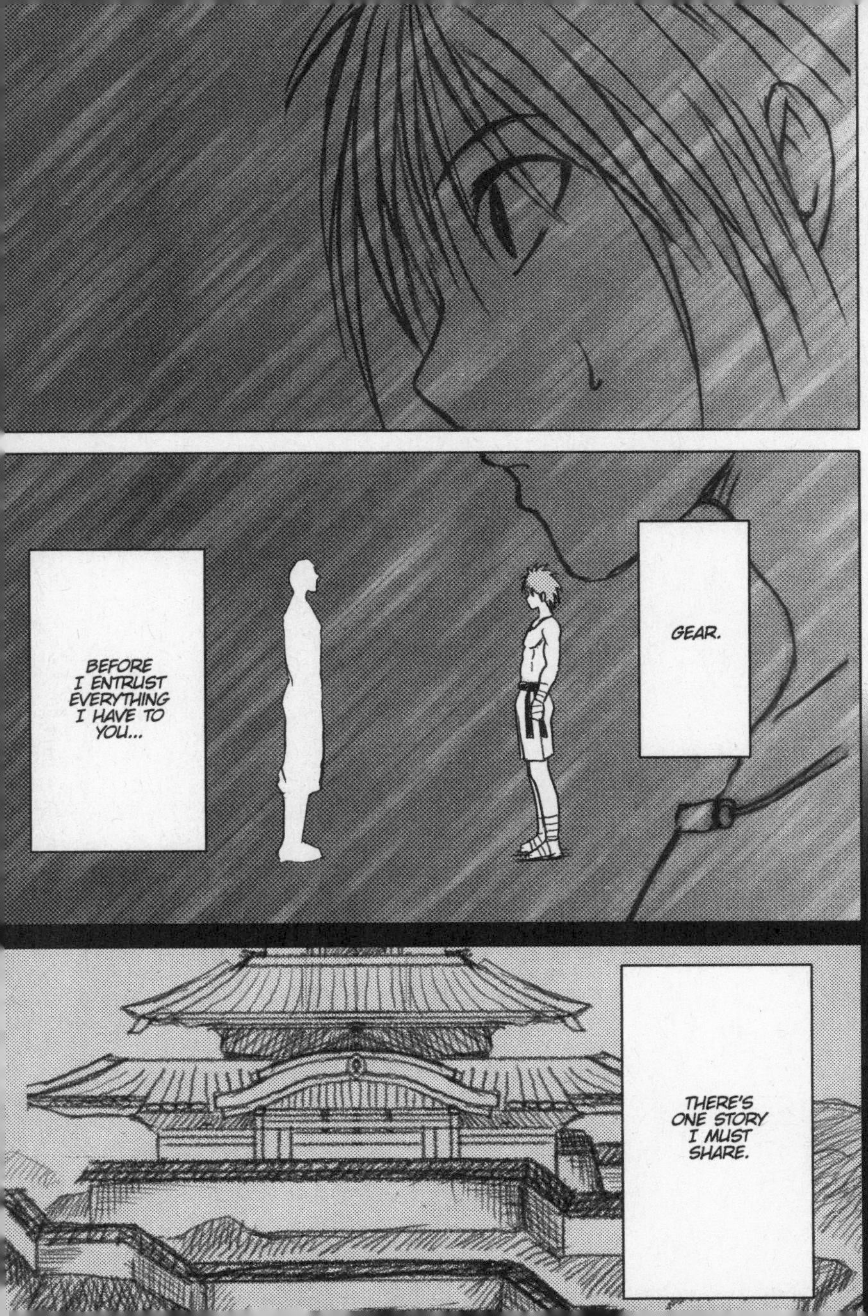
GEAR.
BEFORE I ENTRUST EVERYTHING I HAVE TO YOU...
THERE'S ONE STORY I MUST SHARE.

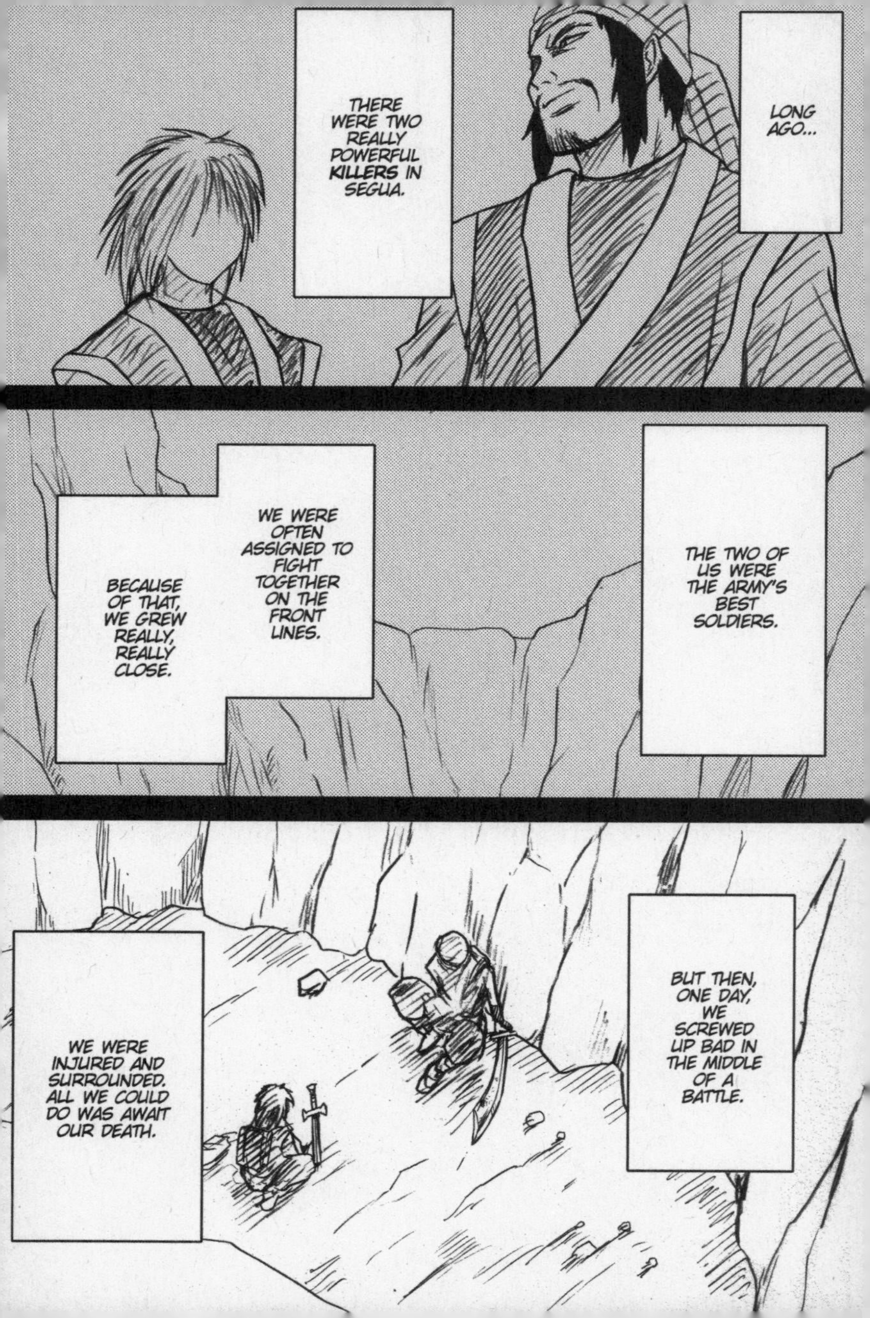
LONG AGO...
THERE WERE TWO REALLY POWERFUL **KILLERS** IN SEGUA.
THE TWO OF US WERE THE ARMY'S BEST SOLDIERS.
WE WERE OFTEN ASSIGNED TO FIGHT TOGETHER ON THE FRONT LINES.
BECAUSE OF THAT, WE GREW REALLY, REALLY CLOSE.
BUT THEN, ONE DAY, WE SCREWED UP BAD IN THE MIDDLE OF A BATTLE.
WE WERE INJURED AND SURROUNDED. ALL WE COULD DO WAS AWAIT OUR DEATH.

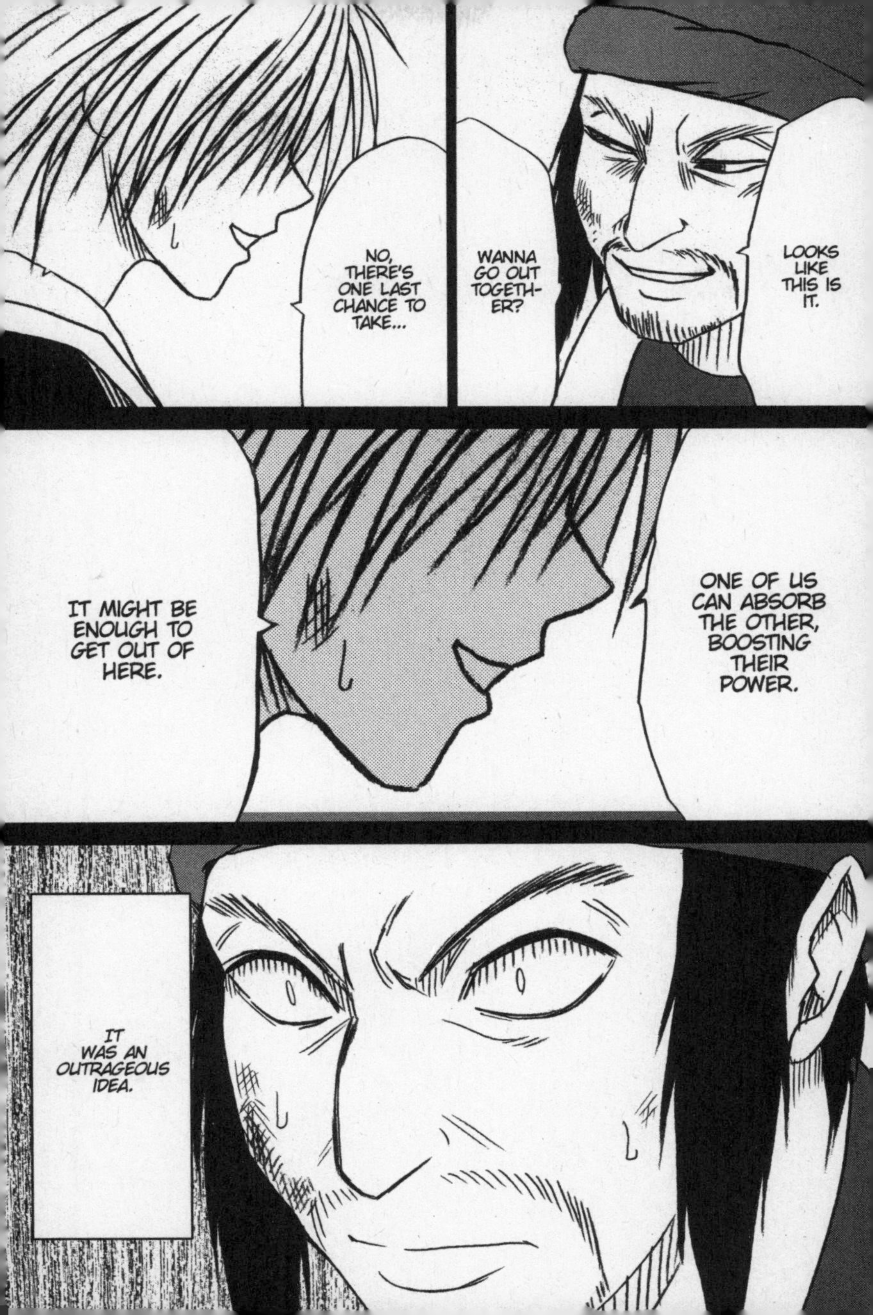
LOOKS LIKE THIS IS IT.
WANNA GO OUT TOGETHER?
NO, THERE'S ONE LAST CHANCE TO TAKE...
ONE OF US CAN ABSORB THE OTHER, BOOSTING THEIR POWER.
IT MIGHT BE ENOUGH TO GET OUT OF HERE.
IT WAS AN OUTRAGEOUS IDEA.

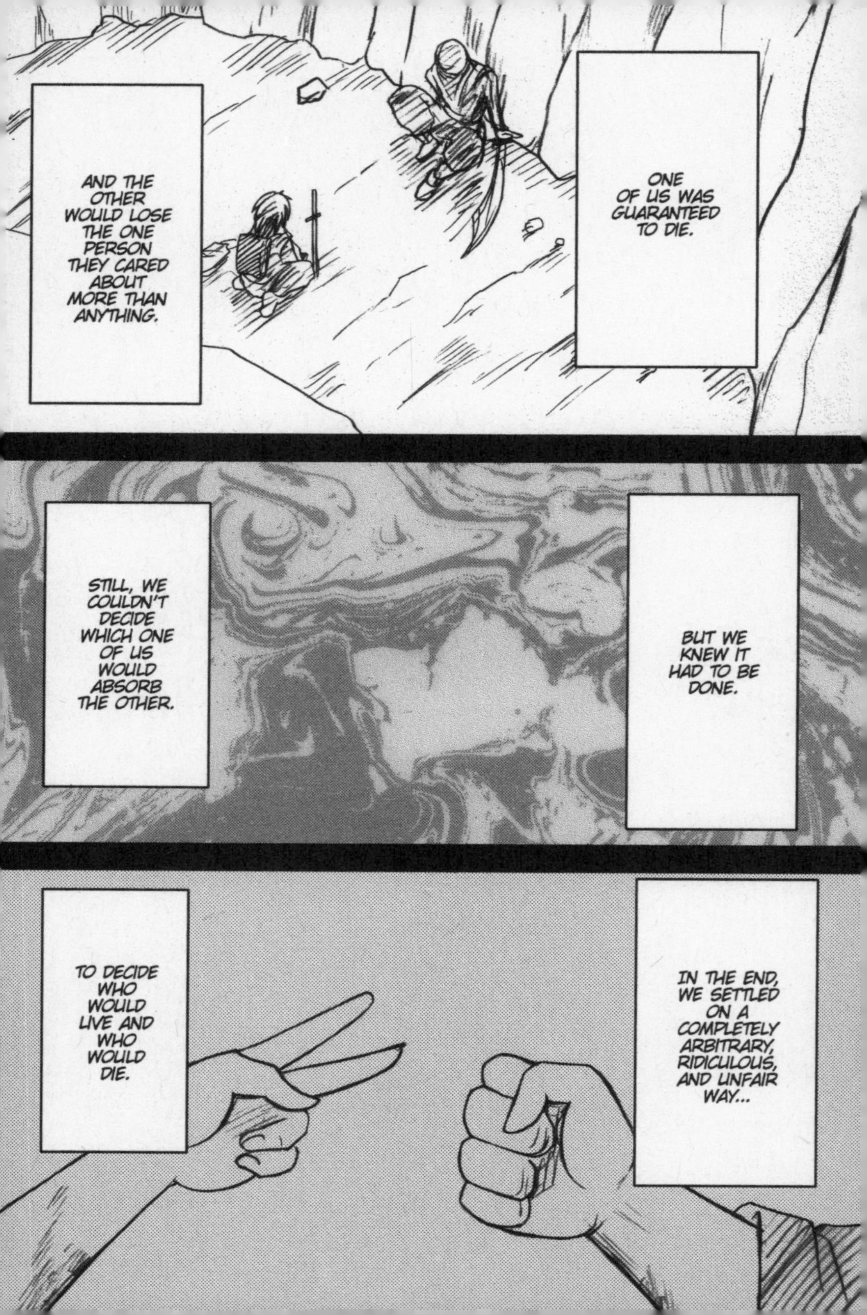
ONE OF US WAS GUARANTEED TO DIE.
AND THE OTHER WOULD LOSE THE ONE PERSON THEY CARED ABOUT MORE THAN ANYTHING.
BUT WE KNEW IT HAD TO BE DONE.
STILL, WE COULDN'T DECIDE WHICH ONE OF US WOULD ABSORB THE OTHER.
IN THE END, WE SETTLED ON A COMPLETELY ARBITRARY, RIDICULOUS, AND UNFAIR WAY...
TO DECIDE WHO WOULD LIVE AND WHO WOULD DIE.

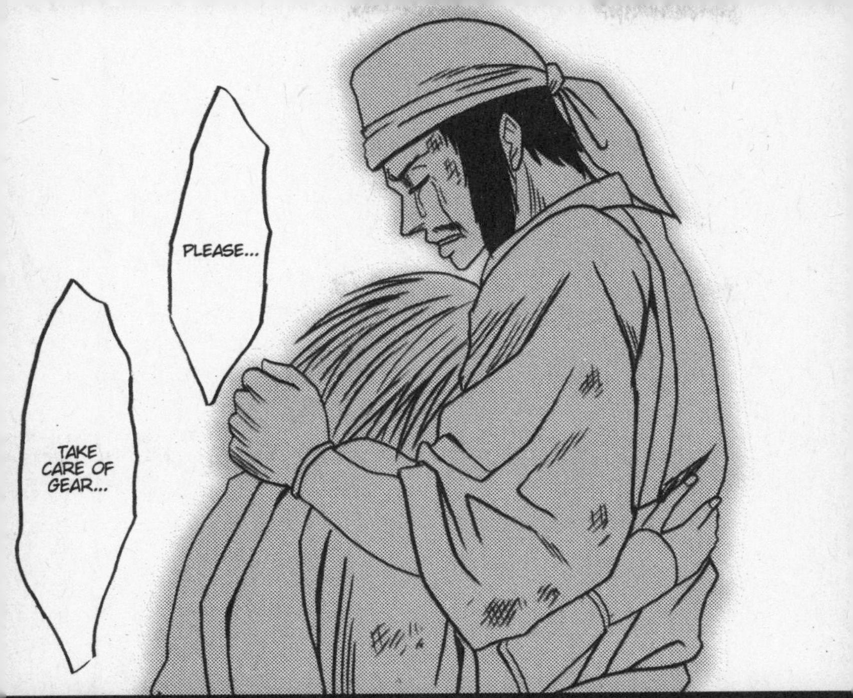
PLEASE...
TAKE CARE OF GEAR...

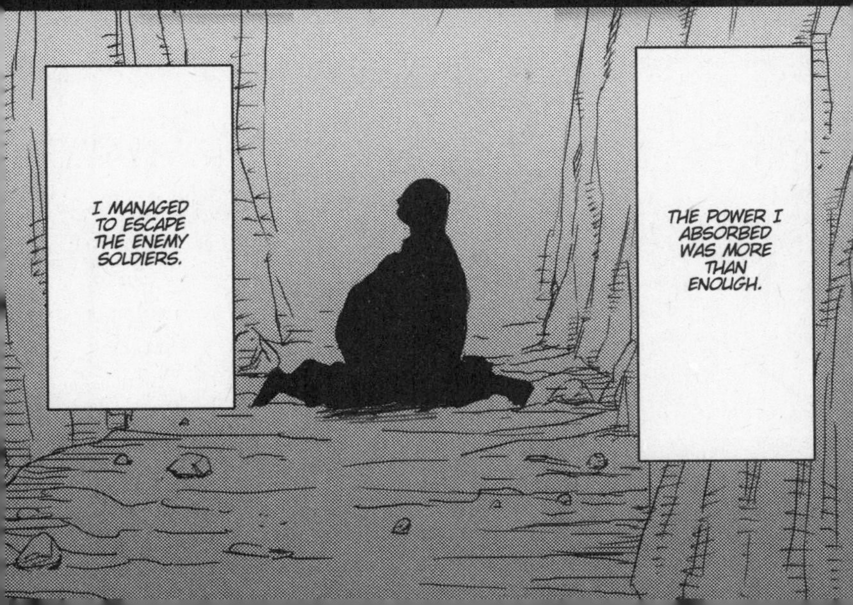
THE POWER I ABSORBED WAS MORE THAN ENOUGH.
I MANAGED TO ESCAPE THE ENEMY SOLDIERS.

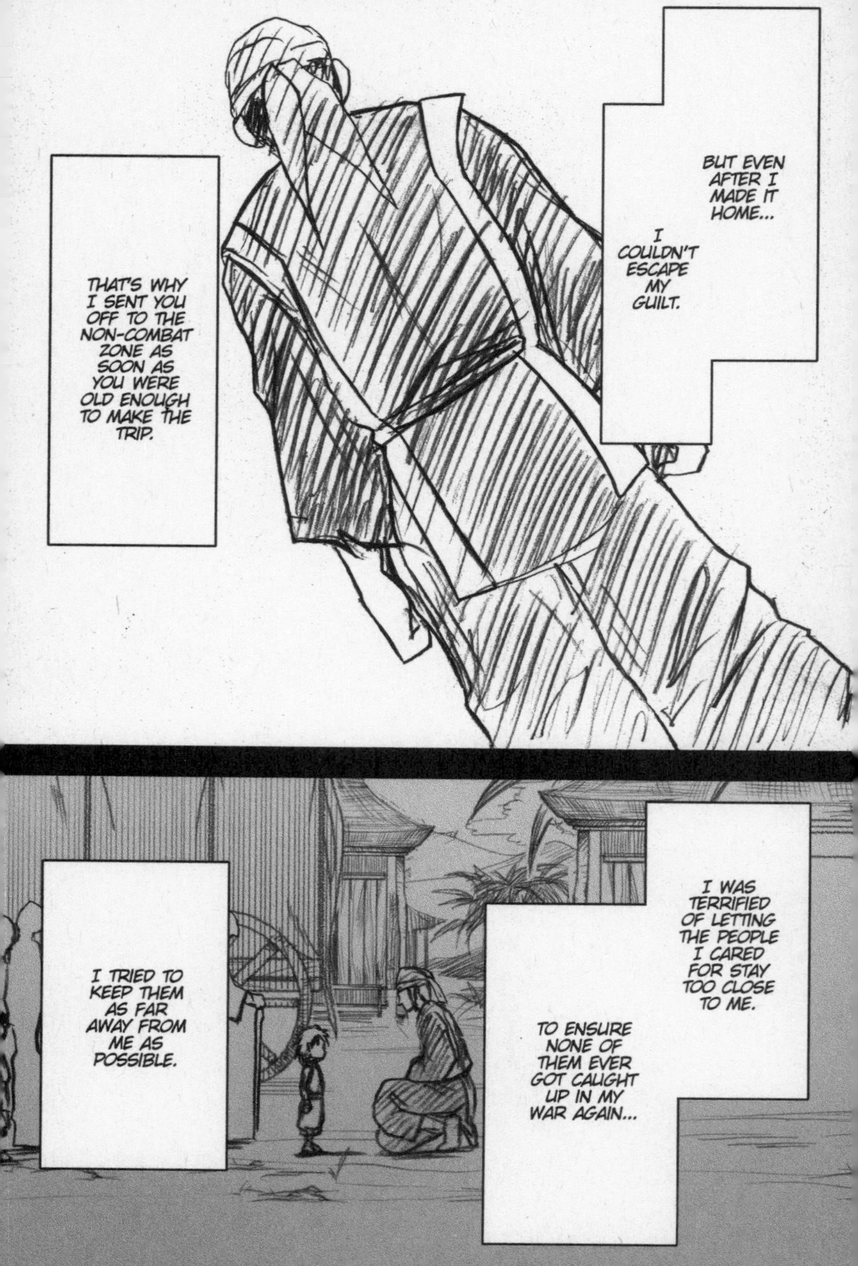
BUT EVEN AFTER I MADE IT HOME...
I COULDN'T ESCAPE MY GUILT.
THAT'S WHY I SENT YOU OFF TO THE NON-COMBAT ZONE AS SOON AS YOU WERE OLD ENOUGH TO MAKE THE TRIP.
I WAS TERRIFIED OF LETTING THE PEOPLE I CARED FOR STAY TOO CLOSE TO ME.
TO ENSURE NONE OF THEM EVER GOT CAUGHT UP IN MY WAR AGAIN...
I TRIED TO KEEP THEM AS FAR AWAY FROM ME AS POSSIBLE.

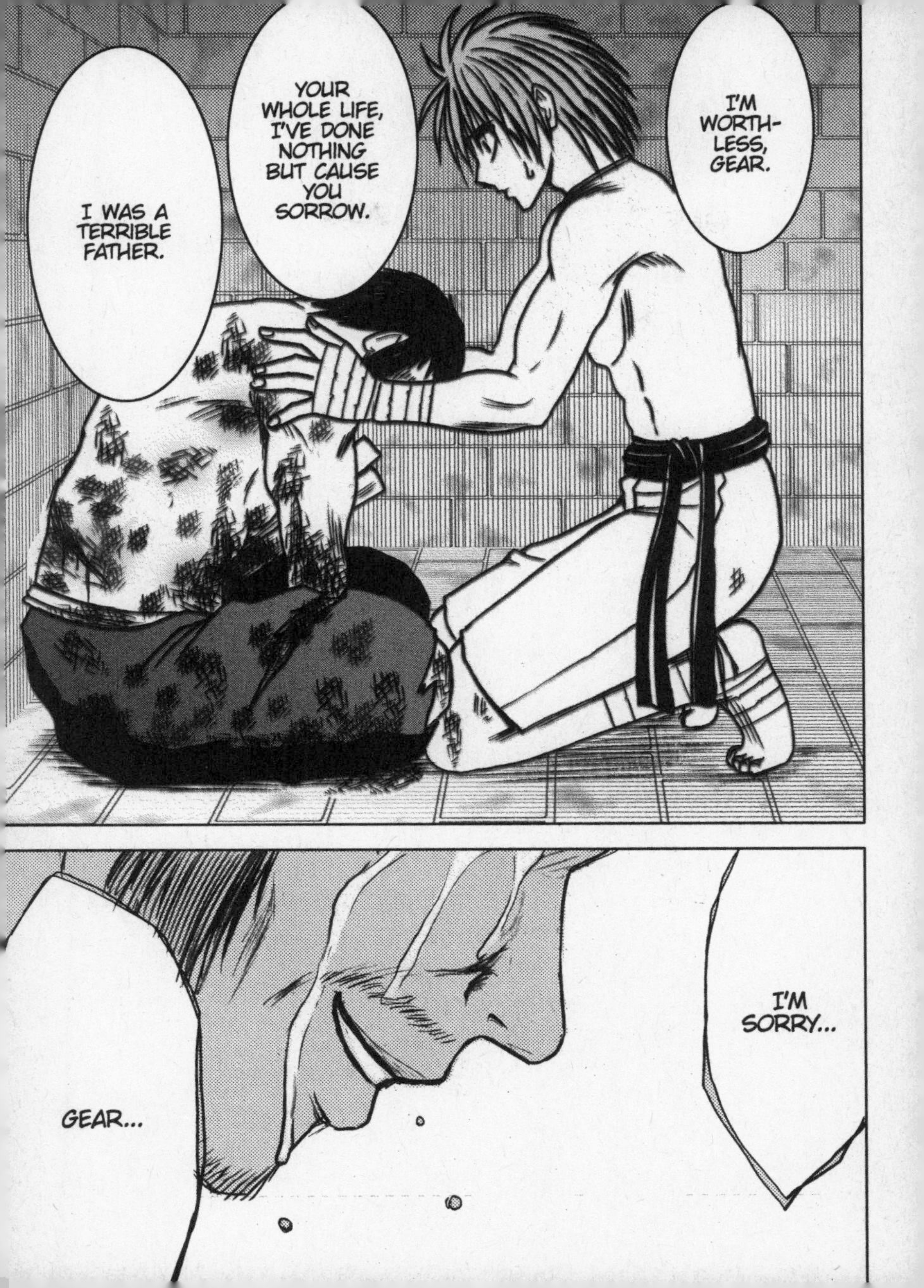
I'M WORTH-LESS, GEAR.
YOUR WHOLE LIFE, I'VE DONE NOTHING BUT CAUSE YOU SORROW.
I WAS A TERRIBLE FATHER.
I'M SORRY...
GEAR...

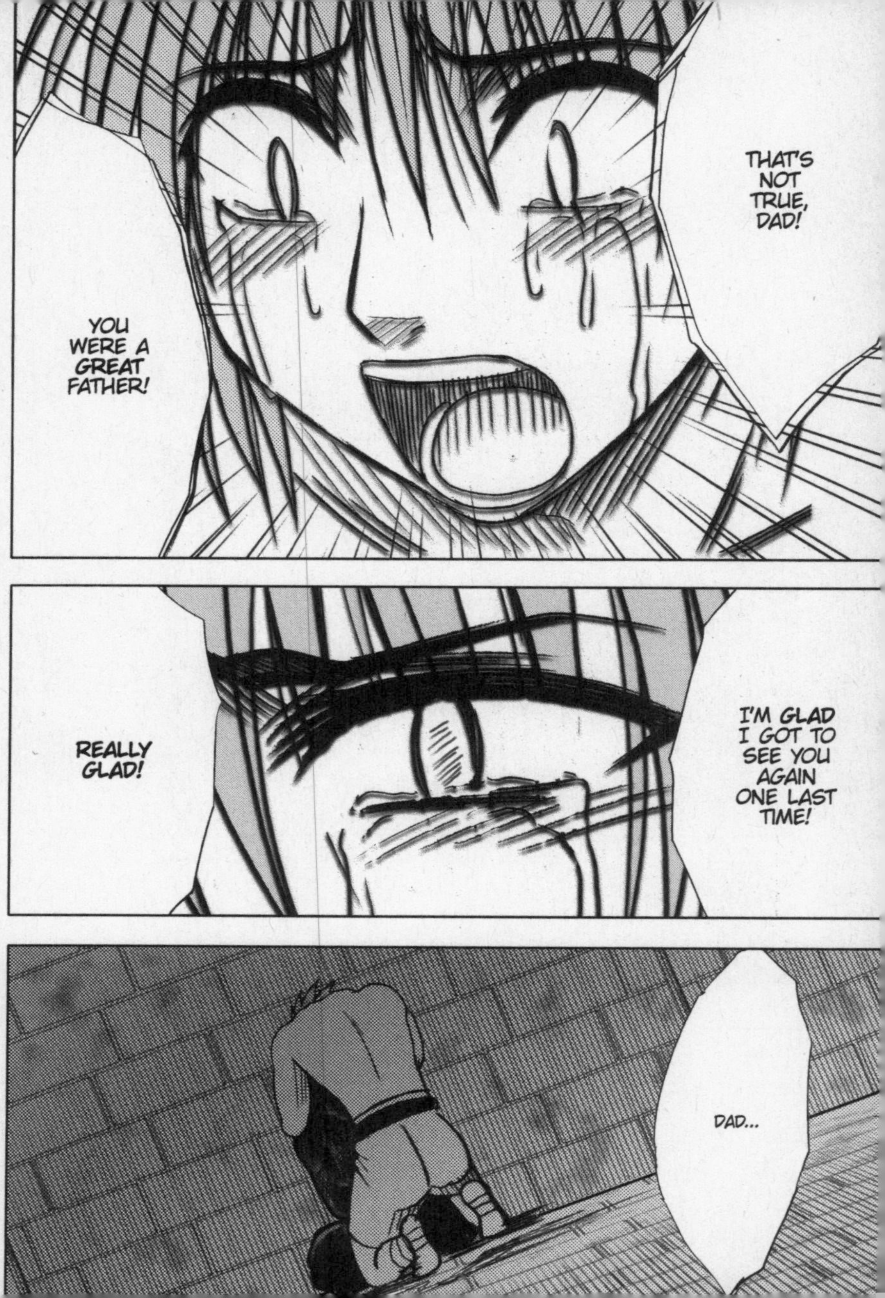
THAT'S NOT TRUE, DAD!
YOU WERE A GREAT FATHER!
I'M GLAD I GOT TO SEE YOU AGAIN ONE LAST TIME!
REALLY GLAD!
DAD...

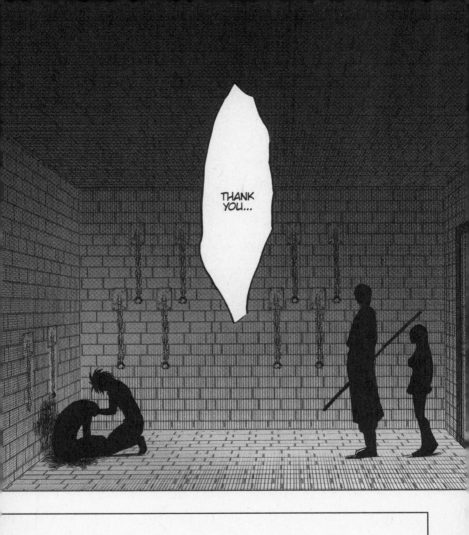

THANK
YOU...

THAT DAY, I ABSORBED MY FATHER.

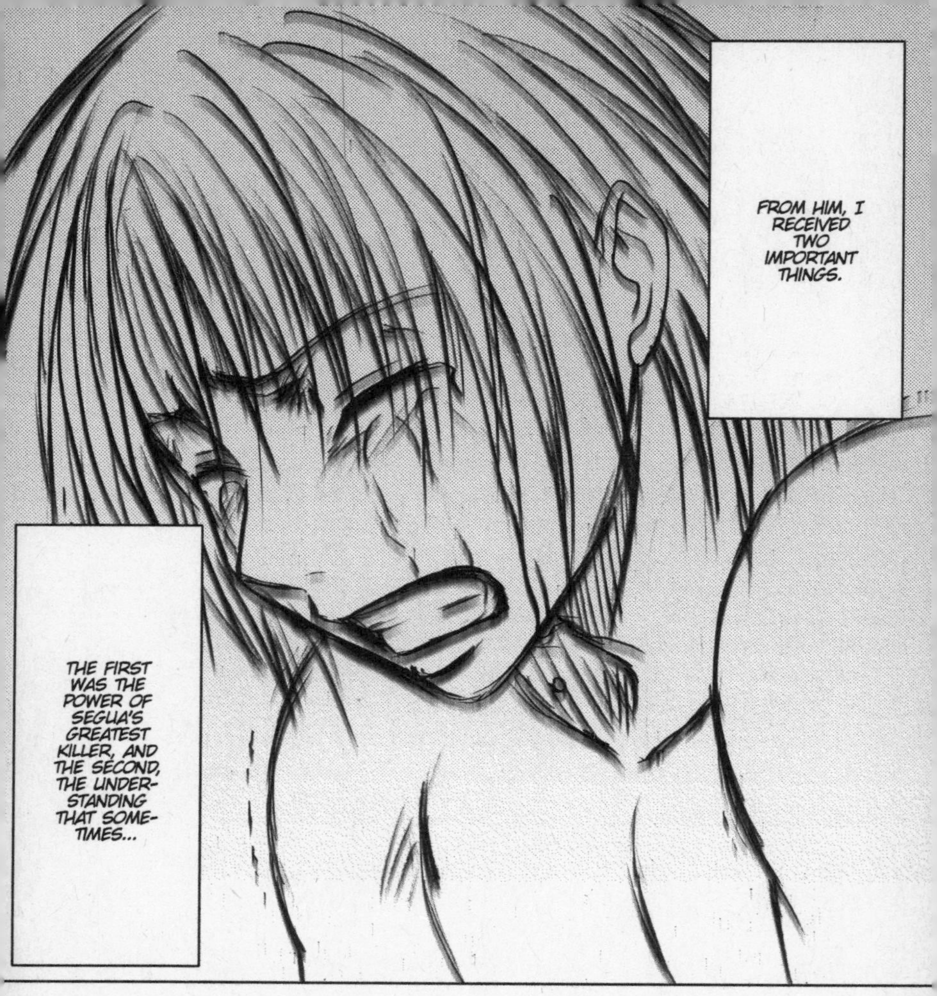
FROM HIM, I RECEIVED TWO IMPORTANT THINGS.
THE FIRST WAS THE POWER OF SEGUA'S GREATEST KILLER, AND THE SECOND, THE UNDER-STANDING THAT SOME-TIMES...
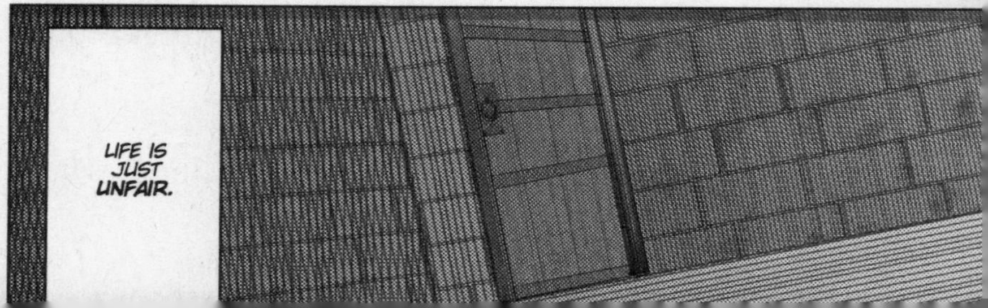
LIFE IS JUST **UNFAIR.**

WORLD WAR BLUE

CHARACTER INTRODUCTION

The Cursed Brothers

VAIZ & VOIZ

Years ago, these Tatrand natives voluntarily accepted the "Curse of the Dragon" to give themselves the power to rescue their lovers, who were trapped at the bottom of a cave 100 floors deep. However, by the time the brothers arrived at the bottom of the cave, their lovers were already dead.

Since then, Vaiz has taken up blowing soap bubbles as fragile as the lives they lost that day, and Voiz has taken up drinking.

Both carry a weapon called a "Rainbow Sickle." Swinging it releases an attack called a *Dragon Bite*.

The elder brother Vaiz is the more powerful fighter, but younger brother Voiz is the one more prone to violence.

Author Comment

I was surprised at how popular Vaiz was with the readers.

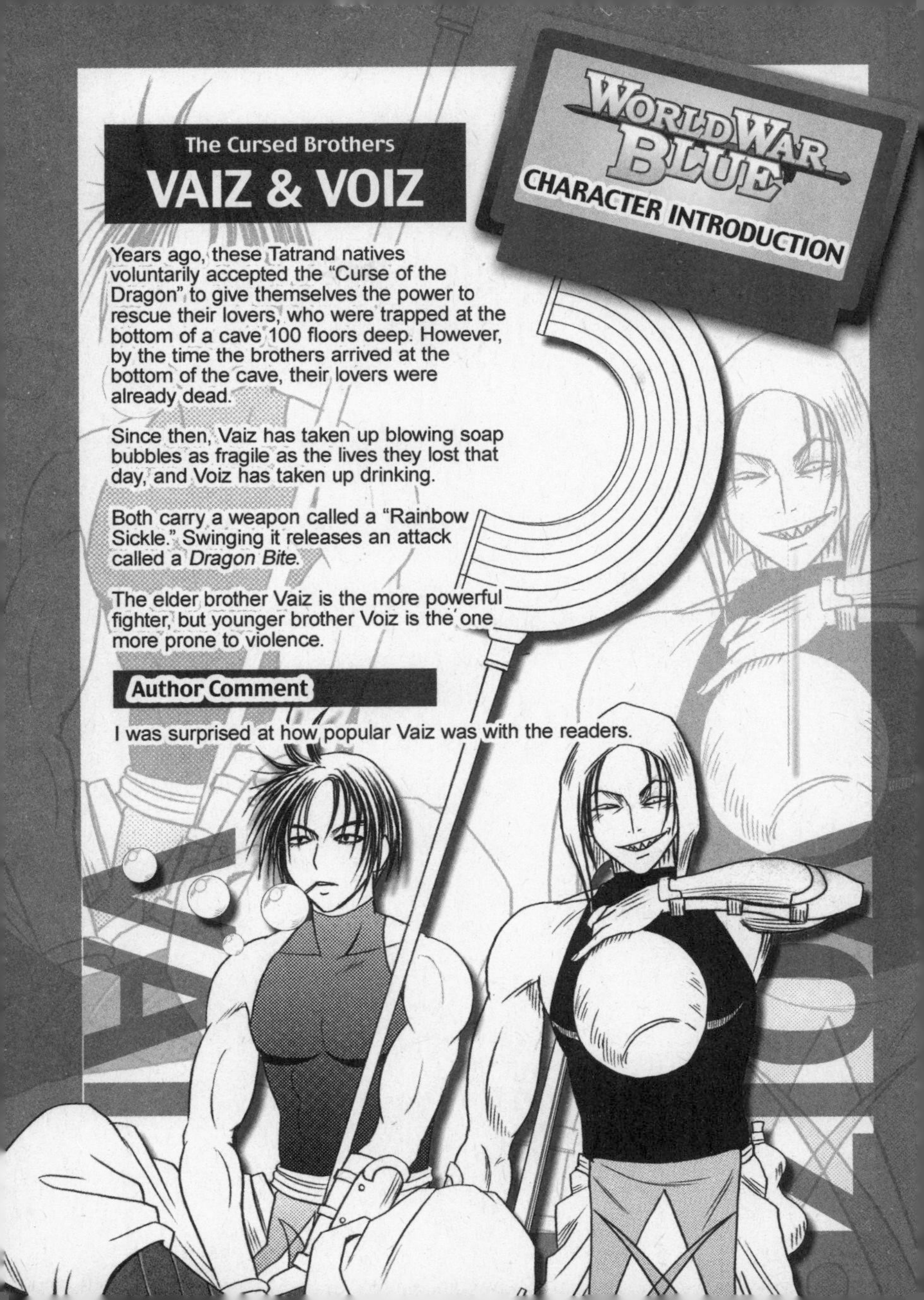

Perusing Video Game History

ON THE EDGE OF THE BLUE WORLD

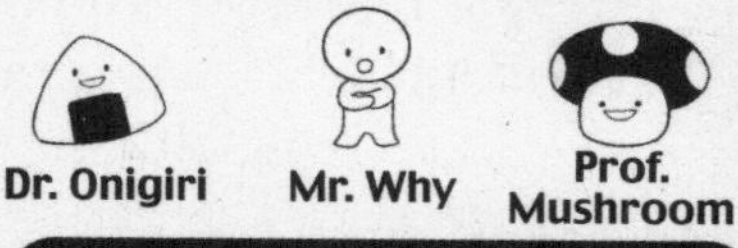
Dr. Onigiri
Mr. Why
Prof. Mushroom

Today's Topic

BUBBLE BOBBLE

Mr. Why: Okay, so I know about *Darius* now. This time, let's talk about *Bubble Bobble.* That's the game where there are colored balls stuck to the top of the screen, and you have to shoot more colored balls at them to match them and make them fall, right?

Prof. Mushroom: A lot of people think that, y'know, since that puzzle game was really popular. But that's actually a *spinoff* of the franchise, called *Puzzle Bobble.* The original *Bubble Bobble* was an action-platformer game.

Dr. Onigiri: Players controlled Bub, who had been transformed into a bubble-blowing dragon by a curse. The object is to make it through 100 stages (plus another 100 bonus stages) of a cave to rescue Bub's girlfriend. The game can be played by two players, with the second player controlling Bub's brother, Bob.

Prof. Mushroom: Yep. They really pushed the 2-player aspect of it. Heck, the catch-phrase for the game was "Let's try together!" There were loads of ways to earn points, from beating an enemy and transforming it into fruit, or catching the cake that sometimes fell from the top of the screen. One of the popular ways to beat enemies was to trap them in a bubble when they got really close, and then immediately touch them with your spikes. It looked so much like you were eating the enemies, fans started calling that attack "biting." Oh, and by the way, the final boss attacked you by throwing sake bottles at you.

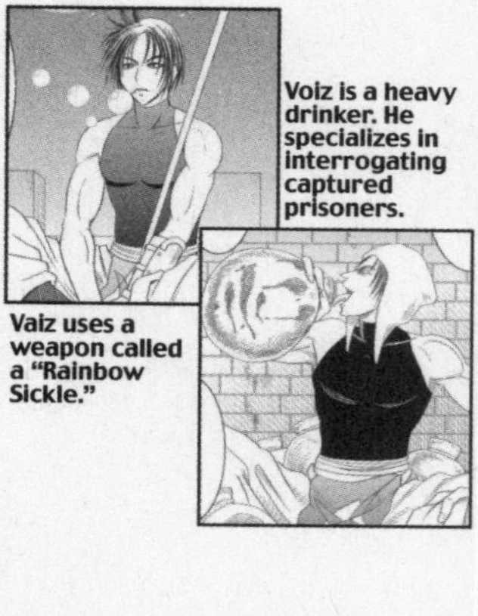

Voiz is a heavy drinker. He specializes in interrogating captured prisoners.

Vaiz uses a weapon called a "Rainbow Sickle."

Dr. Onigiri: At the end of *Bubble Bobble*, Bub and Bob are returned to human form. From there, they go on to the sequel game, *Rainbow Island*, where you use rainbows to move around. Then there's other spinoff games, like the previously mentioned *Puzzle Bobble*, too. *Bubble Bobble* became one of Taito's most beloved franchises.

To Be Continued...

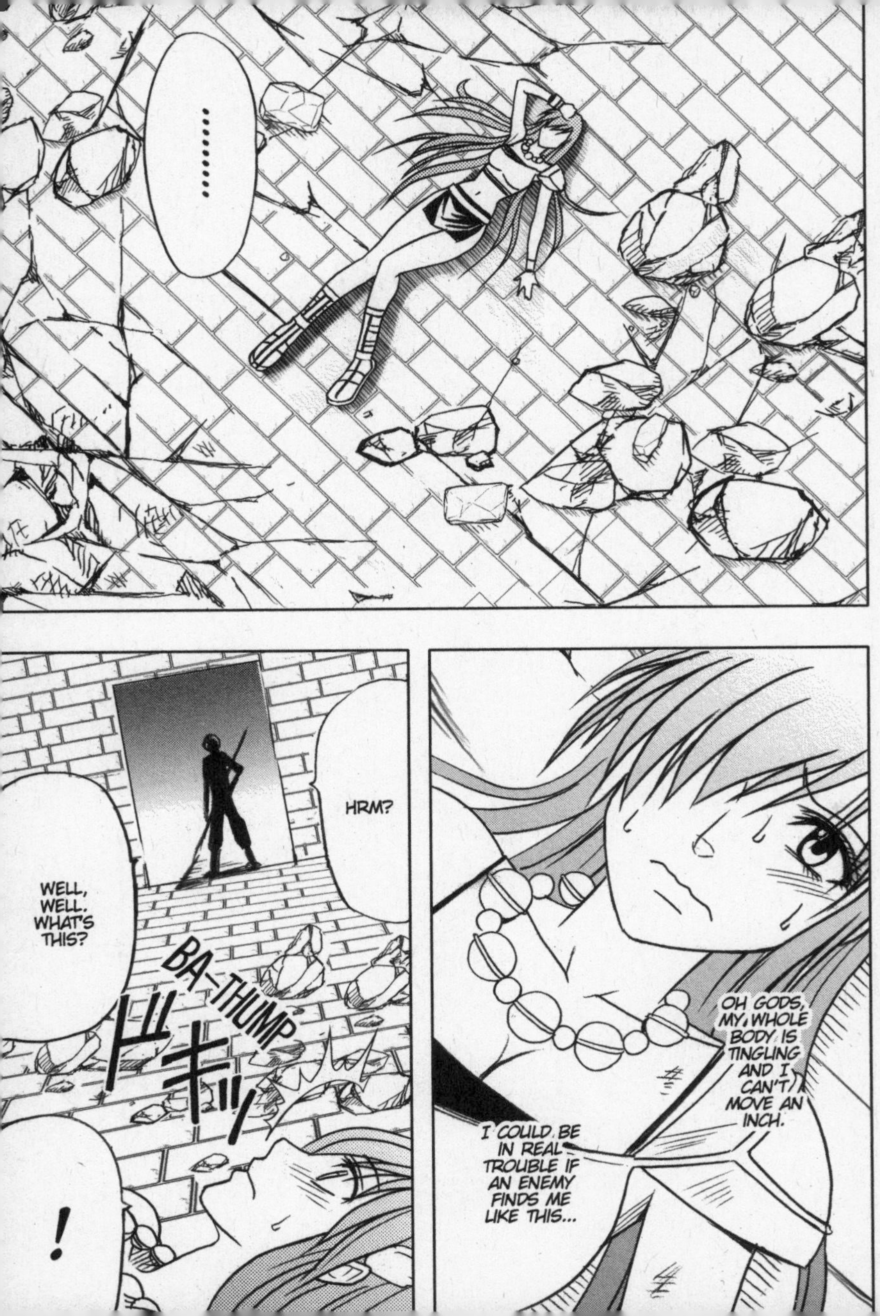
......
OH GODS, MY WHOLE BODY IS TINGLING AND I CAN'T MOVE AN INCH.
I COULD BE IN REAL TROUBLE IF AN ENEMY FINDS ME LIKE THIS...
HRM?
WELL, WELL. WHAT'S THIS?
BA-THUMP
ドキッ
!

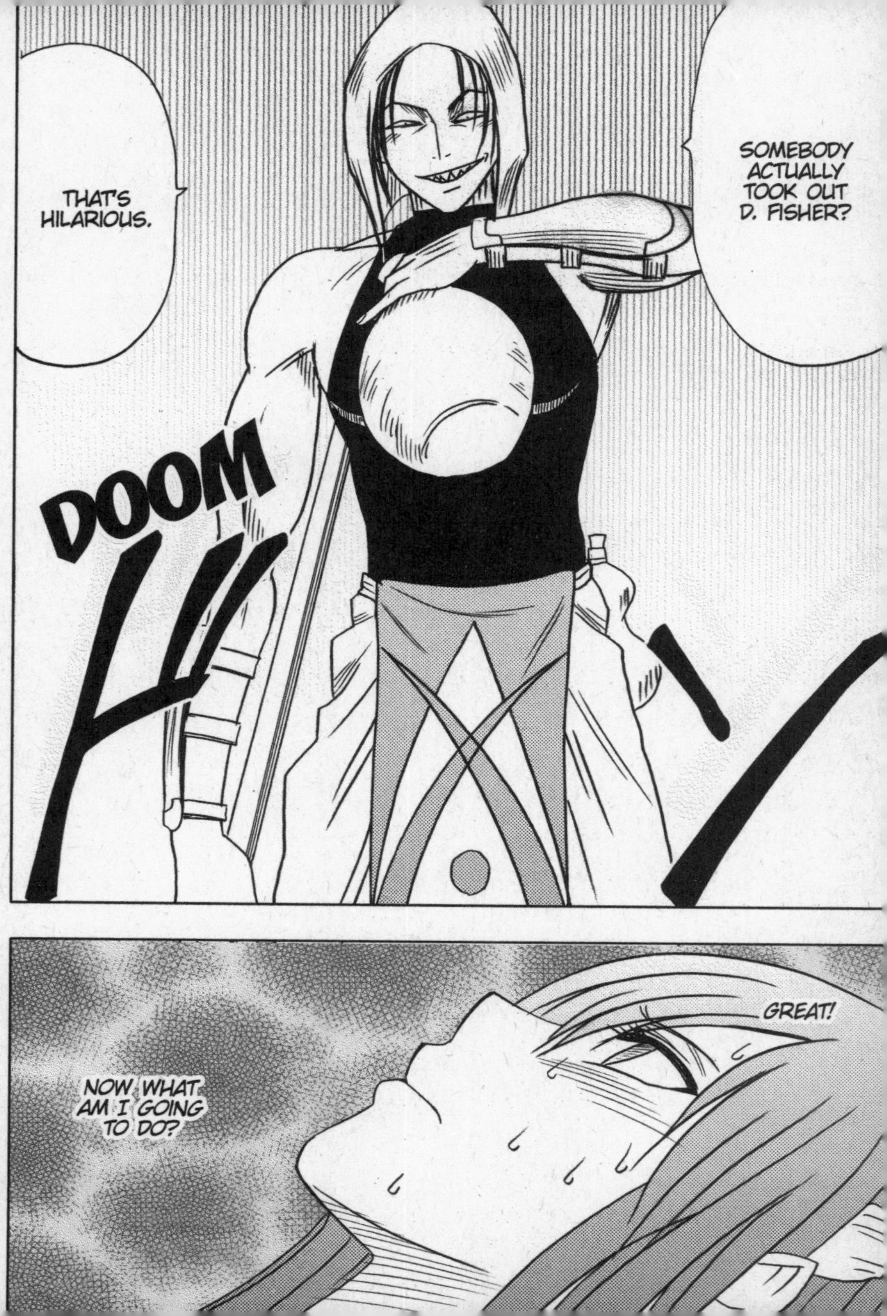
SOMEBODY ACTUALLY TOOK OUT D. FISHER?
THAT'S HILARIOUS.
DOOM
GREAT!
NOW WHAT AM I GOING TO DO?

FINAL CHAPTER

KID

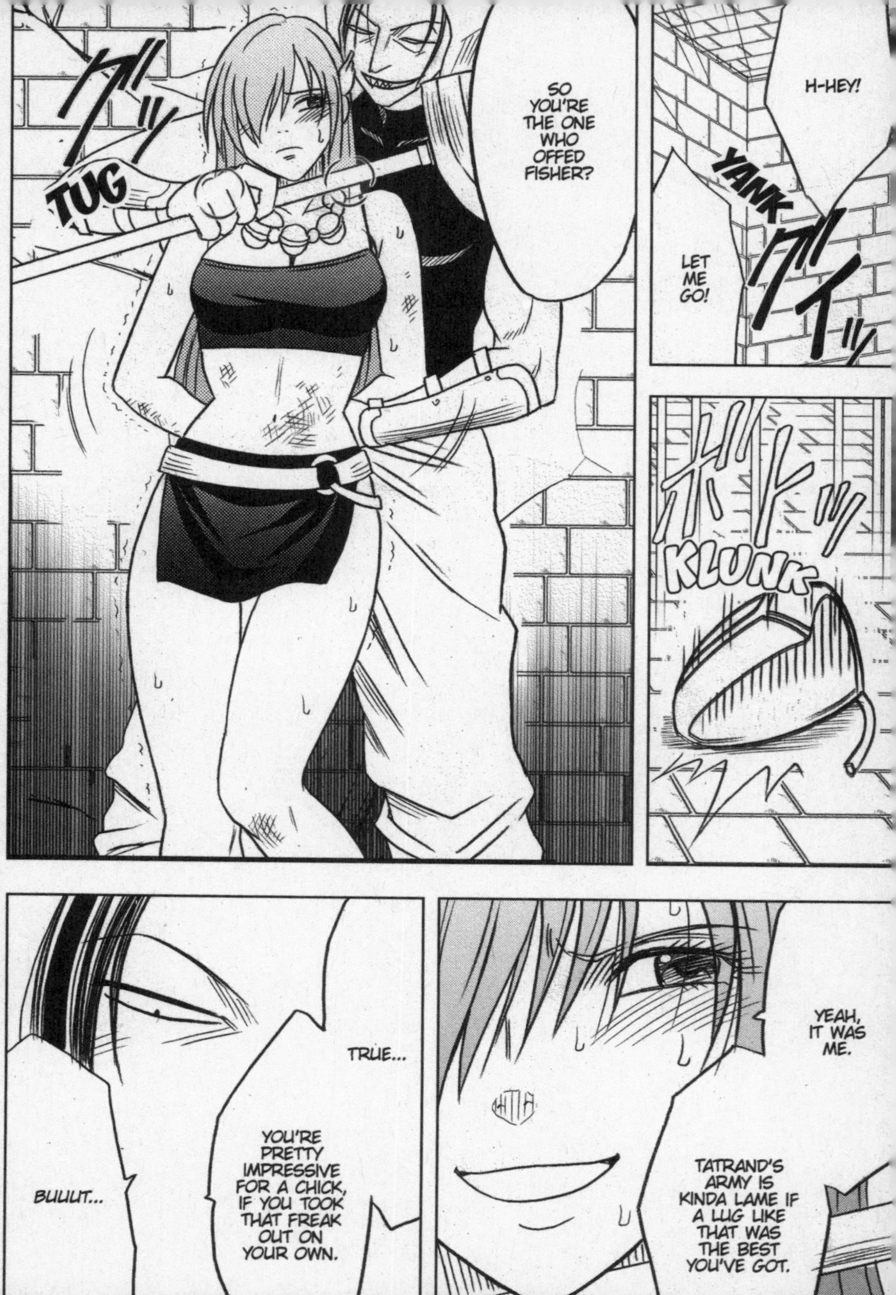
H-HEY!
YANK
LET ME GO!
KLUNK
SO YOU'RE THE ONE WHO OFFED FISHER?
TUG
YEAH, IT WAS ME.
TATRAND'S ARMY IS KINDA LAME IF A LUG LIKE THAT WAS THE BEST YOU'VE GOT.
TRUE...
YOU'RE PRETTY IMPRESSIVE FOR A CHICK, IF YOU TOOK THAT FREAK OUT ON YOUR OWN.
BUUUT...

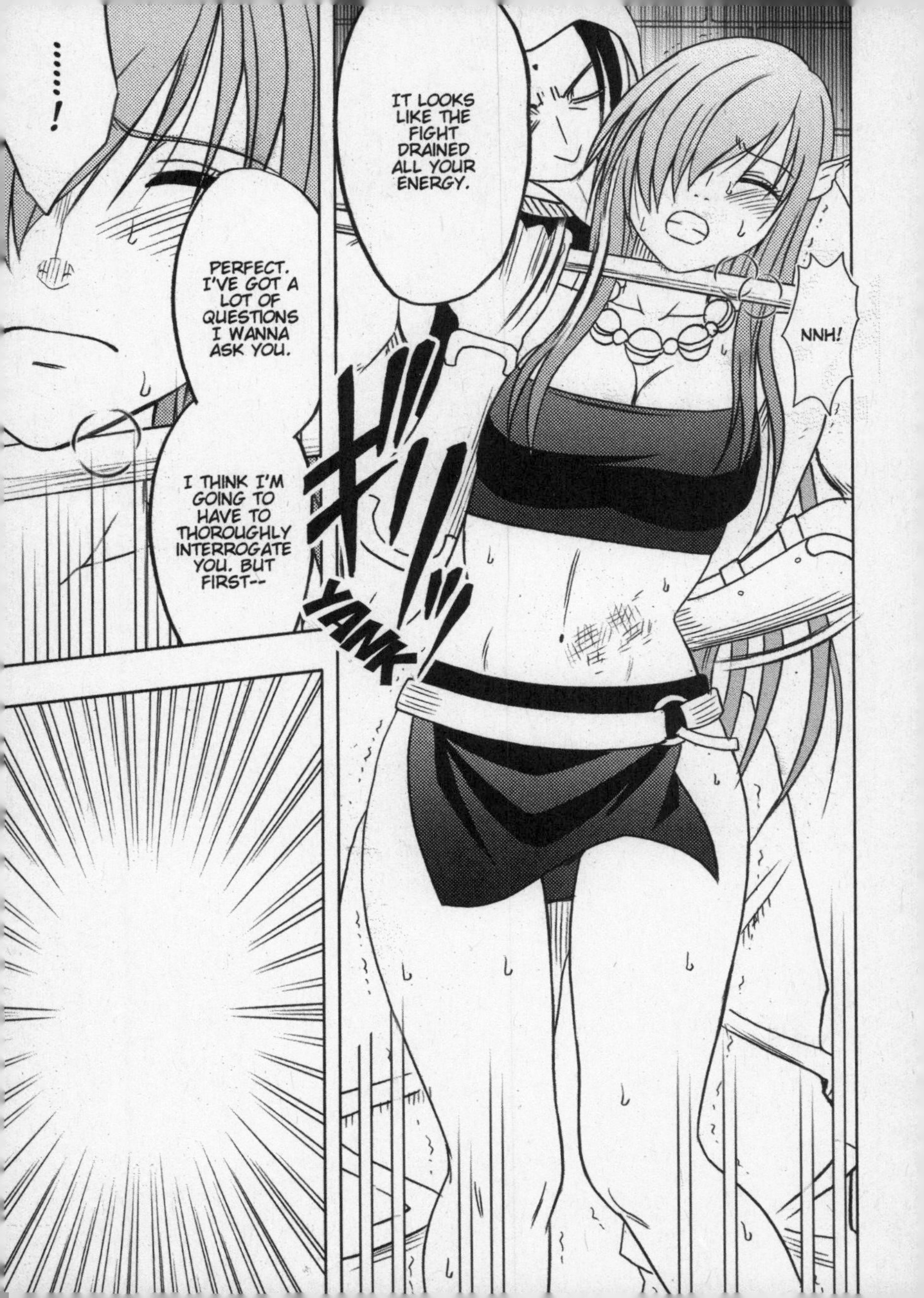
IT LOOKS LIKE THE FIGHT DRAINED ALL YOUR ENERGY.
NNH!
YANK
......!
PERFECT. I'VE GOT A LOT OF QUESTIONS I WANNA ASK YOU.
I THINK I'M GOING TO HAVE TO THOROUGHLY INTERROGATE YOU. BUT FIRST--

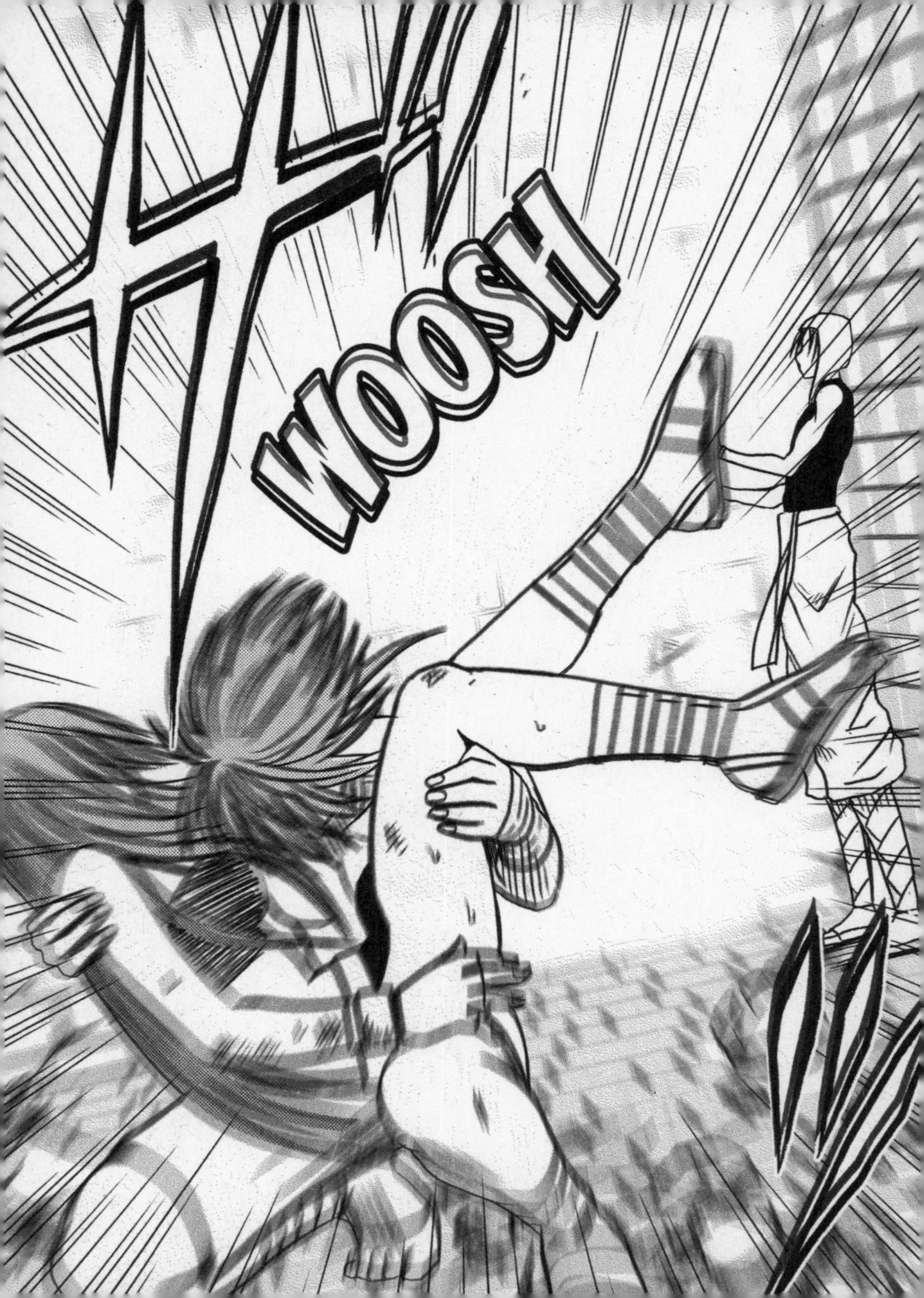
WOOSH

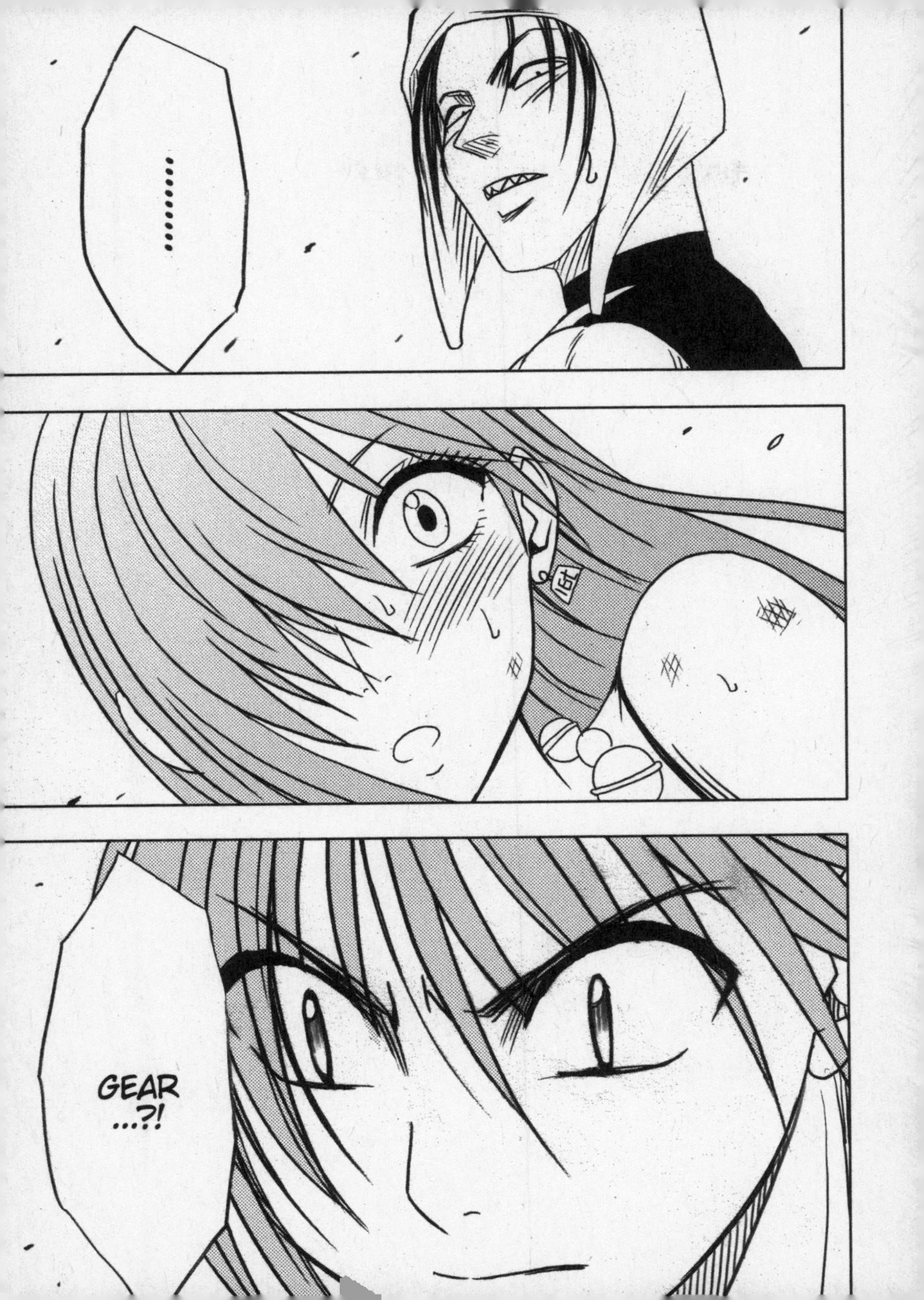

....
GEAR ...?!

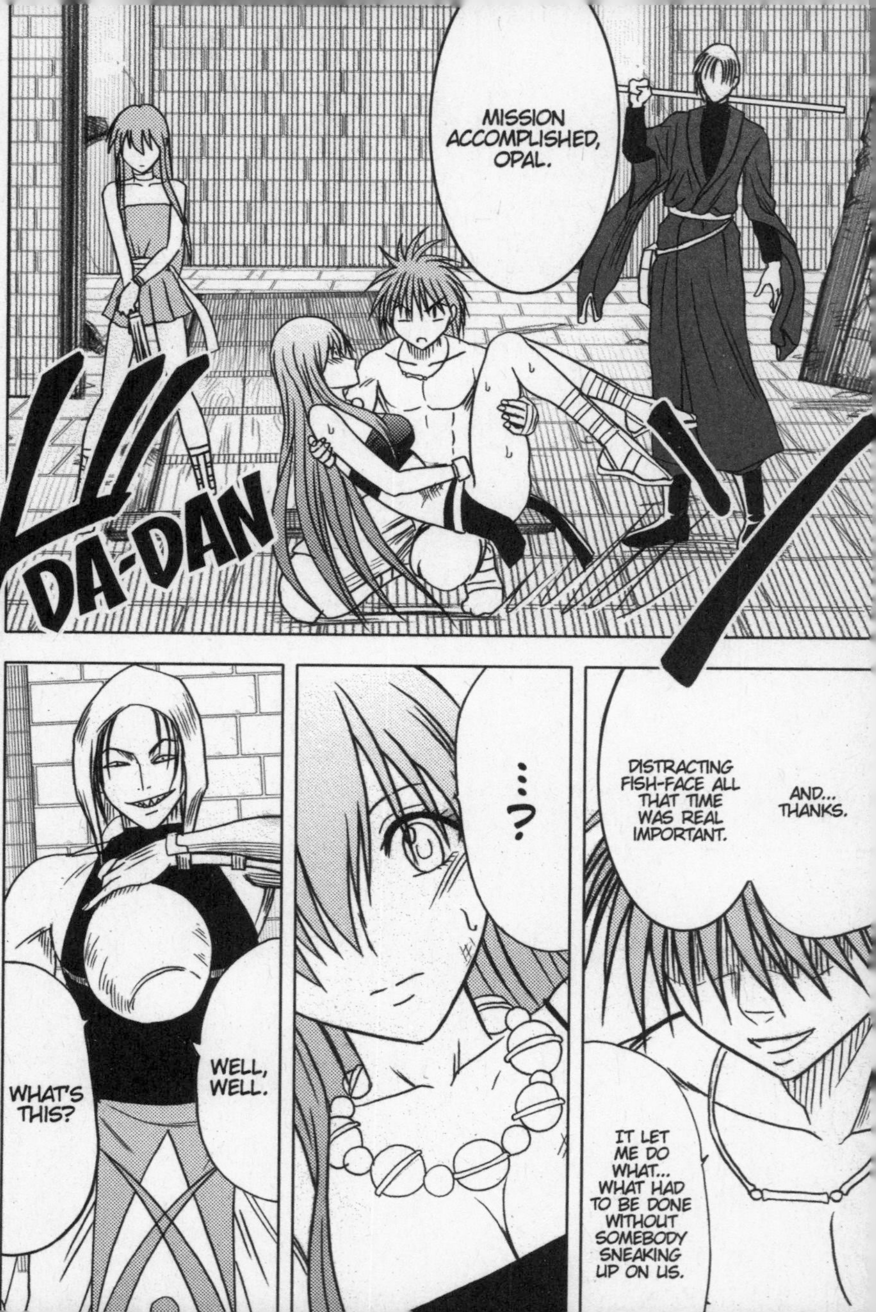
MISSION ACCOMPLISHED, OPAL.
DA-DAN
AND... THANKS.
DISTRACTING FISH-FACE ALL THAT TIME WAS REAL IMPORTANT.
IT LET ME DO WHAT... WHAT HAD TO BE DONE WITHOUT SOMEBODY SNEAKING UP ON US.
...?
WELL, WELL.
WHAT'S THIS?

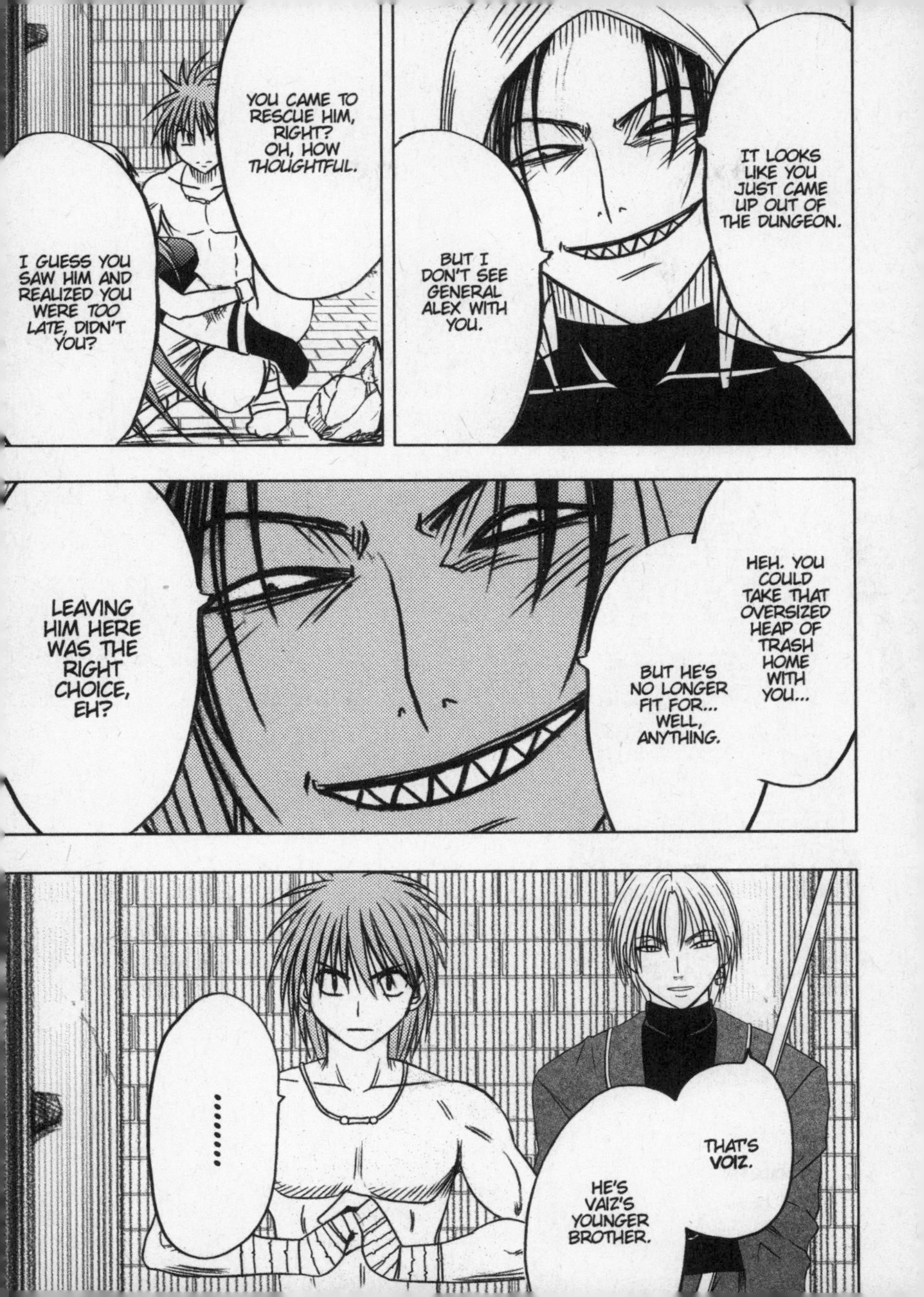

IT LOOKS LIKE YOU JUST CAME UP OUT OF THE DUNGEON.
BUT I DON'T SEE GENERAL ALEX WITH YOU.
YOU CAME TO RESCUE HIM, RIGHT? OH, HOW THOUGHTFUL.
I GUESS YOU SAW HIM AND REALIZED YOU WERE *TOO* LATE, DIDN'T YOU?
HEH. YOU COULD TAKE THAT OVERSIZED HEAP OF TRASH HOME WITH YOU...
BUT HE'S NO LONGER FIT FOR... WELL, ANYTHING.
LEAVING HIM HERE WAS THE RIGHT CHOICE, EH?
THAT'S VOIZ.
HE'S VAIZ'S YOUNGER BROTHER.
....

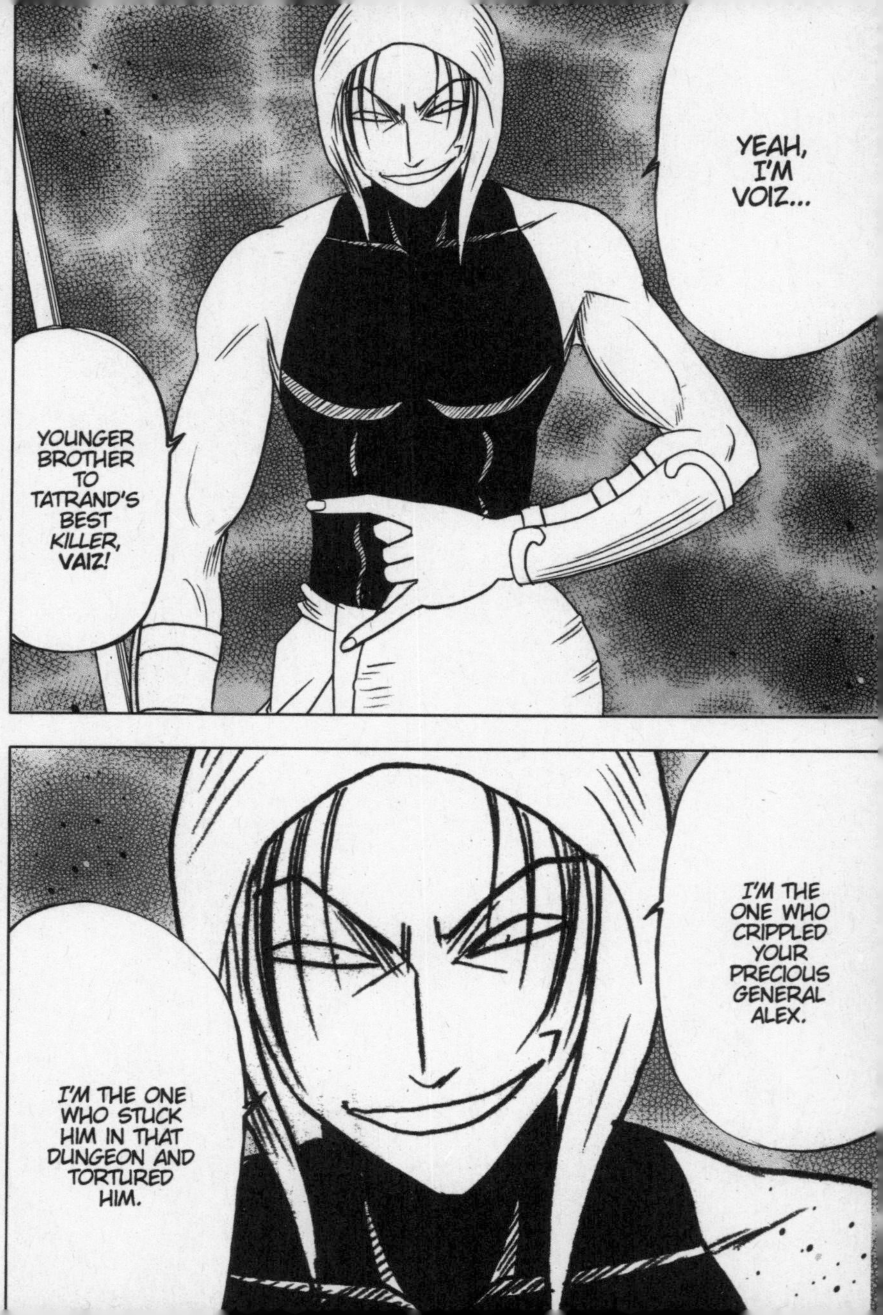
YEAH, I'M VOIZ...
YOUNGER BROTHER TO TATRAND'S BEST KILLER, VAIZ!
I'M THE ONE WHO CRIPPLED YOUR PRECIOUS GENERAL ALEX.
I'M THE ONE WHO STUCK HIM IN THAT DUNGEON AND TORTURED HIM.

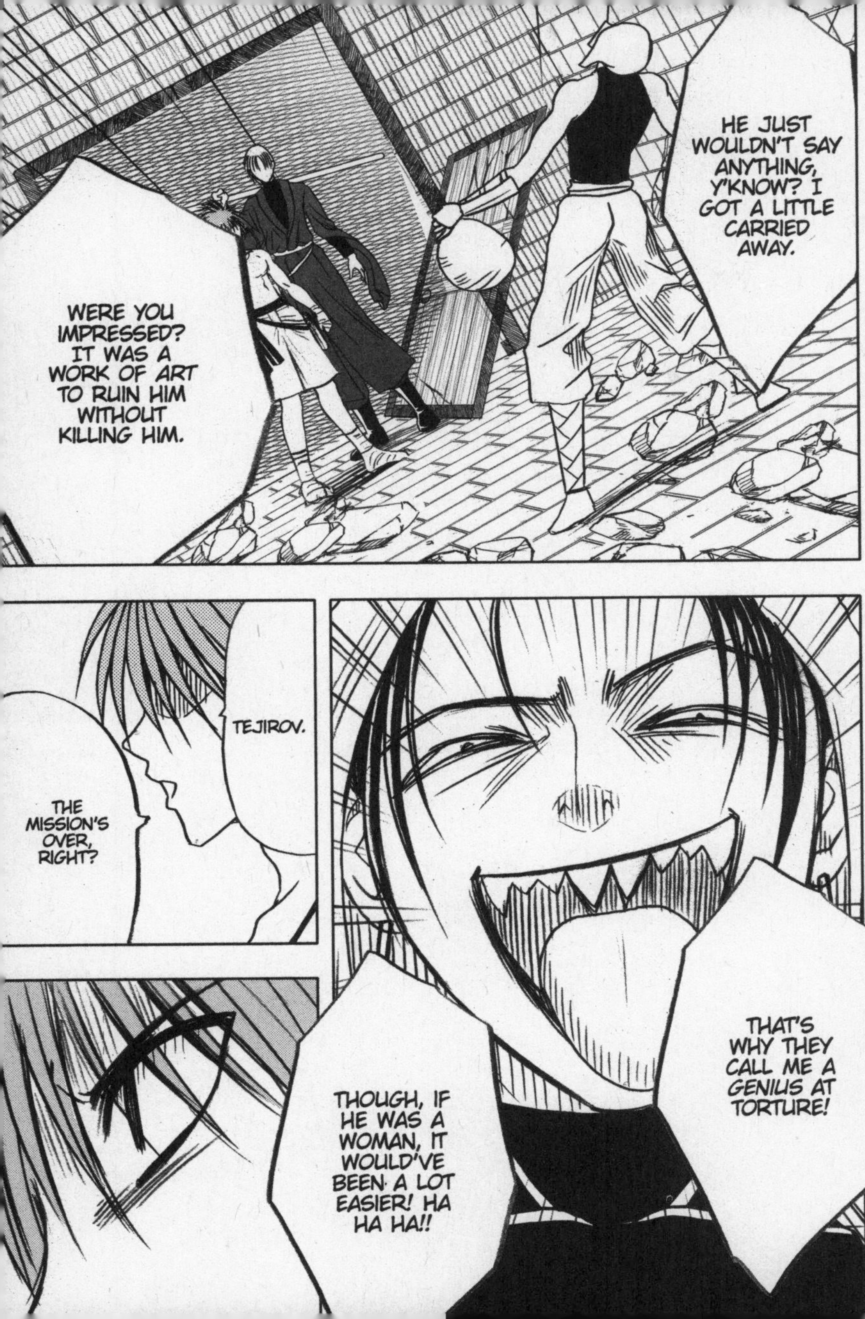

HE JUST WOULDN'T SAY ANYTHING, Y'KNOW? I GOT A LITTLE CARRIED AWAY.
WERE YOU IMPRESSED? IT WAS A WORK OF ART TO RUIN HIM WITHOUT KILLING HIM.
THAT'S WHY THEY CALL ME A GENIUS AT TORTURE!
THOUGH, IF HE WAS A WOMAN, IT WOULD'VE BEEN A LOT EASIER! HA HA HA!!
TEJIROV.
THE MISSION'S OVER, RIGHT?

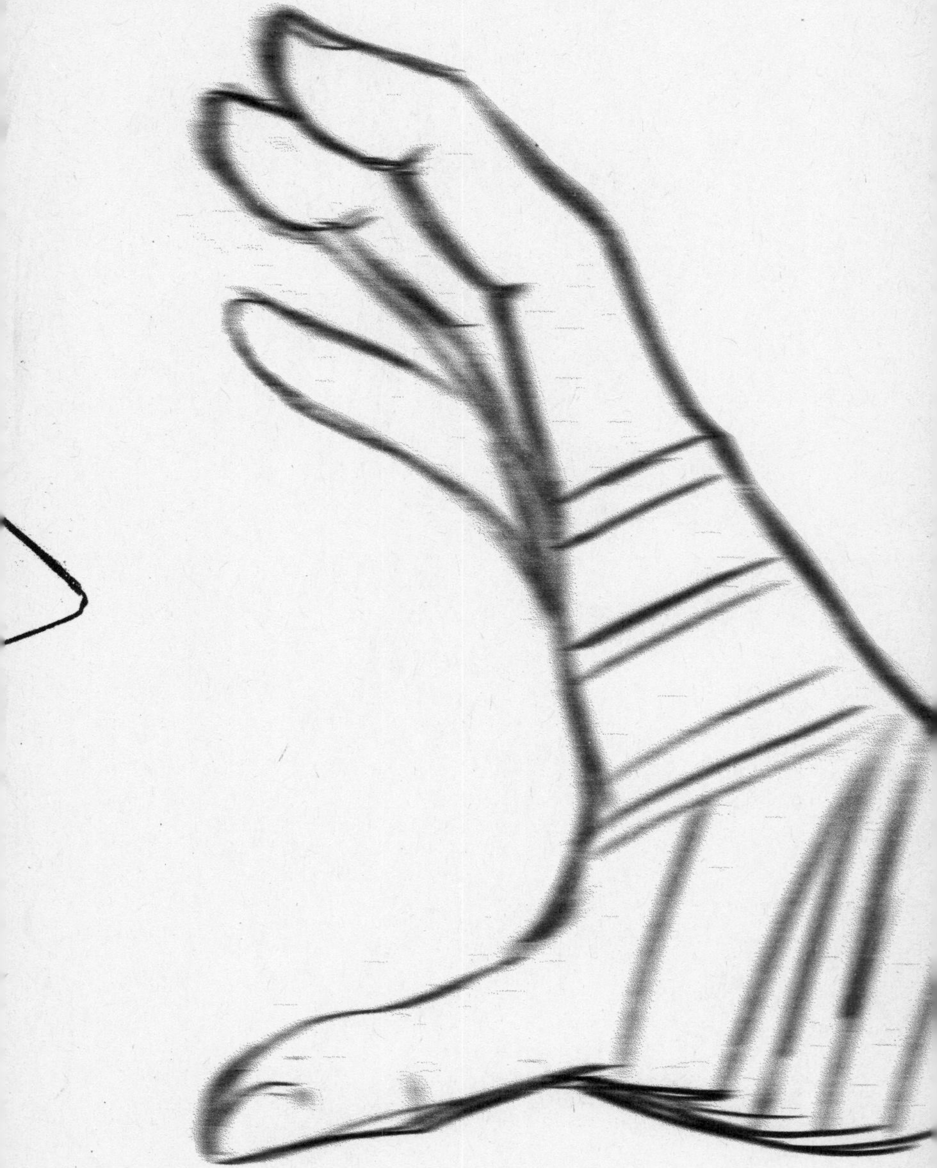

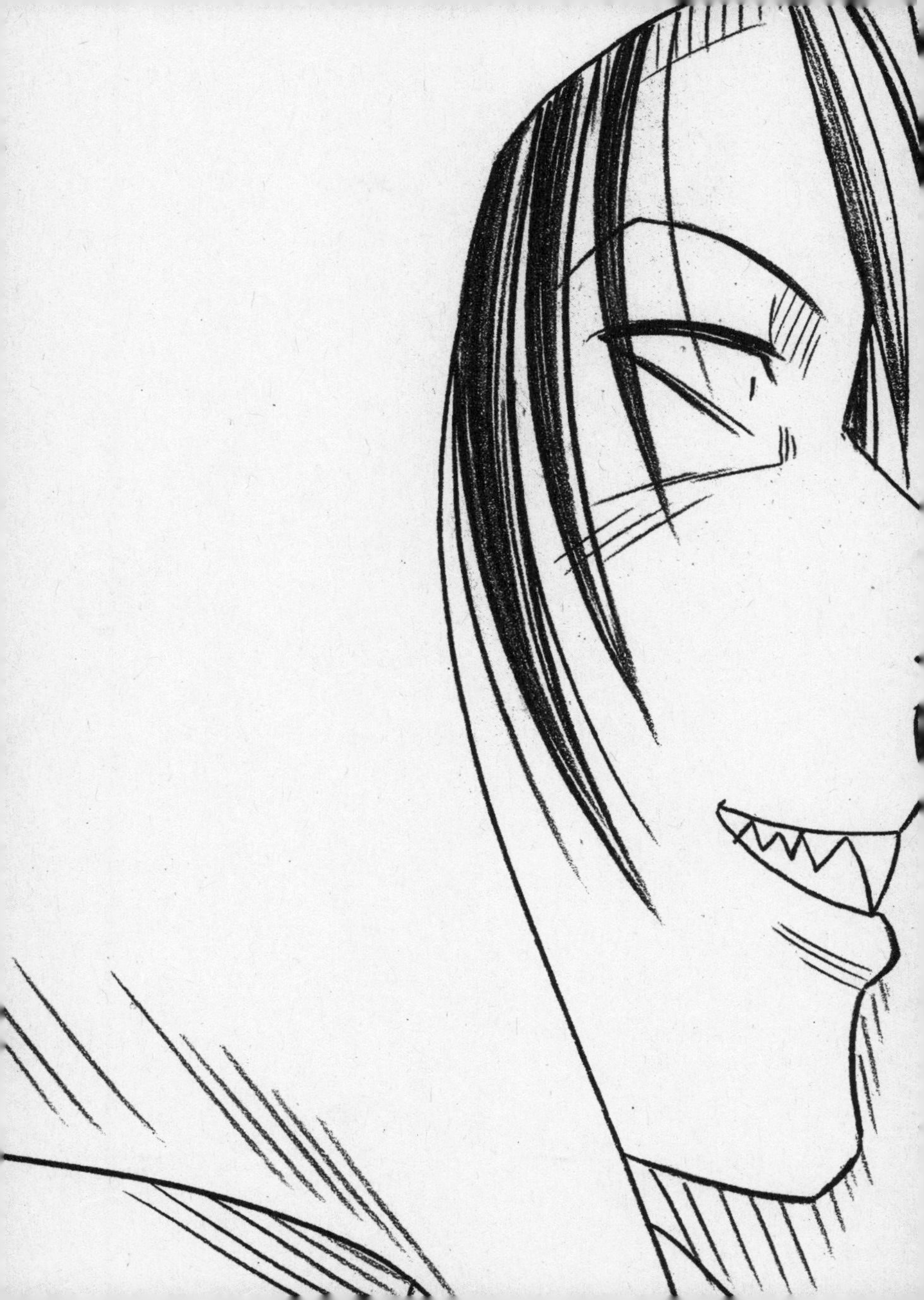

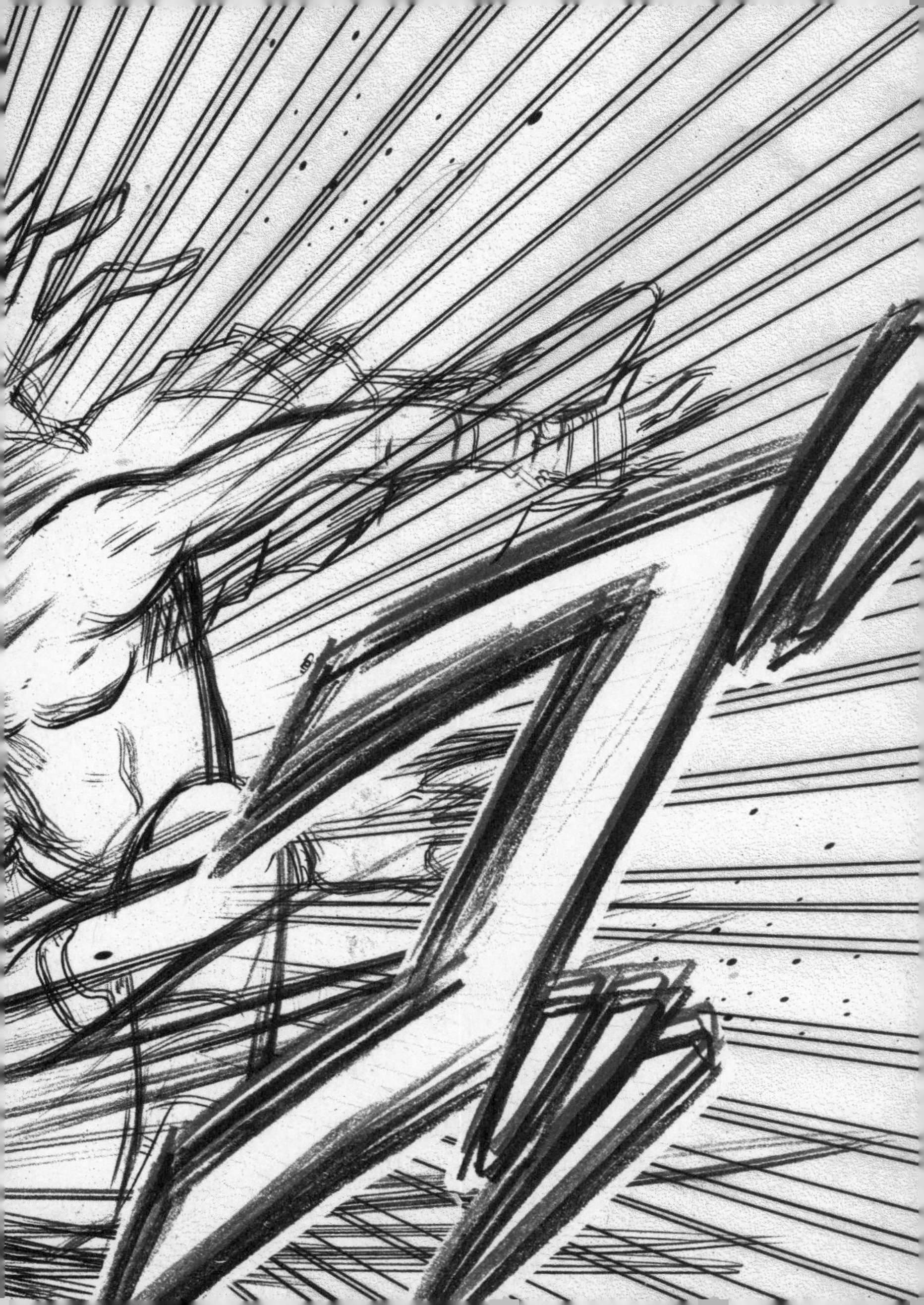

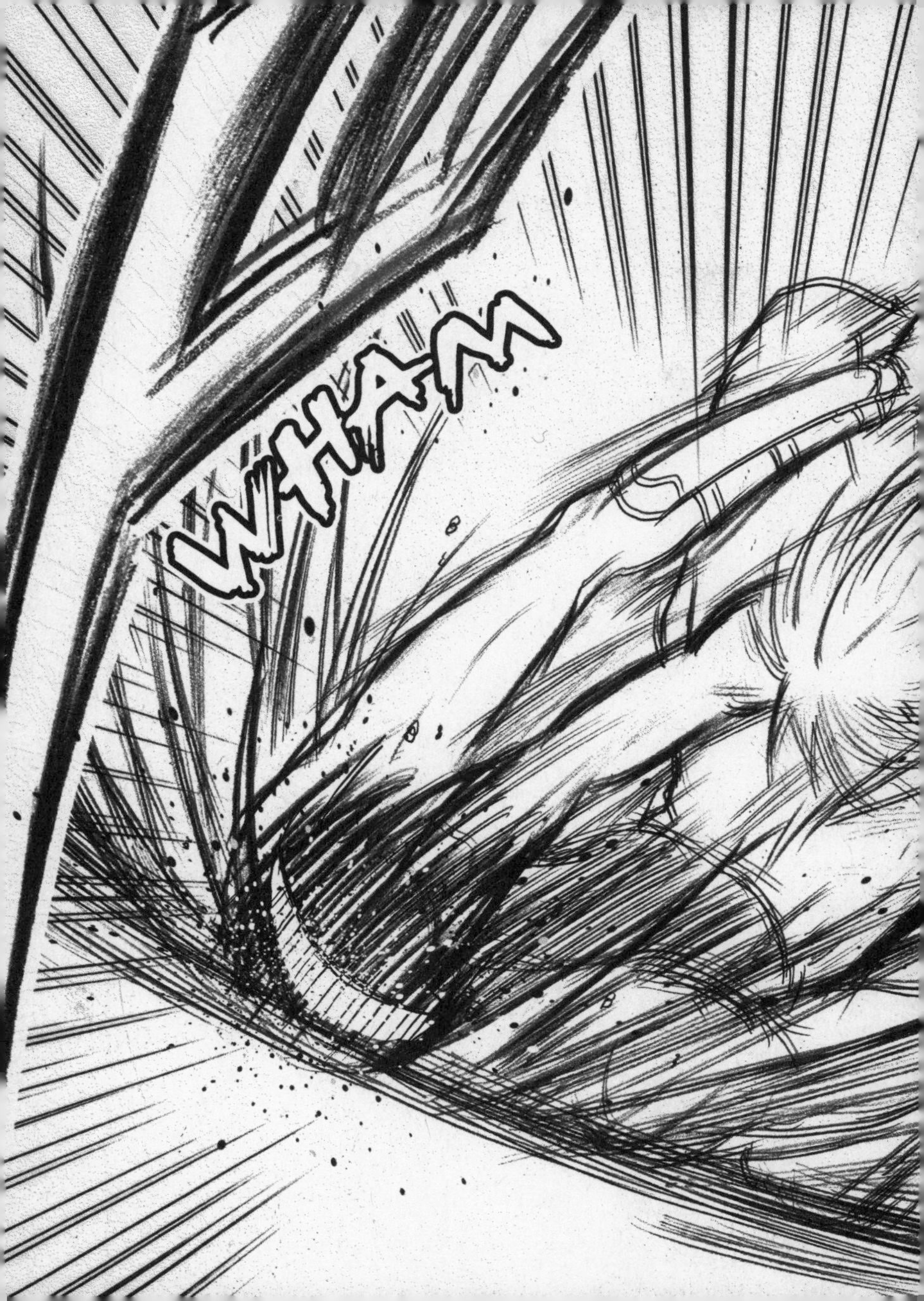
WHAM

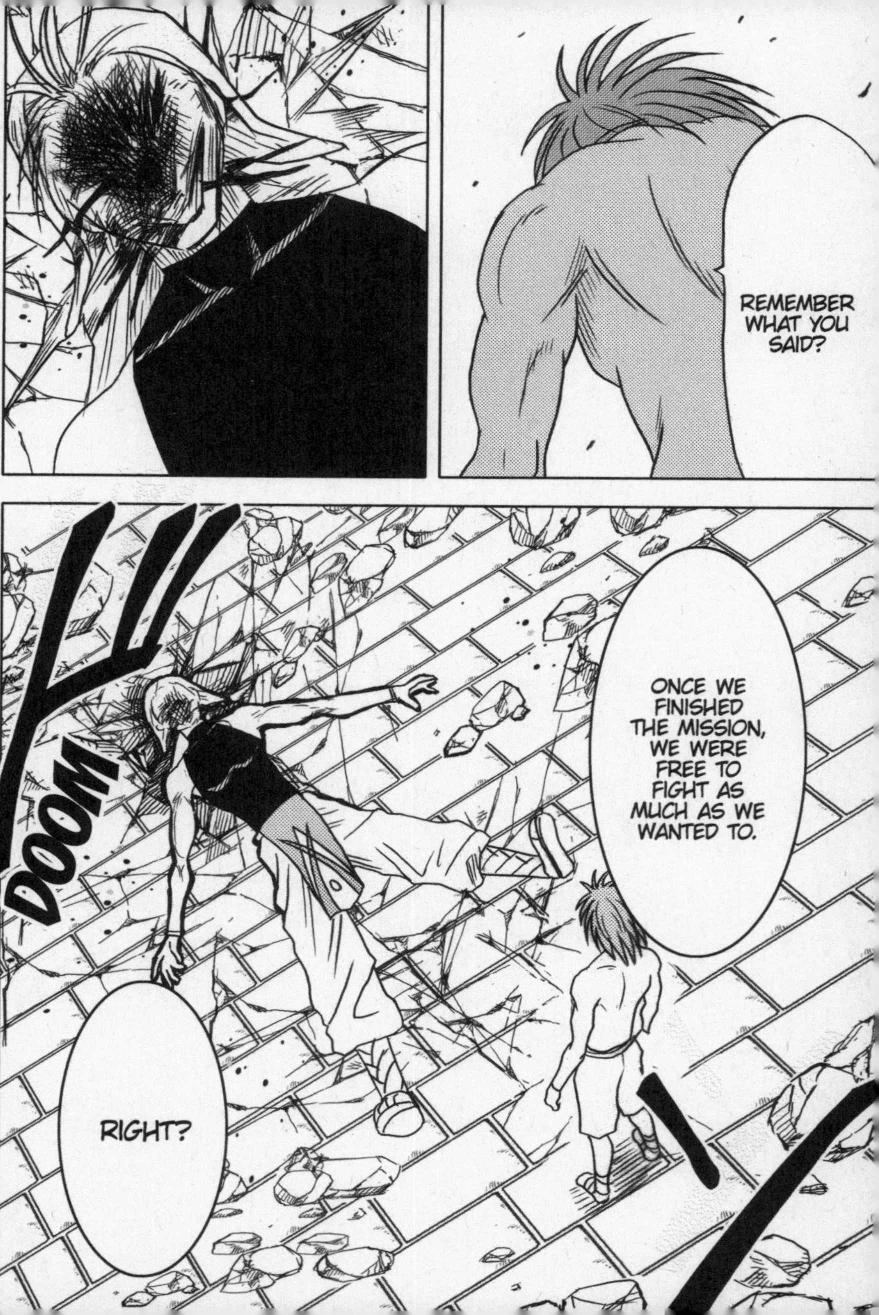
REMEMBER WHAT YOU SAID?
ONCE WE FINISHED THE MISSION, WE WERE FREE TO FIGHT AS MUCH AS WE WANTED TO.
DOOM
RIGHT?

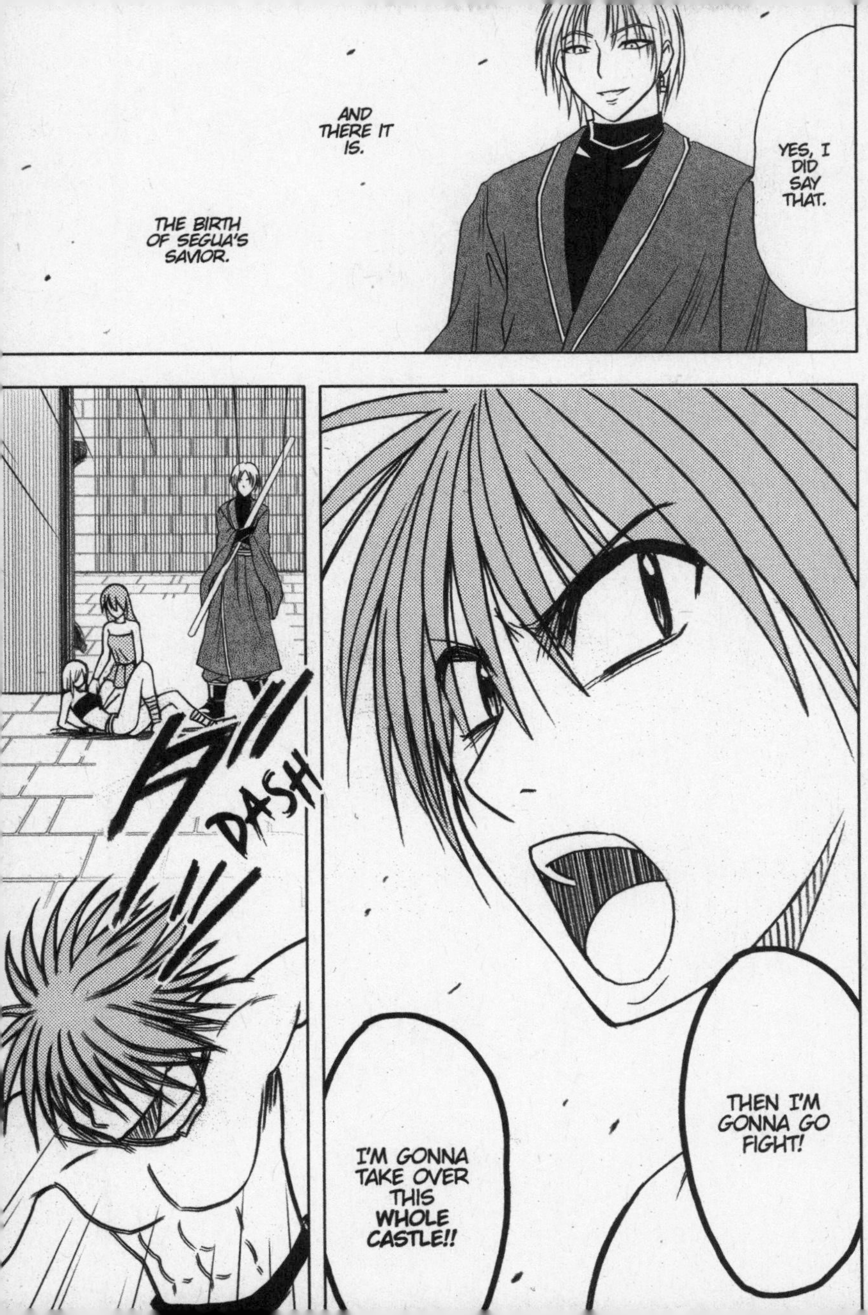
YES, I DID SAY THAT.
AND THERE IT IS.
THE BIRTH OF SEGUA'S SAVIOR.
THEN I'M GONNA GO FIGHT!
I'M GONNA TAKE OVER THIS WHOLE CASTLE!!
DASH

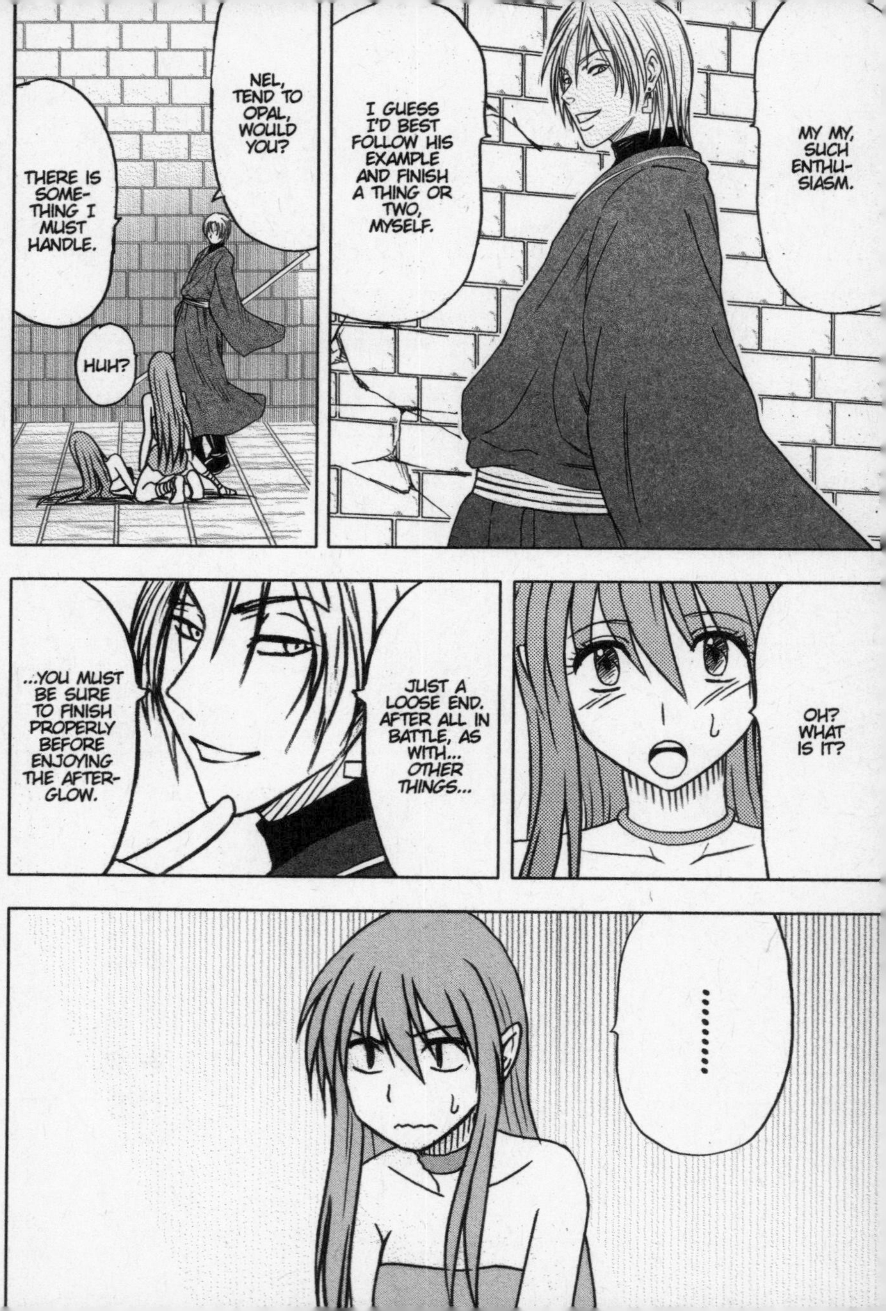
MY MY, SUCH ENTHUSIASM.
I GUESS I'D BEST FOLLOW HIS EXAMPLE AND FINISH A THING OR TWO, MYSELF.
NEL, TEND TO OPAL, WOULD YOU?
THERE IS SOMETHING I MUST HANDLE.
HUH?
OH? WHAT IS IT?
JUST A LOOSE END. AFTER ALL IN BATTLE, AS WITH... *OTHER* THINGS...
...YOU MUST BE SURE TO FINISH PROPERLY BEFORE ENJOYING THE AFTERGLOW.
......

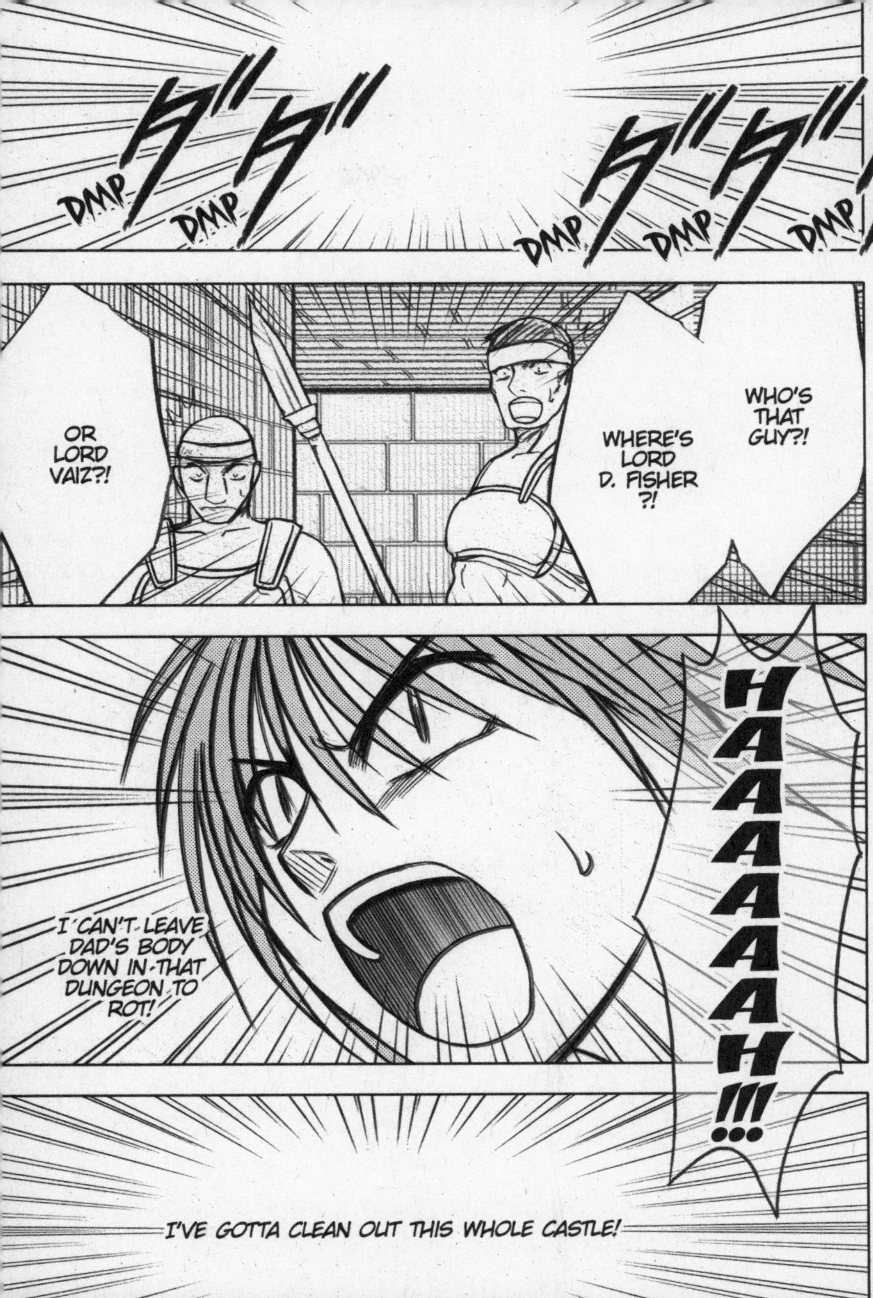
DMP DMP DMP
DMP DMP
WHO'S THAT GUY?!
WHERE'S LORD D. FISHER ?!
OR LORD VAIZ?!
HAAAAAAH!!!
I CAN'T LEAVE DAD'S BODY DOWN IN THAT DUNGEON TO ROT!
I'VE GOTTA CLEAN OUT THIS WHOLE CASTLE!

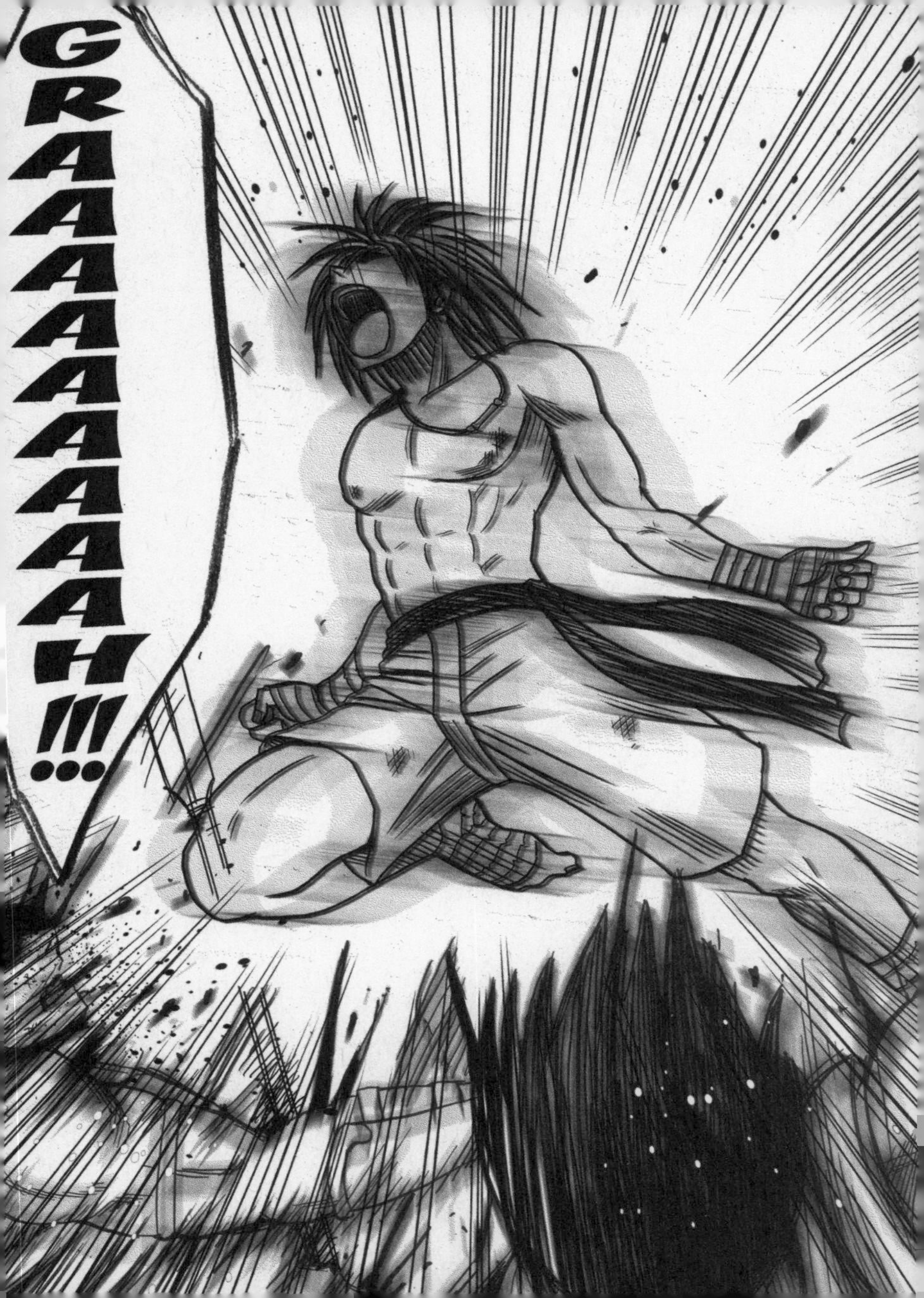
GRAAAAAAAAAH!!!

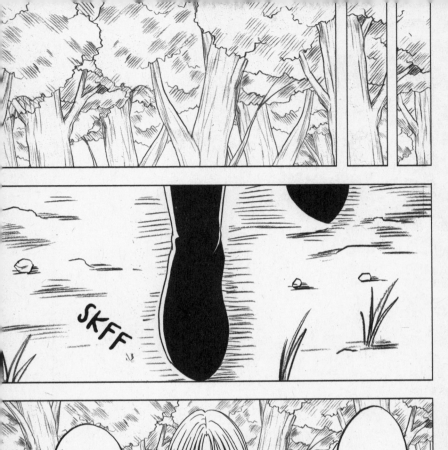

SKFF

IT LOOKS LIKE YOU MANAGED TO ESCAPE ON YOUR OWN.

I CAN'T SAY I'M SURPRISED.

WELL.

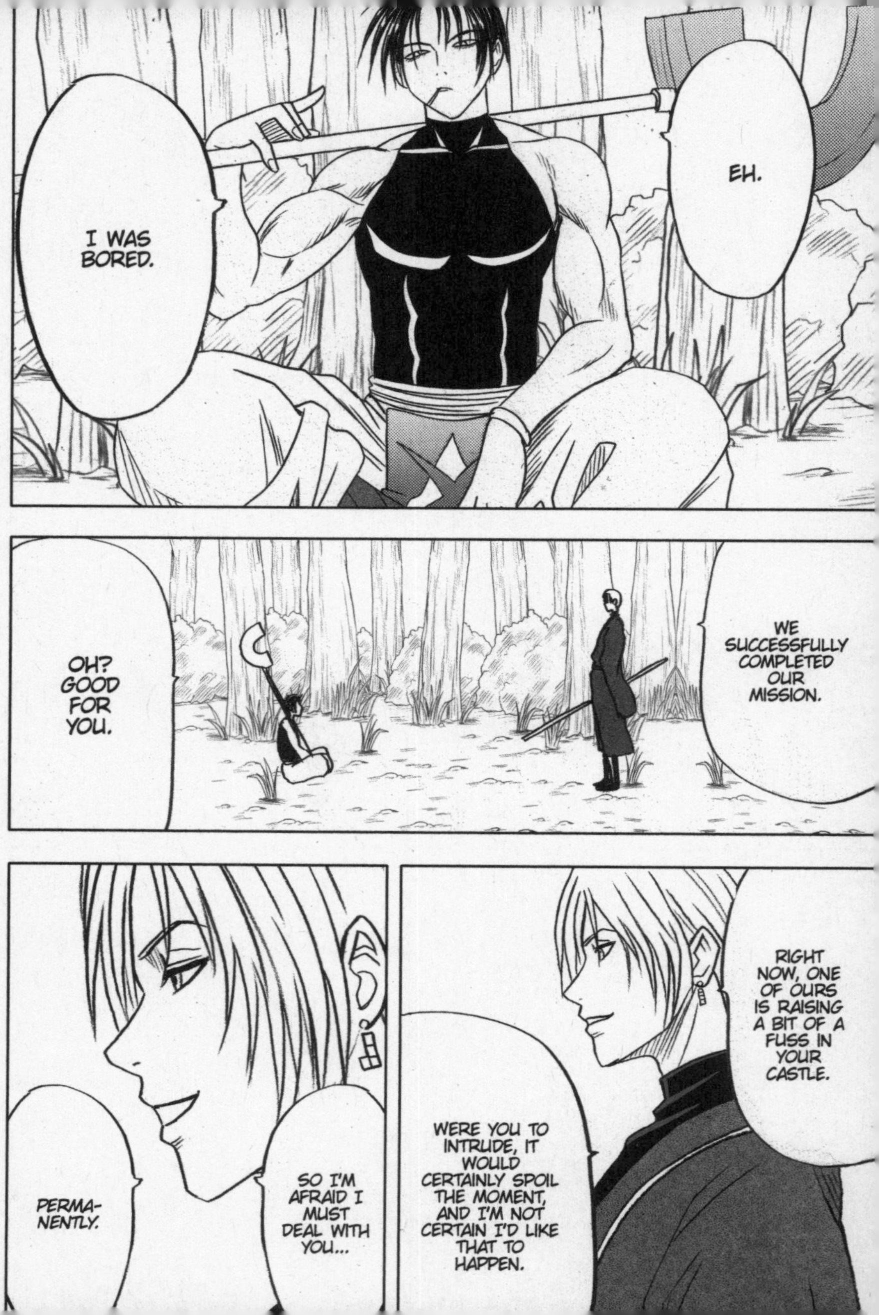
EH.
I WAS BORED.
WE SUCCESSFULLY COMPLETED OUR MISSION.
OH? GOOD FOR YOU.
RIGHT NOW, ONE OF OURS IS RAISING A BIT OF A FUSS IN YOUR CASTLE.
WERE YOU TO INTRUDE, IT WOULD CERTAINLY SPOIL THE MOMENT, AND I'M NOT CERTAIN I'D LIKE THAT TO HAPPEN.
SO I'M AFRAID I MUST DEAL WITH YOU...
PERMA-NENTLY.

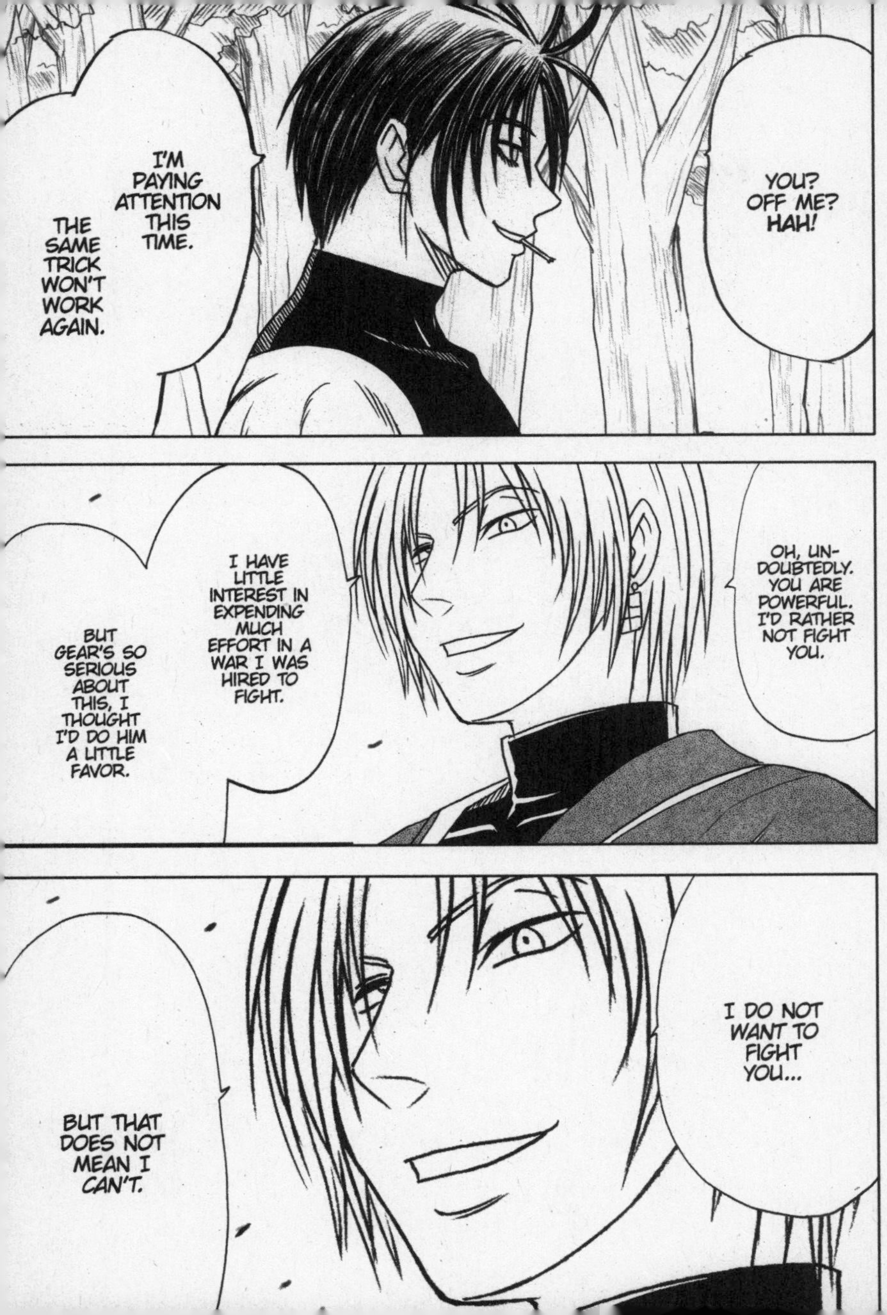
YOU? OFF ME? HAH!
I'M PAYING ATTENTION THIS TIME.
THE SAME TRICK WON'T WORK AGAIN.
OH, UN-DOUBTEDLY. YOU ARE POWERFUL. I'D RATHER NOT FIGHT YOU.
I HAVE LITTLE INTEREST IN EXPENDING MUCH EFFORT IN A WAR I WAS HIRED TO FIGHT.
BUT GEAR'S SO SERIOUS ABOUT THIS, I THOUGHT I'D DO HIM A LITTLE FAVOR.
I DO NOT WANT TO FIGHT YOU...
BUT THAT DOES NOT MEAN I CAN'T.

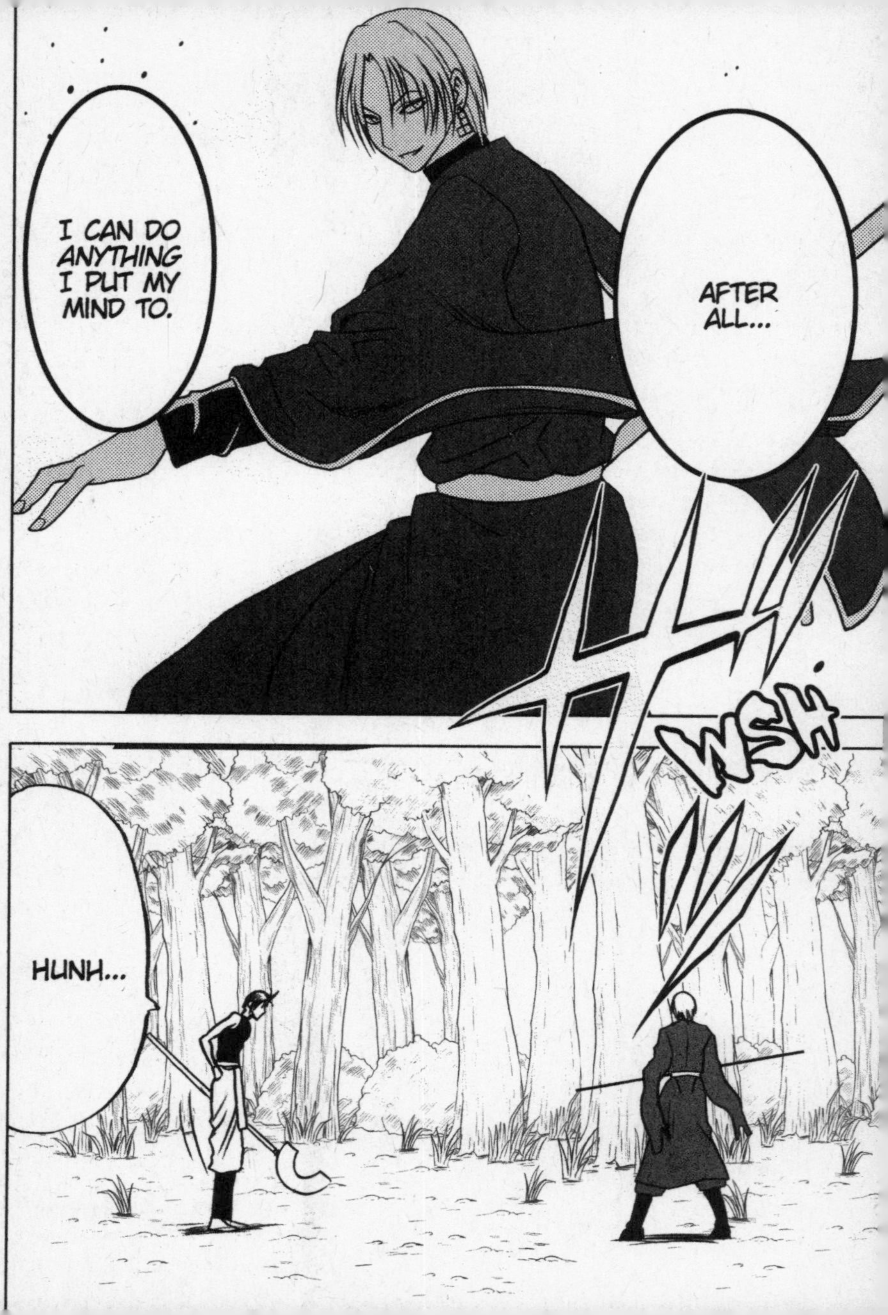
AFTER ALL...
I CAN DO ANYTHING I PUT MY MIND TO.
WSH
HUNH...

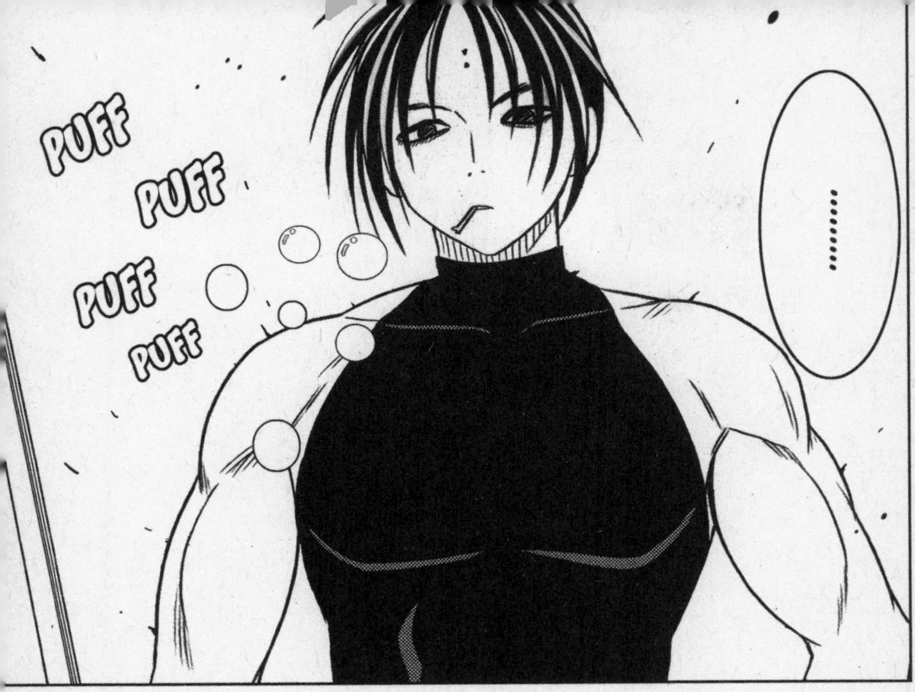
……
PUFF
PUFF
PUFF
PUFF

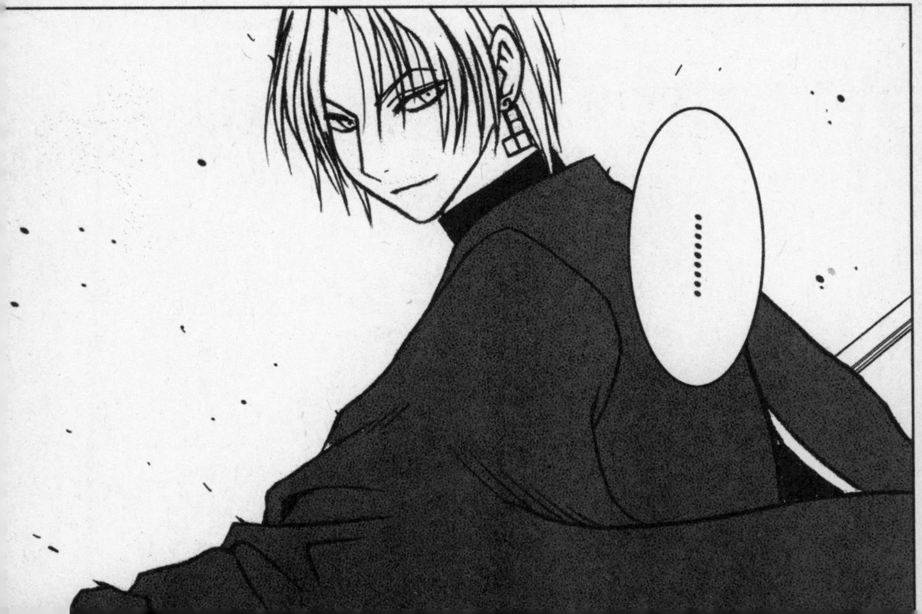
……

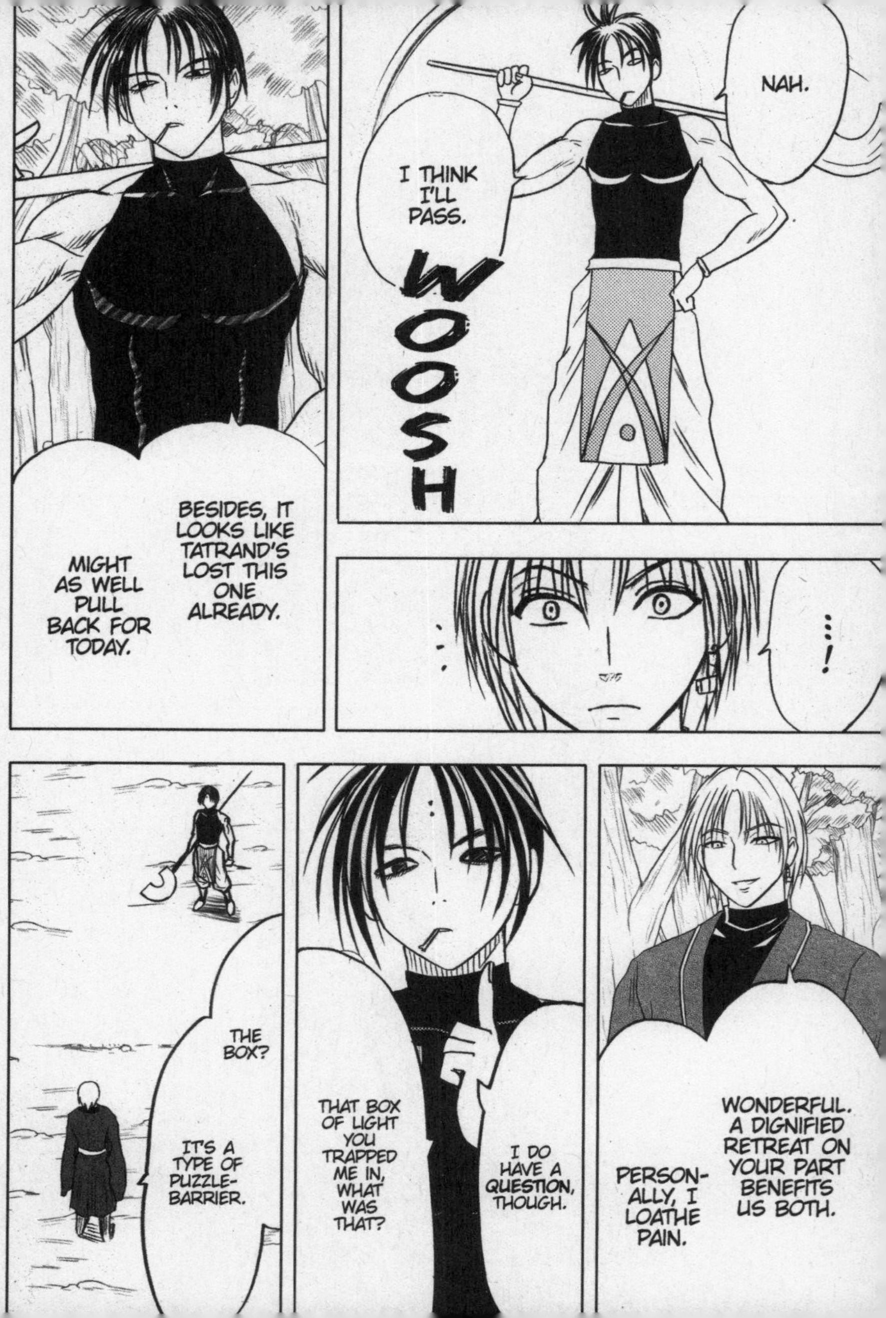
NAH.
I THINK I'LL PASS.
WOOSH
...!
BESIDES, IT LOOKS LIKE TATRAND'S LOST THIS ONE ALREADY.
MIGHT AS WELL PULL BACK FOR TODAY.
WONDERFUL. A DIGNIFIED RETREAT ON YOUR PART BENEFITS US BOTH.
PERSON-ALLY, I LOATHE PAIN.
I DO HAVE A QUESTION, THOUGH.
THAT BOX OF LIGHT YOU TRAPPED ME IN, WHAT WAS THAT?
THE BOX?
IT'S A TYPE OF PUZZLE-BARRIER.

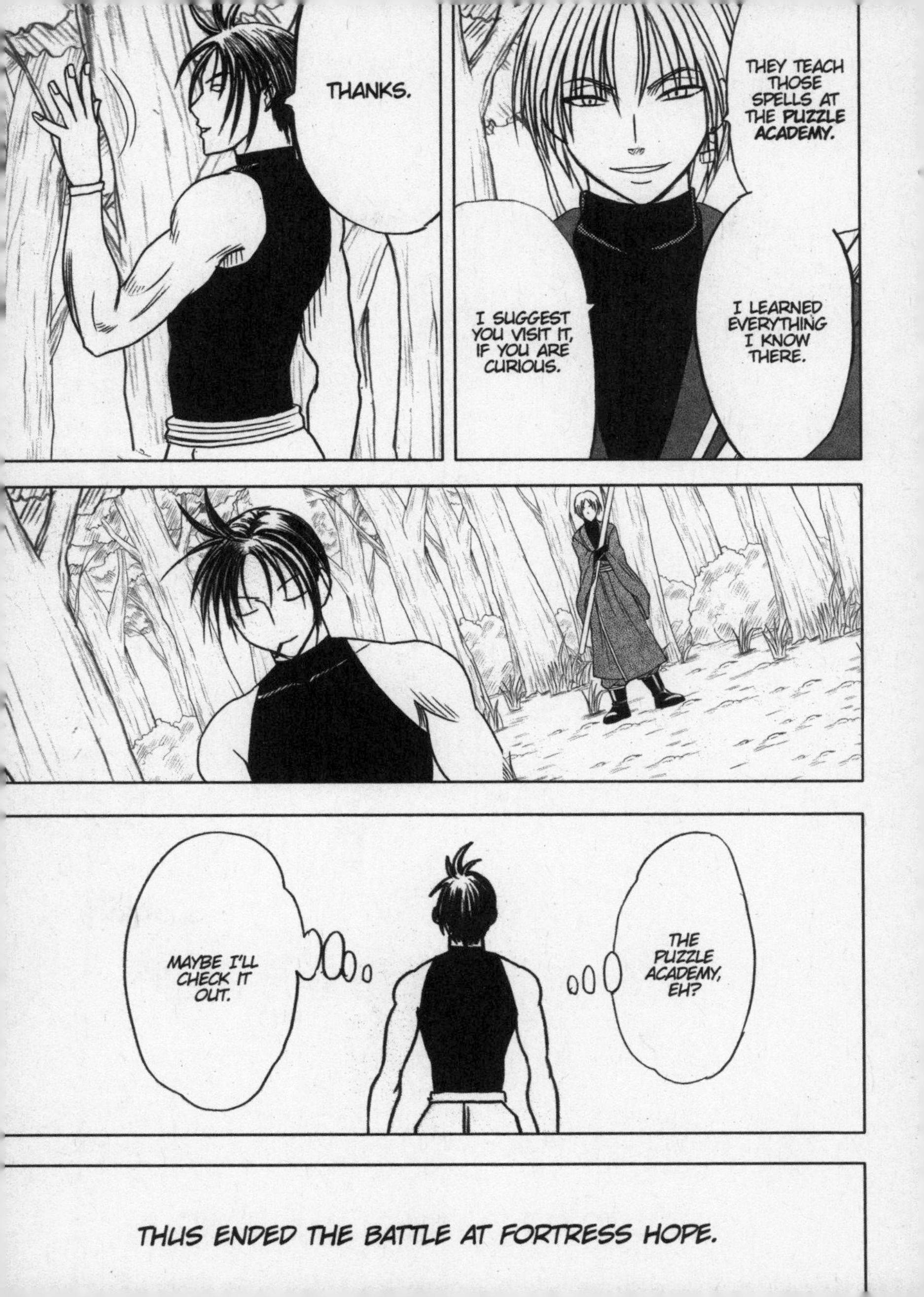
THEY TEACH THOSE SPELLS AT THE PUZZLE ACADEMY.
I LEARNED EVERYTHING I KNOW THERE.
I SUGGEST YOU VISIT IT, IF YOU ARE CURIOUS.
THANKS.
THE PUZZLE ACADEMY, EH?
MAYBE I'LL CHECK IT OUT.
THUS ENDED THE BATTLE AT FORTRESS HOPE.

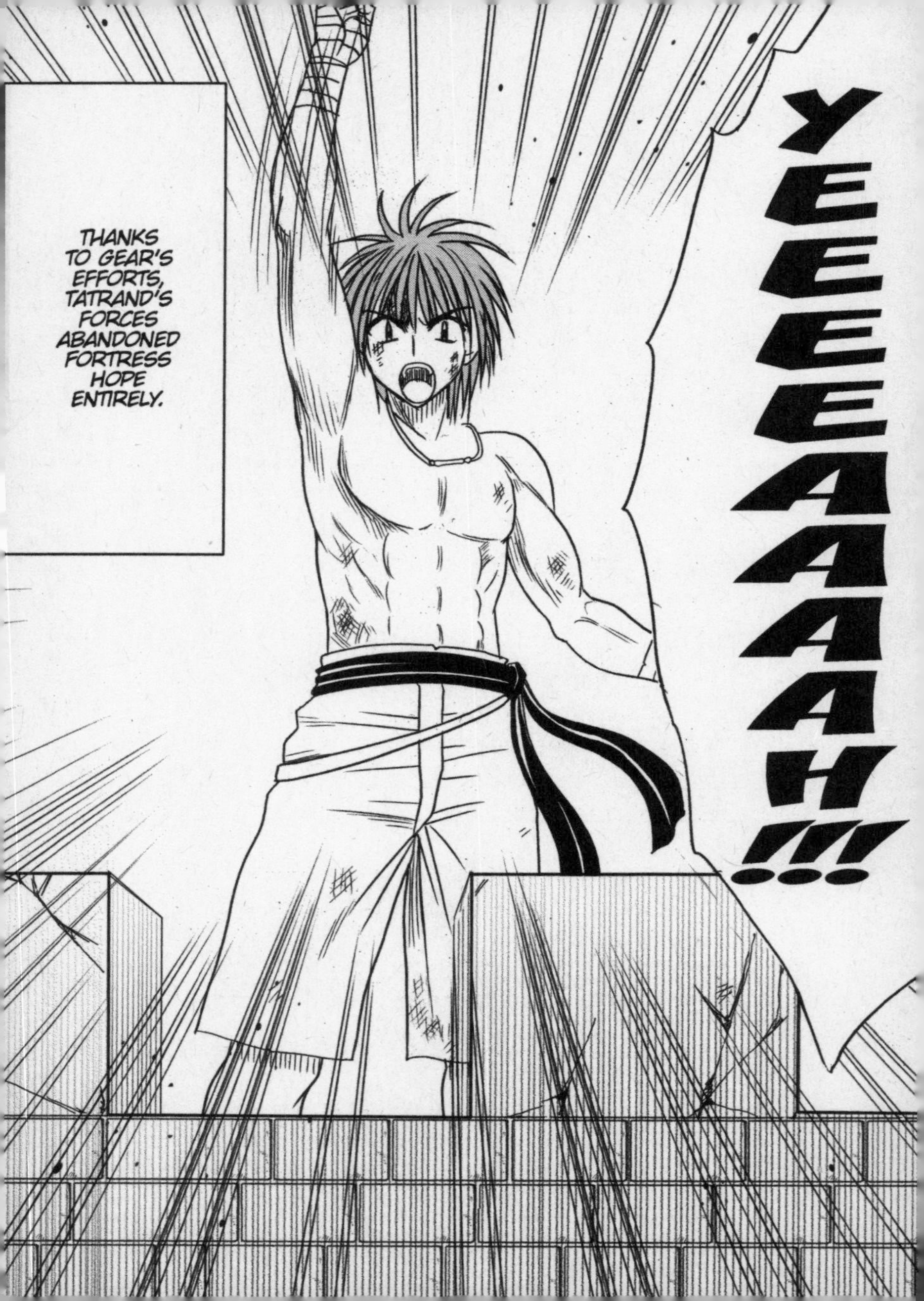
THANKS TO GEAR'S EFFORTS, TATRAND'S FORCES ABANDONED FORTRESS HOPE ENTIRELY.
YEEEEAAAAH!!!

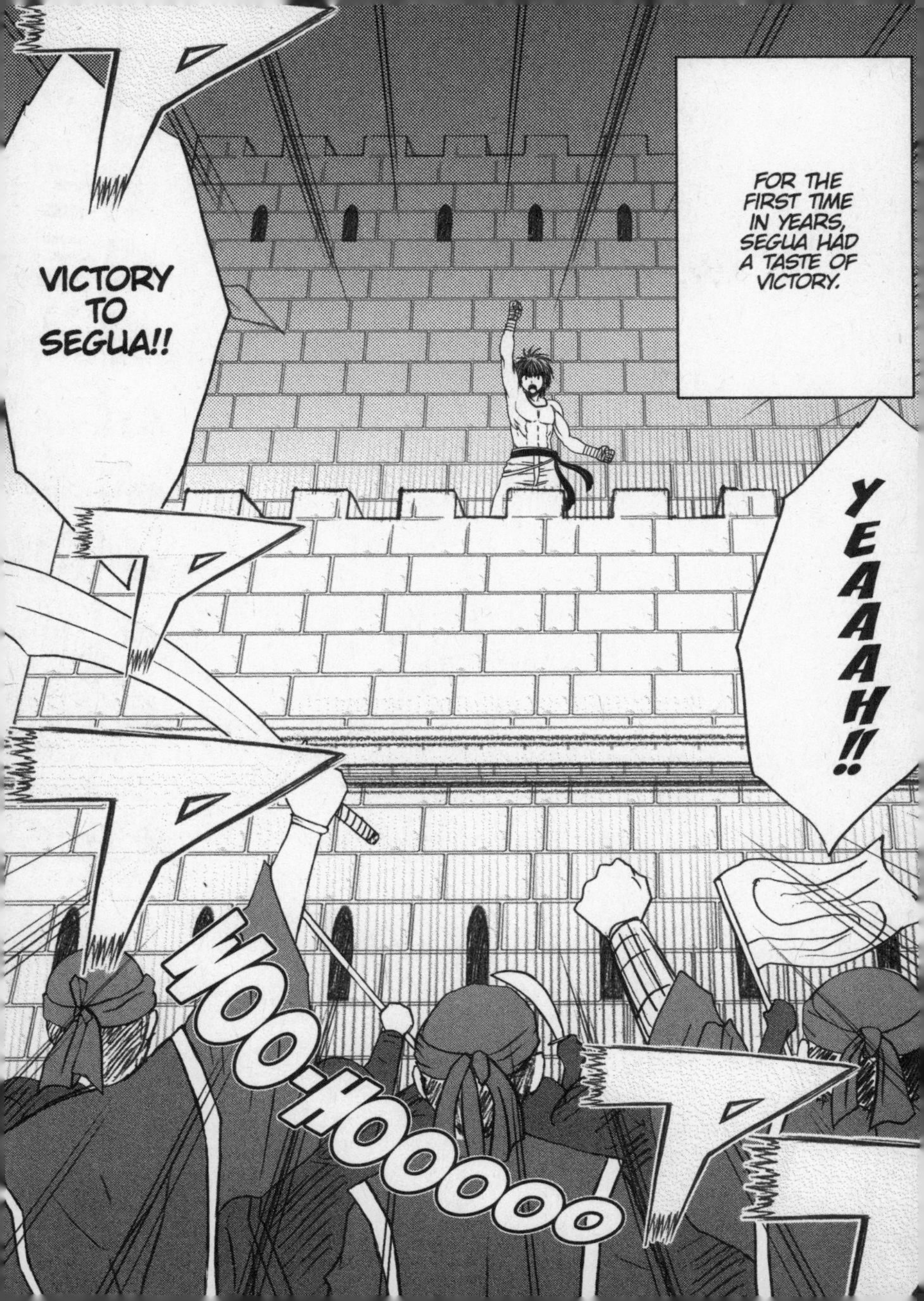
FOR THE FIRST TIME IN YEARS, SEGUA HAD A TASTE OF VICTORY.
YEAAAAH!!
VICTORY TO SEGUA!!
WOO-HOOOOOO

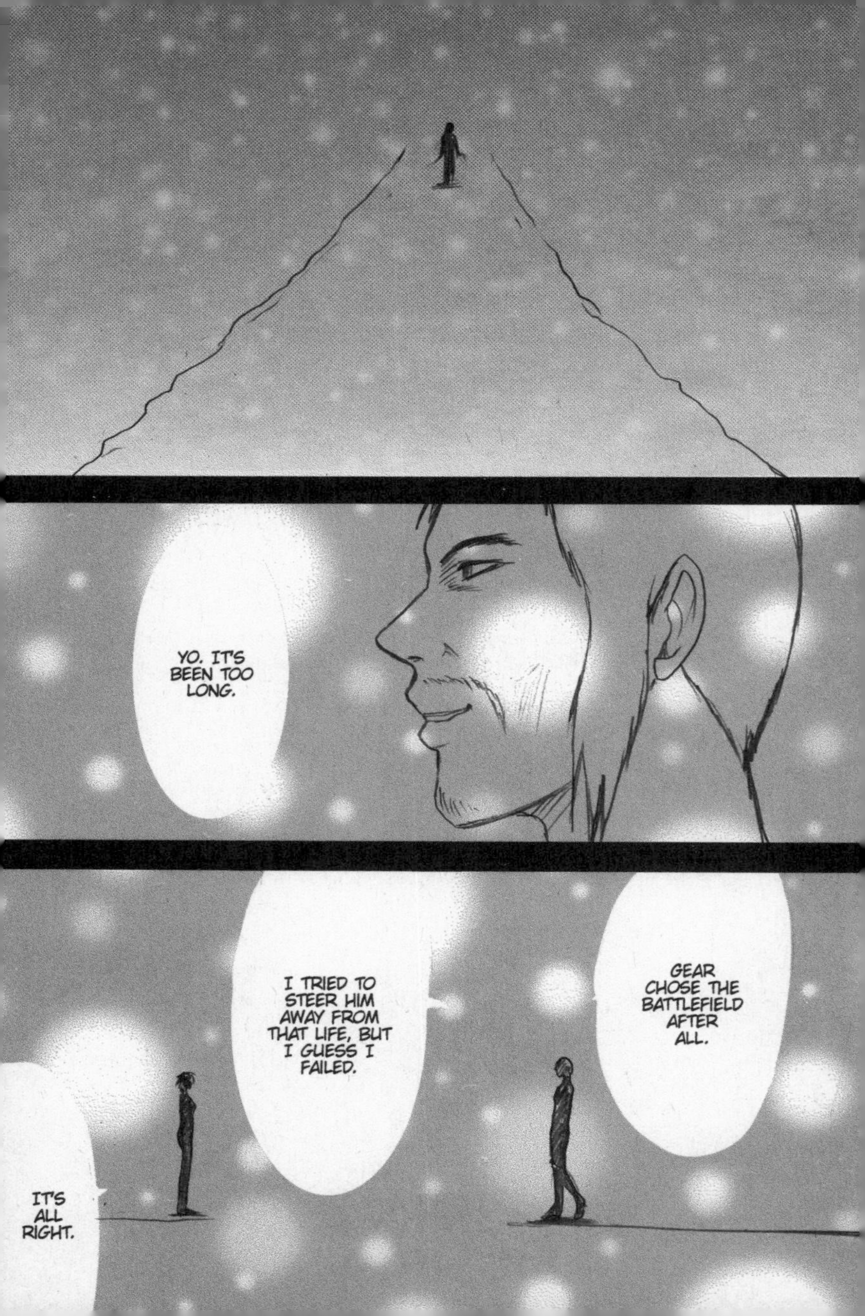
YO. IT'S BEEN TOO LONG.
GEAR CHOSE THE BATTLEFIELD AFTER ALL.
I TRIED TO STEER HIM AWAY FROM THAT LIFE, BUT I GUESS I FAILED.
IT'S ALL RIGHT.

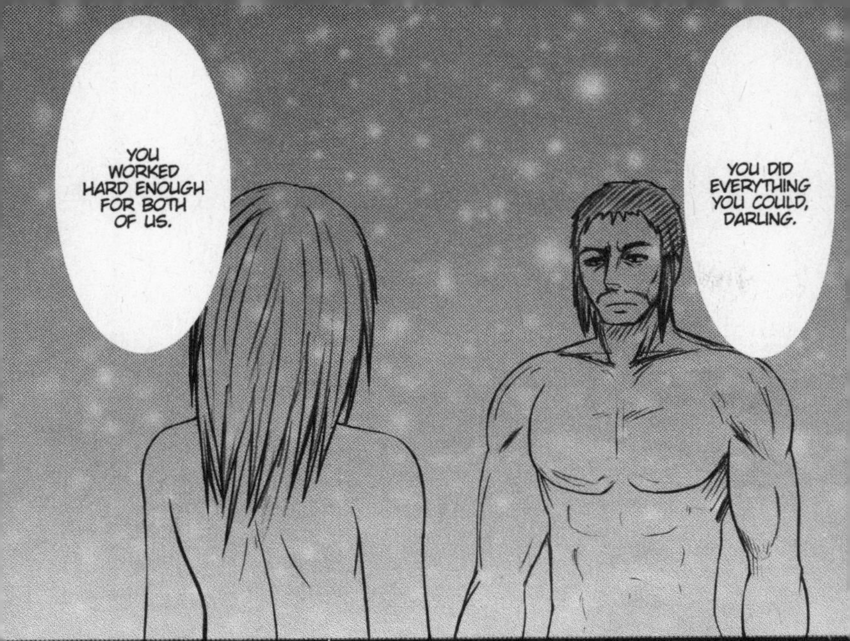
YOU DID EVERYTHING YOU COULD, DARLING.
YOU WORKED HARD ENOUGH FOR BOTH OF US.
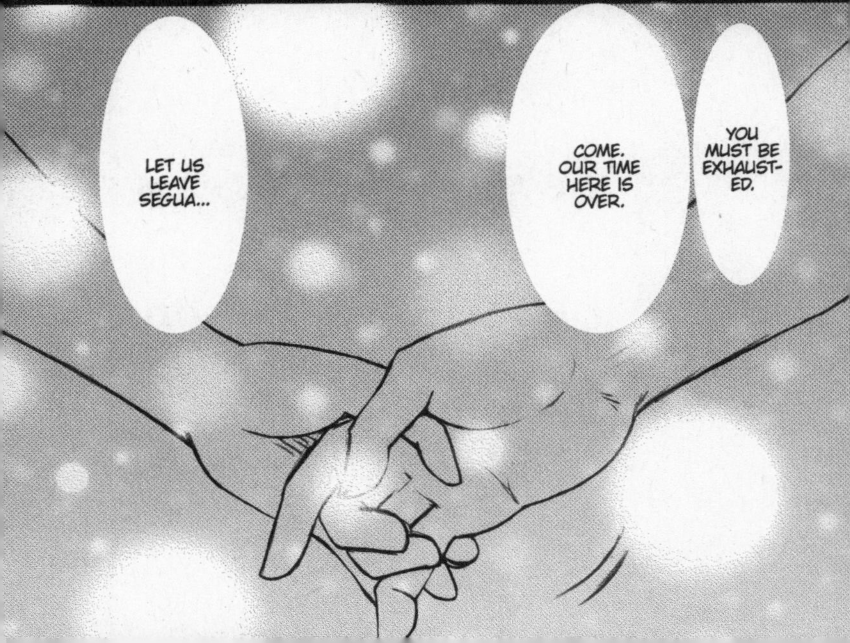
YOU MUST BE EXHAUST-ED.
COME. OUR TIME HERE IS OVER.
LET US LEAVE SEGUA...

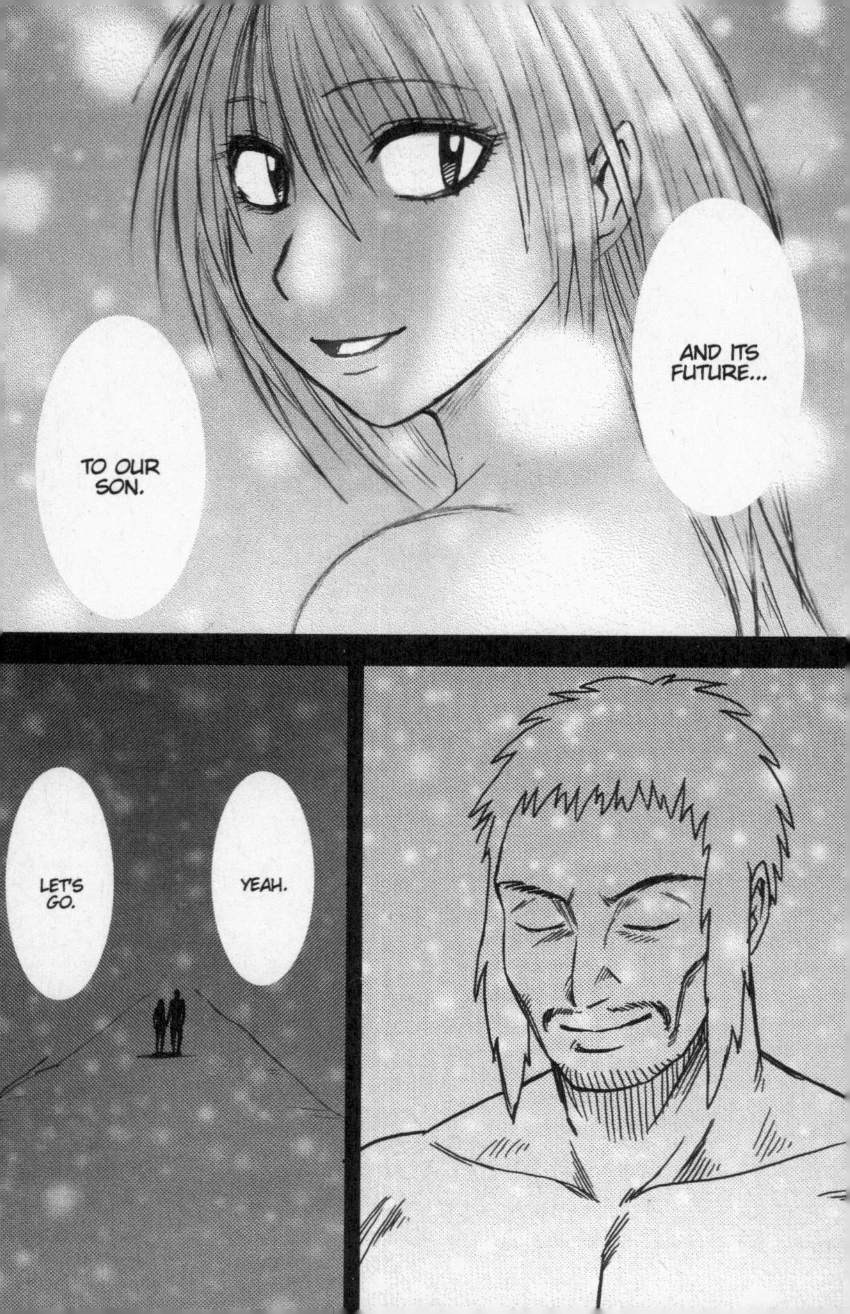
AND ITS FUTURE...
TO OUR SON.
YEAH.
LET'S GO.

WORLD WAR BLUE

END OF PART 1

WORLD WAR BLUE

On the End of Part 1

So that's the end of Part 1. The story so far has been focused on the hero beginning his journey and meeting his companions, and the dawning of a new era in Segua. This is still just the prologue. Moving forward, we'll begin to see the "war" in earnest.

To write this story, I spent a long time studying the history of games in Japan. I read piles of books and articles on the subject, interviewed people employed in the industry, and combed all the related sites I could find on the internet. I thought I was already fairly knowledgeable on the subject, but I discovered there was a lot that I didn't know. Then there were the things that I had forgotten, and subjects I vaguely knew, but didn't realize were such a big deal. All this research taught me that there are still tons of loyal fans out there for retro titles that were great back in the day. It was a rewarding and entertaining study. I plan on using all those small and interesting details I learned to add more depth to the plot.

When we first began serializing this story on the internet, I had to wonder if anyone would be interested in reading a webmanga. After all, isn't reading a paper book easier than trying to flip through a bunch of screens online? And isn't it a pain to go to a website just to read my story? But in the end, a large number of people visited the site and read the manga. Just thinking about it makes me ecstatic. I am thankful to each and every one of my readers.

The Characters of Part 1

I have to admit, my favorite character from Part 1 is Tejirov. Generally, when Japanese people think of Russian characters, they tend to think of chilly and standoffish people, people fanatically loyal to their superiors, or frighteningly violent people, like soldiers and assassins.

But Tejirov's concept started as someone who liked to fill in holes and gaps, and from there it grew into his present friendly, yet filthy, "loves to let his mind wallow in the gutter" character. I love how he completely bucks the trend of Russian characters, and that he is incredibly lewd, despite his normal-guy looks.

Gear was the main character of Part 1, and I aimed to make him as much of a standard shonen-manga hero as I could. He has blinding speed and, like many shonen heroes, a drive to move forward and overcome obstacles. I thought about giving him some more distinguishing features from the start, but I decided that, as the main character, it would be better if he was more relatable. Besides, I figured I could add some unique traits to him as his character grows within the story.

Of all the female characters, Opal is my favorite. I decided to make her determined and strong-willed. There are other parts about her I like, but as they are spoilers, I won't share them here. Like Tejirov, I wanted to distance Opal from the stereotypical manga heroine, so I made her stylish and beautiful, but also prone to making (really bad) puns. Though in Opal's case, there is probably more emphasis on her looks and physical design than on her personality.

I intended Nel to be the "little sister" character. She is proving difficult to use, as she is not the sort to go out and do things for herself. She didn't do very much at all in Part 1, though she will have a bigger role to play in Part 2.

Ramses is another character who hasn't done much yet. She will have more chances to shine later in the story.

In Part 2, lots of new characters will be introduced, many of them from countries other than Segua. I hope you're looking forward to it!

Perusing Video Game History

ON THE EDGE OF THE BLUE WORLD

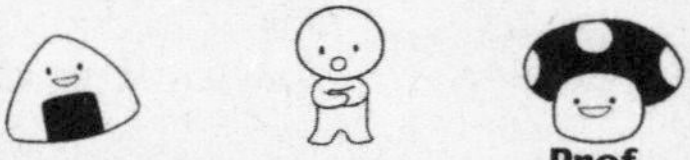

Dr. Onigiri　Mr. Why　Prof. Mushroom

Today's Topic

ALEX KIDD

Mr. Why: Okay, so I get how Sonic became Sega's mascot when his game came out for the Sega Genesis. But did Sega have a mascot before him?

Dr. Onigiri: Bwa ha ha! I am SO glad you asked! Yes! Sega *did* have a mascot, as early as the Sega Mark III era!

Prof. Mushroom: Well, you sure sound excited.

Dr. Onigiri: The year was 1986. That year, a new action hero was born–one destined to rival none other than Nintendo's newly-released juggernaut *Super Mario Bros.*! That hero's name was Alex Kidd, and he debuted in Sega's came *Alex Kidd in Miracle World!*

Mr. Why: He went up against *the* Mario?

Dr. Onigiri: That he did. If Mario destroyed blocks by punching them from below, then Alex would destroy them by punching them from the side! If Mario jumped using the "A" button, Alex would jump using the "B" button! Plus, his favorite food was rice-balls, giving him mass-appeal! Oh! Oh! And the stages were brilliantly designed, with ladders to climb up and cliffs you could climb down! And there were so many different vehicles you could use, too! It was crammed full of ideas grand enough to beat even Mario!

Mr. Why: Wow, that sounds amazing! So it was a big hit, right?

Dr. Onigiri: Well, um... *ahem.* It, uh, got a reputation for being a teensy-weensy bit hard when it first came out. I mean, the jump button was switched from where other games had it, making it awkward to play.

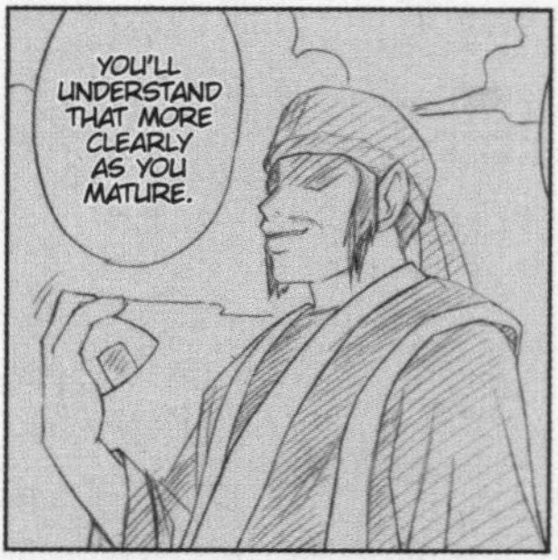
YOU'LL UNDERSTAND THAT MORE CLEARLY AS YOU MATURE.

General Alex loved rice-balls and rock-paper-scissors.

Dr. Onigiri: And, for some reason, the outcome of all of the boss battles were determined by rock-paper-scissors. You could be super skilled at making it through the levels, but then get stuck at the boss because you couldn't win a game of rock-paper-scissors. Players thought that was kinda, well... *unfair.* The game could have leapfrogged over Mario, but I guess it kinda jumped in the wrong direction. Also, the name of the place he trained was a little silly. In Japanese, it was "Maunten-zan," which translates to "Mountain Mountain." The English version fixed that, though...

Mr. Why: ......

Dr. Onigiri: But life is all about learning to accept that some things are unfair, right? Right!! The great Alex Kidd wouldn't let little things like that get him down! Bring on *Alex Kidd: The Lost Stars*, his arcade game debut!!

Prof. Mushroom: Getting a little desperate, are we?

Dr. Onigiri: Mario has Princess Peach, right? So Alex got a female companion named Stella. And she was playable!! Two players could play simultaneously, one as Alex and one as Stella! Even better, the unpopular rock-paper-scissors aspect of the previous game was totally dropped!

Mr. Why: That's great! So this one was a smash-hit, right?

Dr. Onigiri: Uhmmm... well... to be blunt, it was *still* too hard. The cutesy pastel graphics, combined with the crushingly high difficulty level sent most gamers running. It was eventually ported to the Sega Mark III, but then, for some reason, Stella wasn't in it any more. To gamers, it all seemed kinda... pointless.

Mr. Why: ......

Dr. Onigiri: Anyway, thanks to that, Alex Kidd never did get his day in the sun. But I like to think that the work and effort put into those games is what eventually led to Sonic.

Prof. Mushroom: Or they could, y'know, be completely unconnected.

Dr. Onigiri: Thank you, Alex...

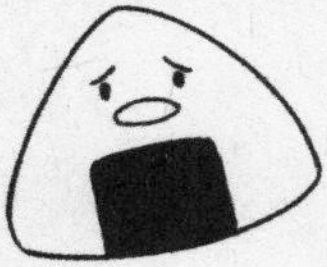

To Be Continued...

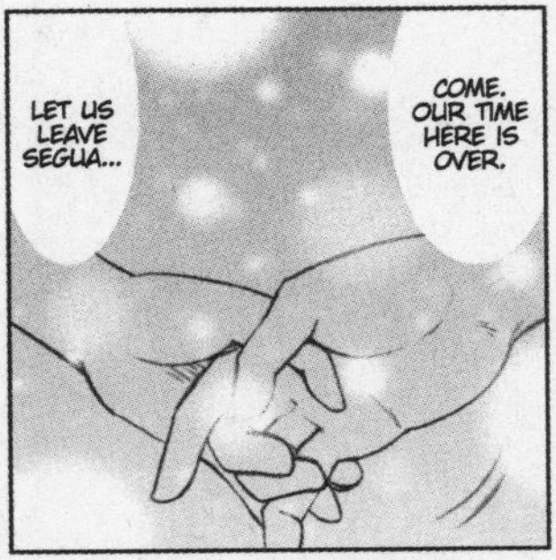
COME. OUR TIME HERE IS OVER.
LET US LEAVE SEGUA...

And so the power and promise of one generation is entrusted to the next.

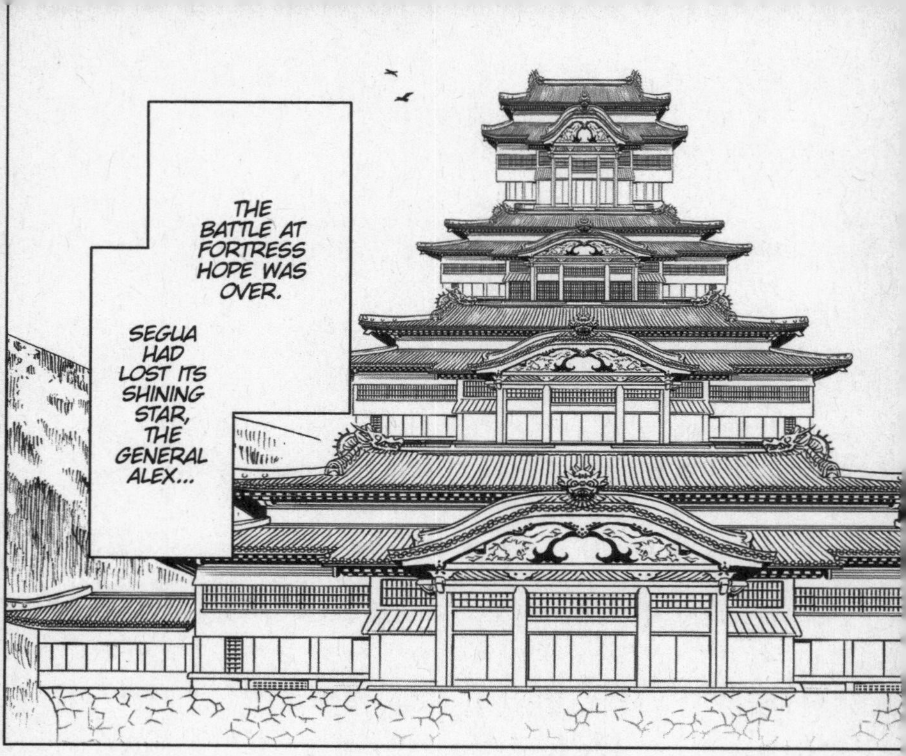
THE BATTLE AT FORTRESS HOPE WAS OVER.
SEGUA HAD LOST ITS SHINING STAR, THE GENERAL ALEX...
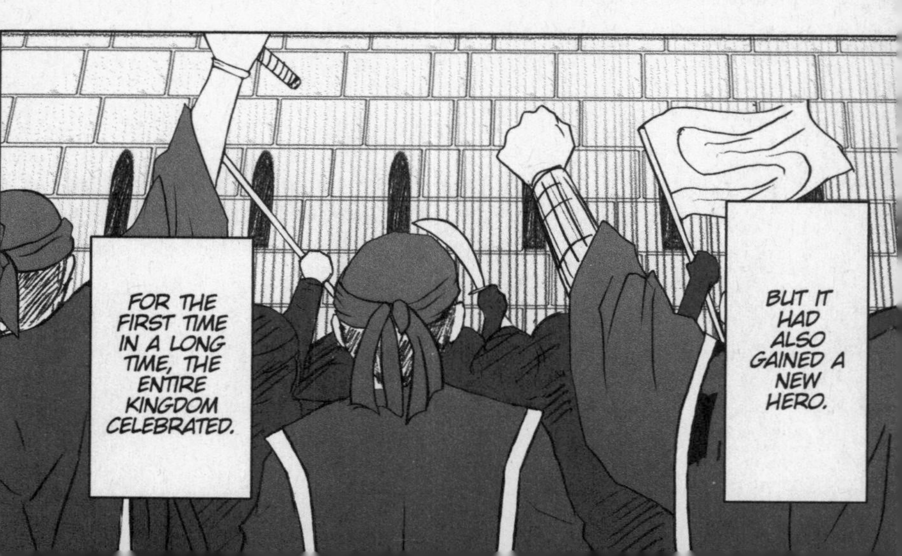
BUT IT HAD ALSO GAINED A NEW HERO.
FOR THE FIRST TIME IN A LONG TIME, THE ENTIRE KINGDOM CELEBRATED.

Part 2

CHAPTER 1

GREEN HILL

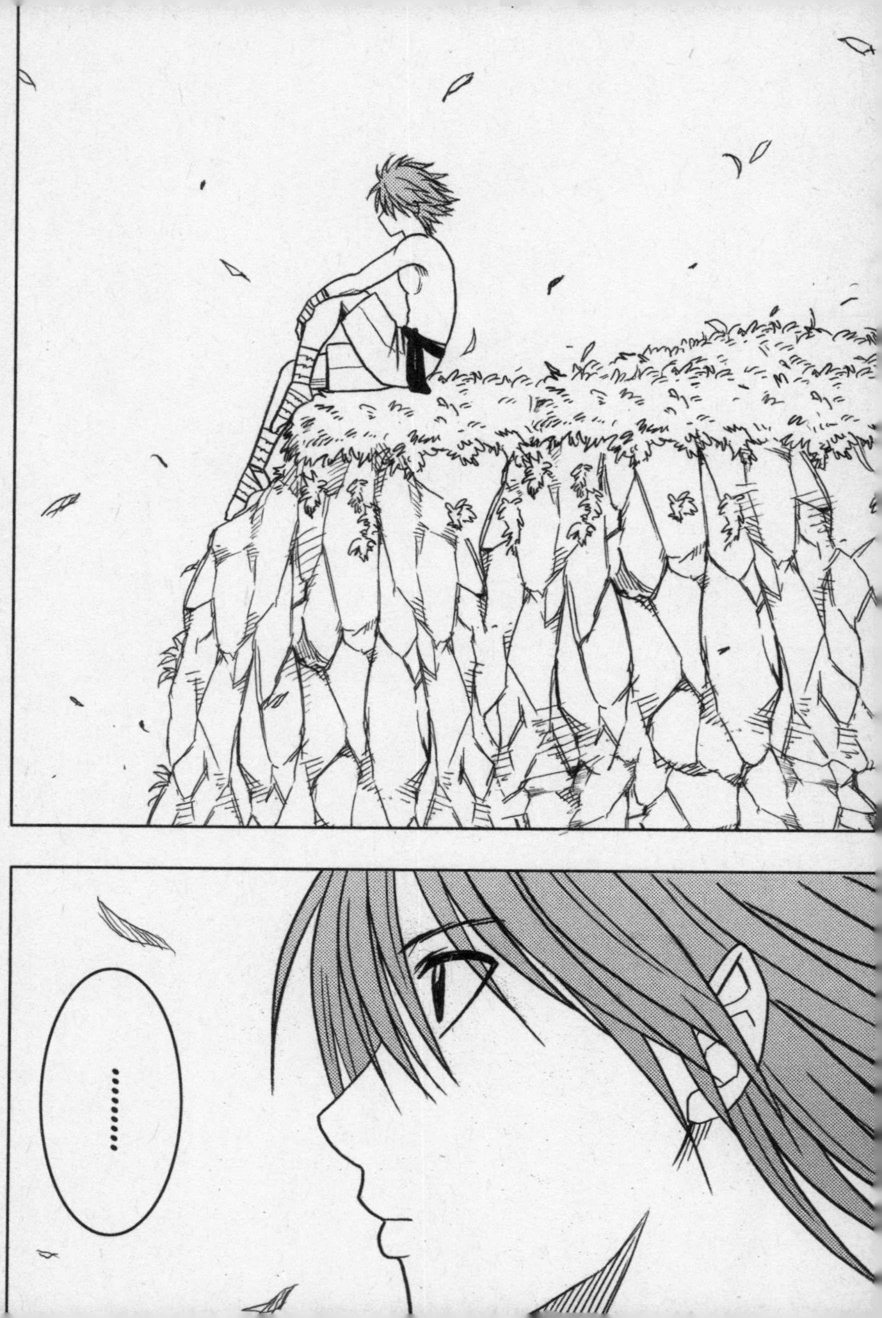
……

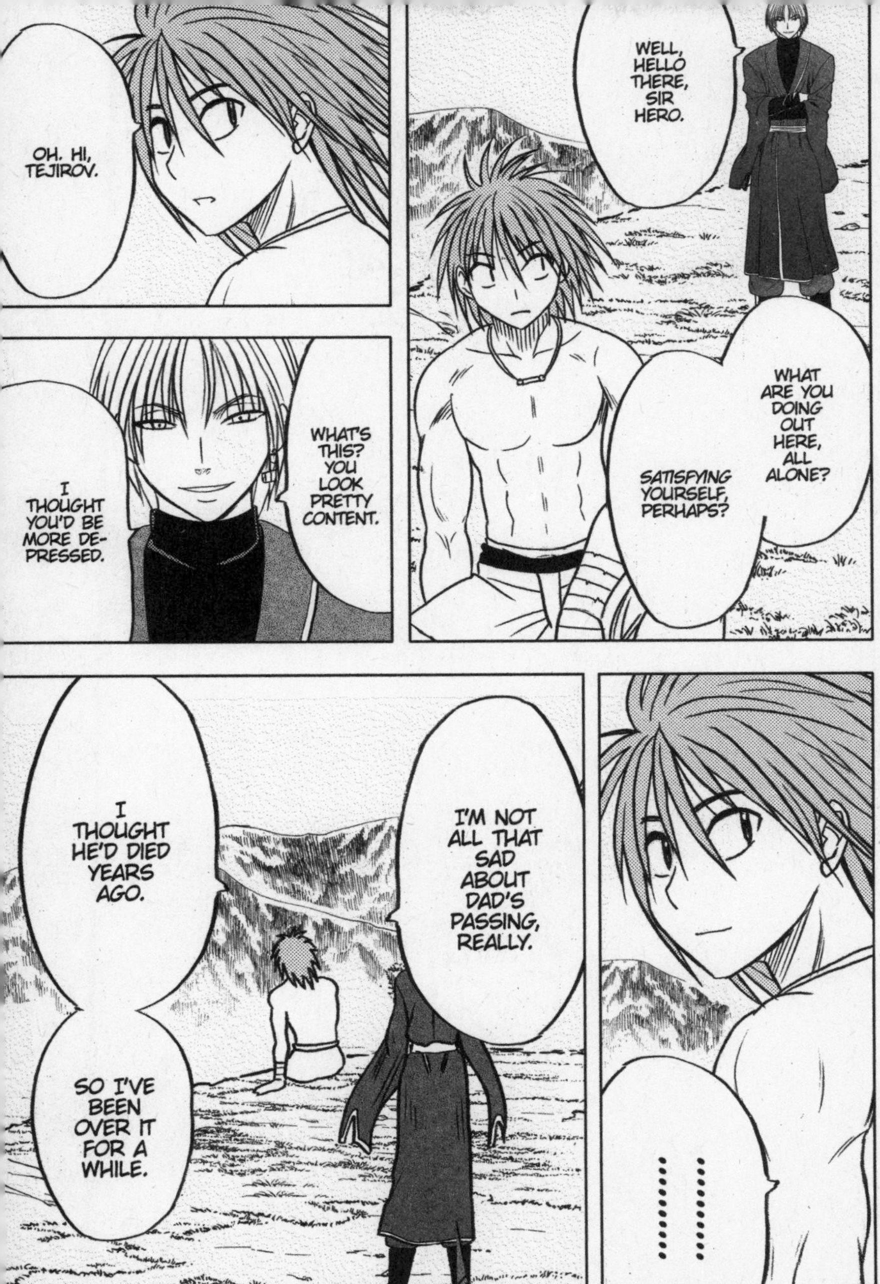
WELL, HELLO THERE, SIR HERO.
WHAT ARE YOU DOING OUT HERE, ALL ALONE?
SATISFYING YOURSELF, PERHAPS?
OH. HI, TEJIROV.
WHAT'S THIS? YOU LOOK PRETTY CONTENT.
I THOUGHT YOU'D BE MORE DE-PRESSED.
......
I'M NOT ALL THAT SAD ABOUT DAD'S PASSING, REALLY.
I THOUGHT HE'D DIED YEARS AGO.
SO I'VE BEEN OVER IT FOR A WHILE.

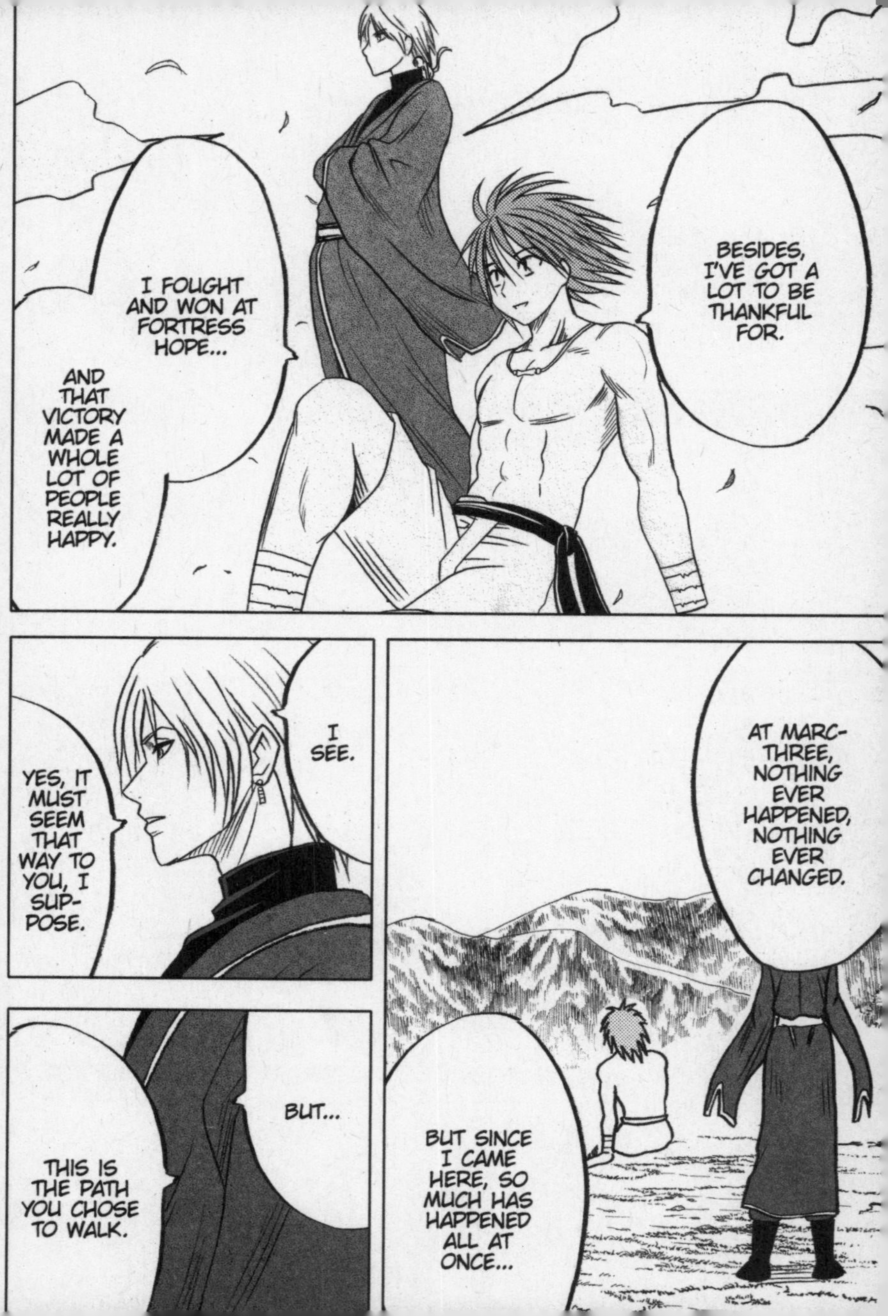
BESIDES, I'VE GOT A LOT TO BE THANKFUL FOR.
I FOUGHT AND WON AT FORTRESS HOPE...
AND THAT VICTORY MADE A WHOLE LOT OF PEOPLE REALLY HAPPY.
AT MARC-THREE, NOTHING EVER HAPPENED, NOTHING EVER CHANGED.
BUT SINCE I CAME HERE, SO MUCH HAS HAPPENED ALL AT ONCE...
I SEE.
YES, IT MUST SEEM THAT WAY TO YOU, I SUPPOSE.
BUT...
THIS IS THE PATH YOU CHOSE TO WALK.

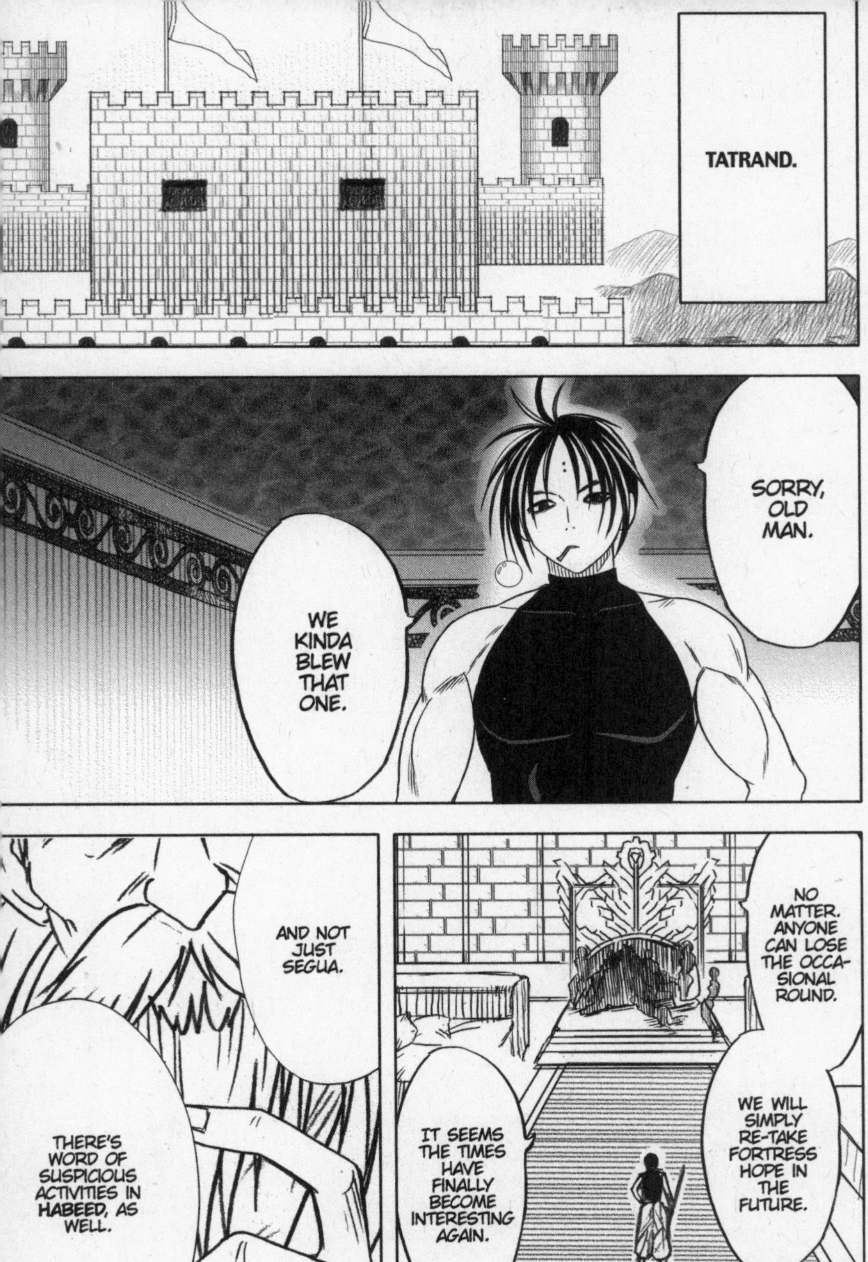
TATRAND.
SORRY, OLD MAN.
WE KINDA BLEW THAT ONE.
NO MATTER. ANYONE CAN LOSE THE OCCASIONAL ROUND.
WE WILL SIMPLY RE-TAKE FORTRESS HOPE IN THE FUTURE.
IT SEEMS THE TIMES HAVE FINALLY BECOME INTERESTING AGAIN.
AND NOT JUST SEGUA.
THERE'S WORD OF SUSPICIOUS ACTIVITIES IN HABEED, AS WELL.

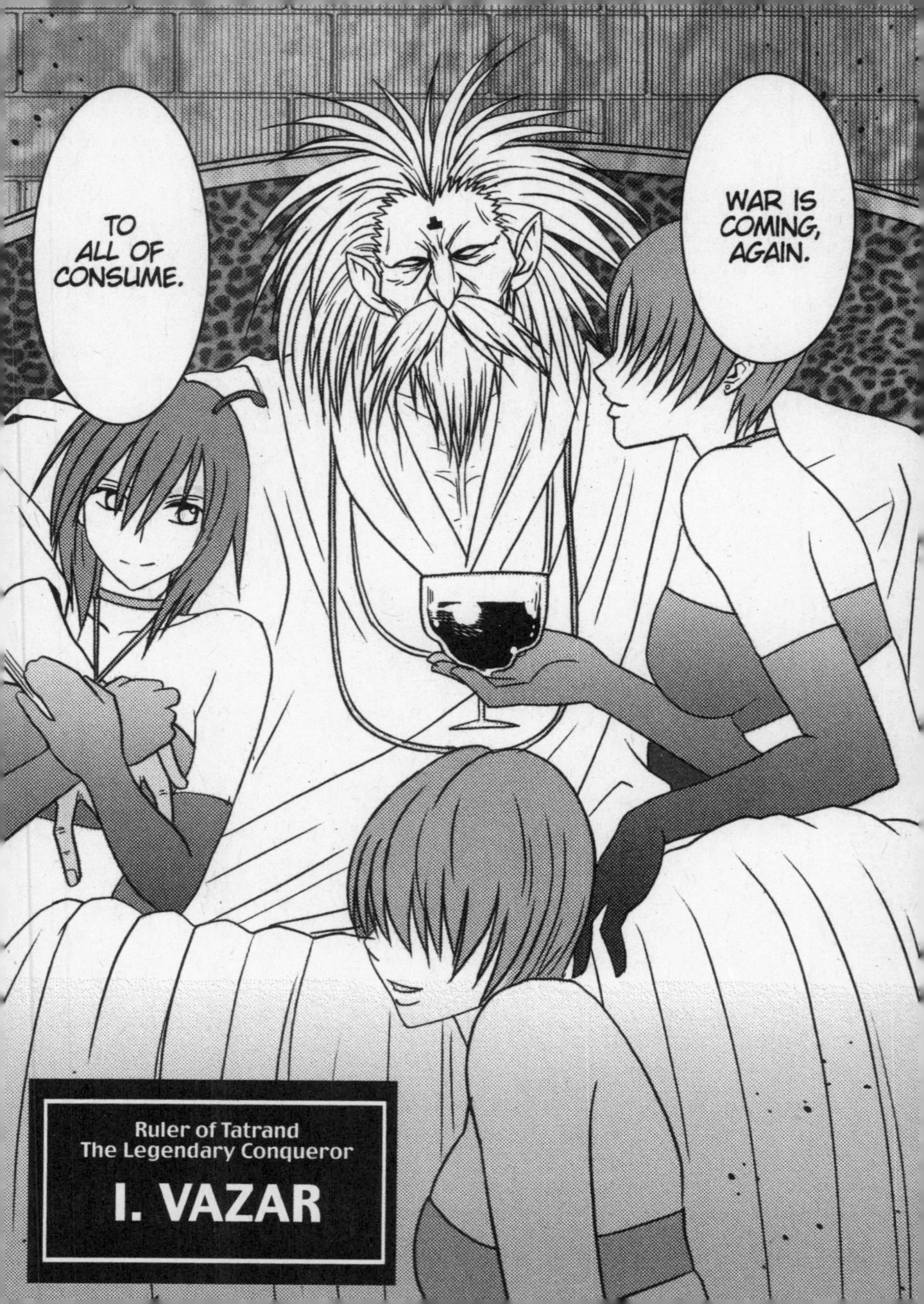
WAR IS COMING, AGAIN.
TO ALL OF CONSUME.
Ruler of Tatrand
The Legendary Conqueror
I. VAZAR

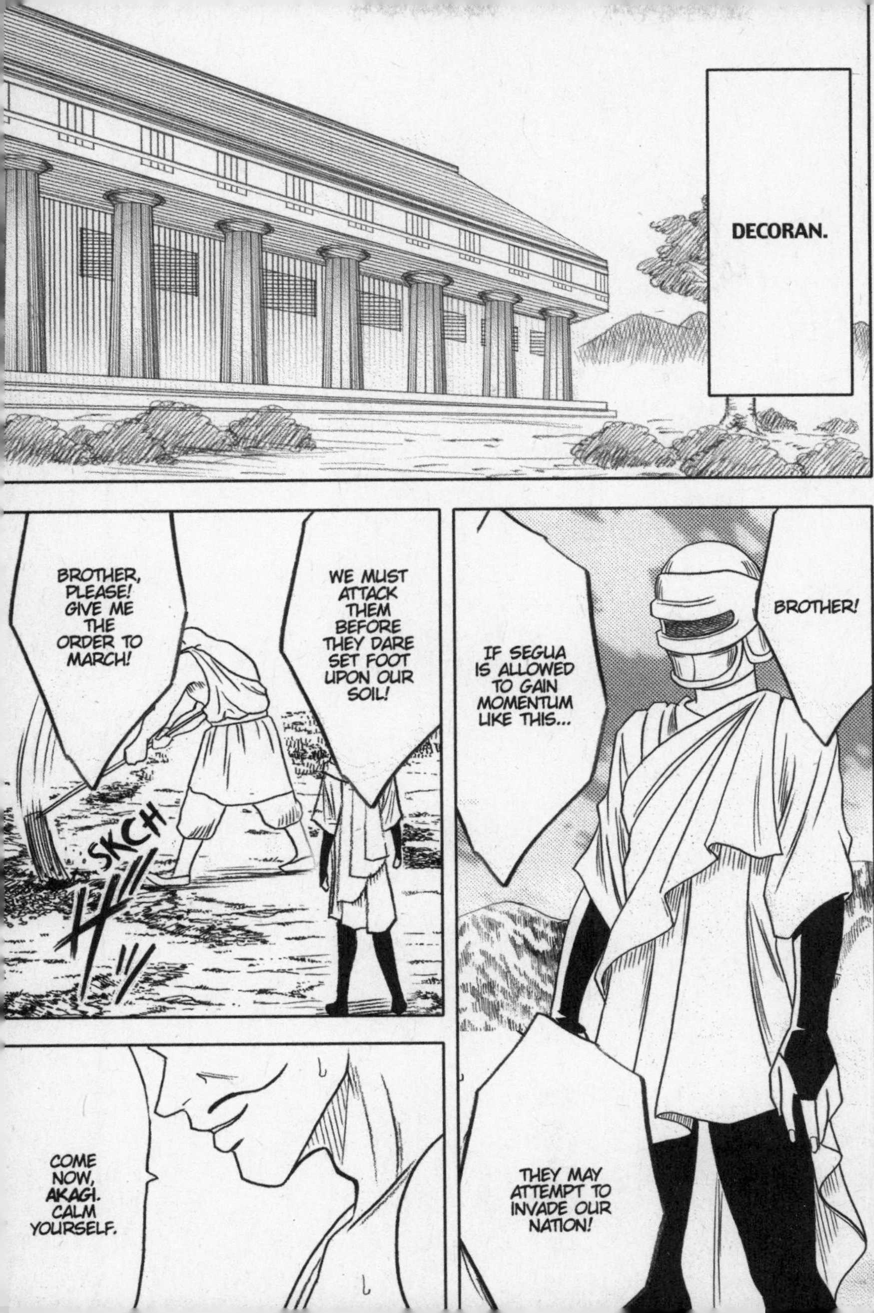
DECORAN.
BROTHER!
IF SEGUA IS ALLOWED TO GAIN MOMENTUM LIKE THIS...
THEY MAY ATTEMPT TO INVADE OUR NATION!
WE MUST ATTACK THEM BEFORE THEY DARE SET FOOT UPON OUR SOIL!
BROTHER, PLEASE! GIVE ME THE ORDER TO MARCH!
SKCH
COME NOW, AKAGI. CALM YOURSELF.

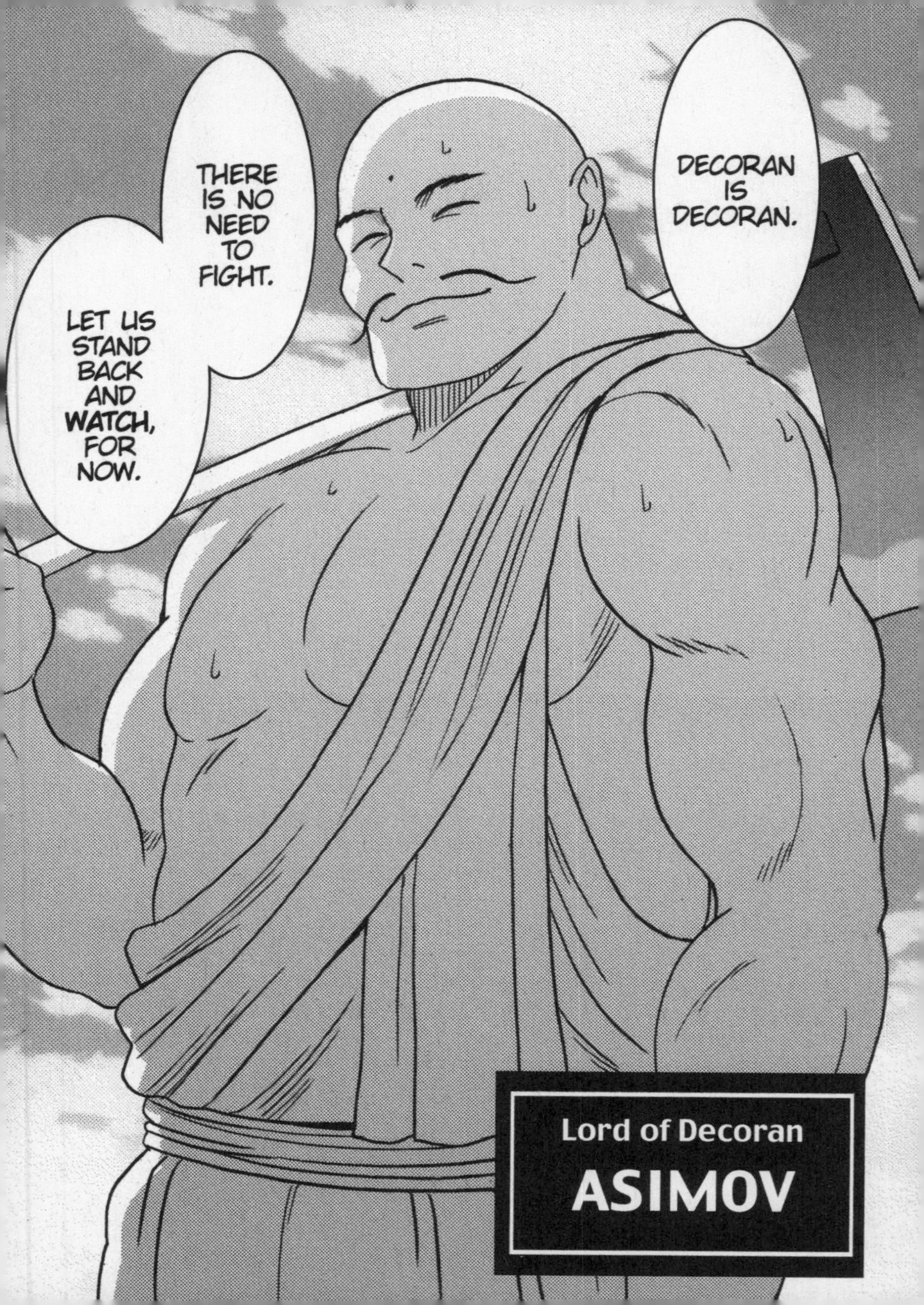
DECORAN IS DECORAN.
THERE IS NO NEED TO FIGHT.
LET US STAND BACK AND WATCH, FOR NOW.
Lord of Decoran
ASIMOV

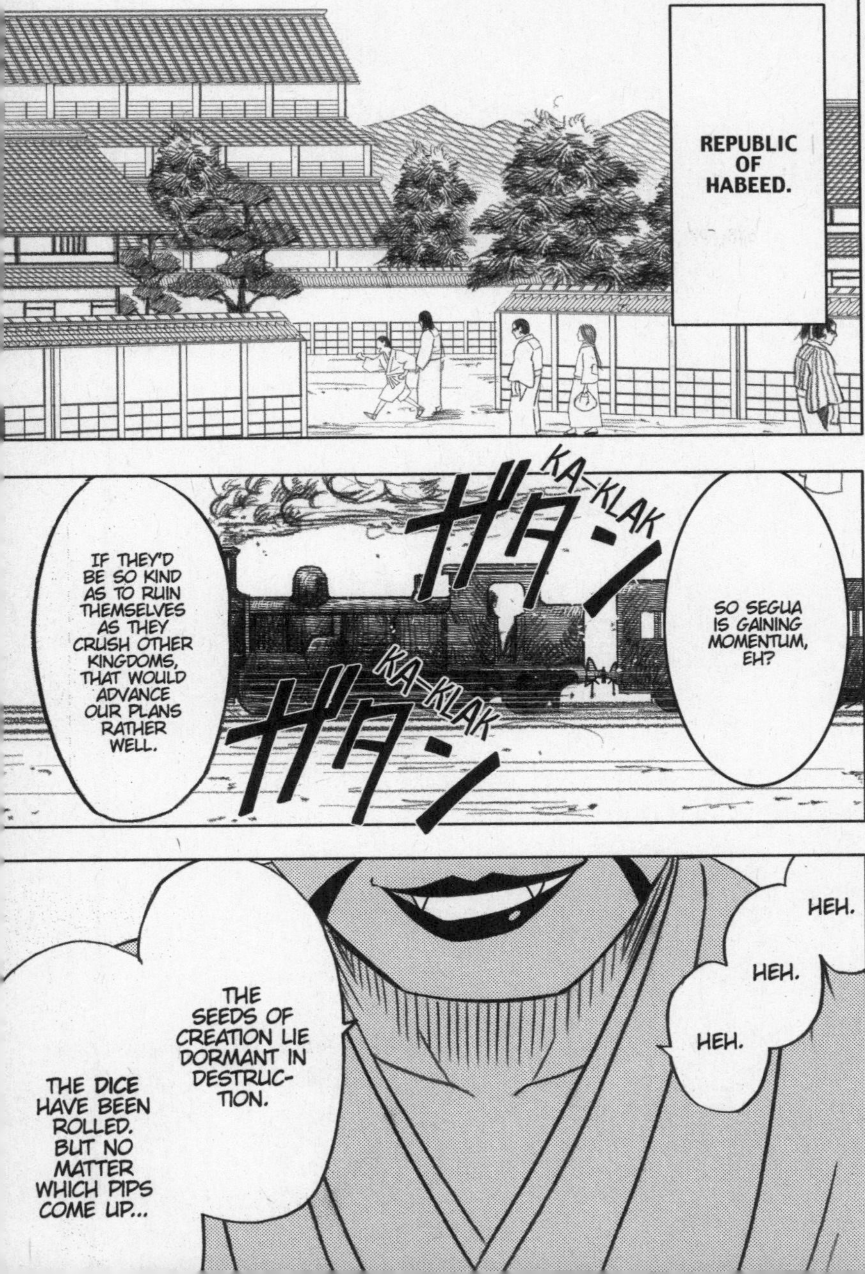
REPUBLIC OF HABEED.
SO SEGUA IS GAINING MOMENTUM, EH?
KA-KLAK
ガタン
KA-KLAK
ガタン
IF THEY'D BE SO KIND AS TO RUIN THEMSELVES AS THEY CRUSH OTHER KINGDOMS, THAT WOULD ADVANCE OUR PLANS RATHER WELL.
HEH.
HEH.
HEH.
THE SEEDS OF CREATION LIE DORMANT IN DESTRUC-TION.
THE DICE HAVE BEEN ROLLED. BUT NO MATTER WHICH PIPS COME UP...

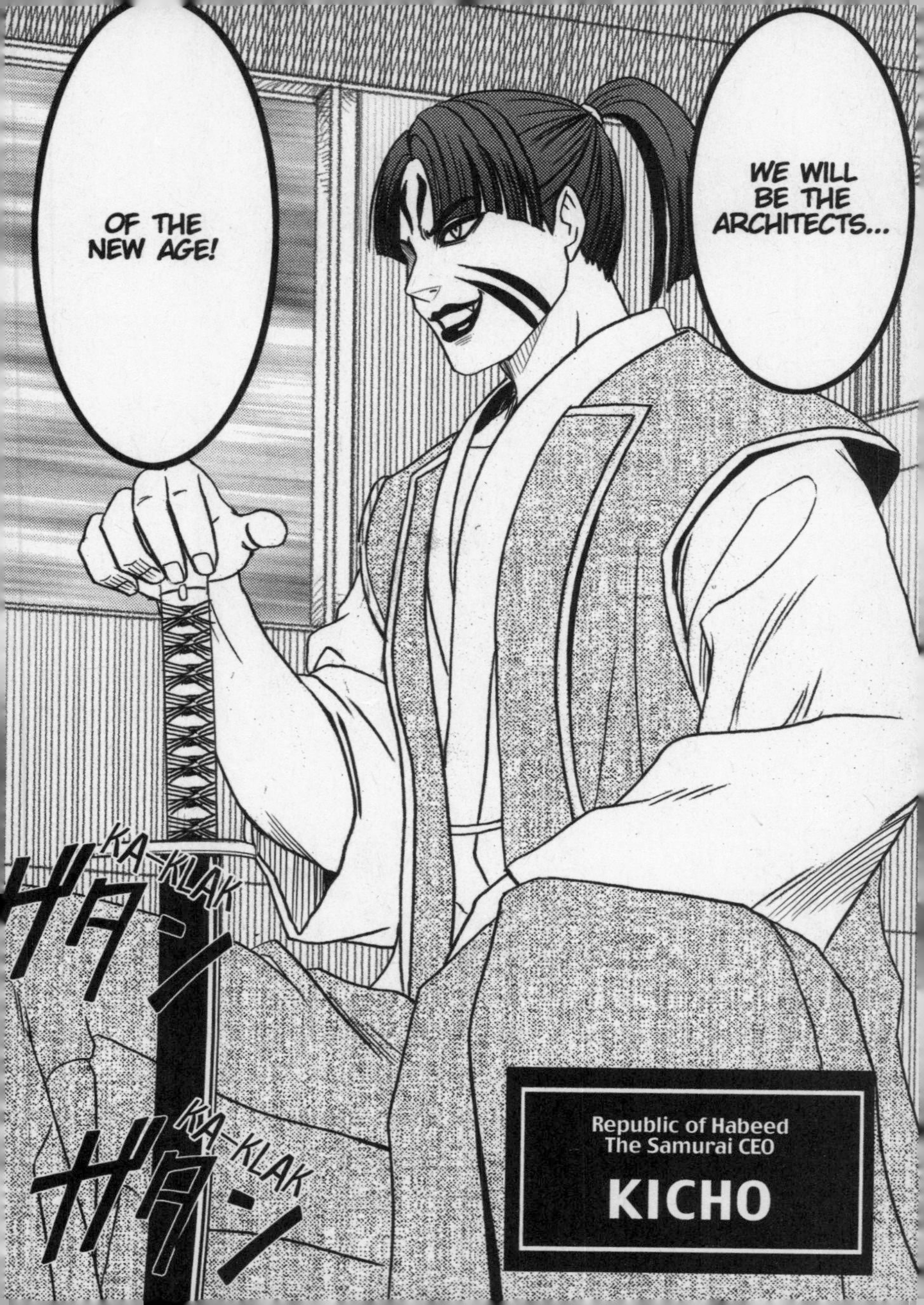
WE WILL BE THE ARCHITECTS...
OF THE NEW AGE!
KA-KLAK
KA-KLAK
Republic of Habeed
The Samurai CEO
KICHO

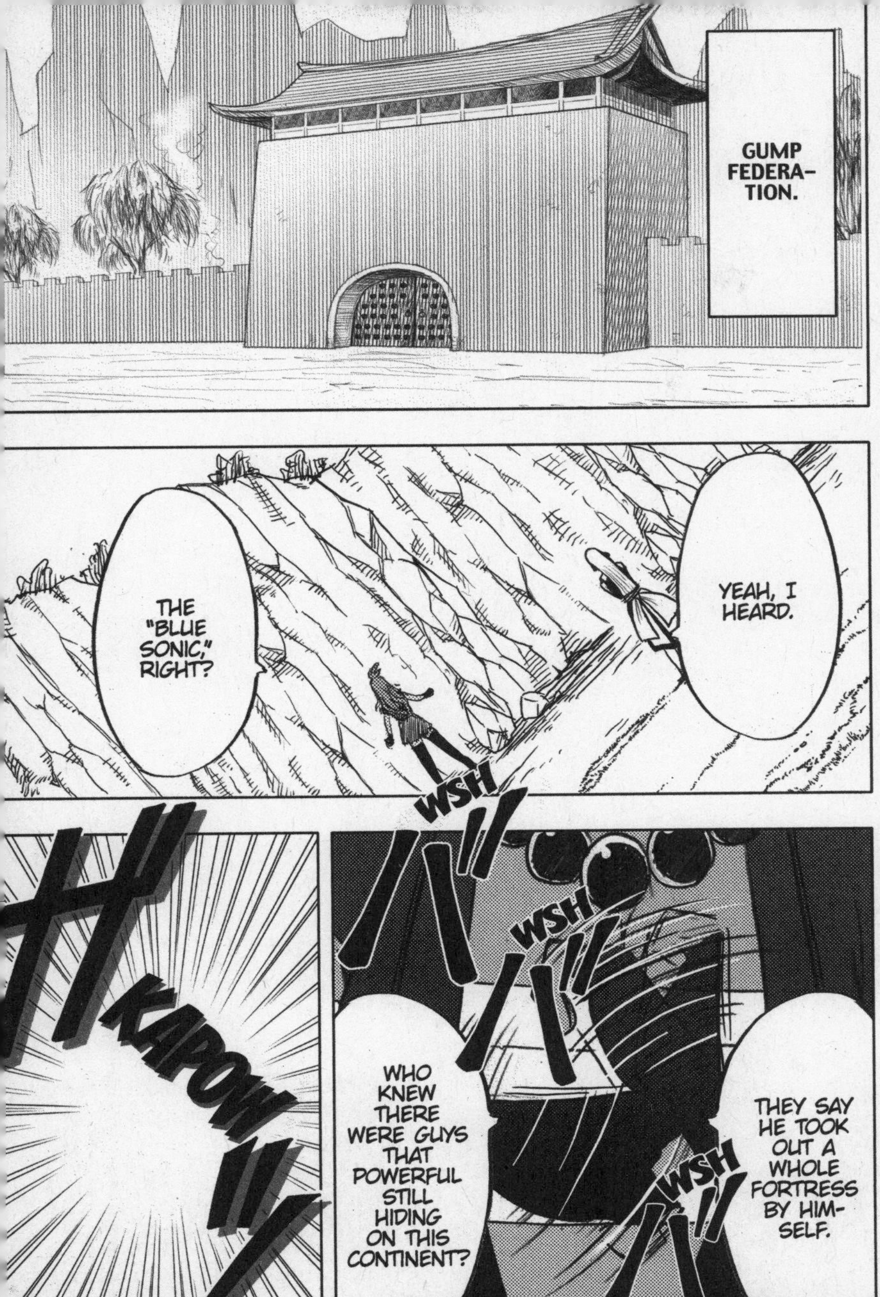
GUMP FEDERATION.
YEAH, I HEARD.
THE "BLUE SONIC," RIGHT?
WSH
WSH
THEY SAY HE TOOK OUT A WHOLE FORTRESS BY HIMSELF.
WSH
WHO KNEW THERE WERE GUYS THAT POWERFUL STILL HIDING ON THIS CONTINENT?
KAPOW

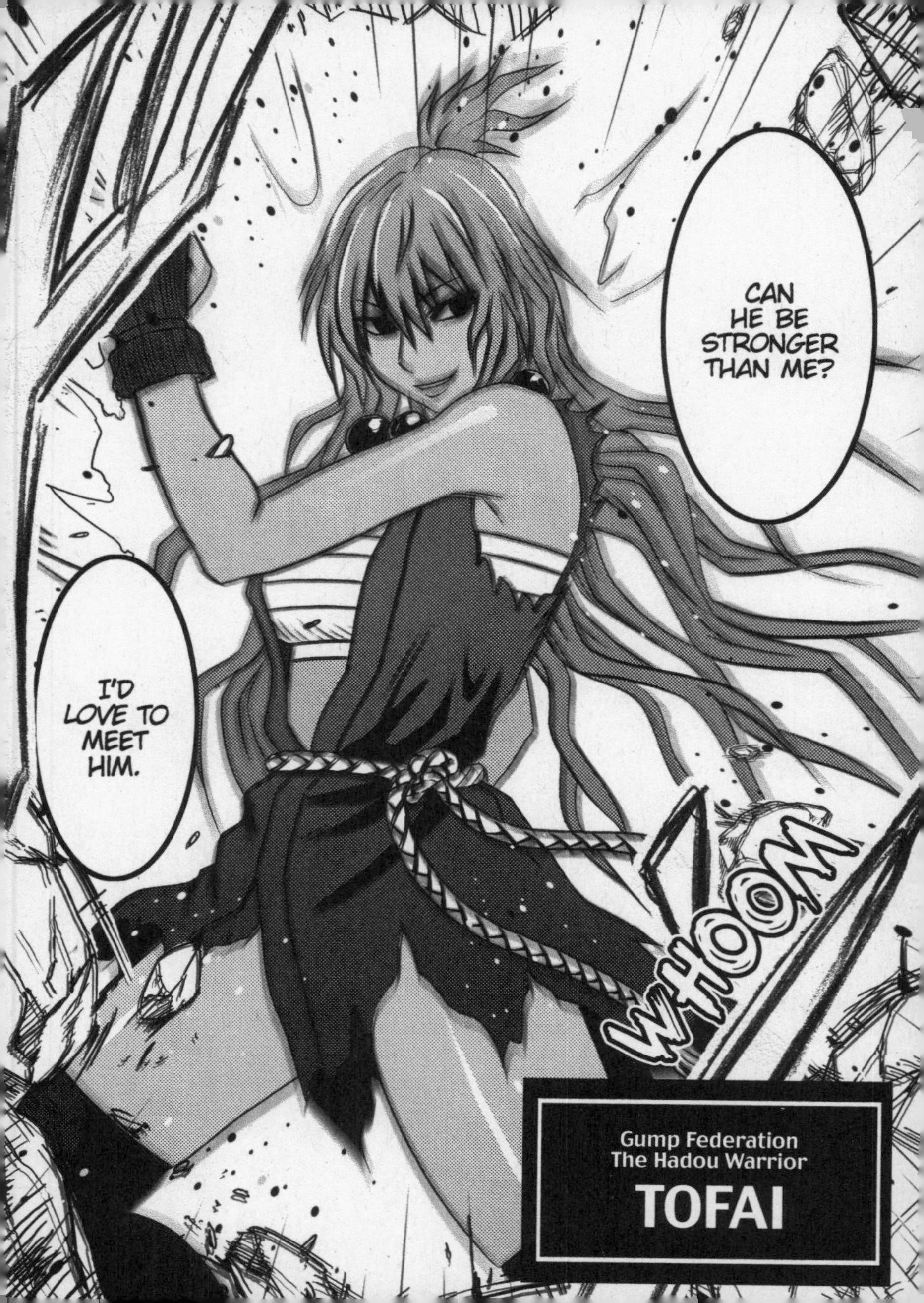
CAN HE BE STRONGER THAN ME?
I'D LOVE TO MEET HIM.
WHOOM
Gump Federation
The Hadou Warrior
TOFAI

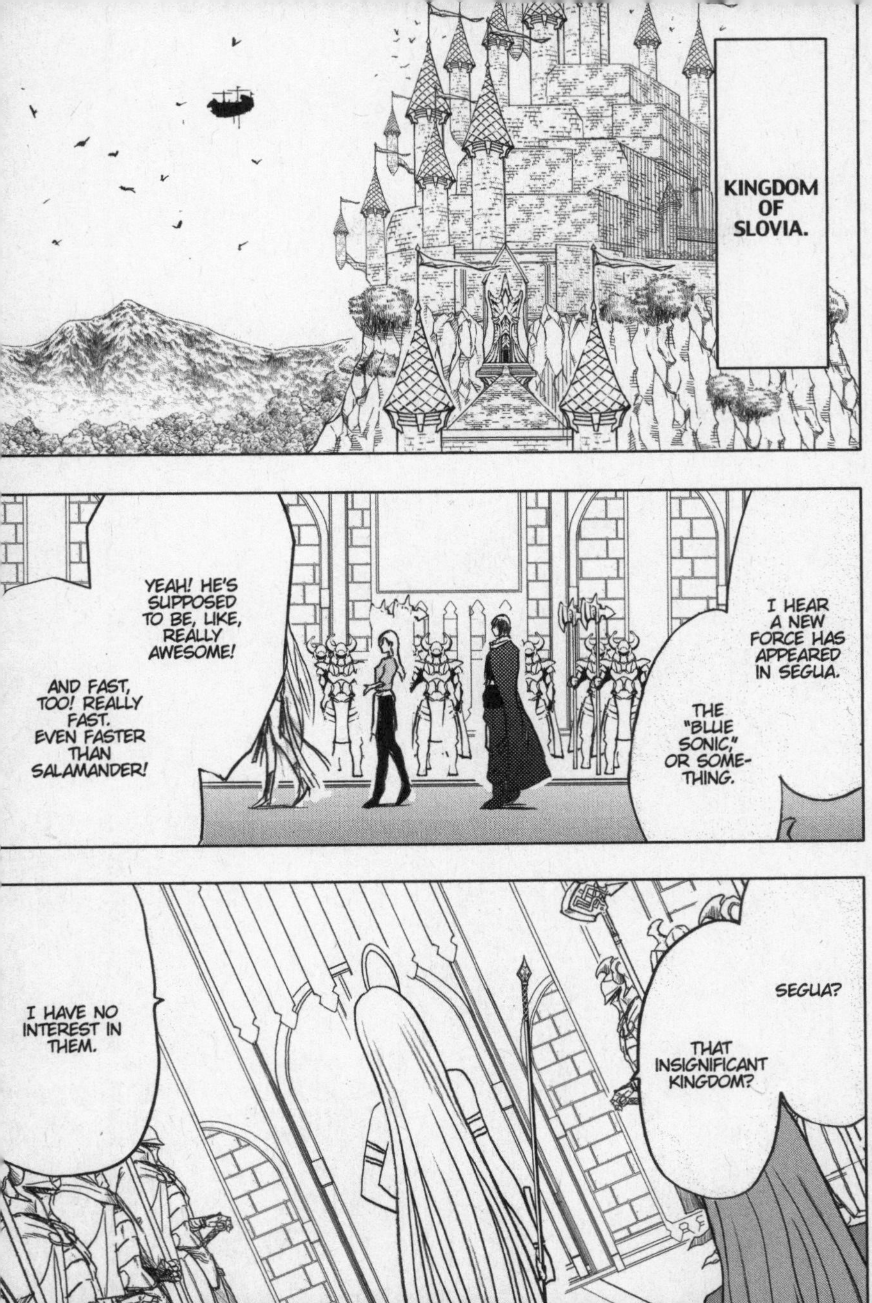
KINGDOM OF SLOVIA.
I HEAR A NEW FORCE HAS APPEARED IN SEGUA.
THE "BLUE SONIC," OR SOME-THING.
YEAH! HE'S SUPPOSED TO BE, LIKE, REALLY AWESOME!
AND FAST, TOO! REALLY FAST. EVEN FASTER THAN SALAMANDER!
SEGUA?
THAT INSIGNIFICANT KINGDOM?
I HAVE NO INTEREST IN THEM.

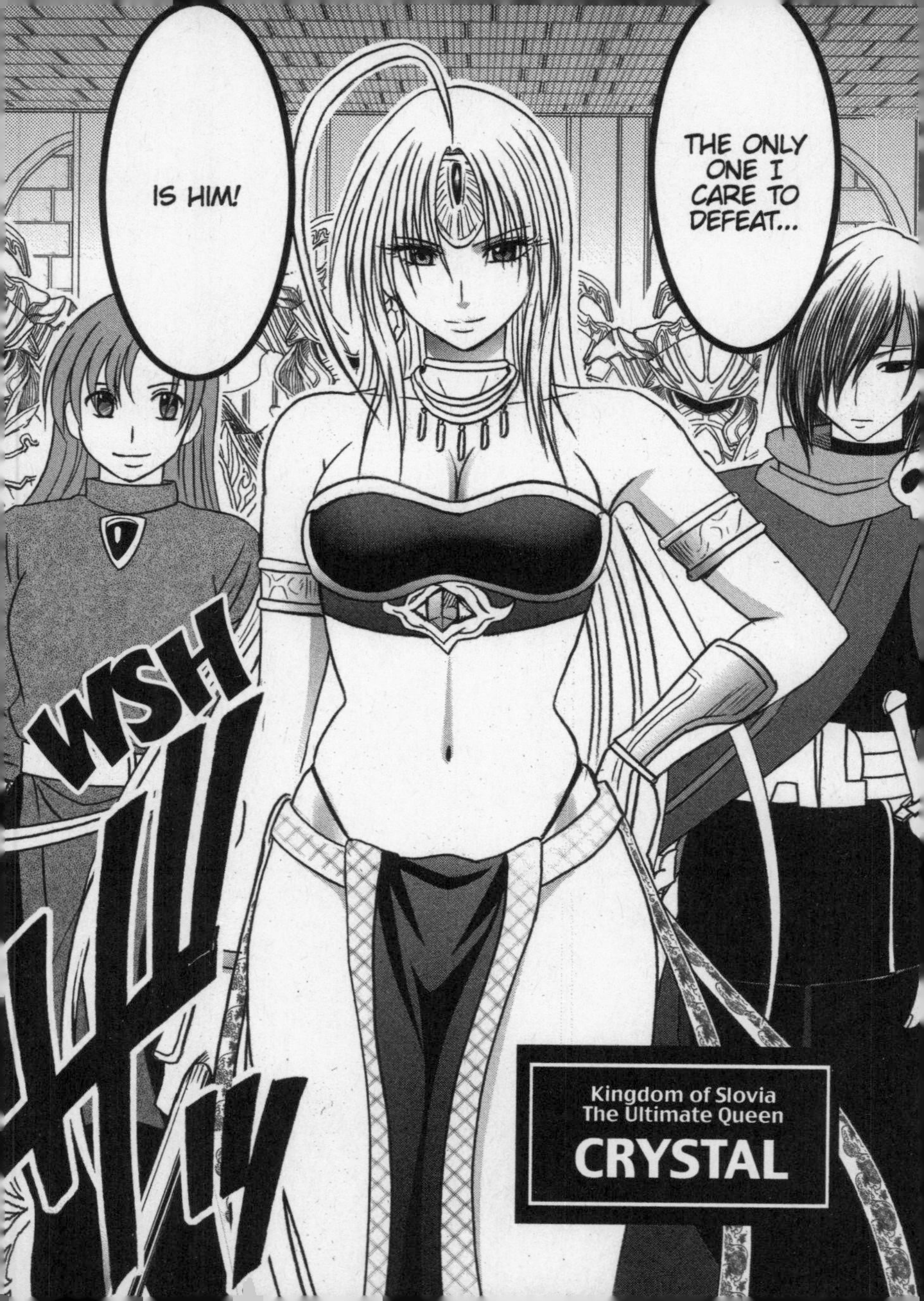
THE ONLY ONE I CARE TO DEFEAT...
IS HIM!
WSH
Kingdom of Slovia
The Ultimate Queen
CRYSTAL

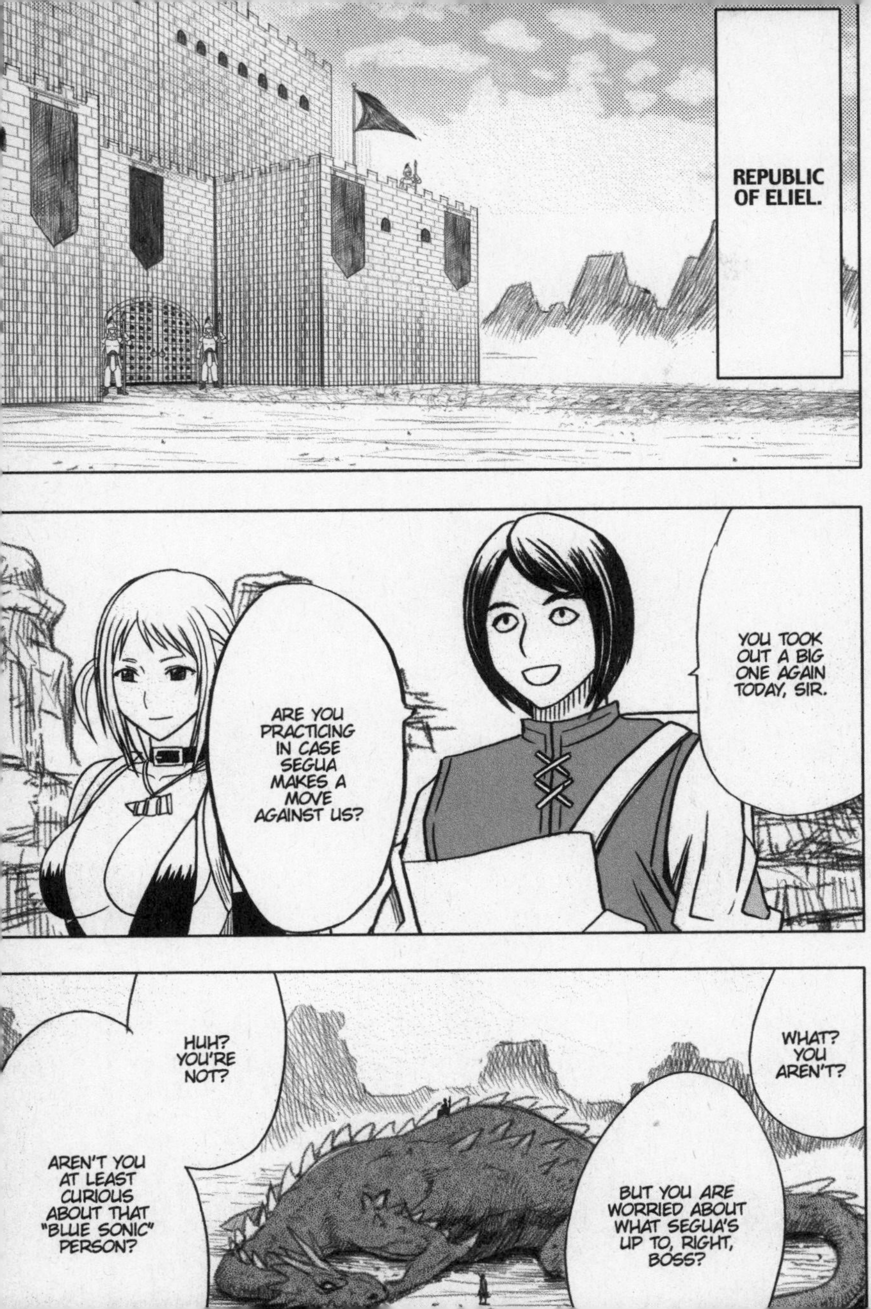
REPUBLIC OF ELIEL.
YOU TOOK OUT A BIG ONE AGAIN TODAY, SIR.
ARE YOU PRACTICING IN CASE SEGUA MAKES A MOVE AGAINST US?
WHAT? YOU AREN'T?
HUH? YOU'RE NOT?
BUT YOU ARE WORRIED ABOUT WHAT SEGUA'S UP TO, RIGHT, BOSS?
AREN'T YOU AT LEAST CURIOUS ABOUT THAT "BLUE SONIC" PERSON?

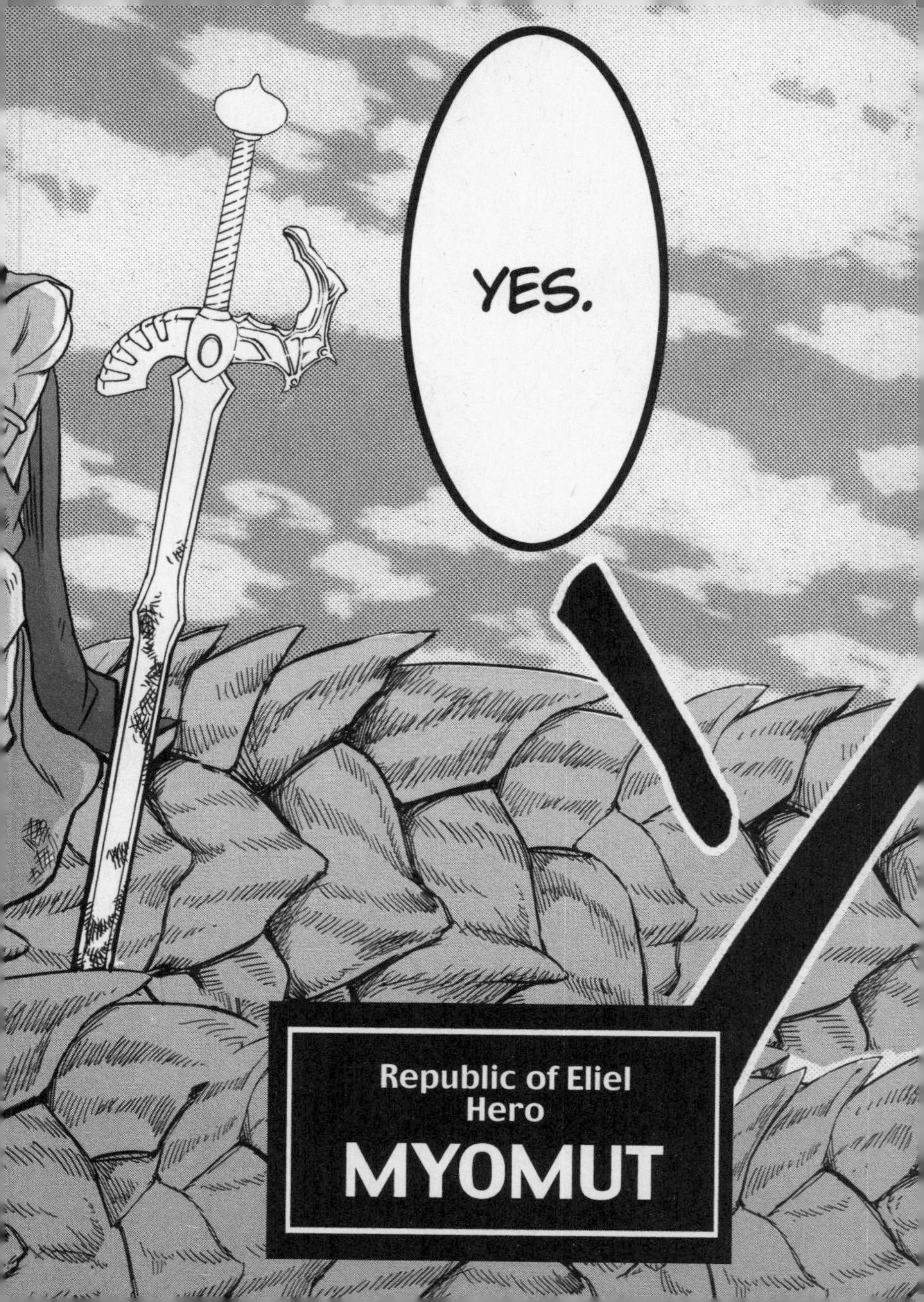
YES.
Republic of Eliel
Hero
MYOMUT

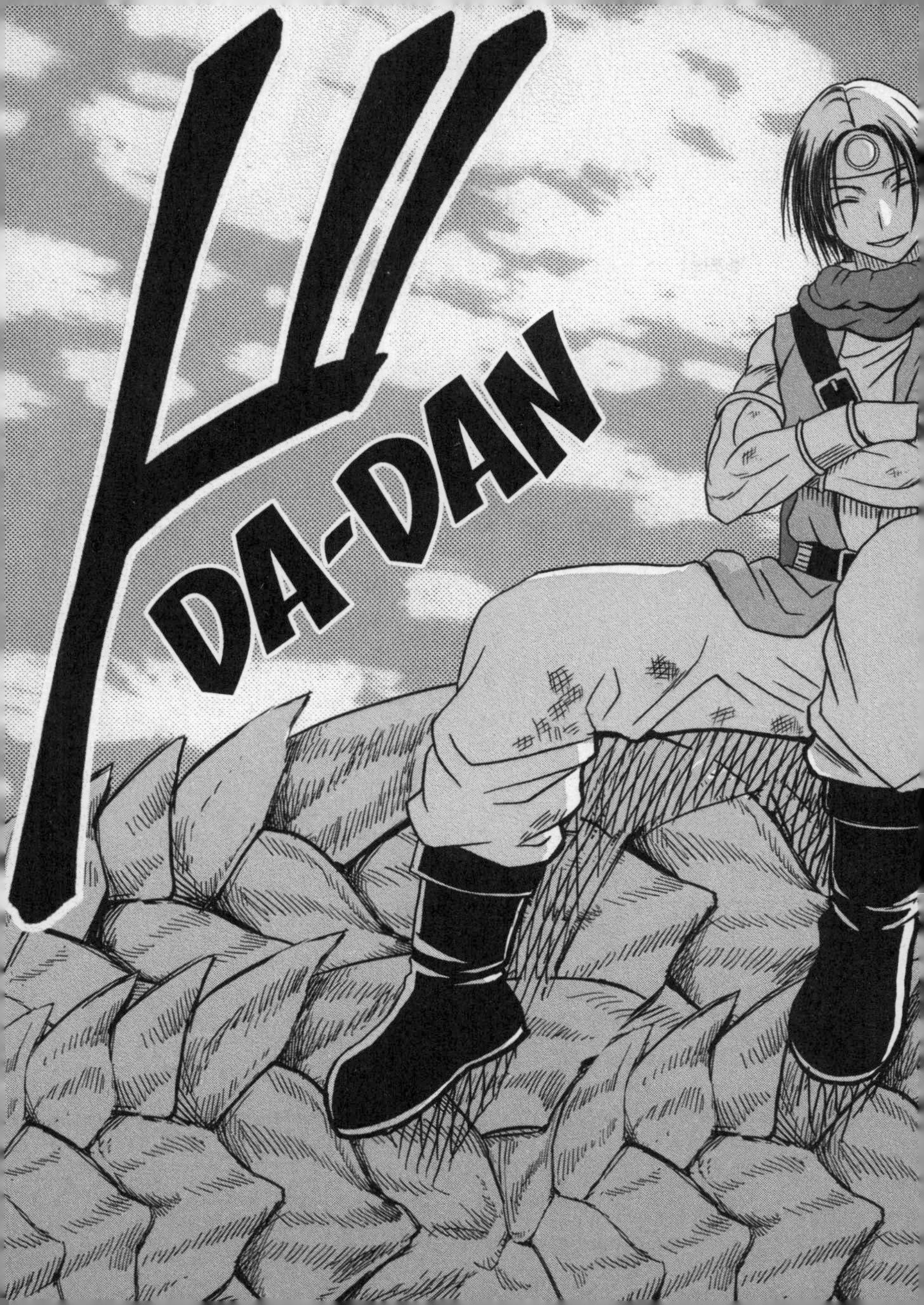
DA-DAN

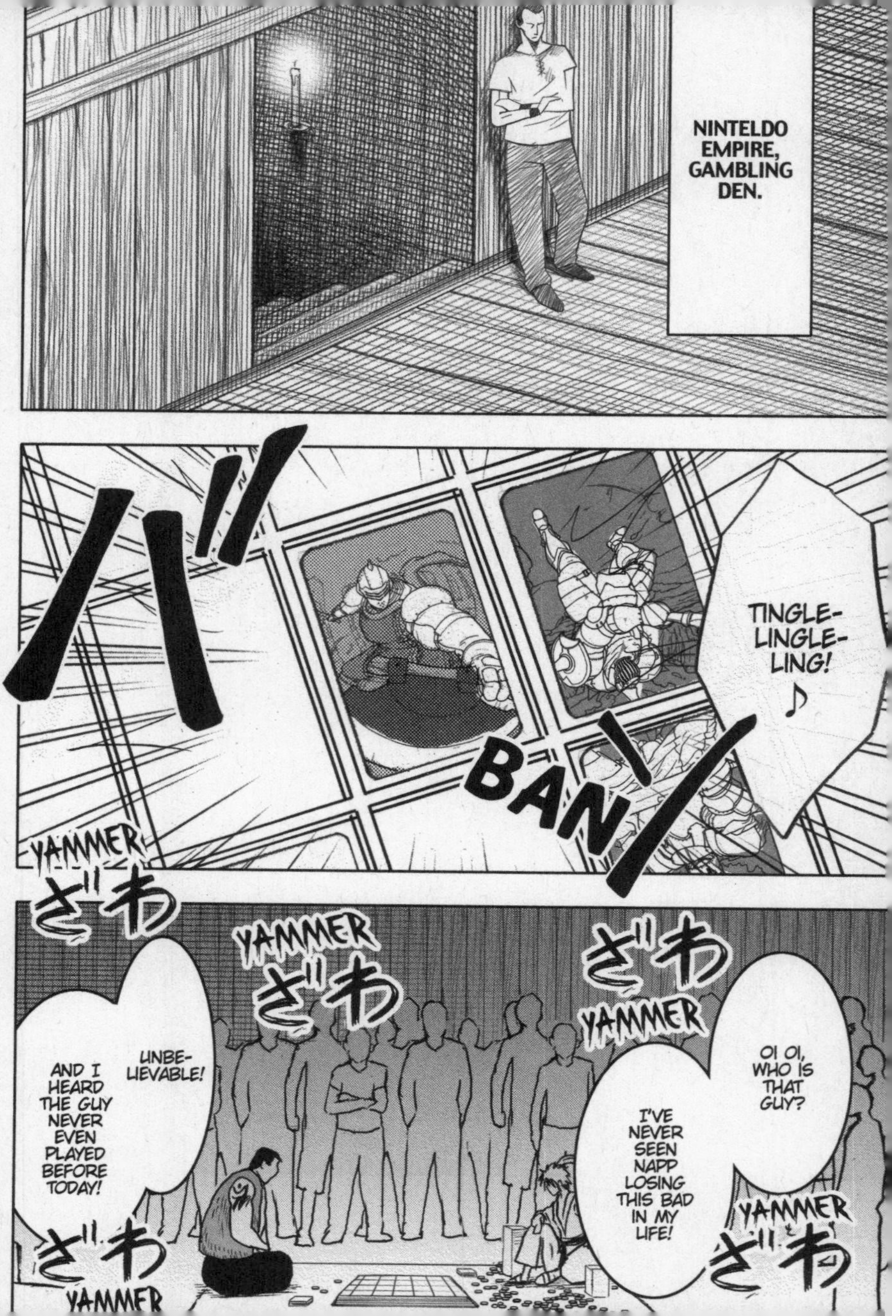
NINTELDO EMPIRE, GAMBLING DEN.
TINGLE-LINGLE-LING! ♪
BAN
バ
OI OI, WHO IS THAT GUY?
I'VE NEVER SEEN NAPP LOSING THIS BAD IN MY LIFE!
YAMMER
ざわ
ざわ
YAMMER
YAMMER
ざわ
UNBE-LIEVABLE!
AND I HEARD THE GUY NEVER EVEN PLAYED BEFORE TODAY!
YAMMER
ざわ
ざわ
YAMMER

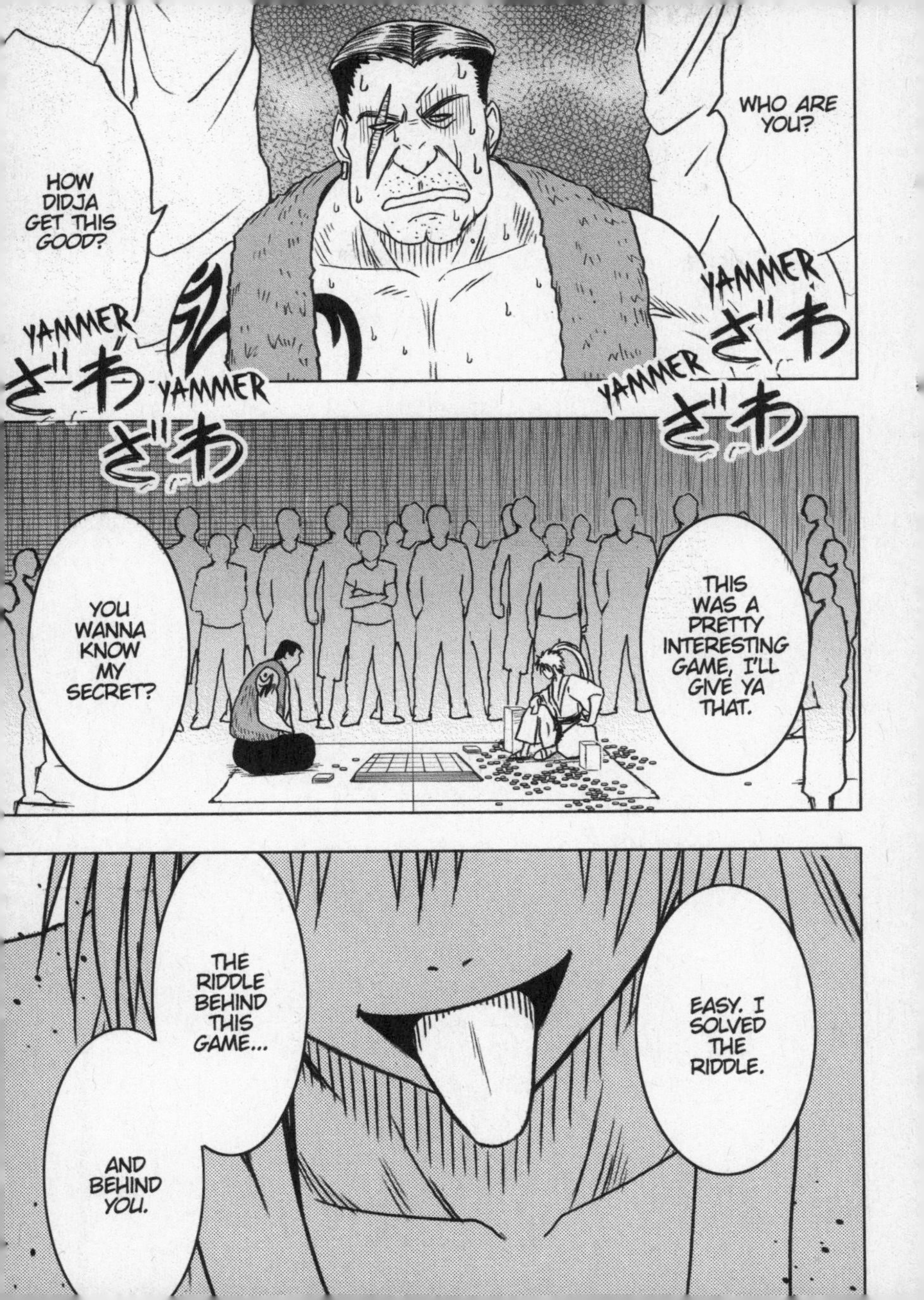
WHO ARE YOU?
HOW DIDJA GET THIS GOOD?
YAMMER ざわ
YAMMER ざわ
YAMMER ざわ
YAMMER ざわ
THIS WAS A PRETTY INTERESTING GAME, I'LL GIVE YA THAT.
YOU WANNA KNOW MY SECRET?
EASY. I SOLVED THE RIDDLE.
THE RIDDLE BEHIND THIS GAME...
AND BEHIND YOU.

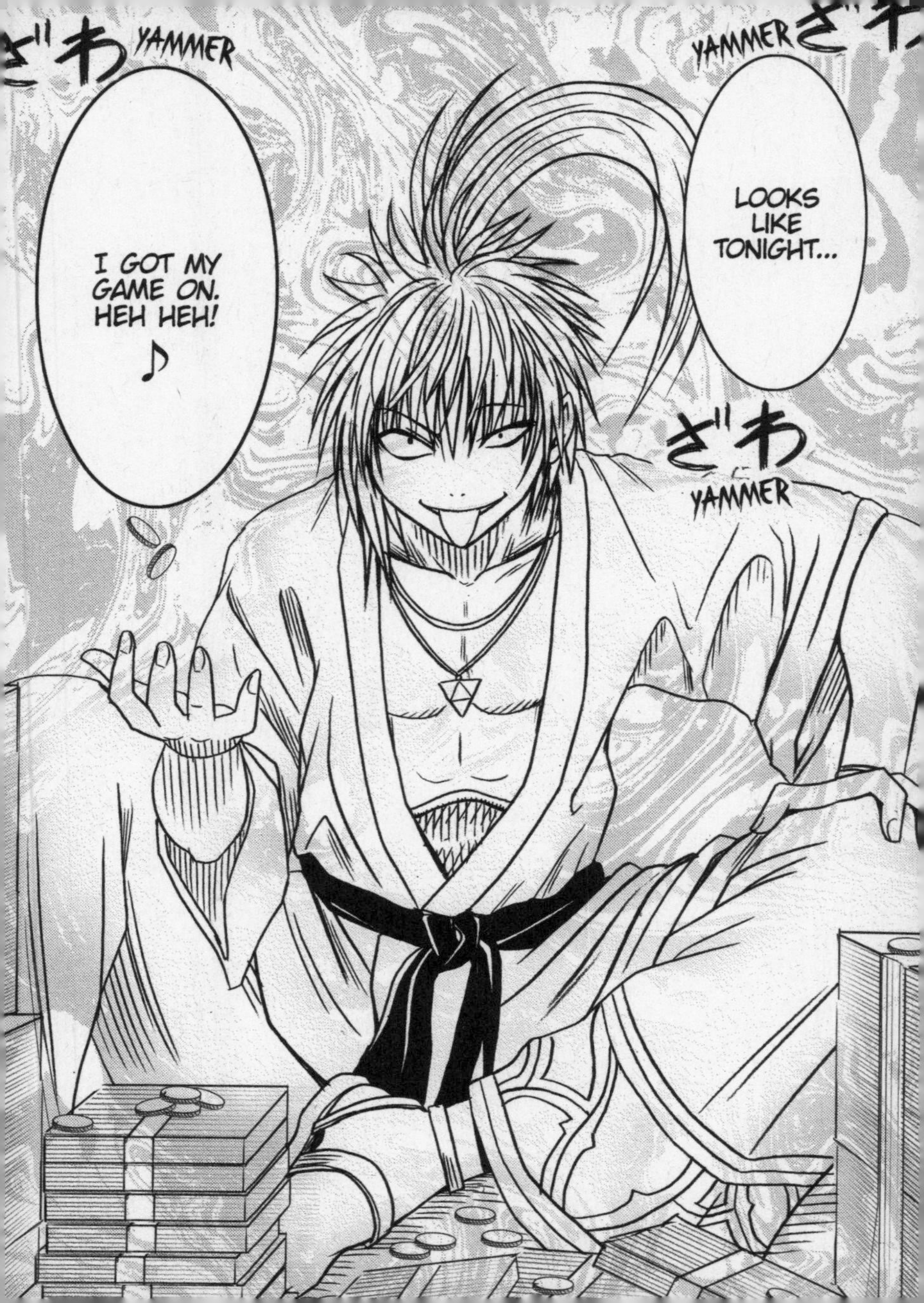
YAMMER
LOOKS LIKE TONIGHT...
ざわ
YAMMER
ざわ
YAMMER
I GOT MY GAME ON. HEH HEH! ♪

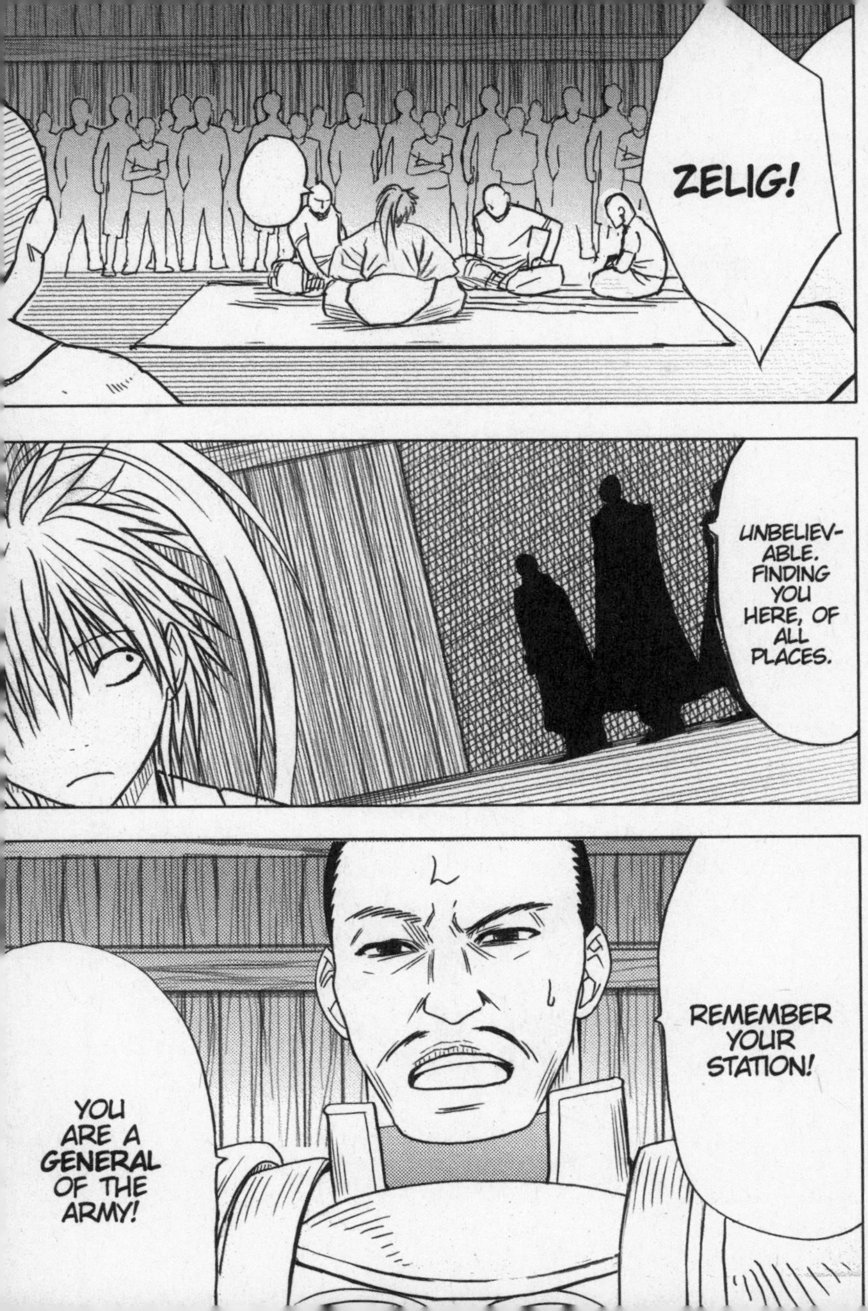
ZELIG!
UNBELIEV-ABLE. FINDING YOU HERE, OF ALL PLACES.
REMEMBER YOUR STATION!
YOU ARE A GENERAL OF THE ARMY!

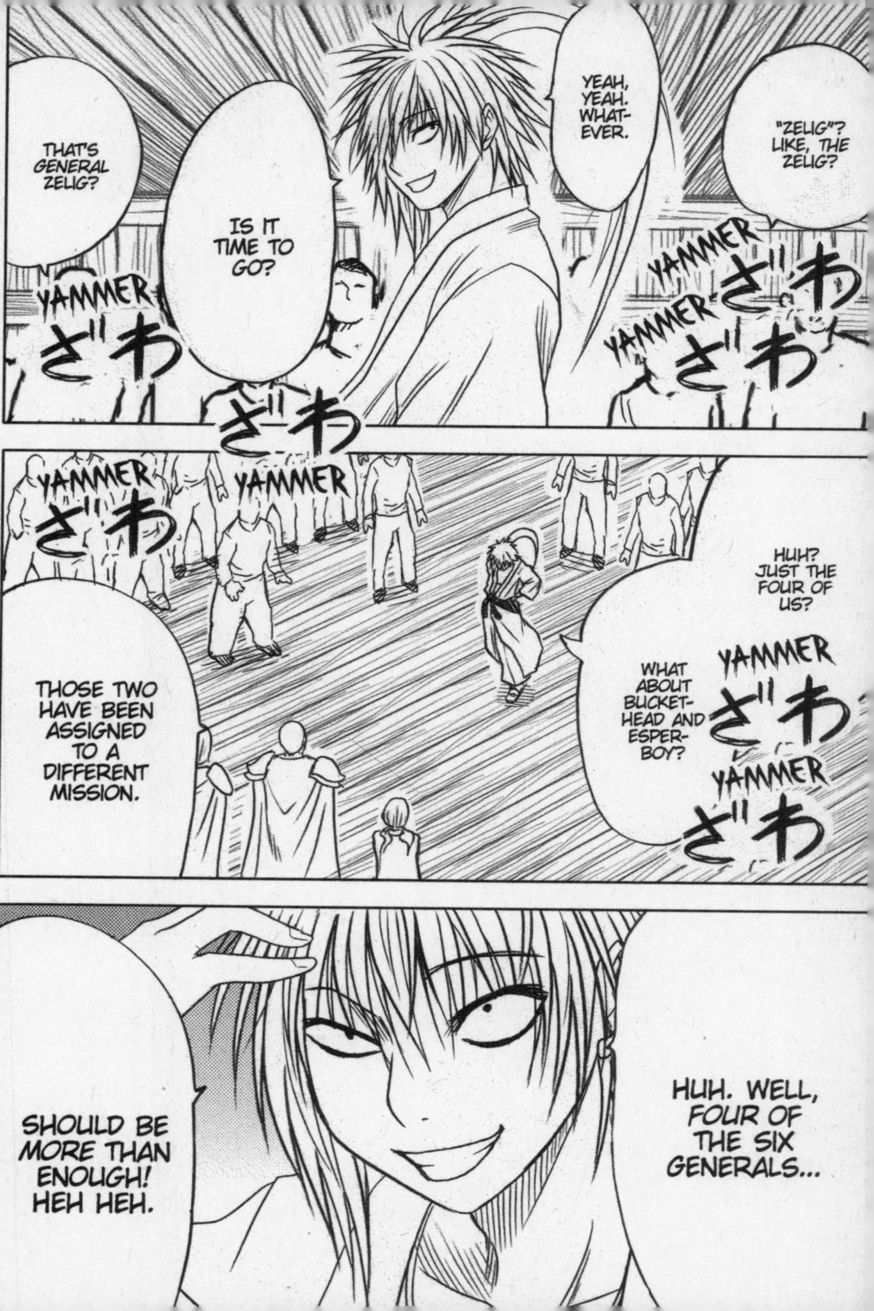
"ZELIG"? LIKE, THE ZELIG?
YAMMER ざわ YAMMER ざわ
YEAH, YEAH. WHAT-EVER.
IS IT TIME TO GO?
THAT'S GENERAL ZELIG?
YAMMER ざわ
ざわ
HUH? JUST THE FOUR OF US?
WHAT ABOUT BUCKET-HEAD AND ESPER-BOY?
YAMMER ざわ YAMMER ざわ
YAMMER YAMMER ざわ
THOSE TWO HAVE BEEN ASSIGNED TO A DIFFERENT MISSION.
HUH. WELL, FOUR OF THE SIX GENERALS...
SHOULD BE MORE THAN ENOUGH! HEH HEH.

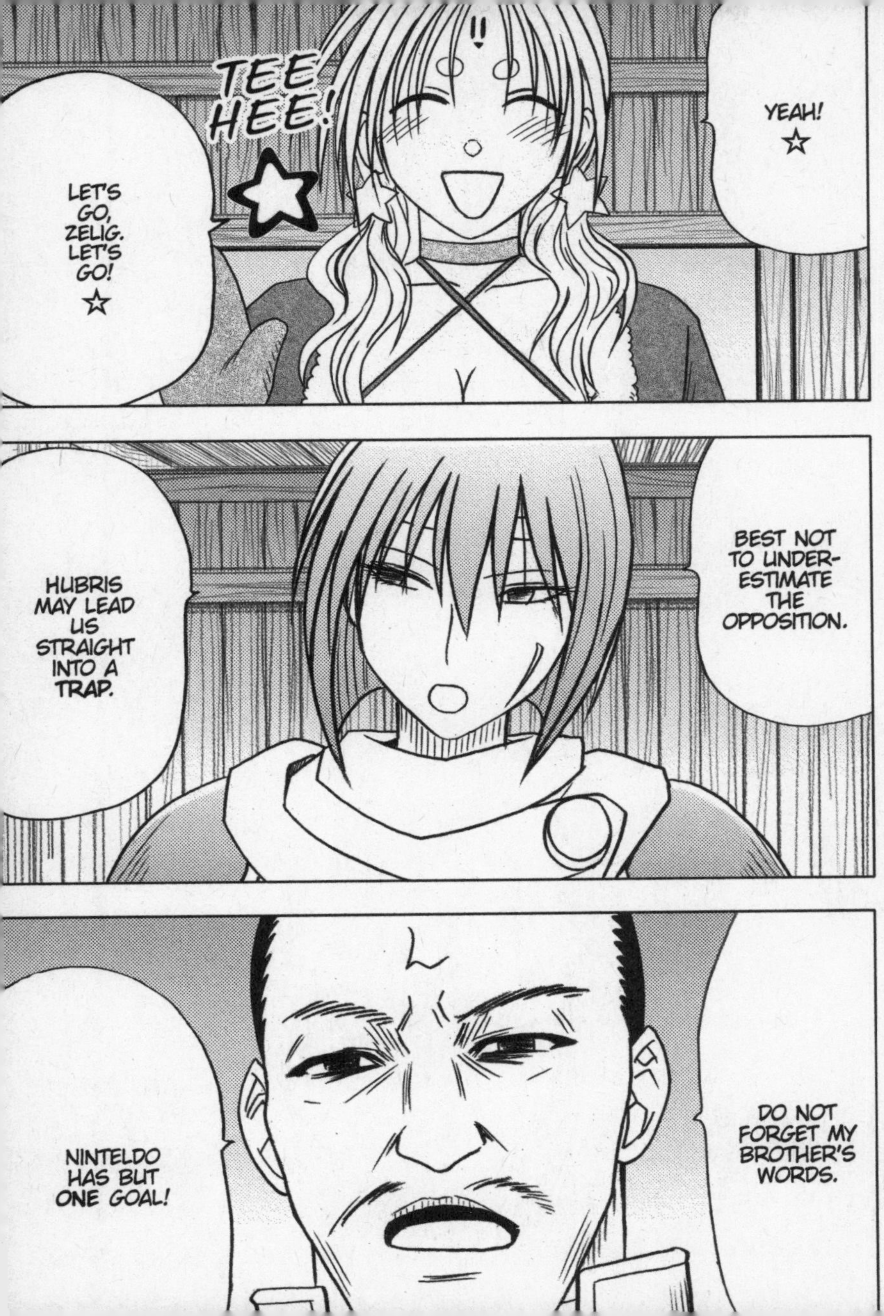
YEAH! ☆
!!
TEE HEE!
LET'S GO, ZELIG. LET'S GO! ☆
BEST NOT TO UNDER-ESTIMATE THE OPPOSITION.
HUBRIS MAY LEAD US STRAIGHT INTO A TRAP.
DO NOT FORGET MY BROTHER'S WORDS.
NINTELDO HAS BUT ONE GOAL!

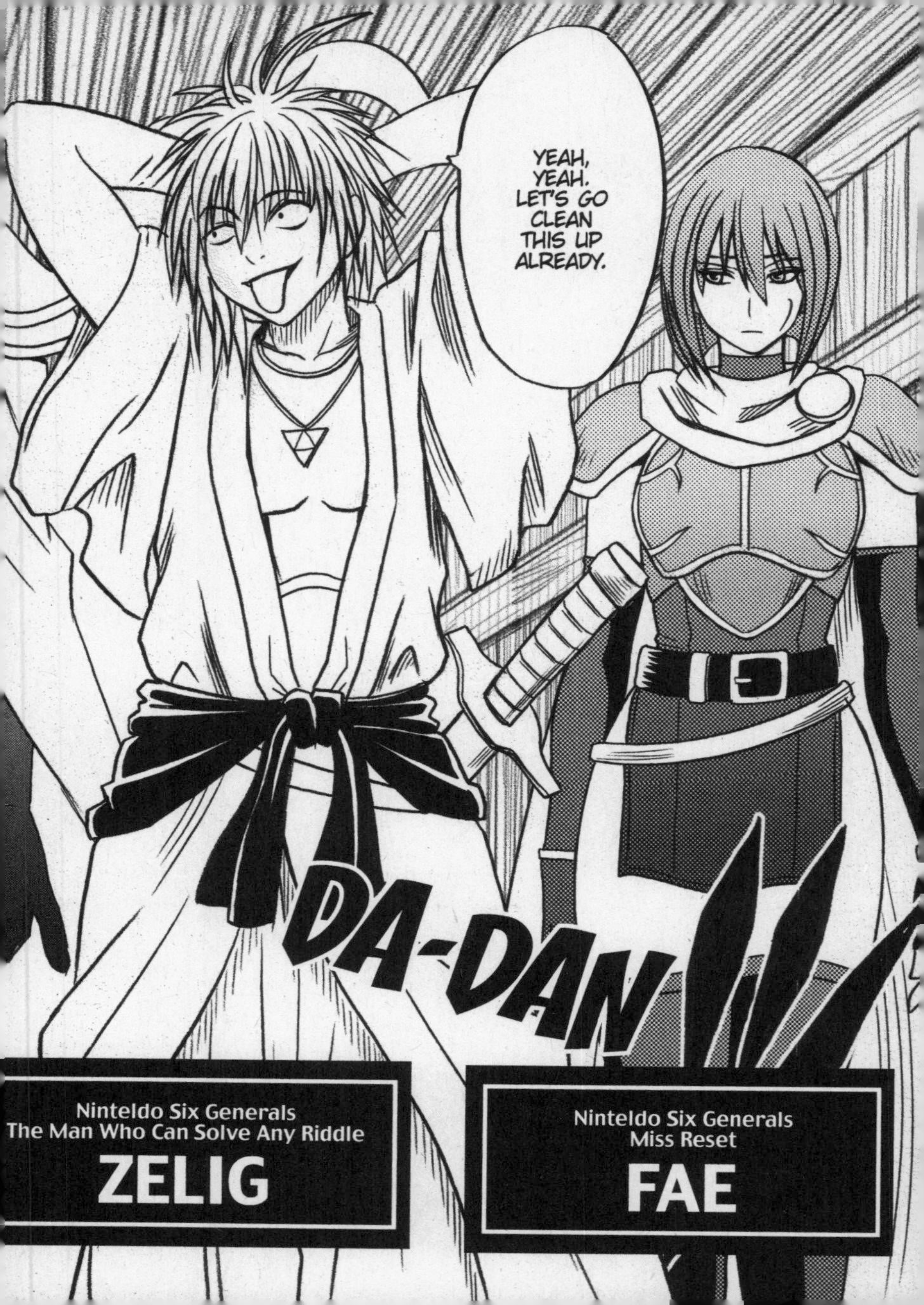
YEAH, YEAH. LET'S GO CLEAN THIS UP ALREADY.
DA-DAN
Ninteldo Six Generals Miss Reset FAE
Ninteldo Six Generals The Man Who Can Solve Any Riddle ZELIG

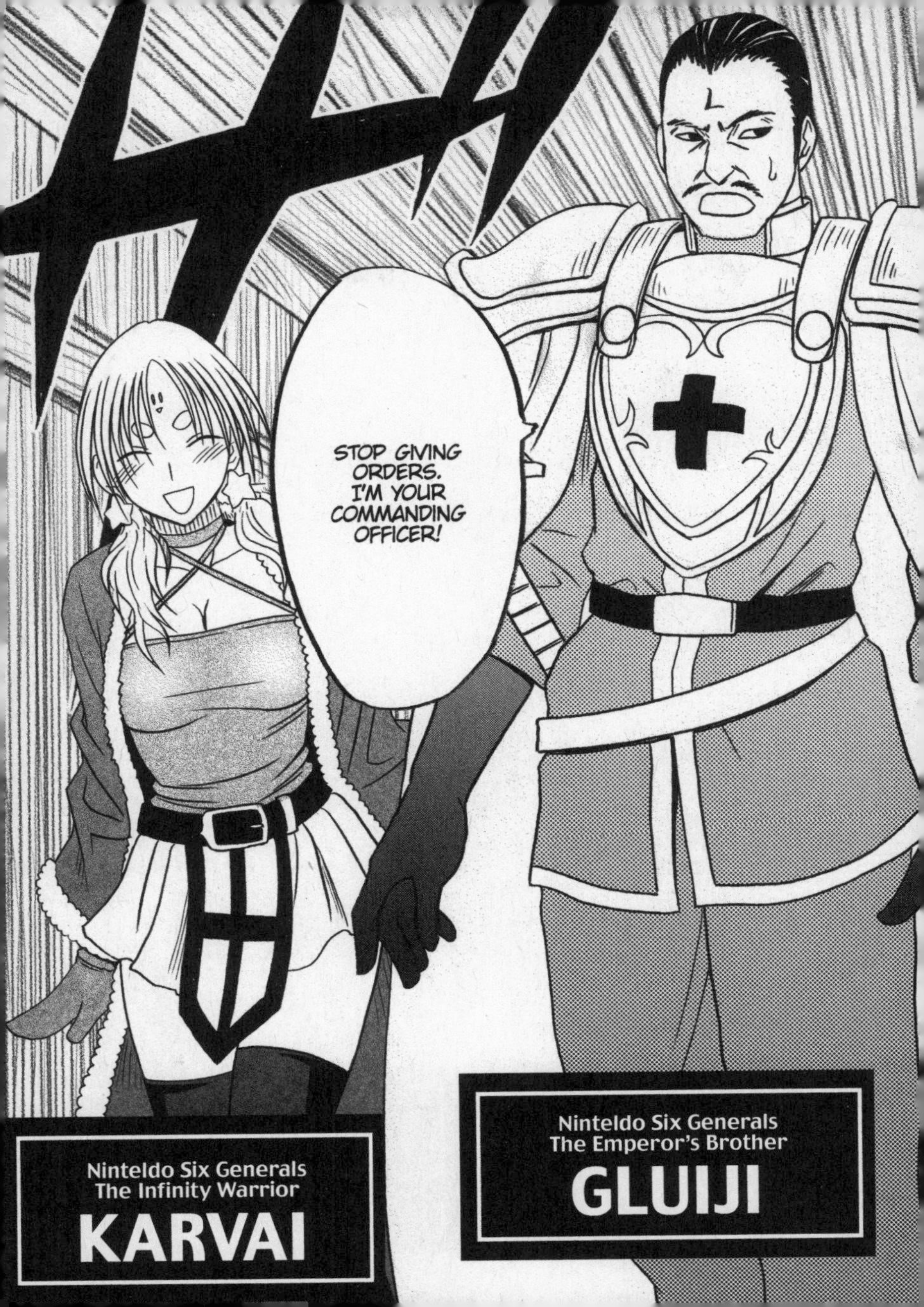

STOP GIVING ORDERS. I'M YOUR COMMANDING OFFICER!
Ninteldo Six Generals The Emperor's Brother GLUIJI
Ninteldo Six Generals The Infinity Warrior KARVAI

Perusing Video Game History

ON THE EDGE OF THE BLUE WORLD

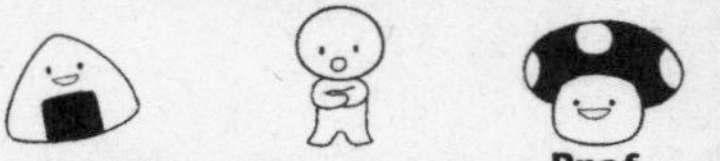

Dr. Onigiri Mr. Why Prof. Mushroom

Today's Topic

THIRD PARTY DEVELOPERS: PART 2

Mr. Why: It looks like we've got a lot of ground to cover this time.

Prof. Mushroom: Huh? Whaddya mean?

Dr. Onigiri: Don't worry about it. Let's just dive into today's topic, okay?

Prof. Mushroom: Uh, right. Okay, last time we talked about Taito, so this time we thought we'd bring up some major games from other publishers.

Dr. Onigiri: Let's start with Data East.

Prof. Mushroom: In the grand scheme of things, they were a pretty minor player, though.

Mr. Why: Really?

Prof. Mushroom: Yeah. Most of their big titles were one-hit wonders. Take their action title, *Midnight Resistance.* People don't remember the game itself so much as the hulking, masked and armored *little sisters* that show up during the opening. Then there's *Atomic Runner,* which gave weird names to things, like calling the standard guided missile the "Mount Akagi Missile." Most of their titles were just downright *strange.*

Dr. Onigiri: *Kamov* was probably their one game that got famous for the weirdest reasons. I mean, a muscle-bound, half-naked old guy with a Chinese mustache who was supposedly from Russia is the *main character.* He looks like a mini-boss from some old Jackie Chan movie. The game itself was a pretty orthodox action side-scroller, though.

Prof. Mushroom: Then add in that Data East had a side-business selling dried mushrooms.

Mr. Why: Mushrooms?

Dr. Onigiri: "To each his own" goes for companies as well as people, I guess. Anyway, moving on!

Prof. Mushroom: Right! Moving on!

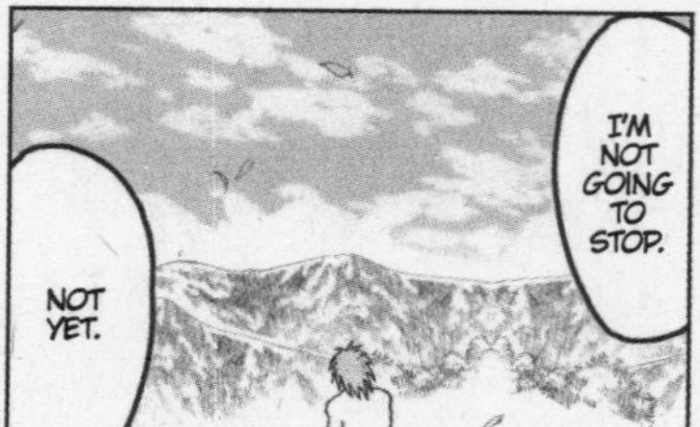
I'M NOT GOING TO STOP.
NOT YET.

The name of the first stage in the first *Sonic the Hedgehog* game is "Green Hill Zone." That is where it all began.

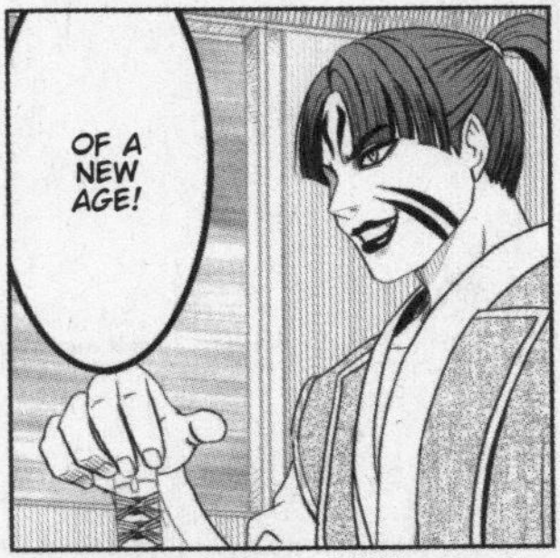
OF A NEW AGE!

Kicho of Habeed. A powerful Killer, but also a skilled businessman.

Prof. Mushroom: Next up is Hudson Soft. They had a pile of killer games to their name, but their longest running series was *Momotaro Dentetsu (The Legend of Momotaro).*

Mr. Why: I know that one! It has King Bonbi in it, right?

Prof. Mushroom: Yep! It was an RPG based on a Japanese fairy tale called *Momotaro Densetsu* at first, but the characters were so popular, they fiddled with the name a little and made it *Momotaro Dentetsu (Momotaro's Rails).*

Dr. Onigiri: Players play the CEO of their own company, rolling dice to move their trains along a track to buy commodities and move towards their goal. It's a really simple and enjoyable game. That's why it's lasted as long as it has, I guess.

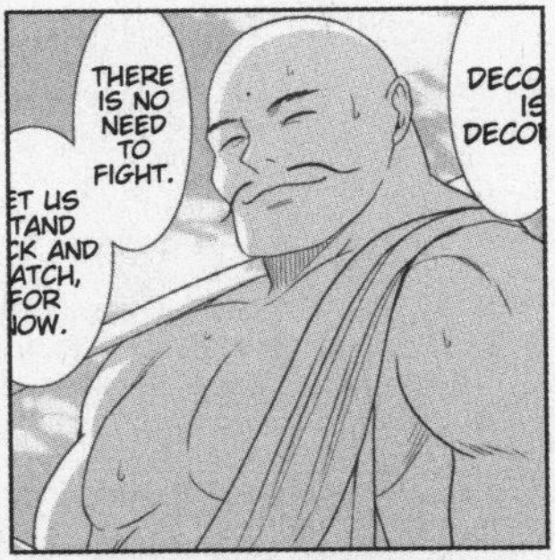
THERE IS NO NEED TO FIGHT.

Lord of Decoran, Asimov is not fond of fighting. He prefers to walk a more peaceful path.

Prof. Mushroom: It's known for going more over-the-top with each new version, too. Later games have the insanely powerful "Hurricane Bonbi" enemy, who says, "In destruction lies the beginning of creation." Then there's the biggest commodity of the game, "Momotaro Land," which increases in value at a staggering rate. It's a game chock-full of crazy stuff.

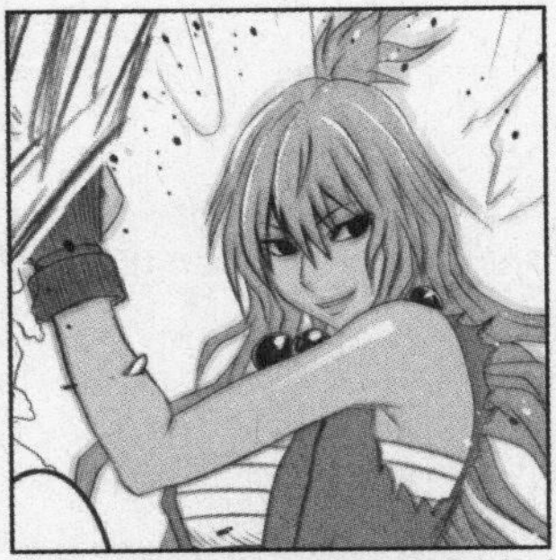

Tofai founded the "Command Action" style of fighting. It's said no one can stand up to her in a one-on-one fight.

Dr. Onigiri: And it is still the go-to title for party games in Japan.

Prof. Mushroom: Now, we've really talked up *Momotaro Dentetsu*, but the RPG series, *Momotaro Densetsu*, is still going pretty strong, too.

Dr. Onigiri: By the way, the best password* in the first game of the series was one letter long. Seriously, just one.

Prof. Mushroom: Right!

*In the old days before even memory cards and battery-powered backups, games were saved using passwords. Correctly entering certain passwords would let you start from the stage where you last left off.

IS HIM!

THE ONLY ONE I CARE TO DEFEAT...

Crystal is the ultimate Queen. She pursues both strength and beauty in all things.

Prof. Mushroom: Now, one developer you can't ignore is Capcom. They've got a metric ton of killer action games. The recent mega-hit series *Monster Hunter* is one of theirs.

Dr. Onigiri: Another Capcom title completely changed the face of arcades: *Street Fighter II*. Being able to execute certain moves by inputting a string of button presses, like down-downright-right-punch (*Hadoken!*), was a revolutionary idea, and ignited a fighting game boom.

Prof. Mushroom: If you go to an arcade nowadays, I'm not kidding when I say half the games there'll be fighters.

Dr. Onigiri: The slogan for the game, "I seek to fight someone stronger than me," was pretty awesome, too.

Prof. Mushroom: Moving on to graphics, nobody has prettier games than Square. They pay special attention to the screen, with each new *Final Fantasy* game showing off even more jaw-droppingly gorgeous graphics. An RPG series, *Final Fantasy* gives off a really thick "fantasy" vibe, with airships and magic and stuff.

Dr. Onigiri: I thought *Phantasy Star* was pretty slick for its time, too, y'know.

Prof. Mushroom: And the manly-man RPG to Square's beautiful *Final Fantasy* was Enix and their smash hit *Dragon Quest*. Now, Enix had put out some pretty great adventure games, like *Portopia Serial Murder Case*, but *Dragon Quest* was so massive, it outshone even gems like that.

Dr. Onigiri: Yeah. When a game gets that big, it can even change a company's entire image.

The Greatest Hero, Myomut. He travels Consume with his two retainers, Manos and Patry.

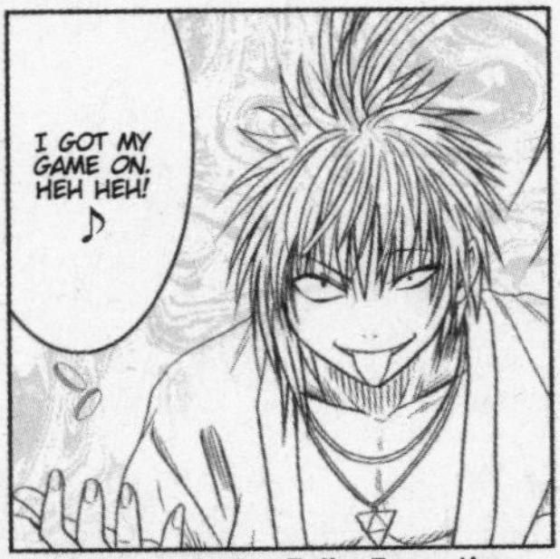
I GOT MY GAME ON. HEH HEH! ♪

Genius swordsman Zelig. Every time he solves a puzzle, he hears a particular tune play in his head.

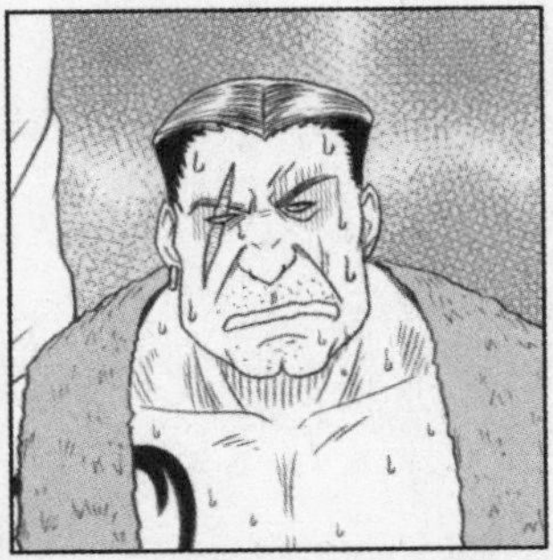

Napp was confident he could win any game until he came up against Zelig.

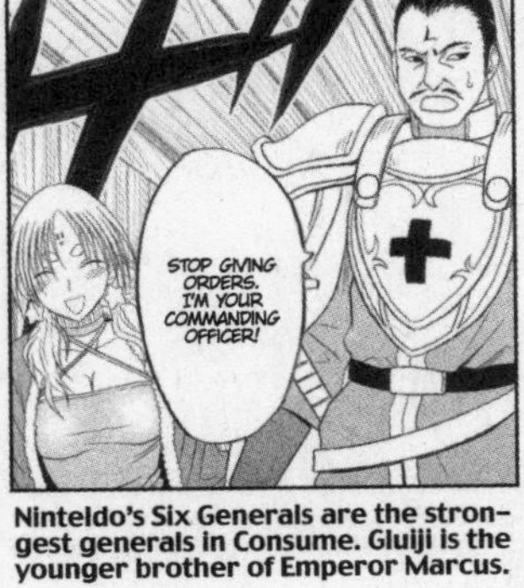
STOP GIVING ORDERS. I'M YOUR COMMANDING OFFICER!

Ninteldo's Six Generals are the strongest generals in Consume. Gluiji is the younger brother of Emperor Marcus.

Dr. Onigiri: By the way, *Dragon Quest II's* ultimate secret password (called Scrolls of Resurrection) was "yuuteimiyaoukimukouhoriyuujitoriyamaakirapep-epepepepepepepepepepepepepep-epepepepepepepepepepepepe." Input that and you would get to start the game as the highest-level hero, named "Moyomoto."

Prof. Mushroom: But if we're talking about truly killer apps, we have to mention the king of all first-party developers, Nintendo. Even just a glimpse of their catalogue reveals killer game after killer game. First, there's the pinnacle of all action-puzzle games, *The Legend of Zelda.* It has a traditional story, where the hero Link goes to rescue the Princess Zelda. But the gameplay is spiced up by clever puzzles, making it an addictive game that kept players up all night.

Then there's the simulation RPG that kept players playing, despite the number of times they'd hit the reset button: *Fire Emblem*. And don't forget *Kirby*, the action game about an adorable pink glutton. Seriously, Nintendo had a *really* diverse line-up. Oh, and by the way, it may surprise you, but Nintendo has made a lot of playing-card decks and hanafuda cards. Their "NAP" series is a staple of all playing-card series.

Mr. Why: Wow, they really are the king of all game makers.

To Be Continued in Volume 3!

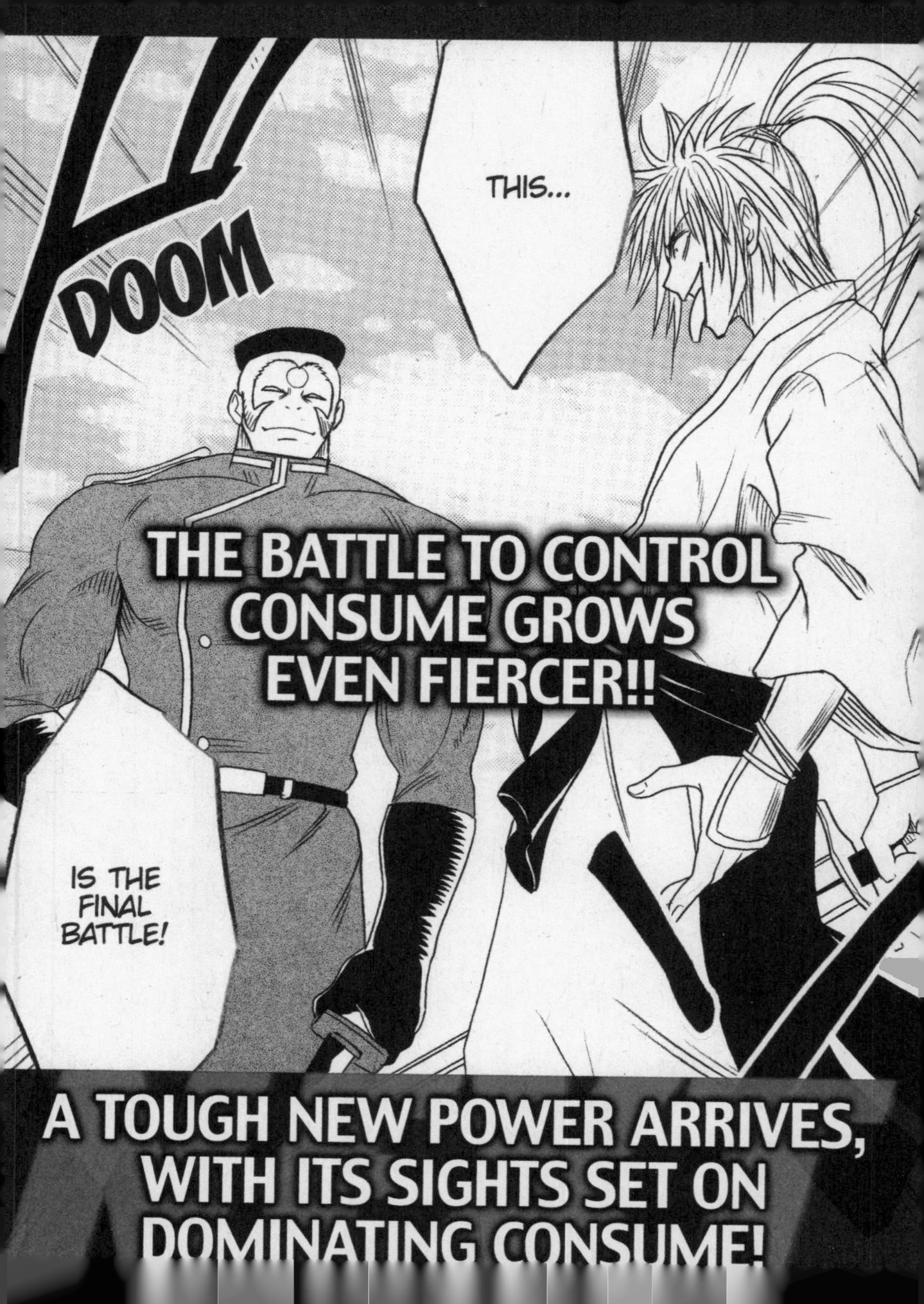
THIS...
DOOM
IS THE FINAL BATTLE!
THE BATTLE TO CONTROL CONSUME GROWS EVEN FIERCER!!
A TOUGH NEW POWER ARRIVES, WITH ITS SIGHTS SET ON DOMINATING CONSUME!

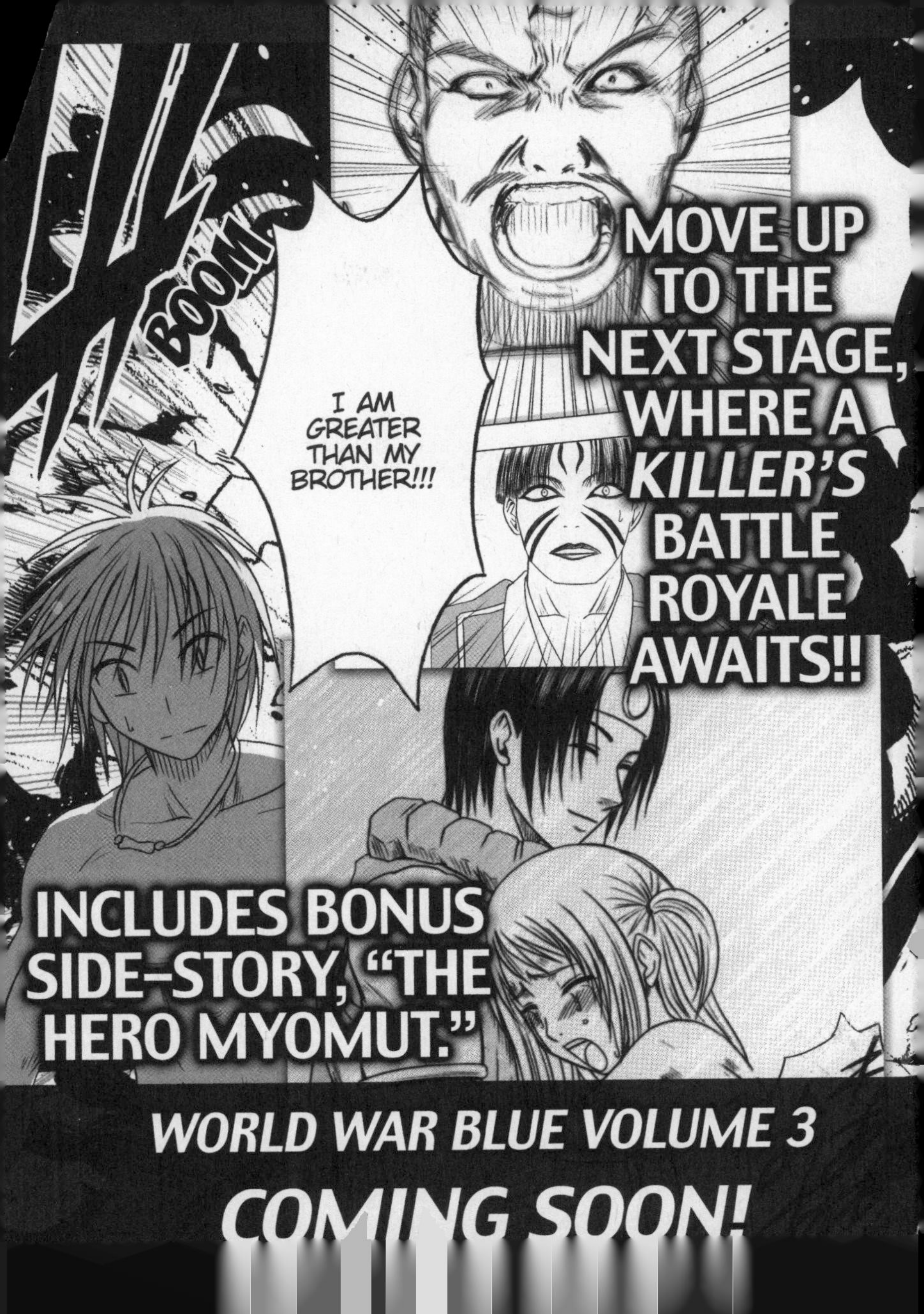
MOVE UP TO THE NEXT STAGE, WHERE A *KILLER'S* BATTLE ROYALE AWAITS!!
I AM GREATER THAN MY BROTHER!!!
BOOM
INCLUDES BONUS SIDE-STORY, "THE HERO MYOMUT."
WORLD WAR BLUE VOLUME 3
COMING SOON!

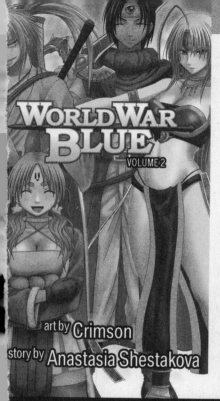

STAFF CREDITS

translation	**Adrienne Beck**
adaptation	**Patrick King**
lettering	**Laura Scoville**
logo design	**Courtney Williams**
cover design	**Nicky Lim**
proofreader	**Janet Houck**
editor	**Adam Arnold**
publisher	**Jason DeAngelis**
	Seven Seas Entertainment

AOI SEKAI NO CHUSINDE KANZENBAN VOL. 2
© 2010 ANASTASIA SHESTAKOVA / © 2010 CRIMSON
This edition originally published in Japan in 2010 by
MICROMAGAZINE PUBLISHING CO., Tokyo. English translation
rights arranged with MICROMAGAZINE PUBLISHING CO., Tokyo
through TOHAN CORPORATION, Tokyo.

No portion of this book may be reproduced or transmitted in any form without
written permission from the copyright holders. This is a work of fiction.
Names, characters, places, and incidents are the products of the author's
imagination or are used fictitiously. Any resemblance to actual events, locals,
or persons, living or dead, is entirely coincidental.

Seven Seas and the Seven Seas logo are trademarks
of Seven Seas Entertainment, LLC. All rights reserved.

ISBN: 978-1-937867-97-3
Printed in Canada
First Printing: August 2013
10 9 8 7 6 5 4 3 2 1

FOLLOW US ONLINE: **www.gomanga.com**

READING DIRECTIONS

This book reads from *right to left*, Japanese style.
If this is your first time reading manga, you start
reading from the top right panel on each page and
take it from there. If you get lost, just follow the
numbered diagram here. It may seem backwards
at first, but you'll get the hang of it! Have fun!!